PIMLICO

740

'HURRAH FOR THE BLACKSHIRTS!'

Martin Pugh was Professor of Modern British History at Newcastle University until 1999, and Research Professor in History at Liverpool John Moores University from 1999 to 2002. He has written ten books on aspects of nineteenth- and twentieth-century history and is on the board of *BBC History Magazine*.

'HURRAH FOR THE BLACKSHIRTS!'

Fascists and Fascism in Britain Between the Wars

————

MARTIN PUGH

PIMLICO

Published by Pimlico 2006

2 4 6 8 10 9 7 5 3 1

Copyright © Martin Pugh 2005

First published in Great Britain by Jonathan Cape in 2005

Pimlico edition 2006

Pimlico
Random House, 20 Vauxhall Bridge Road,
London SW1V 2SA

Random House Australia (Pty) Limited
20 Alfred Street, Milsons Point, Sydney,
New South Wales 2061, Australia

Random House New Zealand Limited
18 Poland Road, Glenfield,
Auckland 10, New Zealand

Random House South Africa (Pty) Limited
Isle of Houghton, Corner of Boundary Road & Carse O'Gowrie,
Houghton 2198, South Africa

Random House UK Limited Reg. No. 954009

A CIP catalogue record for this book is available from the British Library

ISBN 1844130878
ISBN 9781844130870 (From Jan 2007)

Papers used by Random House UK Ltd are natural, recyclable products
made from wood grown in sustainable forests. The manufacturing processes
conform to the environmental regulations of the country of origin

Printed and bound in Great Britain by Cox & Wyman Ltd, Reading, Berkshire

Think of what our Nation stands for,
Books from 'Boots' and country lanes,
Free speech, free passes, class distinction,
Democracy and proper drains.

Sir John Betjeman, *In Westminster Abbey*, 1940

'You have great contempt for democracy?'
'Yes.'

Diana Mosley at the Advisory Committee
on her detention, 2 October 1940

I went to a party at Chips Channon's . . . There in
his room were gathered the Nurembergers and the
Munichois celebrating *our* victory over *their* friend
Herr von Ribbentrop. I left in haste, leaving my coat
behind me. A voice hailed me in Belgrave Square. It
was Charles, seventh Marquis of Londonderry,
Hitler's friend. As we walked towards his mansion in
Park Lane, he explained to me how he had warned
the Government about Hitler, how they would not
listen to him; but for him, we should not have had
the Spitfires.

Harold Nicolson on VE Day, in his *Diaries and Letters
1939–1945* (1967), 458–9

CONTENTS

Illustrations

Rotha Lintorn-Orman in 1923 *(Getty Images)*.

Alan Ian Percy, 8th Duke of Northumberland, pictured by the *Saturday Review*, 7 April 1934.

Sir Patrick Hannon MP at an Anglo-German conference in 1926 *(Hartley Library, University of Southampton)*.

Arnold Leese, Director of the Imperial Fascist League *(PRO)*.

Gerrard V. Wallop, Viscount Lymington MP (9th Earl of Portsmouth), pictured by the *Saturday Review*, 24 March 1934.

Food convoys in the East India Dock Road during the General Strike, 1926.

Viscount Rothermere launches the *Daily Mail*'s campaign for the British Union of Fascists, 15 January 1934.

Oswald Mosley and BUF members with Italian fascists in Rome, April 1933 *(Birmingham University Special Collections)*.

Oswald Mosley with William Joyce *(Getty Images)*.

Major-General J. F. C. Fuller *(Getty Images)*.

Lady Lucy Houston, millionaire owner of the *Saturday Review* and sponsor of the 'Flight over Everest', 1933.

Maud, Lady Mosley, Sir Charles Petrie and Sir John Squire at a January Club dinner at the Savoy *(Imperial War Museum)*.

Oswald Mosley inspects women fascists in the Limehouse Branch, 4 July 1937 *(British Union Collection, University of Sheffield Library)*.

Oswald Mosley basking in the admiration of his supporters during a march from Kentish Town to Trafalgar Square, 4 July 1937 *(British Union Collection, University of Sheffield Library)*.

Oswald Mosley speaking from the top of a loudspeaker van in London, July 1938 *(British Union Collection, University of Sheffield Library)*.

Communists demonstrate against a BUF march, 4 July 1937 *(British Union Collection, University of Sheffield Library)*.

Lord Redesdale, Lady Redesdale, their daughter Unity Mitford and Dr Fitz-Randolph of the German Embassy, at an Anglo–German Fellowship concert, December 1938 *(Getty Images)*.

Sir Archibald Henry Maule Ramsay MP with his wife at Lords, July 1937 *(Getty Images)*.

Admiral Sir Barry Domvile with Arthur Bryant in 1933.

Lord Mount Temple at an Anglo–German Fellowship dinner, July 1936 *(Hartley Library, University of Southampton)*.

BUF Women's Drum Corps at the Earl's Court Peace Rally, 16 July 1939 *(British Union Collection, University of Sheffield Library)*.

The scene at the BUF's Peace Rally at Earl's Court, 16 July 1939 *(British Union Collection, University of Sheffield Library)*.

ACKNOWLEDGEMENTS

I would like to express my thanks to those who have helped me in various ways in the preparation of this book, notably Eugenio Biagini, David French, Julie Gottlieb, Thomas Linehan, Lewis Mates, Philip Murphy, John Ramsden, Colin Simms, Dan Stone and Pat Wilson. I am also very grateful to Jörg Hensgen at Jonathan Cape for his perceptive and constructive reading of the manuscript. Special thanks are due to all the staff of the library of the Literary and Philosophic Society of Newcastle-upon-Tyne, to Dr Alison Rosie at the Scottish Record Office for the trouble she took over access to the sources, and to Lawrence Aspden at Sheffield University Library. I am also grateful to the archivists and librarians at the following institutions at which I have worked: Birmingham University Special Collections, Blair Castle, Bradford University (J. B. Priestley Library), Cambridge University Library, Churchill College Archives Centre (Churchill College, Cambridge), Durham County Record Office, Hampshire County Record Office, the House of Lords Record Office, the Imperial War Museum, Leeds University (Brotherton Library) Liddell Hart Centre for Military Archives (King's College, London), the National Archives of Scotland, the National Maritime Museum, the National Museum of Labour History, the Public Record Office (Kew), the RAF Museum (Hendon), the Royal Archives (Windsor Castle), Sheffield University Special Collections, Southampton University (Hartley Library).

For permission to make quotations I am indebted to the following individuals and institutions: Her Majesty Queen Elizabeth II for material in the Royal Archives, His Grace the Duke of Atholl, His Grace the Duke of Buccleuch, His Grace the Duke of Hamilton and Brandon, The Earl of Portsmouth, Lord Kelvedon, Lord Norwich, Lady Lloyd of Dolobran, Sir John Gilmour, Sir Vere Harmsworth, Captain J. Headlam and Durham County Record Office, Jay Luttman-Johnson, Alexander Mosley, Nicholas Mosley, Nigel Nicolson, the Friends of Oswald Mosley (Saunders Papers), the Trustees of the Broadlands Archives (Lord Mount Temple Papers), and the Trustees of the Liddell Hart Centre for Military Archives (Arthur Bryant Papers). I am grateful for assistance in obtaining photographs for the book from Birmingham University Special Collections, the British Library Newspaper Library, Getty Images, the Imperial War Museum, the National Archives, the National Maritime Museum, Sheffield University Special Collections and Southampton University (Hartley Library). Every attempt has been made to contact copyright holders. The author and publisher would like to apologise to those with whom attempts to make contact were unsuccessful and for any inadvertent infringements of copyright.

Introduction

Fascism in inter-war Britain was not just a failure, it was an *inevitable* failure. While it flourished in Italy and Germany, the British simply failed to see its relevance to them. In fact, fascism seemed fundamentally alien to British political culture and traditions; the British people were too deeply committed to their long-standing parliament, to democracy and the rule of law to be attracted by the corporate state, and they found the violent methods employed by Continental fascists offensive. Fascist organisations arrived late in Britain and when they did they were easily marginalised by the refusal of conventional right-wing politicians to have anything to do with them. When the fascist movement under Sir Oswald Mosley showed itself in its true colours in 1934 the government took prompt and effective action to suppress the violence and the paramilitary organisation. The outbreak of war in 1939 promptly put an end to the movement.

Such assumptions reflect a comforting and widely held British view that fascism is simply not part of our national story. Yet, although these beliefs are not wholly wrong, they are, without exception, misleading and are based as much on prejudice as on the evidence. In fact, doubts about the received wisdom were sown as long ago as 1975 when Robert Skidelsky published his biography of Oswald Mosley. By demonstrating that fascism was not simply a matter of mindless thuggery but involved a set of well-thought-out ideas, Skidelsky forced us to take the subject more seriously. And by showing how a typical member of the war generation could arrive at a fascist position as a result of his experiences, he implicitly issued a warning against simplistic psychological explanations of fascism as the product of a warped mentality.

Since then our understanding of fascism in Britain has been hugely extended by a succession of outstanding books and articles by scholars including Richard Thurlow, Tony Kushner, Kenneth Lunn, Richard Griffiths, G. C. Webber, D. S. Lewis, Stuart Rawnsley, Thomas Linehan,

I

Julie Gottlieb, Dan Stone, Philip Coupland, Stephen Cullen and David Baker. However, the academic community is as conservative as most professions, and it has not always proved easy to convince those outside the circle of specialists of the importance of this work. As recently as 2001 one reviewer of Julie Gottlieb's *Feminine Fascism* praised the book, but confessed himself perplexed that so much effort had been devoted to so insignificant a subject.[1] Against this background the aim of the present volume may seem ambitious as it is intended to carry the subject of British fascism to a wider audience by suggesting that it is part of the national story.

However, this perspective is difficult to convey if one approaches fascism through detailed studies of small fascist organisations. By contrast this book can be read almost as a history of the inter-war era in that it examines all the main issues and themes of our history: the aftermath of the Great War, the rise of Labour, the General Strike, the dominance of the Conservatives and the National Government, the growing threat to the Empire, the Abdication Crisis, and the controversy over rearmament and appeasement. In many ways fascism was a reaction to these developments, and the vicissitudes of British fascism cannot be adequately explained unless it is seen in this context. This approach makes it immediately clear that fascism was much more central to British inter-war history than has traditionally been appreciated; it makes its relevance and credibility for contemporaries more obvious, and helps to throw light on its relative weakness and eventual failure.

Ironically the current obsession with the rise and fall of Nazi Germany in schools and on television seems to have done little to improve our understanding of the phenomenon in Britain, except, perhaps, to strengthen traditional assumptions. This was clear from the unthinking hostility with which the death of Lady Diana Mosley was treated by the press and by the BBC recently. Most people start from a view of inter-war fascism as a political contagion, arriving, like most unpleasant things, from abroad, and from which the British enjoyed a natural immunity. Britain's liberal political tradition, her respect for the parliamentary system, and her rejection of political violence deprived fascism of any natural base in British society. Consequently, developments after the First World War, when countries such as Italy, where parliamentary traditions were fragile and superficial, rapidly succumbed to fascism, appear to have little or no relevance to British politics. As Britain emerged victorious from war, her institutions, her values and her social system gained prestige rather than being undermined. Although some fascist organisations emerged in the 1920s, they are seen as very small, extremely marginal to the political system, and perhaps not authentically fascist at all. Even during the 1930s, when Germany fell to Nazism and Spain to Franco's Nationalists, Britain displayed a marked reluctance to follow Continental trends towards authoritarianism. Not until 1932 did the British Union of Fascists emerge under the leadership of Sir Oswald Mosley. For a brief period from January to June 1934 Mosley's organisation gained thousands of members and enjoyed extensive publicity courtesy of Lord Northcliffe who used the *Daily Mail* and the *Sunday Dispatch* to promote the movement; but thereafter it rapidly collapsed.

Traditionally the BUF is seen largely in terms of street-fighting, paramilitary organisation and anti-Semitism in the East End of London, which underlines its alien character and its marginal status. Mosley himself is regarded as vain, opportunistic, and not taken seriously by his contemporaries. What little support the BUF won was alienated by reactions to the notorious rally at Olympia in June 1934 when the press and the politicians were finally alerted to the real nature of the movement by scores of eyewitness accounts of the violence meted out by fascist thugs on anyone who intervened to ask a question. A popular anti-fascist movement sprang up which mobilised thousands of people and checked the BUF, notably at the famous Battle of Cable Street in 1936. The government clamped down with the Public Order Act of 1936 which, among other things, banned political uniforms and empowered the police to stop marches designed to provoke the local inhabitants such as those of the Jewish districts of London's East End. In the form of the National Government from 1931 onwards Britain enjoyed an effective bulwark against the extremes of both right and left to which other countries had succumbed. Those politicians who might have been sympathetic towards fascism, and thus given it respectability, marginalised it by repudiating any association with it or its ideas. As a result, in the later 1930s Mosley's movement languished on the sidelines of politics, becoming increasingly pro-Nazi and keen to stop Britain going to war with Hitler. Eventually, the subversive nature of the movement was recognised when hundreds of fascists were arrested, admittedly rather late in the day, in May 1940 in the belief that they represented a fifth column working for the German invasion that now appeared imminent.

Among other things this book draws attention to the fact that fascism enjoyed a longer history in Britain than is usually recognised and that it was far from being simply an import from abroad. Chapter 1 sketches the preconditions for a fascist movement that were present in Britain before 1914, and Chapter 2 examines the proximate reasons for the emergence of fascist organisations shortly after the end of the war. In fact, the political and economic impact of the war did expose Britain to the challenge of fascism; and many men embarked on the road to fascism as a result of their disillusionment in the aftermath of that war. As early as 1923 Britain's first fascist organisation had been formed, only months after Mussolini's 'March on Rome'. The explanation for our reluctance to see the significance of Italy is that

British perspectives on fascism have been, and still are, excessively coloured by the 'Churchillian' view of the inter-war period, that is, by an obsession with Nazi Germany. In fact, the Italian model exercised a much more prolonged and positive influence.

During the 1920s fascism took root in British fears about national degeneracy, the lack of virile leadership, and international conspiracies allegedly orchestrated by Bolsheviks and Jews. Seen from the fascist perspective, 1920s Britain was perpetually on the edge of a crisis that seemed likely to lead to chaos and the collapse of law and order, the danger points being the first Labour government in 1924, the General Strike of 1926, the economic-political upheaval of 1929–31 that produced the National Government, and the Abdication of 1936. Far from being marginal, fascists and their ideas were centrally involved in many of the major controversies of the inter-war period including the General Strike, the handling of mass unemployment, the defence of the Empire, the preservation of European peace, and the role of the monarchy; indeed, the relationship between fascism and monarchy, a hitherto neglected theme, constitutes a key element in the fortunes and thinking of British fascism.

Although perceptions of inter-war fascism have been heavily coloured by the movement's paramilitary aspects, Mosley never expected to get into power by means of violence, except perhaps briefly during the Second World War. Rather, he anticipated being invited in by right-wing politicians during some political crisis – just as Mussolini and Hitler had been. Accordingly, he developed strategies designed to advance this aim which have not been sufficiently recognised. This involved creating an election machine for a general election around 1939–40; it involved cultivating MPs and peers who were entrenched within the system but were also fascists awaiting the opportunity to replace the decayed parliamentary system; it involved creating front organisations such as the January Club and hoping to use the armed forces as, in effect, fronts.

It is usually, and understandably, believed that the real history of fascism in Britain has been obscured by the reluctance of the authorities to release the official records. But in recent years a good deal of material has become available at the Public Record Office. However, in some respects this compounds an already biased view because it concentrates on street violence, anti-Semitism, the East End and some big cities, as well as on the Mosleys and several notorious villains such as William Joyce. In fact much of the fascist effort was focused on agricultural England, medieval market towns and centres of declining industry where meetings usually passed off without violence or even serious interruption, and the movement took on a distinctly respectable form. The reports by MI5 and Special

Branch in the PRO material give little idea of this movement. It is striking that the only records we have for a local BUF organisation (held in the University of Sheffield's collection) are for Dorset. Moreover, little use has been made of the papers now available of respectable MPs who were involved with fascism in various ways including those of Viscount Lymington, Henry Drummond Wolff, Sir Patrick Hannon, Wilfred Ashley (Lord Mount Temple), Lieutenant Colonel J. T. C. Moore-Brabazon (Lord Brabazon of Tara), Alan Lennox-Boyd, the Marquis of Clydesdale (later Duke of Hamilton and Brandon) and Commander Robert Bower. So far from fascism being repudiated and marginalised by the conventional politicians, there was a flourishing traffic in ideas and in personnel between fascism and the Conservative Right throughout the inter-war period. This was not simply a case of youthful flirtations with fascism leading to respectable careers later in life; it proved comparatively easy to maintain dual membership of fascist and Conservative organisations without disadvantaging oneself; some of the individuals involved rose to become ministers in the 1930s, 1940s and 1950s. These links are a reminder that although fascism had some distinctive ideas, much of what fascists had to say was not particularly distinctive. The common ground was advantageous in that it enabled them to address the concerns of a large body of potential recruits and sympathisers; on the other hand it led many disillusioned right-wingers to retain a footing in conventional Conservative politics rather than commit themselves wholly to fascism.

Although no definition of fascism commands complete acceptance, some core elements are fairly clear. Fascism may be seen as a revolutionary movement with long-term roots in European society but which emerged as a reaction to the perceived crisis facing liberal democracy at the end of the First World War and to its inability to handle the material hardship caused by the collapse of the nineteenth-century economy. In a sense fascism took on the character of a generational revolt by those who had experienced the war and felt angered and betrayed by the retention of power by the old men who had been responsible for the disaster. Fascism also reflected an obsession with the moral, physical and racial degeneracy afflicting Western societies, and saw itself as a cleansing and purifying force capable of ushering in the rebirth of the nation. It is frequently defined in terms of negatives: anti-Communist, anti-liberal, anti-bourgeois. But on the positive side fascism exalted the authority of the state against what it regarded as a divisive and outworn individualism; it emphasised loyalty to the group, the promotion of national unity, belief in generating national consensus, and the cult of leadership. Although obviously hostile to democracy, fascism cannot simply be equated with tyranny or dictatorship, for it sought to channel popular emotion into support for the great leader and into building national unity.

However, while certain features can be regarded as central, the movement has varied both from one country to another, and also over time especially in the sense that fascism in power has not always been faithful to the ideas used en route to power. For example, though fascist rhetoric was often anti-capitalist, fascist regimes proved fairly accommodating to big business. Even within Britain, fascist organisations differed in some respects. Despite the reputation of the movement as an expression of virile masculinity, the British Union of Fascists welcomed female participation and saw the corporate state as a means of defending the interests of women both as housewives and as workers. Although from left-wing perspectives fascism appears indisputably anti-proletarian, this is not consistent with the actual composition and programme of the BUF which drew heavily on former Socialists who saw it as a means of combining patriotism with Socialism. Again, fascist leaders such as Mosley depicted their movement as a modernising one, but others were frankly reactionary, finding inspiration in a medieval past whose virtues would be recaptured by the fascist state.

The example of Britain underlines the dangers of trying to identify too rigidly the boundaries between fascism and other adjacent ideologies and movements. The arguments deployed by fascists enjoyed a lengthy pedigree extending into the late-Victorian era. Consequently, when expressed by fascists in the 1920s and 1930s they did not always appear as novel or alien, but rather as developments of British thinking. Moreover, any attempt to measure fascism simply in terms of the membership of fascist organisations (for which there is no reliable, comprehensive evidence anyway) is bound to misrepresent a phenomenon that extended far more widely through British society. Fascism is best understood not in terms of tight categories, but as part of a spectrum; although the main colours are clear enough, the point is that half the range actually comprises broad bands in which the colours are blurred, making it difficult to say where one ends and another begins.

ONE

The Origins of British Fascism

'Germany is organised not only for war but for peace. We are organised for nothing but party politics.'

Winston Churchill to H. H. Asquith,
29 December 1908

On 19 September 1870 the troops of the Prussian army completed their encirclement of Paris, making almost inevitable the capitulation of the French capital four months later. But their unexpectedly swift victory did more than bring down the curtain on the empire of Napoleon III: it levered Europe into a new era of insecurity and struck at the foundations of British complacency. During the previous twenty years Britain, by sheer serendipity, had reached the peak of her industrial, commercial and imperial strength without being challenged by a major power. However, from the 1870s to the outbreak of the First World War in 1914 the conditions that had under-pinned her success steadily unravelled. In the process confidence in her system of free trade and parliamentary government was undermined, and suspicious were voiced about the moral decline and racial degeneracy of the British people.

The late-Victorian and Edwardian period is usually examined in the light of *progressive* political developments: the extension of the vote to some working men, the emergence of an organised labour movement, the campaigns for female emancipation, the creation of state-funded social welfare. This is entirely valid. However, this ought not to prevent us from recognising a different history. During the forty years before the First World War the ideas that prepared the ground for fascism were abundantly in evidence in British politics and society; like other European countries Britain had a pre-fascist tradition, and consequently there is no reason, other than hindsight, for regarding Britain as inherently less likely to generate a fascist movement after 1918 or for seeing British fascism as a mere import from the Continent.

Although the Victorians prided themselves on giving the world a model of parliamentary government, British confidence in parliamentary democracy has been greatly exaggerated. In the pre-1914 period Britain still fell a considerable way short of being a democracy, and in some respects lagged behind the United States and France, for example. Before 1918 four out of every ten men, and all women, still failed to qualify as voters. Historically, voting in Britain was largely linked to property rights as manifested in land ownership and payment of rates and taxes; from this it followed that those who depended on the Poor Law were automatically barred from voting. The notion of people as citizens who possessed individual rights was regarded as abstract and alien; rather, the vote was extended to people who had a stake in the country and did their duty to the state.*

Moreover, in the absence of a formal constitution British people enjoyed few of the rights and liberties of citizens. Contemporary claims by A. V. Dicey, the eminent Victorian jurist, that civil liberties were protected by the common law, were simply wrong.[1] In effect, whatever rights people enjoyed had to be specifically conferred on them by parliament. But by the same token they could be withdrawn or curtailed. After the 1914–18 war, for example, parliament deprived conscientious objectors of their vote for a five-year period, and it suspended general elections from 1915 until the end of 1918. During the Edwardian period the government took advantage of the preoccupation with spies and subversion to launch a serious attack on political freedom in the 1911 Official Secrets Act. Passed with scarcely an hour's discussion on a quiet Friday afternoon in an empty House of Commons, the legislation allowed the authorities to arrest and prosecute anyone on mere suspicion of harbouring an intention 'prejudicial to the safety or interests of the state'; it was unnecessary to prove that the accused was a spy or had committed an act of subversion. Despite assurances that 'in no case would the powers be used to infringe any of the liberties of His Majesty's subjects', for the next century the Act enabled governments to stifle legitimate criticism on the plea of protecting the security of the state.[2]

Just how ruthless a British government could be in responding to its critics had been demonstrated by the largely successful suppression of the Women's Social and Political Union (WSPU) from 1912 to 1914. In March 1912 detectives raided WSPU headquarters in Clement's Inn where they seized quantities of documents for use in prosecuting its leaders. Christabel Pankhurst fled to Paris where she remained in exile until after the outbreak of war. The Home Secretary, Reginald McKenna, allowed the police to remain in occupation of suffragette offices for lengthy periods, against the advice of the

---

* In some ways this remains true today. For example, homeless people are largely denied the vote; and prior to the election of 1992 the names of a million people who had not paid their poll tax disappeared from the electoral registers.

Attorney General, and signed warrants authorising the police to cut off their telephones and divert their mail. The government censored copy for *The Suffragette*, prosecuted its printers and seized copies printed abroad at the ports.[3] McKenna also collected information about forty leading financial backers of the WSPU against whom he was about to institute legal proceedings when the war interrupted him. With some justification Emmeline Pankhurst complained that Liberals would have reacted with indignation if the forcible feeding inflicted on women in Holloway had been applied to people who campaigned for political rights in Turkey and Russia. Yet although a handful of MPs protested, the government remained undeterred, if embarrassed; and despite continuing action by individual suffragettes, the organised campaign among the militants had effectively been suppressed by 1914.

Thus, despite its reputation for liberalism, British politics was also notably authoritarian in some respects. Many politicians were less impressed by the parliamentary tradition and more attracted by the alternative, autocratic mode of government adopted in the empire. Ireland enjoyed a hybrid form of government involving an essentially imperial rule mitigated by Irish representation in both houses of parliament. But above all it was India that commanded the frank admiration of large numbers of influential politicians who enjoyed experience as viceroys, governors or as secretaries of state. In India, as one viceroy put it, 'we are all British gentlemen engaged in the magnificent work of governing an inferior race'. According to Lord Lytton, 'India is a field of administration which furnishes us with the practical confutation of a great many liberal fallacies.' There, so the argument ran, government was neutral and focused on the national interest; governments could proceed to implement their policy unhindered by the sectional demands, party pressures, elections and assemblies that enfeebled representative systems. Inevitably imperialists contrasted this favourably with domestic British politics. After returning to Britain in 1870 Fitzjames Stephen noted: 'There [in India] you see real government. Here you see disorganized anarchy which is quickly throwing off the mask.'[4] For Lord Salisbury and Lord Curzon, who regarded the growing trend towards popular participation in politics with contempt, India appeared an enviable field for promoting efficient administration, autocratic rule and feudal values. These pre-1914 sentiments remained lively during the inter-war period amongst pro-fascist MPs such as Viscount Lymington and Alan Lennox-Boyd who fought against concessions to Indian nationalism and were deeply moved by the deferential, pre-industrial societies of Asia and Africa which they believed were being ruined by western education and the ideas of liberal democracy.

This anti-democratic tradition enabled inter-war fascists to present their case within a British historical context rather than simply in terms of

Continental states. In fact, they based their analysis on the claim that Britain had taken a false turn during the eighteenth century, under the influence of liberal and egalitarian notions imported from France, by diminishing royal authority, promoting commercial interests and setting a course towards parliamentary reform. They argued that the original British system took no cognisance of votes for individuals; rather, the state granted representation to interests, corporations and communities by allotting two MPs to specified parliamentary boroughs. In a similar spirit, under fascism the corporate state would give recognition to all the country's economic interests rather than to the political parties, which merely promoted divisions damaging to the national interest. Fascists also commended the medieval guilds for sustaining an economic and social system based on communities; the guilds controlled output, prices and wages in the interests of consumers and workers just as the corporate system would do. The fall of feudalism and the guilds had opened the way for rapid economic development, but it had also promoted the damaging cult of the individual and accelerated competition leading to the destruction of stable communities.[5] In short, with the aim of restoring a sense of community, nationhood, kingship and hereditary leadership, fascism presented itself as a return to English traditions, not as an alien innovation.

Of course, for much of the Victorian period British liberals had taken comfort from the belief that anti-parliamentary values were anachronistic, part of a world that was steadily giving way to economic progress, international understanding and political enlightenment. However, towards the end of the century liberalism was forced on to the defensive by the growing obsession with external rivals, aggressive nationalism and xenophobia. Under the threat of a huge, efficient Germany army capable of mobilising rapidly, all the European powers felt obliged to reconsider their military strategies. Even Britain, despite the protection offered by the Channel and the Royal Navy, felt increasingly vulnerable to naval rebuilding by France and Russia, and to the emergence of the German High Seas Fleet in the late 1890s. Germany's dramatic victory over France in 1870 inspired an influential article in *Blackwood's Magazine* entitled 'The Battle of Dorking'. This inaugurated a tradition of writing about fictional invasions of the British Isles in which a negligent government and a complacent people were taken by surprise. A generation grew up, fearful that one dark and misty night a Continental enemy would slip his fleet across the Channel, land his troops on the south coast and march up through the pinewoods of Surrey by breakfast, en route for London.

During the Edwardian period, as Germanophobia reached its peak, invasion scares were successfully exploited by a succession of authors including Erskine Childers in *The Riddle of the Sands* (1903), William Le Queux in

The Invasion of 1910 (1906), H. G. Wells in *The War in the Air* (1908) and John Buchan in *The Thirty-Nine Steps* (1915). It became an article of faith that the country had been infiltrated by up to 100,000 German spies and saboteurs who served quietly as clerks, waiters and barbers against the day when they would emerge to assist the invading forces. The press magnate, Alfred Harmsworth, invited readers of the *Daily Mail* to report sightings of suspicious foreigners, and he advertised the likely invasion routes which invariably passed through towns where the *Mail*'s circulation required a boost. The climax came in the form of baseless scare stories around 1908 to the effect that the Germans were building the new Dreadnought-type battleships at a faster rate than Britain. In this way the British fell victim to insecurity, anti-alienism, and disillusionment with their political leaders.

Moreover, Britain's unpreparedness to meet an invasion was seen as symptomatic of a wider deterioration afflicting all aspects of society and politics. The 1870s triggered a protracted debate about whether Britain had entered a period of economic decline. After decades of industrial supremacy she experienced falling prices, narrower profit margins and stiff competition from German and American manufacturers who benefited from larger domestic markets and greater natural resources. 'The day of small nations has long passed away,' declared Joseph Chamberlain, the leading architect of economic revisionism, in 1904, 'the day of Empires has come.'[6] Although Britain possessed an extensive and still-expanding empire, much of her territory remained thinly populated and vulnerable to rival powers. Imperialists correctly saw that Britain often failed to exploit the economic potential of her overseas possessions. They attributed this to the prevalence of free trade which led Britain to buy food and raw materials from foreigners and to invest extensively in their industries. During the 1870s the large-scale imports of cheap grain from North America triggered a long-term decline in agriculture, marked by falling rents and land values, which left a generation of country gentlemen and aristocratic landowners disillusioned with conventional Conservatism and was eventually to make them susceptible to extremist politics. Protectionists and imperialists also complained about unfair competition by foreigners who protected their own markets with tariffs and dumped their goods on Britain at below cost price; they vented their anger on British financial interests for supporting these rivals and undermining the British economy to promote their own profits. Hence arose the thesis that policy was dictated by 'cosmopolitan' financiers, 'Radical Plutocrats', and wealthy Jews who showed no loyalty towards the country that sheltered them. The alternative strategy involved abandoning free trade in goods, labour and investment in order to expand the domestic market for British manufactures.

Although this protectionist programme was championed by Joseph Chamberlain in 1903 and soon became the orthodox Conservative position, it was for years frustrated by popular hostility to dearer food. From the 1890s onwards the Conservative Party was consumed with a bitter internal battle over protectionism, but it was not until 1932 that its leaders eventually succeeded in replacing free trade with a general policy of tariffs, though by then it was too late to arrest the decline of much of British manufacturing industry. All the characteristic elements in this debate – the protection of British jobs, the development of the empire, the exclusion of foreign products, and the attack on the influence of Jews and financiers – reappeared, albeit in more extreme form, in the inter-war propaganda of Sir Oswald Mosley and the British Union of Fascists. Fascists cited the betrayal of British farmers and manufacturers over many years as proof of their thesis that the parliamentary politicians had become too flabby and emasculated by liberalism to stand up for British interests.

This long-term controversy over economic and imperial strategy had major implications for fascism in Britain because it fostered the interaction between fascists and Conservatives. It is often argued that British fascism inevitably failed because it made no appeal to conventional right-wing forces. In fact the problem lay more in the extent to which conventional Conservatism managed to satisfy the concerns that animated fascists or offered a vehicle for their aims. It proved relatively easy for Tory MPs to operate in both fascist and Conservative organisations simultaneously during the inter-war period. Some of them frankly characterised fascism as a more virile expression of their party's creed. Mosley's programme for empire and industry carried conviction on the right because it spoke to long-standing grievances and tapped a pervasive feeling that the Tory leaders had betrayed their own principles. Of course, endorsing the fascist economic-imperial programme did not make Conservatives into fascists; it was when they embraced the idea that the parliamentary system was played out, accepted that Britain stood in need of an authoritarian system along the lines of the corporate state, and countenanced the use of force, that they decisively crossed the line.

Beneath these concerns over industry, agriculture and the empire lay a wider unease about the moral condition of British society during the last twenty years of the nineteenth century. The assumptions of a generation of writers, academics and politicians had been influenced by Darwinian notions about survival, adaptation and degeneracy. With their passion for classifying the animal species of the world, many Victorians also perceived the human races in terms of certain indelible qualities and characteristics. In the Indian Empire, for example, they minutely distinguished the 'martial' races recruited into the army from the 'effete' types suitable only for employment as 'baboos' or pen-pushers. But if Darwin was right, even the British could not afford to sit back and bask in their superiority indefinitely. Revelations by Charles Booth and Seebohm Rowntree in the late 1890s about the extent of urban poverty provoked fears about the spread of a physically degenerate population in the cities, which in turn raised doubts about Britain's future as an imperial power. A similar concern led Victorians to worry about the tendency of younger women to postpone marriage and about the steady decline in the birth rate, especially among the middle classes, from 35 per thousand population in the 1870s to 24 per thousand by 1914.[7]

One by-product of this pessimistic thinking was the interest in genetic engineering which gained respectability from the work of Francis Galton during the 1880s. Many late-Victorian and Edwardian intellectuals believed that a liberal society encouraged the procreation of the least fit members, which was a certain recipe for industrial, military and imperial decline. They saw eugenics as an appealing remedy.[8] In *The Moral Basis of Socialism* (1880) Karl Pearson argued for the need to strengthen the power of the state, which he believed to be inhibited by liberal individualism, and to improve the population by additions of superior stock. Similarly, Benjamin Kidd in his book *Social Evolution*, published in 1894, emphasised the role of the state in developing the corporate life of the nation and thus promoting 'social efficiency'. Perhaps the most influential member of this school was Houston Stewart Chamberlain, author of *The Foundations of the Nineteenth Century* (1899), who believed the race was threatened by racial impurity or mixing, the worst agents of which were the Jews; as he put it: 'a mongrel is frequently very clever, but never reliable; morally he is always a weed.'[9] From this it followed that the state had a clear duty to encourage selection with a view to maximising the proportion of pure Teutonic blood in the population; the logical conclusion was the elimination of the 'degenerate' elements in the national stock.[10]

These debates in the 1890s about moral degeneracy, racial rejuvenation, national unity and the Jews remind us that Britain played her part in laying the foundations for inter-war racist and fascist thinking. Indeed, the work of Kidd was influential in Germany, and Hitler is known to have drawn on Chamberlain's anti-Semitic writing for his own race theory.[11] In Britain racist and eugenic ideas were disseminated by, among others, Arnold White, a scaremongering journalist and propagandist who wrote *Efficiency and Empire*, and by Anthony Ludovici, a prolific polemicist who produced fifty books and pamphlets and became an important influence on inter-war fascist organisations including English Mistery and English Array. Ludovici and White despised the liberal state for its effete value system and for nurturing the feeble, which they attributed to the debilitating influence of Judaic-Christian ideas and to the revolutionary belief in equality and feminism. Instead they looked to a revival of virile, aristocratic leadership and royal authority which would somehow push aside the liberal democracy that currently hampered Britain in her role as a great imperial power. According to Ludovici, civilisation could not be expected to maintain its forward march without the use of violence and the physical elimination of the unfit: 'the time has come to recognise the inevitability of violence and sacrifice, and consciously to select the section or elements in the world or the nation that should be sacrificed.'[12]

Perhaps the most obvious of the preconditions for inter-war fascism was anti-Semitism which was rife throughout British society and across the political spectrum. Its best-known advocates were the writer and MP, Hilaire Belloc, and his friends Cecil Chesterton and G. K. Chesterton who used their journals, the *Eye Witness* and *My Weekly* as vehicles for anti-Semitic propaganda, notably during the Marconi Scandal of 1912–13 when they targeted two ministers, Rufus Isaacs and Herbert Samuel, for corrupting British politics. They fostered the stereotyped view of Jews as 'a non-Christian culture, embedded for ages in what has always been a Christian culture, [which] acts as an irritant and to some extent as a parasite, because it trades and schemes but does not plough or produce'.[13] They blamed Jews for virtually all historic and recent disasters including the Boer War and the revolutionary movements in Russia; and condemned them as basically disloyal. 'Cosmopolitan Jews ... for some unexplained reason are almost always prepared to do Germany's work', as Leo Maxse put it in 1913.[14] Protesting their desire to 'solve' the Jewish problem, some of the anti-Semites and eugenicists of Edwardian Britain advocated Zionism and even approved the use of the 'lethal chamber' to eliminate undesirable elements from society.[15]

British fears about national decline and degeneracy reached a climax amid the disasters of the war in South Africa between 1899 and 1902. Accustomed to easy victories over poorly armed African and Asiatic opponents, the British faced a shrewd and resourceful enemy in the shape of the Boer settlers who inflicted humiliating defeats at the battles of Colenso, Stormberg and Magersfontein, and besieged British forces at Ladysmith, Mafeking and Kimberley. As a result of these setbacks, earlier misgivings crystallised into a thesis of 'National Decadence'. In turn this generated a fashionable doctrine of 'National Efficiency', designed to improve the health and fitness of British youth, to reform education, introduce compulsory military training and to institute a state-funded social welfare system. 'What is the use of talking about Empire', asked the future prime minister, H. H. Asquith, 'if here, at its very centre, there is always to be found a mass of people, stunted in education, a prey of intemperance, huddled and congested beyond the possibility of realising in any true sense either social or domestic life ?'[16]

National Efficiency attracted those who felt detached from the political parties, including Conservatives (Lords Milner and Curzon), Liberals (Lord Rosebery and Richard Haldane) and Fabian Socialists (Sidney and Beatrice Webb). Their characteristic complaint was the decay of the parliamentary system and the incompetence of amateur party politicians in tackling complex issues; Salisbury's handling of the Boer War epitomised the problem. As Rosebery put it: 'Party is an evil; its operation blights efficiency.' National Efficiency enthusiasts sought to remedy matters by reducing the role of parliament and of elected local authorities and replacing them with experts and successful entrepreneurs capable of promoting the national interest without being diverted by party, doctrine or sectional interest. A conspicuous example of this thinking was the establishment of the Committee of Imperial Defence in 1902. Essentially a private body comprising a few ministers, soldiers, sailors and military experts, this committee was designed to develop British strategy for the next war by bypassing both parliament and the garrulous twenty-member cabinet. As such it represented a threat to parliamentary democracy. But it was the wartime administration of David Lloyd George from 1916 to 1918 that most closely reflected National Efficiency thinking, by incorporating businessmen and non-political experts into government ministries, and thus reducing the role of party politicians. While National Efficiency was not fascism, it represented a halfway house to the corporate state, preparing the way for it by fostering a disparaging view of parliament and by promoting the obsessive belief in national decadence that was at the heart of post-1918 fascism.

If long-term trends were unfavourable to liberalism, this did not prevent British Liberals winning a landslide victory at the general election of 1906. The Asquith governments remained firmly in control, winning three general elections and achieving major policy goals. However, popular perceptions of the Edwardian period have been dominated by *The Strange Death of Liberal England*, a book published by George Dangerfield in 1935. This offered a vivid account of an elected government wilting under attack by a succession of violent or unlawful movements: a wave of strikes, suffragette militancy, the peers' rejection of Lloyd George's 1909 'People's Budget' and the constitutional conflict with the House of Lords, and the physical resistance to Irish Home Rule by the Ulster Unionists. Written from the perspective of a Europe in which democracy had succumbed to totalitarian regimes of left and right, the book saw the Edwardian controversies as the first symptoms of the current malaise.

In fact, however, the defining characteristic of the Edwardian era was a crisis of *Conservatism*. Alarmed by the pace of social change and the rise of the labour movement, and frustrated by its own impotence, sections of the Edwardian right began to display a dangerous disillusionment with conventional politics. Not only did Conservatives lose three elections in 1906 and 1910, but the Liberals' electoral pact with Labour and, in effect, the Irish Nationalists, appeared capable of excluding the Tories from power indefinitely. Quite suddenly the political agenda had changed. The Liberals engineered a stream of innovations including graduated taxation of incomes, old age pensions, minimum wages for miners, health insurance and labour exchanges; and by 1914 they threatened to introduce land taxation and minimum wages for agricultural labourers. Many Conservatives attacked this programme as tantamount to Socialism, but privately they feared they had lost the ideological battle. For several years rebellious Tories vented their anger on their own leader, A. J. Balfour, for leading them to three defeats. In 1911 the 'Balfour Must Go' campaign forced him out, the first of a succession of party leaders to perish at the hands of his own followers; throughout the new century disloyalty was to be the Conservatives' secret weapon.

Before long the leaders of this 'Radical Right' began to display the paranoia of a displaced ruling class. They included MPs such as Lord Willoughby de Broke and peers such as Lord Halsbury, who demanded all-out resistance to Liberal reforms, and propagandists including Leo Maxse of the *National Review*, Anthony Ludovici and Arnold White. Deploring the fashion for Liberalism, Socialism and feminism, and the influence of trade unions, Jews and foreigners, they saw the best hope for Britain in an aristocratic revival; and their growing alienation from parliamentary politics made them vulnerable to the appeal of physical force. Though Conservatives, they felt deeply frustrated by what they saw as the limp, compromising leadership of Balfour and others. They despaired of the camaraderie shown by leaders of the rival parties, strengthened by their common social life and their experience as lawyers: 'they do love one another so!' as Willoughby de Broke put it.[17] He believed that too many politicians treated politics as essentially a game, pursued almost frivolously without regard to the national interest – precisely the charge levelled by Mosley and other inter-war fascists against conventional politicians.

This left the Radical Right perpetually suspicious of betrayal and very susceptible to conspiracy theories to explain their setbacks. Consequently, though its members operated within the parliamentary system, they became distinctly ambivalent towards it. Sir George Lloyd, an extreme right-winger who entered the Commons in 1910, quickly fell into despair over what he saw as the failure to introduce tariff reform and to respond to the challenge of Germany: 'sixty years of Cecils in a cosmopolitan system have killed much patriotism and national feeling,' he complained. Only a year after becoming an MP Lloyd contemplated resignation: 'I hate the House of Commons so badly that I despise myself for not having the initiative to abandon it,' he admitted.[18] Lloyd was typical of the Radical Right in his unsophisticated approach to politics; anxious to find simple, immediate solutions they yearned for a patriotic, virile leader. Baffled by the complexities of urban, industrial Britain, they sought to recreate a deferential, rural past, which is why, like Lloyd himself, they found an imperial role more congenial than domestic politics. For them, the outbreak of war in 1914 came as an enormous relief because it united the nation and created one simple, over-riding cause.

For the Radical Right the nadir of Edwardian politics was the constitutional crisis of 1910–11 when the Asquith government managed to enact the Parliament Act curtailing the veto powers of the House of Lords – with the reluctant acquiescence of many Tory peers and MPs. This opened the way to further radical attacks on causes they regarded as sacred, notably the Union with Ireland. In this crisis Ludovici and de Broke wanted the aristocracy to seize the initiative and thrust aside the traitorous politicians. In his book, *A Defence of Aristocracy*, Ludovici advanced a bold case in favour of aristocratic rule as against democratic or representative government. For him aristocracy represented the finest achievement of the race insofar as it maintained strict control of heredity and avoided mixing with lesser races. What, then, had gone wrong in Britain? Ludovici claimed that the House of Lords had lost prestige because it had been diluted by upstart capitalists, plutocrats and bourgeois who lacked a proper stake in the country, by which he meant landed wealth. Unhappily for the Radical Right, the Tory leaders now regarded the peers as an electoral handicap after their trouncing by Lloyd George over the budget and after their role in the two elections of 1910. Thus, although they promised to restore the powers of the upper chamber and to reform its composition, they never did so.

To many on the extreme right it seemed that the conspiracy had penetrated even to the monarchy itself. The diehard supporters of the peers were outraged to find that the King had promised to create enough Liberal peers to enact Asquith's Parliament Bill if the Tory majority refused to do so. In an extraordinary debate in the Commons on 24 July 1911 the prime minister stood at the despatch box for half an hour while leading Tory members shouted hysterically, 'Traitor!' and 'Who killed the King ?' By the 1920s this notion of 'The King in Chains' had given rise to an influential thesis to the effect that the King's authority had been usurped by parliamentary politicians over many years, effectively relegating him to a largely decorative role. A revival of royal power became an important element in fascist thinking partly because it appealed to their need for virile leadership and because it enabled them to cast fascism in a patriotic, British form. As things stood, many Edwardian critics believed that after 1911 Britain's traditional tripartite system, based on a sharing of powers between King, Lords and Commons, had been subverted in favour of one-chamber government; in effect this meant a prime-ministerial dictatorship sustained by corrupt deals with small parties. From this it was a short step to the argument that although the government had been elected, it was not *legitimate*.

The right argued that the Liberals lost their independent majority in 1910 but still retained office through informal coalitions; the Labour members had been bought with the payment of salaries to MPs in 1911, and the Irish with a commitment to introduce a Home Rule Bill. The critics also condemned the creation of a vast spoils system as a result of the Liberals' social policies; new bodies such as Labour Exchanges and the National Insurance Commission had generated 7,000 jobs by 1913.[19] If this were not bad enough, the Liberal Party was alleged to enjoy a corrupt relationship with its commercial and industrial backers who were rewarded with honours for their donations; these were the 'Radical Plutocrats' who happily subsidised policies calculated to subvert British interests and traditions. This attack on the financiers of Liberalism took on an anti-Semitic and xenophobic tone because of the prominence of such entrepreneurs as Sir Alfred Mond and Sir John Brunner in the party. They were cited as evidence that anti-British elements had insinuated themselves into positions of influence where they could betray the national interest. Amid the war scares of the Edwardian years it was tempting to lump them together with pacifists and aliens as men intent on playing the Kaiser's game by inhibiting the government from arming against Germany.

These attacks on the legitimacy of elected governments became dangerous only insofar as they fostered a cult of violence. Although few were prepared to give explicit endorsement to violence, Anthony Ludovici argued that it was healthy and essential in driving the expansionism which was the engine of civilisation.[20] While the British had apparently perfected the art of changing their governments peacefully, physical force remained a lively tradition particularly during parliamentary elections, and the law permitted the organisers of political meetings to use 'stewards' to beat up their opponents if their heckling was considered to be disruptive. The stakes were, however, raised by the Edwardian controversies which prompted the losers to contemplate resorting to force when thwarted at the ballot box. The upsurge of trade union militancy provoked this kind of thinking. Arnold White, for example, advocated establishing a committee of public safety and creating a volunteer police force to defeat strikes by coal miners. This was precisely the role British fascists aspired to fill during the General Strike in 1926.

Moreover, several authorities in constitutional law, including Professor Goldwin Smith and A. V. Dicey, had advanced the thesis that since the law rested ultimately on physical force, the sovereignty of parliament would be jeopardised by any legislation enacted in the face of male opposition.[21] Though originally employed by the opponents of votes for women, it was used to lend respectability to those who were determined to resist the establishment of a Home Rule parliament for Ireland. Under the Parliament Act the Home Rule Bill, which was announced in February 1912, could become law, despite rejection by the peers, if passed three times by the House of Commons. Angry that their last line of defence had been removed, the Ulster Unionist leaders, Sir Edward Carson and Sir James Craig, gave notice of their intention of defying London by establishing a provisional government. By signing the 'Ulster Covenant', Unionists pledged themselves to refuse to recognise the authority of a Dublin parliament. Yet they held only 17 parliamentary seats out of 103, and after losing one to a Home Ruler in 1913, they were in a minority even in Ulster. When Winston Churchill arrived in Belfast to support Home Rule in February 1912 he had to be spirited away by the police because of the violent response among Protestants, and as the legislation slowly made its way through parliament they resorted to increasingly violent methods to intimidate their opponents.

In this they received backing from the leaders of the Conservative and Unionist Party in Britain, many of whom regarded the ending of the Union with Ireland as a strategic mistake and as the start of a retreat from empire. At a notorious rally at Blenheim Palace in July 1912 Andrew Bonar Law, who had replaced Balfour as Conservative leader, denounced the Liberal government as 'a revolutionary committee which has seized by fraud upon despotic power'; he went on to endorse Unionist tactics by claiming that even though the Bill might be passed, 'there are things stronger than Parliamentary majorities . . . if an attempt were made to deprive these men of their birthright – as part of a corrupt Parliamentary bargain – they would be justified in resisting such an attempt by all means in their power, including force.'[22] To this end the opponents of Home Rule established the Ulster Volunteer Force which, along with the Orange Lodges and the Ulster rifle clubs, undertook military training with a view to intimidating and ultimately resisting the authority of a Home Rule parliament. In April 1914, 20,000 rifles were illegally imported to arm the volunteers.

Whether this would have resulted in a civil war remains a matter of speculation as the European war interrupted developments. Although there was an element of bluff and brinkmanship on Bonar Law's part, Unionist tactics certainly promoted the creeping militarisation within the Radical Right; it encouraged them to believe that in a crisis the officers of the British army would take their side rather than follow instructions from a government of which they disapproved. For this reason Sir Edward Carson and his volunteers have been seen as the precursors of the fascist paramilitary organisations that sprang up in Britain during the 1920s. Long before Mussolini's rise to power, his movement had given concrete form to the notion of virile and authoritarian leadership capable of sweeping aside an effete, unpatriotic elected government. With the Home Rule Bill ready for the Royal Assent by the summer of 1914, the outbreak of the First World War could not have come at a more crucial moment.

TWO

Decadence, Democracy and Revolution

'If [the Tsar] had shot a few hundred Socialists and governed firmly Russia would have been all right today.'

Lady Bathurst to Leo Maxse, June 1918

On 29 July 1914 the First Lord of the Admiralty, Winston Churchill, instructed the British Home Fleet to leave Portland, where it had recently mobilised, for Scapa Flow in the Orkneys. 'Picture this great Fleet,' wrote an exultant Churchill, 'with its flotillas and cruisers, streaming slowly out of Portland Harbour, squadron by squadron, scores of gigantic castles of steel wending their way across the misty, shining sea, like giants bowed in anxious thought.'[1] That night a procession of warships eighteen miles long passed through the Straits of Dover without lights to occupy their places in the coming struggle with the Kaiser's Germany. After the controversies of the previous years Britain's declaration of war in August 1914 came as a great relief to the critics of parliamentary government.

Despite all the naval scares Britain enjoyed a comfortable lead over her rival in Dreadnought-standard ships; the navy swept German shipping off the seas, it kept open the overseas trade on which the population depended, and it deterred the German High Seas Fleet from any attempt to invade the British Isles. Meanwhile, the navy conveyed the British Expeditionary Force to France in time to join the French in checking the outer swing of the German armies attempting to encircle Paris. The German war plan thus failed, and the Allies won time in which to bring the weight of Russian manpower and British industrial output to bear against the Central Powers. In due course Britain mobilised a massive army and generated hitherto unimaginable quantities of munitions for four years of war. This represented a triumph for the Edwardian governments that had diagnosed the key strategic problem posed by a war with Germany and reoriented British diplomacy and military planning to deal with it; in no war in her modern history has Britain been so well prepared at the outset.

Yet before long contemporaries began to see a different picture. In the absence of any dramatic naval or military victories it appeared that Britain was losing the war. On the Western Front Sir John French, struggling to come to terms with trench warfare, claimed that his offensives would have achieved a breakthrough if he had been supplied with more munitions; though impossible to prove, this gave him and other mediocre generals a good alibi because the public preferred to believe them rather than the politicians. On the home front Britain's entry into the war encouraged the warring parties to show their patriotism by agreeing to a political truce. However, partisan controversy was fully maintained by the newspapers, led by Lord Northcliffe's *Daily Mail*. Refusing to accept that Britain had been prepared for war, Northcliffe argued that the failure to score any decisive victories was a reflection of the lack of enthusiasm for war on the part of Asquith's Liberal government and proof that the war effort was hamstrung by spies and traitors entrenched in government and the civil service.

As a result, much of the next four years was taken up with attempts to root out all alien influences in British institutions. People with German-sounding names who became immediate targets for popular hysteria made judicious changes; the MP, Sir Charles Schwann, became Swan, and Prince Louis of Battenberg adopted the name Mountbatten, though he was still forced to give up his post as First Sea Lord. Among politicians the chief victim was the former Secretary of State for War, Richard Haldane, who by reorganising the army so as to produce the expeditionary force had done more than anyone to prepare the country for war, but was traduced by the Northcliffe press for his interest in Germany philosophy. Northcliffe was briefly frustrated when Asquith appointed Britain's foremost military hero, Lord Kitchener, as Secretary of State for War, hardly a sign of lack of enthusiasm for the war. Unfortunately, Kitchener, who felt nothing but contempt for the press, banned journalists from reporting on the British Expeditionary Force. Although Northcliffe reluctantly accepted that censorship was justified he continually challenged the government to 'have the courage to tell the British people the truth', and he attempted to discredit Kitchener as the best means of undermining the government.[2] He took his revenge in May 1915 in an editorial on the latest offensive entitled 'Lord Kitchener's Grave Error': 'What we do know is that Lord Kitchener has starved the army in France of high explosive shells'.[3] Yet although sales of the *Daily* Mail plummeted for a time and copies were burnt in the streets of London, its claim that the war effort was being hampered by domestic subversion commanded wide sympathy.

In 1914 Britain's arrangements to counter espionage were still rudimentary. She relied on the Special Branch of the Metropolitan Police, and a Secret Service Bureau formed in 1909 as a result of official recognition that 'an extensive system of German espionage exists in this country'. This bureau subsequently became known as MI5. It was led by a professional soldier, Captain Vernon Kell, whose staff comprised nine army officers, three civilians, four female clerks and three policemen to deal with espionage at home and throughout the empire. Kell's main method involved building a card index of suspects which held 25,000 names by 1925. But on 4 August 1914 just twenty-one alleged spies were arrested of whom only one was prosecuted. In the charged atmosphere of wartime this modest tally was interpreted as proof of the skill of the enemy spy network and its influential connections within the system. During 1915 the press circulated rumours to the effect that the prime minister's wife, Margot Asquith, organised tennis parties for imprisoned German officers; in 1916 it was alleged that she supplied them with what *The Globe* called 'dainties and comestibles', and concealed military secrets inside their food parcels.[4] Although Margot Asquith successfully sued for libel on both occasions, such absurd stories enjoyed currency throughout the war because the public had become wholly credulous about conspiracy, sabotage and betrayal in high places, encouraged by witch-hunts against alien influence in the newspapers.

Hysteria reached a peak in 1917 as a result of articles in *Vigilante*, a journal published by Pemberton Billing, who had been elected to parliament as an Independent with Northcliffe's support. Billing employed one Harold Spencer, an obsessive anti-Semite who had been dismissed from Army Intelligence for 'delusional insanity'. Spencer's articles publicised a so-called 'Black Book', a list of 47,000 'perverts' compiled by the Germans comprising the names of prominent British people, including cabinet ministers, their wives, and privy councillors, and details of their sexual habits. In May 1918 Pemberton Billing was prosecuted at the Old Bailey for accusations against an actress, Maud Allen, over her production of Oscar Wilde's play, *Salome*, which 'ministered to sexual perverts'. By way of defence Billing cited the 'Black Book' and discomforted the judge, Mr Justice Darling, with the claim that his own name was among the 47,000 listed perverts. The jury's decision to acquit Billing was received with acclaim. Among 'superpatriots' the existence of the 'Black Book' was regarded as proof of a conspiracy, backed by German, Jews and Bolsheviks, to bring down Lloyd George's Coalition Government and restore Asquith to power with a view to suing for peace.

These wild claims about decadence and disloyalty within the British establishment gained credibility from the pre-war obsession with spies and the attacks on collusion and betrayal among leading party politicians. Such fears were accentuated by the wartime political truce and by the failure to win clear victories on land or at sea. When Asquith's Liberal government fell in May 1915, the critics thought they had finally destroyed the enemy within.

Northcliffe, meeting Emmeline Pankhurst on the day the government fell, was 'quite like a lunatic, bouncing up and down on the leather seat of his armchair, crying out: "I did it"'.[5] However, the triumph proved brief, for the new coalition included many of the old ministers and merely formalised the existing collusion between the parties. Moreover, the Coalition freed the politicians from their worst fear: a wartime general election. Although parliament's life ran out in December 1915, the lists of voters had become hopelessly inaccurate owing to the migration away from their homes of thousands of workers to the armed forces and to munitions factories. Now that the three main parties had joined the government, there seemed no need to hold an election. In July 1915 registration of voters was abandoned, making the registers even more outdated, and from December onwards parliament simply prolonged its own life by stages, usually for eight months at a time, until the end of the war; by then it was three years beyond its proper term.[6] This created the precedent for suspending elections during the Second World War which spared the country an election from 1935 to 1945.

Long before the fall of Asquith's government it had become apparent that liberalism would be an early casualty of the war. On 12 August 1914 the Defence of the Realm Act (DORA) conferred on the government wide powers to issue regulations in order to maintain national security and defence without consulting parliament.[7] In effect this allowed it to control the activities of opponents of the war and to impose extensive restrictions on civil liberties. The military authorities gained powers to take over private property; meetings could be prohibited, buildings closed and curfews imposed. A major restriction on the civil liberties of women was the introduction of Regulation 40D which made it an offence for women with venereal disease to have sex with members of the armed forces; as a result, in some areas the authorities imposed curfews on women, banned them from public houses and subjected them to up to 62 days in prison. The state also enjoyed the right to deport individuals from one part of the country to another merely on suspicion that they might act 'in a manner prejudicial to the public safety or the defence of the realm'. This was used against David Kirkwood, one of the leaders of the Clyde Workers' Committee, who was awoken at three in the morning by police with a warrant under the DORA; he was put on a train and court-martialled in his absence with no opportunity to offer a legal defence; the military authorities had been empowered to take cases from the civil courts for trial by courts martial. As it often proved difficult to find evidence to sustain prosecutions, the authorities used their right to detain suspects under Regulation 14B of DORA, a power they retained until 1923. The government also banned any unauthorised communication of information, suppressed several anti-war newspapers, and censored newspapers for printing 'anything calculated to be or [that] might be directly or indirectly useful to the enemy', which in effect covered all criticism of the war effort or official policy.

However, none of these restrictions caused as much political controversy as the decision by the new Coalition Government to replace Britain's traditional policy of voluntary recruiting with military conscription; this was applied to single men in January 1916 and to married men in June. Despite the massive response of men to the call for volunteers, the country still seemed a prey to fears, originating in the Boer War, that its young men were too corrupted by materialism and leisure to respond willingly to the call to arms. By the summer of 1915 the press was denouncing 'shirkers' for holding back, and young women had started distributing white feathers to men seen in public wearing civilian clothes. These were the first symptoms of the post-war obsession with declining masculinity, the spread of effeminacy and the influence of homosexuality in Britain. Condemning the 'great flood of luxury and sloth' of pre-war days, Lloyd George claimed the war had helped the nation to see 'the fundamental things that matter in life, that have been obscured from our vision by the tropical growth of prosperity'.[8] It became fashionable to see the war as the means of recreating a virile, imperial nation and saving Britain from her effete and decadent recent past. Admittedly, parliament allowed those who could convince a tribunal that they had a conscientious objection an exemption from military service. However, in 1917 this concession was qualified when MPs decided to include in the Representation of the People Bill a clause barring accredited conscientious objectors from having a vote for a five-year period after the war. This retrospective punishment imposed on men who had merely availed themselves of an exemption granted by parliament was perhaps the most blatant attack on the liberties of British citizens and the most signal evidence of the erosion of liberal attitudes during wartime.[9]

In fact, by the time Asquith's premiership came to an end in December 1916 most of the key liberal causes had been abandoned. Its unqualified commitment to the outright military defeat of Germany and its refusal to allow anything to stand in the way of victory at home, should have reassured right-wing critics. On the contrary, however, the close collaboration between Lloyd George and the leading Conservatives heightened existing suspicions about the conventional parties and accentuated what they saw as the subversion of true Tory principles; in this way the Edwardian contempt for parliament and party politics was carried forward into the inter-war period. Well before the war had been won it was clear that the government had paid a heavy price in the form of sweeping pledges to introduce state-financed social reform, the retention of higher taxes and a massive extension of voting rights.

When the military situation unexpectedly turned in the Allies' favour in the summer of 1918, Lloyd George capitalised on his popularity as 'The Man Who Won The War' by arranging a general election before Christmas. The Conservative leader, Andrew Bonar Law, judged that his party stood in need of Lloyd George's prestige to win the support of the millions of new working-class voters at this election: 'We must never let the little man go,' he reportedly insisted. Consequently he readily agreed to fight the election in alliance with Lloyd George, which meant extending his premiership into peacetime for an apparently indefinite period.

This strategy worked insofar as it led to an overwhelming victory for the coalition. The election ushered in a period of almost continuous office for the Conservatives which lasted until 1945, interrupted by two brief Labour governments in 1924 and 1929–31. They had other reasons to feel reassured. While monarchies were falling and empires disintegrating all over Europe, Britain's victory in 1918 enhanced national pride, bestowed fresh prestige on her national institutions and her empire and thus went some way to stabilising her political and social system. As a result, in the immediate post-war period Britain was to be less obviously susceptible to anti-parliamentary challenge than countries like Italy and Germany whose regimes had been severely discredited by the experience of war. On the other hand, even in Britain four years of mass war helped prepare the ground for a fascist movement by severely weakening liberalism both as an idea and as an organised political force. It was not that the war introduced new ideas, rather it made many of the pre-war concerns about race, decadence, anti-Semitism and internal subversion appear more acute. Those who championed these fears became less marginal because the war and its aftermath appeared to have proved their warnings justified and their critique of British traditions valid.

Certainly the euphoria induced by victory in November 1918 proved ephemeral. Within a year of the election Conservatives began to behave as though they were condemned to opposition rather than entrenched in power. This generated a fractious, embattled mentality which persisted throughout the inter-war period. The explanation for this is that many of them saw Britain as a victim of external subversion and betrayal from within. The evidence for such fears seemed too obvious to ignore. During the war trade union membership had increased from 4.1 to 6.5 million, and reached 8.3 million by 1920. From 1917 onwards workers increasingly went on strike, apparently forgetting the patriotism that had inhibited them at the start of the war. Six million working days were lost in 1918; and the end of the war found Britain engulfed in militancy, losing 35 million days in 1919, 26 million in 1920 and 86 million in 1921 – half as many as in the General Strike itself.

It was tempting to see the strikes as inspired by the Bolshevik Revolution and by a Russian regime committed to exporting revolution, destroying capitalism and overthrowing empires.

Some British Socialists, enthused by the downfall of Tsarism, flirted with Marxism and aspired to create 'Soviets' of workers designed to run industry and bypass the parliamentary system on the Russian model. 'Parliament is a decaying institution,' proclaimed Sylvia Pankhurst, 'it will pass away with the capitalist system.'[10] For a time around 1919–20 the idea of 'direct action' by industrial workers gained favour in the Labour movement partly because the huge majority enjoyed by Lloyd George's government seemed to make parliamentary action irrelevant to the needs of the workers. In 1920 dockers at the East India docks refused to load a ship, the *Jolly George*, with munitions intended by the government to assist counter-revolutionary forces in Russia, and stopped it sailing. Such actions led many people on both the left and the right to anticipate the spread of the revolution to Britain. Admittedly, the organisations on the far left were so small, so quarrelsome and so starved of resources, according to Special Branch intelligence, that their chances of launching a revolution in Britain were negligible. On the other hand, they were known to be receiving subsidies from 'the eye of Moscow' and other exotically named sources, and Soviet agents tried hard to persuade the quarrelling factions to join together. Eventually a Unity Convention, held in July 1920, led to the formation of the Communist Party of Great Britain. However, the Communists spent much of their time fruitlessly trying to persuade the Labour Party to allow them to affiliate. Although they were consistently rebuffed, their efforts to infiltrate larger organisations gave some grounds for the exaggerated right-wing fears about Bolshevik influence in the trade unions, the Labour Party and the national movements in Ireland and India.

Around 1920 these new fears about Bolshevism became inextricably entwined with existing obsessions with the idea of a worldwide Jewish conspiracy. In May of that year a *Times* correspondent reported on a new publication, *The Jewish Peril*, based on the book, *The Protocols of the Elders of Zion*, which had been published in Russia by Professor S. Nilus in 1905 and had been in circulation among army officers and at the peace conference at Versailles. 'Never before have a race and a creed been accused of a more sinister conspiracy,' commented the newspaper.[11] *The Jewish Peril* described a secret, centuries-old, international organisation of Jews animated by hatred of Christianity; its goal was the destruction of the Christian national states and their replacement with international Jewish dominion. This was to be achieved by weakening the status quo by the infusion of disintegrating political ideas including Liberalism, Socialism and

Communism, culminating in national division and chaos. Political leaders were to be turned into puppets manipulated by the hidden hand of the Elders. Since all key institutions – parliament, the press, the law, the stock exchange, science, the arts –were ultimately controlled by money, they too could be used to promote the materialism that would enfeeble the whole system.

The interesting feature of this is how quickly the wild claims in *The Protocols* gained currency. Initially the book gained respectability from the endorsement of *The Times* and of H. A. Gwynne, the editor of the *Morning Post*, who described it as 'a most masterly exposition'. Although the *Times* correspondent acknowledged it might be a forgery, he argued that it presented a credible account of Jewish influence in Russia since 1905; and the paper printed further letters claiming that of the 556 principal state functionaries in Russia no fewer than 488 were Jews.[12] In August 1921 *The Times* printed three articles revealing *The Protocols* as a forgery; but although it was discounted in all but the most fanatical circles, its underlying thesis about Jewish influence continued to command widespread support throughout the post-war period. Propagandists like Leo Maxse who had spent years denouncing the Jews as malignant wirepullers, now felt vindicated by the Russian Revolution: 'Whoever is in power in Downing Street, whether Conservatives, Liberals, Radicals, Coalitionists, or pseudo-Bolshevists – the International Jew rules the roost.'[13] Above all, *The Protocols* gained credibility from the neurotic mood of post-war society which grasped eagerly at any plausible working hypothesis to explain the perils surrounding it. A reputable publisher, Eyre & Spottiswoode, had printed 30,000 copies of the first edition, followed by second and third editions in August and September 1920. In 1923 a new translation was made by Victor Marsden, a former *Morning Post* correspondent, and from 1922 onwards it was kept in print by an extreme anti-Semitic organisation, The Britons.[14]

Founded in July 1919 by Henry Hamilton Beamish, The Britons defined their aim as 'to protect the birthright of Britons and to eradicate Alien influence from our politics and industries'. Its membership was restricted to those who could prove that their parents and grandparents were of British blood. Beamish himself was a forty-five-year-old officer who had served in South Africa during the war and had attempted to launch himself on a parliamentary career by standing twice as an Independent candidate at Clapham in 1918. Despite his enthusiasm for 'ousting the Hun and making Germany pay for the war' and appeals for the votes of ex-soldiers, Beamish was heavily rejected, and his failure left him increasingly a prey to anti-democratic ideas and conspiracy theories. By the 1920s he had become an eccentric and fanatical racist who advanced lurid claims about the role of

Jews as the perpetrators of the white slave traffic; he wanted to ostracise any English person who 'betrays the purity of his white blood' by marrying a Jew. Beamish's solution to the Jewish problem was not the homeland in Palestine to which Britain was officially committed by the Balfour Declaration of 1917, but compulsory transportation to Madagascar, a suitably remote and unhealthy island.[15] In 1919 he denounced the Liberal MP and 'Radical Plutocrat', Sir Alfred Mond, as a traitor, for trading with the enemy, and as 'the head of the International Jewish gang who . . . are selling our dear old England'. When his victim sued, Beamish was fined £5,000. To avoid paying he fled to South Africa in 1920 and spent much of the inter-war period in Italy, Germany and Southern Rhodesia, propagating his ideas about an international crusade against the Jews.

Although The Britons folded in 1925 when its journal, the *Hidden Hand*, ceased publication, it continued until 1932 in the form of the 'Britons Publishing Society' whose main role was to keep *The Protocols* in print. It created the seedbed from which many of the British fascist organisations sprang, and it stimulated anti-Semitism among men such Arnold Spencer Leese and John Beckett who later became prominent fascists. 'Everything in this little book [*The Protocols*] rang true,' wrote Leese, 'I simply could not put it down until I had finished it.'[16] These 1920s anti-Semites were often men from a military background like Leese, or an imperial one such as Lord Sydenham of Combe, a former Governor of Victoria and of Bombay, or from a landed background such as George Pitt-Rivers, the author of a popular pamphlet entitled 'The World Significance of the Russian Revolution'. During the 1920s the conspiracy thesis was endlessly rehearsed in right-wing journals. In 1922 Alan Ian Percy, the eighth Duke of Northumberland, a man completely obsessed with the idea of a world conspiracy, even founded a new, proto-fascist journal, *The Patriot*, to publicise the threat posed by the 'Hidden Hand'. Like Maxse, who continued to denounce 'Pro-Germanism in High Places', the Duke believed that Germany maintained its agents in Britain in the shape of Jewish financiers who exercised influence over government policies.[17]

Perhaps the most prolific propagandist was Nesta Webster whose books – *World Revolution* (1921), *Secret Societies and Subversive Movements* (1928) and *The Surrender of an Empire* (1931) – won the approbation of the right-wing journals. In *World Revolution* Webster traced the origins of Europe's current problems from the philosophers of the eighteenth century and the intrigues of secret societies in bringing about the French Revolution. The subversive ideas of that revolution, in the shape of Liberalism and Socialism, spread across Europe leading to periodic upheavals including the revolutions of 1830 and 1848, the Paris Commune in 1871, Fenianism in Ireland

and the anarchist and Socialist movements in Russia. These developments culminated in the revolution of 1917 which was the work of Bolsheviks and Jews now acting as the agents of Satan in his grand plan to destroy Christianity.[18] In this way, during the 1920s the new obsession with Bolshevism became inextricably mixed up with existing anti-Semitism.

For fascists the refusal of conventional politicians to take this conspiracy thesis seriously was merely proof of the dangerous complacency and degeneracy that had overtaken the parliamentary parties after 1918. In a sense this represented the fascist take on the fashionable view that the three-quarters of a million British war deaths had swept away the cream of the nation's future leaders, leaving her with an enfeebled and even unpatriotic political elite. As a result, during the 1920s many fascists looked with especial concern to the next generation of British youth, regarding it as vulnerable to alien influence. They particularly condemned the Americanisation of popular culture as manifested in the Hollywood-dominated cinema, an industry largely under Jewish control. In the 1920s Hollywood was seen as undermining British imperial values; while in the 1930s Charlie Chaplin, whose film, *The Gold Rush*, was banned in Germany, was denounced as a Jewish intellectual. 'One of the first duties of Fascism', noted A. K. Chesterton,'will be to recapture the British cinema for the British nation.' Similarly fascists hoped to recover the theatre for the national cause. Looking fondly back to Elizabethan England as the culmination of British cultural achievement, they liked to claim that Shakespeare would have been a fascist. In this way the perceived need to counter the degeneracy afflicting both society and the political system became a characteristic theme in fascist propaganda throughout the inter-war period.

Fears about external subversion also gained force as the political elite woke up to the realisation that its grip on power had suddenly become greatly imperilled as a result of the massive extension of the vote in 1918. The eight million electorate of pre-war days had mushroomed to over twenty-one million. 'Democracy has arrived at a gallop in England,' observed Stanley Baldwin, one of the more relaxed and liberal Conservatives; 'can we educate them before the crash comes ?'[19] The extra five million male voters had been enfranchised with little debate on the basis that their patriotic conduct during the war removed any doubts about their loyalty. By contrast the claims of women had been a source of continuous controversy since the 1860s; but most previous proposals envisaged granting a vote to a mere one million women – not the 8.4 million enfranchised in 1918. Inevitably, once victory had been secured the implications of this unprecedented increase alarmed many politicians.

For its critics the new electorate posed a threat by virtue of the social class, gender and even age of the new voters. The Victorian and Edwardian

generations felt particularly sceptical about the values of youthful pa
pation in politics. Although twenty-one was the legal age for voting, in
tice many men did not register until later in life, usually when they married
and became head of their own household. By introducing a simpler system
enabling people to vote on the basis of their normal place of residence, the
1918 reform swept on to the registers millions of relatively young people,
whom the politicians regarded as naive, politically ignorant and thus susceptible to Socialist propaganda. Subsequently some Conservatives advocated
twenty-five as a more suitable age, though they conceded the impossibility
of withdrawing the vote from those already enfranchised.[20]

As a result a sharp generation gap developed in the aftermath of war.
Many of the younger Tories, including Anthony Eden, Harold Macmillan
and Oswald Mosley, who had seen active service as junior officers and entered
parliament in the 1920s, resented the attitude of the older generation and
came to despair of its incompetence as war gave way to economic depression and unemployment. 'The old gang continued to play musical chairs
for office,' commented A. K. Chesterton (second cousin to G. K. Chesterton)
after returning to Britain from South Africa.[21] The feeling that power had
been monopolised by the elderly and enfeebled at the expense of the virile
young men who had sacrificed themselves in the war was to be one of the
most compelling arguments wielded by Mosley in his efforts to discredit
the entire parliamentary system, and it enabled fascism to speak to a large
constituency of the disillusioned.

The class composition of the new electorate also aroused apprehension
at a time when the labour movement was fast expanding and showing itself
susceptible to syndicalist and Communist ideas. Many critics of the 1918
reforms argued that a mass franchise was inherently destructive of democracy because 'what everyone possesses, no one values'. They depicted
democracy as perverse and dangerous because it handed power to the least
able and it demoralised men of intellect who were driven out. The Duke of
Northumberland, a good example of an extreme Tory deeply disillusioned
with conventional politics, pointed to the sale of honours to disreputable
men by Lloyd George's honours' touts as proof of his view that a mass electorate inevitably lowered standards of political morality.[22] Other critics
simply warned that as the landowners, rentiers and professionals were now
outnumbered, middle-class people would be taxed for the benefit of the
working classes.[23]

Such opinions were not confined to a reactionary fringe, but gained an
airing in the mainstream press. 'The fact is', commented Lord Rothermere's
Daily Mail, 'that quite a large number of people now possess the vote who
ought never to have been given it.'[24] The *Mail* was not alone in objecting

to the abolition in 1918 of the rule excluding anyone dependent on the Poor Law: 'It is obviously unjust to the community ... that persons in receipt of public relief, who are living on the taxes paid by workers out of their earnings, should have the power to dictate policy and decide elections.'[25] After granting the popular vote in 1918 there was little chance of the political parties attempting to withdraw it. Yet most of the leading right-wing journals, including the *English Review*, the *National Review*, the *Saturday Review* and *The Patriot*, maintained a chorus of complaint about the reformed system throughout the 1920s and came dangerously close to a total repudiation of democracy.

Extreme as these views may seem, the critics of democracy saved their real venom for the new female voters who, at 8.4 million, comprised over 40 per cent of the 1920s electorate. Although the pre-war suffragists had persuaded a majority of MPs to support the cause, they had made much less progress with the wider public whose traditional attitudes towards women's role remained largely intact. Consequently, the praise that had been lavished upon women for undertaking men's jobs during the crisis of wartime proved ephemeral. By 1919 women's attempts to hang on to their employment were more commonly disparaged and attracted virtually no sympathy from the politicians who had so recently granted them the vote. One of the most shrill critics of female emancipation was Anthony Ludovici, the aristocratic revivalist of the Edwardian period, who became a leading propagandist for several of the inter-war fascist organisations. Keen to disparage their patriotism, Ludovici argued that during wartime women 'had never had such a good time, nor had they ever been so well paid for having a good time'.[26] In enfranchising them, he claimed, the Coalition Government had acted without a mandate 'in this atmosphere steeped in emotionalism, sentimentality, and abnormally stimulated servile ardour'. Women's suffrage, according to the *Saturday Review*, had merely raised expectations about the effects of the vote that were doomed to disappointment, for 'nothing will cure women of perverted ambition except experience'.[27]

Such embittered remarks underline the effect of the war in first creating full employment for men but then casting many of them, including returning soldiers, into long-term unemployment from 1920 onwards. This proved damaging to traditional male pride and left many men feeling demoralised by evidence of female emancipation. Those who had not fought for their country were easily antagonised by the sight of women strutting around in the uniforms of the women's police, the Voluntary Aid Detachments, the Women's Army Auxiliary Corps, the Women's Royal Navy Service, the Women's Royal Air Force and the Land Army. They sometimes expressed their personal insecurity by extravagant displays of hostility towards women and became vulnerable to the demands for virile leadership and contempt for democracy.

Although the impact of votes for women now appears to have been modest and gradual, in the immediate aftermath of the war many men saw the implications of female emancipation in exaggerated and even apocalyptic terms. They, of course, assumed that women would use their political weight to win concessions at the expense of men, and believed that the 'Lost Generation' had left British society too enfeebled to resist. In the *English Review* Douglas Jerrold complained that 'women have stepped into dead men's shoes in the labour market and in the professions', and consequently did not need to be rewarded with the vote. In 1917 the MP George Lloyd's wife wrote: 'I know the suffrage nightmare must be poisoning your hours of solitude – and it really is rather hard on you that such an infamy should have been forced upon you when you were almost looking the other way.' Even in the 1920s the Duchess of Atholl, who was herself elected to parliament in 1923, argued that it would be unfair to men to give equal voting rights to women because 'we lost 740,000 precious lives of men in the Great War . . . a great extension of this kind looks like taking advantage of the heroic sacrifices of those men'.[28] Such sentiments suggest a British version of the stab-in-the-back theory popular among Germans who believed their fighting men had been betrayed by feeble politicians. If such views seem slightly bizarre in view of the contribution women had made to winning the war, they do illuminate the post-war mentality of large sections of the political class, and suggest how sceptical it was about the advent of mass democracy.

Anti-feminists were briefly reassured by the fact that female participation had posed no discernible threat to the coalition at the 1918 election – indeed women were thought to have supported it even more strongly than men. Yet for some years to come anti-democrats continued to see the effect of enfranchising women in apocalyptic terms. This reflected fears that the vote was merely one symptom of a confusion of gender roles which profoundly threatened British society and the political system. The consequence of encouraging women to ape men, so the argument ran, was not only damaging to women, but also accelerated the emasculation of *men*; women's progress undermined virility and led to British 'flabbiness'.[29] Misogynists saved their greatest contempt for the single women who were believed to be intent on using their new freedom to retain their wartime employment and thus avoid marriage and motherhood: 'unmarried women are a malignant power because they are bound by no responsibilities; they pursue an erratic course, directed entirely by their abnormal emotions and crazy outlook on life.'[30] As a result of the death of around 750,000 relatively young and marriageable British men, it was natural, in the early 1920s, to assume that the enhanced surplus of women over men would make marriage a practical impossibility for a large number of women. Combined with the continuing fall in birth rates, this implied a dwindling population which, in turn, would undermine Britain's ability to populate and defend her huge but empty empire.

Such fears help to account for the hysterical attacks in the *Daily Mail* and *Daily Express* on the irresponsible behaviour of the 'Flappers', those selfish and irresponsible young women who were alleged to be pursuing an energetic social life and sexual emancipation. In the process, the pundits claimed, they ceased to be real women in both the psychological and even the physical sense. Referring darkly to women 'with short hair, skirts no longer than kilts, narrow hips, insignificant breasts' the *Express* warned: 'this change to a more neutral type can only be accomplished at the expense of the integrity of her sexual organs.'[31] The young Barbara Cartland, who was busily establishing herself as an authority on motherhood in the 1920s, insisted that the 'new slimline girl' would produce unhealthy babies if she produced them at all.[32] Fears about declining motherhood also reinforced men's hostility towards women in uniform, which they interpreted as a sign of masculinity and even lesbian tendencies. Before 1914 British society had shown little awareness of lesbianism, but during the 1920s the idea attracted public debate and condemnation. In 1921, when the House of Commons debated the Criminal Law Amendment Bill which dealt with male miscon- duct, an amendment was introduced to make homosexual acts between women illegal for the first time. In the debate F. A. Macquisten urged the House to 'do its best to stamp out an evil which is capable of sapping the highest and the best in civilisation'. Members took it for granted that lesbianism was a psychological disorder, and Lieutenant Colonel Moore- Brabazon suggested: 'There are only three ways of dealing with these perverts. The first is the death sentence . . .The second is to look upon them as frankly lunatics and lock them up for the rest of their lives . . . The third way is to leave them entirely alone, not notice them, not advertise them.'[33] The amendment was approved by nearly three to one. The episode was symptomatic of the effect of war in accentuating existing obsessions with degeneracy and moral decline in Britain.

These contemporary perceptions of the results of female emancipation would have been much less shrill had society not been in mourning for what came to be known as 'The Lost Generation'. It was widely believed that only the feeble, the cowardly and those who had been psychologically shat- tered by trench warfare had survived. Barbara Cartland recalled that young men returning from France often sought the reassurance of a quick marriage and, if thwarted, became emotional and dramatic even to the extent of threatening suicide; in 1919 she was herself the target of an undiplomatic approach by a forty-five-year-old colonel on the Isle of Wight, the first of no fewer than forty-nine proposals of marriage received up to 1927, all of which she unceremoniously rejected.[34] Even Vera Brittain corroborated this view, describing the 'charming ineffectiveness of so many present-day husbands' and suggesting that the survivors suffered either a lack of vitality or poor physique; as a result she thought Britain was heading for a matriarchal society.[35]

This obsession with the moral and physical deterioration of British men and women, which was characteristic of the 1920s, formed another part of the intellectual milieu from which fascism emerged. Throughout the decade fascists characteristically deplored the loss of virility amongst men which, they argued, had turned Britain's political system into a shabby refuge for a generation of emasculated, unpatriotic, middle-aged nonentities. The epitome of this decline, in their view, was Stanley Baldwin who dominated Conservative politics from 1923 to 1937. Their worst fears about Baldwin were confirmed after his election victory in 1924 when he allowed himself to be pressurised into promising to introduce equal franchise for women, an innovation which threatened to turn women into a majority of the electorate for the first time. The legislation, announced in April 1927, was condemned by the extreme right within his party on the grounds that he had no mandate for further reform: 'There are not too few but too many electors already,' claimed the *National Review*.[36] According to the critics, once women became a majority of the electorate unmarried women would promote feminism even to the extent of launching their own party.[37] They resurrected the old warning that if governments became subject to female pressure Britain would inevitably lose its credibility as an imperial power, especially in Africa and Asia; the fashionable policy of pandering to the League of Nations was symptomatic of this reluctance to stand up for British interests.

These timeworn arguments gained fresh force in the 1920s as a result of the new challenges presented by national movements, particularly in India and Egypt. In the *Daily Mail* Lord Rothermere shrewdly attempted to convince the Conservatives that if young women became voters they would be especially susceptible to Socialist propaganda, a claim which, however preposterous it seems in retrospect, gained credibility from the steady advance of the Labour Party in the 1920s. In a bizarre campaign the *Mail* carried daily headlines that screamed: 'Men Outnumbered Everywhere'; its editorials exploited Conservative fears by suggesting 'Why Socialists Want Votes for Flappers', and they urged 'Stop the Flapper Vote Folly'.[38] It is fair to note that the MPs ignored Rothermere's scaremongering partly through loyalty to the government but also because experience with female voters since 1918 offered some reassurance. But their acceptance of the policy was interpreted, as were all setbacks for the extreme right, as evidence of the extent to which parliamentary politicians had already been corrupted by the pervasive influence of liberalism.

Nonetheless, the reactionary rhetoric reflected the insecurity of a generation of men who had been unsettled by mass male unemployment and by the evidence of female emancipation. They often expressed their personal insecurity by extravagant displays of hostility towards women. Easily persuaded that the new democracy was degenerate, they became vulnerable to the manly appeal of fascism with its characteristic demand for virile, patriotic leadership.

THREE

The Advent of Mussolini

'Though *Fascismo* may be quite specifically Italian in scope and utility, its message to all Europe in ruins is one of hopefulness . . . Europe has begun to revive, that is the lesson.'

Austin Harrison, *English Review*, 35, December 1922

The Italian *fascisti* first appeared during the autumn of 1914. They were largely recruited from patriotic former Socialists who were determined that their country should enter the First World War. By December they had fallen under the leadership of the thirty-one-year-old Benito Mussolini, the editor of the left-wing newspaper *Il Popolo d'Italia*. Disgusted by the politicians for insisting on keeping Italy neutral, Mussolini disparaged parliament as 'that pestiferous plague spot that poisons the blood of the nation'; and by May 1915 he had organised riots and threatened a civil war with a view to forcing the politicians into changing their minds. But in the event, the initiative came from the King, Vittorio Emanuele, who simply ignored the views of the elected parliament and signed a declaration of war against Austria. With some justice Mussolini subsequently claimed this as the beginning of the fascist revolution.[1]

In fact the decision proved disastrous. Italy's ill-prepared army suffered a humiliating defeat at the Battle of Caporetto in October 1916, and the war quickly undermined her precarious economy. However, as these setbacks helped to discredit and destabilise the country's political system, they reinforced the fascists' case for abolishing parliamentary politics altogether. In June 1917, following a bungled training exercise in which an exploding grenade left him with forty metal fragments in his arm, Mussolini was invalided out of the army and thus released to seek a new career. Eventually he launched his fascist party in Milan in March 1919. Though lacking a detailed programme at that stage, the movement was characterised by its extreme patriotism, its syndicalism, and by its contempt for the personnel and apparatus of parliamentary democracy which it regarded as a vulgar deception designed to maintain an effete class in power. Yet despite his use of violence and intimidation, Mussolini's party failed to gain any seats in the elections of 1919 and won just 35 in 1921.

Although the fascists resorted to violence to compensate for their lack of support, Mussolini's organisation could easily have been crushed by the army at this time. Vittorio Emanuele actually approved the introduction of martial law for this purpose. However, he then changed his mind, rejecting his cabinet's advice in the process because he wanted to remove the liberal government, thereby allowing Mussolini to develop a private militia and prepare for his coup. Indeed, in March 1922 the King invited Mussolini, now aged thirty-nine, to become prime minister. But the need to dramatise his victory over a decaying parliamentary system prompted Mussolini to stage a bogus *coup d'état* – the famous 'March on Rome' – in October. In this way the myth was created that he had bravely seized power with the sacrifice of three hundred 'fascist martyrs'. At once the chaos of which Mussolini had complained began to spread, thereby giving him the justification for his *squadristi*, an armed militia designed to intimidate and assassinate his political opponents.

Within a few weeks British politicians enjoyed an opportunity to inspect the new Italian regime when Mussolini arrived in London to participate in a conference about German reparations. While the Italian embassy organised a military parade of Blackshirts to salute his arrival, the new leader was, with difficulty, persuaded to leave behind his *manganello* – the wooden club that symbolised the *squadristi*. Revelling in his status as the first Italian statesman to play a key role in international affairs, Mussolini fed the press twice daily with news of his activities, including the information on one occasion that he could not be disturbed as he was in bed with a girl.[2]

The sophisticated and supercilious politicians of the far right might have been expected to react with disdain to the emergence of so vulgar a figure. But on the contrary, they found the phenomenon intriguing and even inspiring. The British reaction to Italian fascism has never received the attention it deserves, largely because the Churchillian preoccupation with Nazi Germany has dominated and distorted the historiography of the inter-war period. In fact Mussolini's movement had a much more protracted and positive influence in Britain, partly because the British could approach Italian fascism free from the inhibitions surrounding the Germans who had so recently been their chief enemy and because the 1922 coup coincided with a key point in domestic politics. For the British Government fascism in Italy was an experiment deserving of success, and its violent aspects could simply be overlooked. Moreover, from the early 1920s onwards Mussolini attracted the admiring attention of leading Conservative journals including the *English Review*, the *National Review*, the *Saturday Review* and *The Patriot*, as well as several newspapers, notably the *Daily Mail* and the *Morning Post*. They carried explanatory pieces by writers claiming to be well-informed about

Italy, such as Anthony Ludovici, Enrico Corradini, Filippo Virgilii, Luigi Villari and Dr C. Pellizzi, as well as the propaganda freely issued by Mussolini himself, and apologias by, among others, Leo Maxse, Lord Rothermere, Sir Charles Petrie, Captain Basil Liddell Hart, Francis Yeats-Brown, Harold E. Goad and Douglas Jerrold. What united these men was a visceral hostility towards democracy; those who came from a High Tory background had become alienated by what they saw as the vulgar materialism of western liberal society and the impact of capitalism on the poor, which they believed could best be remedied through the corporate state.

Although the British apologists for Mussolini were initially defensive, by the mid-1920s they had become increasingly confident in the superiority of the fascist regime when compared with the perceived failures of democratic government in Britain. Those who met him invariably depicted Mussolini as simple, charming and businesslike, not the bombastic and theatrical figure portrayed in left-wing demonology. They saw him as a resolute patriot – 'Italy finds her Cromwell' – who had brought his country into war on Britain's side. 'What a man!' commented Sir Douglas Haig after meeting him. 'He is really exceptional.' Only Margot Asquith, who recognised that he was 'on his best behaviour' when they met in April 1923, refused to be impressed and delivered a short lecture on Liberalism; 'imprisoning and terrorizing people is not a sign of power, it is a confession of failure,' she told him. The *fascisti* themselves were presented as men who had rejected the dead hand of pacifism and been galvanised by the new menace of Bolshevism into recognising that participation in war would create a better and greater Italy.[3]

But was Mussolini's fascism simply 'an Italian regime for Italians, a product of the Italian mind', in the words of T. S. Eliot? Foreign Office officials liked to see Italians as unstable people who required a dictatorial government; fascism there was not a problem for Britain because it was 'not for export'. Yet the apologists were keen to emphasise the wider moral and social significance of the political upheaval in Italy: 'it is a resurrection of character, something new in politics ... we have in *Fascismo* more than a Mediterranean or volcanic symptom. It is the movement of Youth and of artists, almost a sociological phenomenon ... Italy [was] not afraid to die, and so [is] reborn.'[4] In this way its British sympathisers elevated fascism to a higher plane and suggested its relevance to British conditions.

But why was the Italian example of such interest to the far right in Britain in 1922? Two immediate explanations present themselves. In the first place the advent of Mussolini coincided with a phase of sharp disillusionment over the evolution of the political system with its new mass electorate, and imputations of corruption and careerism. After six years of the Lloyd George

Coalition Government disaffected Conservatives rapidly succumbed to the attractions of an alternative model. Now that popular democracy had arrived many politicians no longer felt convinced that the British were as well suited to the system as they had once believed. According to Lord Rothermere, the proprietor of the *Daily Mail*, the *Sunday Dispatch* and the *Daily Mirror*, Mussolini had exposed the greed and idleness to which democratic politicians pandered; the Italians, so the argument ran, had been badly served by their system and by their corrupt politicians. 'With a criminally weak Government not unlike our own Coalition', wrote Enrico Corradini, 'the only hope of saving Italy from anarchy lay in the strong hand of organised patriotism.' 'The fascist regime', claimed Austin Harrison, 'has stepped into power over a Government afraid and too corrupt to govern.'[5] Whether Italian politics was quite as corrupt as they claimed in 1922 is arguable; but these comments clearly reflected British perspectives after four years of the all-party coalition under Lloyd George. Under the Duke of Northumberland aristocratic Tories were now leading a campaign against the flagrant sale of honours by the premier's touts, Maundy Gregory and Sir William Sutherland who freely offered knighthoods for £12,000–15,000, baronetcies at £40,000 and peerages for still more.[6] Through this system titles were bestowed upon men who had been convicted of fraud, tax dodging, food hoarding and even trading with the enemy.

Disgust at the devaluation of the peerage contributed to the revolt by backbench Conservative MPs in October 1922 when they overthrew their own party leader, Austen Chamberlain, by voting to withdraw from Lloyd George's Coalition. For right-wing rebels it was more than symbolic that this blow for pure and patriotic government coincided with the 'March on Rome'. While Mussolini had purged politics of corruption, so the argument ran, in Britain, by contrast, even the return to normal party government under prime ministers Bonar Law and Stanley Baldwin failed to correct the flaws in British political culture. In a remarkably frank comparison of the two countries in the *English Review* Ludovici derided the British penchant for parliamentary debates – 'lulled into partial somnolence by their soporific effect'– and insisted: 'there are no principles more urgently needed by modern Englishmen than that pursuit of reality, that hatred of fatalism, that suspicion of claptrap and romantic ideals, and, above all, that fervent patriotism which are the heart and soul of the Fascist movement.'[7] That a mainstream Conservative journal had begun to present a fascist system as superior to a liberal parliamentary one was indicative of the disillusionment prevailing in right-wing circles during the 1920s.

The second and most obvious explanation for the favourable reception of Italian fascism lay in the perceived threat of the Bolshevik Revolution.

Since 1917 the political establishment had been gripped by fears that Communist influence was steadily spreading across Europe, taking advantage of economic collapse, labour militancy and unstable regimes. Mussolini's coup offered the first check to the forward march of this revolution. Moreover, while no one believed British society to be as vulnerable as Italian, the experience of the previous four years suggested that she might be on the slippery slope to chaos. Trade union militancy, the popularity of 'direct action', the rise of the Labour Party, the formation of a British Communist Party in 1920 and the government's policy of buying off strikes with large wage increases could be plausibly represented as symptoms of a degenerate politics. Up to a point this diagnosis was even adopted by the Labour Party which, with an eye on its own claims to respectability, blamed the rise of fascism on the militancy and disorder engendered by the far left in Italy.[8]

Before long the extreme right began to use the Italian example to suggest that the resort to 'rough' methods would be justified if governments failed to maintain control in the face of popular disorder. As Leo Maxse wrote in the *National Review*:

> No doubt Labour Bureaux, Co-operative Societies, Workmen's Clubs and Socialist newspaper offices have been destroyed, but many of these were previously engaged in destruction . . . It leaves us comparatively calm . . . Italy has avoided the abyss – in no small measure thanks to the Fascisti whose operations are necessarily of intense interest to those of us who are most anxious that England shall escape this noisome pestilence.[9]

This line of argument was employed by Lord Rothermere, perhaps the most influential single propagandist for fascism between the wars. Notorious for his enthusiastic endorsement of the British Union of Fascists in 1934, Rothermere had been converted to the cause much earlier, largely due to his pronounced anti-Communism. Less than a year after the fascist coup he used the *Daily Mail* to explain 'What Europe Owes To Mussolini'. Making no secret of his 'profound admiration' for Mussolini, Rothermere claimed: 'in saving Italy he stopped the inroads of Bolshevism which would have left Europe in ruins . . . in my judgement he saved the whole Western world. It was because Mussolini overthrew Bolshevism in Italy that it collapsed in Hungary and ceased to gain adherents in Bavaria and Prussia.'[10] However, having adopted this heroic view, the British apologists for fascism felt compelled to remain silent during 1923 as the fascist *squadristi* launched their brutal campaign to suppress Socialists, Communists and even left-wing Catholic opponents. They even turned a blind eye to the kidnapping and murder of Giacomo Matteotti, the most prominent and courageous critic of the regime in June 1924. 'By resolutely grasping the nettle Signor Mussolini violated the accepted canons of Parliamentary and Press statesmanship,' admitted the *National Review* in an editorial that showed that it recognised the real nature of his regime.[11]

Faced with mounting evidence about the violence prevailing in Italy, the British pro-fascists endeavoured to raise the discussion to a higher level, arguing that the movement was no mere anti-Bolshevik spasm but an upheaval of the Italian mind against the tyranny of foreign ideas, especially liberalism and individualism. It represented a real revolution, comparable to the French Revolution of 1789, against a decadent political creed: 'Liberalism is no longer a historic necessity.' From this perspective outworn ideas were simply being replaced by nationalism and patriotism which possessed the power to unify the nation by contrast with the cult of the individual which had merely divided it.[12] In a revealing piece published in 1929 Lord Sydenham of Combe argued that most western states had been led astray by French revolutionary thinking into introducing notions of equality and individualism into their political culture, from which followed much of the weakness and division that now afflicted them: 'of this recoil from a gigantic delusion . . . Italy is the foremost and the most successful example . . . whatever may be the psychological differences between the British and the Latin races, we can all learn from their heroic effort to find a national solution of patent existing evils.'[13]

In fact, for several years after Mussolini's seizure of power it remained uncertain whether he intended to dispense entirely with parliament or would simply reinvigorate the executive within the existing system. He proceeded by stages to strangle the political life of Italy. In 1923 fascist guards, armed with revolvers and daggers, were stationed on the doors and in the galleries of the parliament building to humiliate and intimidate the elected representatives into granting him full emergency powers. By December 1925 parliamentary government had effectively been ended, and by 1926 the political parties had been abolished, made irrelevant by the corporate state. Italy continued to have a Chamber of Deputies comprising four hundred members chosen from a list of a thousand names drawn up by the Fascist Grand Council. This list was placed before the voters – men over twenty-one – in a national plebiscite, the options being to vote 'yes' or 'no' to the entire list, not to select individual candidates.[14]

However, the intimidation of opponents and the manipulation of elections that characterised the fascist system, did not deter the extreme right in Britain from endorsing the Italian model. According to Leo Maxse,

Mussolini was far from being a dictator because he had obtained a mandate for his innovations and implemented his programme constitutionally, though without hindrance from parliament. After visiting Rome in 1927 Winston Churchill commented: 'it is quite absurd to suggest that the Italian government does not rest upon popular bases or that it is not upheld by the active and practical assent of the great masses.' [15] A number of British observers argued that Italians either did not miss their former political rights or felt the price of losing them was well worth paying for the material and moral improvements attained under fascism. 'I could not find an Italian who was aware of any loss of liberty, any sense of grievance because he could no longer by his vote put into office one set or another of disastrous politicians,' wrote one observer. 'On the contrary, everywhere there is manifest in Italy today a new sense of national pride and civic dignity, a new confidence in the future.'[16]

Such a relaxed view of the abolition of political rights is more explicable in the context of what increasingly appeared to be a general retreat from democracy in the 1920s affecting Italy, Spain, Greece, Bulgaria, Hungary and Turkey. Could democracy survive in France and Germany? Even in Britain there was some speculation, not only amongst supporters of fascism, about the durability of parliamentary government in the aftermath of the General Strike of 1926, which had come close to overthrowing the elected government of Stanley Baldwin. In an article in the *English Review*, 'The Safeguarding of British Democracy', the MP Noel Skelton pointed out that among the Continental countries Italy was the dearest to Englishmen because of her cultural heritage and because nineteenth-century Italy had consciously adopted the English rather than the French view of constitutional institutions. Consequently: 'who . . . could not be profoundly moved when modern Italy flings aside democracy and calls to her councils the civic spirit and traditions . . . of ancient Rome?'[17] In fact, despite the general Anglophilia of nineteenth-century Italian politicians, Skelton's contention was debatable.[18]

However, Skelton's perception was significant even if based on a misreading. Impressed by the 'amazing release of energy produced by the Fascist Revolution', he reluctantly admitted that 'the new authoritarianism . . . bears all the marks of being an evolutionary movement discarding and supplanting an outworn form.' Though slightly reassured by the thought that democracy was inevitably at a disadvantage in societies dominated by the authoritarian traditions of the Catholic Church, he speculated: 'is there not spreading in England also an opinion that democracy is outworn?' While the political system was attacked by what Skelton called 'the rabble of political Anglo-Catholics', no one, he noted, spoke up for it in either main party: 'The Conservative Party has always contained a school of thought, not even yet extirpated, which tolerates rather than approves democratic government.'[19] The explanation lay partly in the expansion of popular democracy which was now more complex and burdensome and placed politicians under more pressure to cultivate public opinion. By way of rejuvenating British democracy Skelton came up with the referendum, an expedient to which Conservatives had often resorted when out of office in order to deal with such issues as tariff reform and women's suffrage. The referendum offered a means of squaring popular participation with decisive Conservative government; but to contemplate it, as Skelton did, under a Conservative government blessed with a huge majority was symptomatic of the disillusionment afflicting the party by the later 1920s.

In the early 1920s the fascist apologists had clearly entertained some misgivings about the durability of the Italian regime. 'The critical world continues to watch Signor Mussolini's amazing experiment in government with keen solicitude and with no small hope in its ultimate success', as Maxse put it.[20] But after five years they evinced a growing confidence that the abandonment of parliamentarianism had been justified by what Rothermere called 'the practical benefits of strong and enlightened government . . . for the first time Italy is now experiencing real liberty – the disciplined liberty which secures the fulfilment of duties as well as the enjoyment of rights.'[21] Beyond making general claims about the restoration of Italian national pride and vitality, British observers pointed to material advances. Five years of stable rule had put an end to strikes and the class war; taxation and unemployment had fallen, the balance of payments deficit had been redressed, and the government's annual revenue deficit had become a surplus. In its efforts to raise standards and eradicate corruption the state had expelled tens of thousands of superfluous bureaucrats, especially at the municipal level. Above all, agricultural output had been stimulated, the role of middlemen curtailed, and farmers secured in their occupation of the land.[22] These achievements resonated with many British Conservatives who felt highly aggrieved at the collapse of agriculture under a Tory government during the 1920s; and they help to explain why Sir Oswald Mosley devoted so much attention to farmers after he founded the British Union of Fascists.

British attitudes towards the fascist regime were also conditioned by Italy's role in international affairs. Italians' enthusiasm for Mussolini was partly explicable in terms of the restoration of their country's status in Europe; denied the territorial gains that had drawn them into war, they condemned the Treaty of Versailles and regarded the League of Nations as a mere tool of the victorious powers. For Mussolini it was therefore crucial to avenge the humiliations she had suffered over the peace settlement after the war and thus elevate her to the rank of a great power. As a result Italy posed the most consistent threat to the authority of the League and to the territorial status quo during the 1920s. Although the British were officially supportive of the League, they feared it would damage British imperial interests, and consequently they had no desire to invoke it in order to obstruct Italian ambitions. Mussolini attained his objectives by the unashamed bullying of smaller powers; the South African leader, General Smuts, memorably described him as 'running about biting everybody', a reputation which carried weight with British policy-makers throughout the inter-war period.[23] In 1923 he attacked Greece, seized the island of Corfu, and prepared for war with Turkey with a view to obtaining territory for a new Italian colony. In the following year he annexed Fiume from Yugoslavia, and by 1925 he had effectively imposed a protectorate over Albania, turning King Zog into a puppet of Italy.

Although these actions went a long way to discrediting the League of Nations, they were welcomed in Britain by many Conservatives. When the Baldwin government expressed its reservations about the occupation of Corfu, Lord Rothermere responded that there was nothing provocative in Mussolini's foreign policy: 'Do [the government] know where they are drifting? I do not think so.'[24] According to Rothermere, rather than undermining her position by getting on the wrong side of Mussolini, Britain should cooperate with France and Italy to contain any threats to peace in Europe. Notwithstanding Rothermere's criticism the British government was largely anxious to conciliate Mussolini, despite its protestations of support for the League of Nations, because of Italy's strategic position in the Mediterranean astride Britain's vulnerable lines of communication with India and the Far East. This led the government to exaggerate the strength of the Italian navy and the risks to British shipping by way of justification.

As a result the Italian dictator rapidly acquired an undeserved reputation as the strong man of Europe which was crucial to his image as a great fascist leader. This was strikingly illustrated by his dealings with Germany which the Italians regarded as an obstacle to their expansion. Although under the peace settlement they had gained territory around Trieste and the South Tyrol from Austria-Hungary, they aspired to include many more Italian nationals in the Italian state. However, in the South Tyrol they had acquired a large German and Slovene population which naturally added to Germany's sense of grievance over the peace treaty. Mussolini chose to stand up for Italian interests in the region by confiscating the property of German-speakers, banning the use of their language and closing their schools. In 1926 when the German government backed down after a confrontation over Italy's behaviour in Trentino, Mussolini was hailed by the far right in Britain.

'If only responsible statesmen nearer home would take a leaf out of Signor Mussolini's book instead of imagining that every Anglo-German difficulty is solvable by amicable platitudes,' pronounced the *National Review*, 'the European situation would be measurably more stable.'[25] In fact, this thinking did influence British policy after Hitler's rise to power in 1933 when the government attempted to cultivate Anglo-Italian friendship with a view to using Italy as a check on the ambitions of the Nazi regime. This pro-Italian policy eventually collapsed ignominiously when Mussolini invaded Abyssinia in 1935.

Abyssinia was merely the culmination of an ambitious imperial programme designed to extend Italian influence across much of the Balkans and North Africa and to transform the Mediterranean into the 'Italian Sea' – in effect a visionary scheme to recreate the glory of the Roman Empire. Grandiose as this may seem in hindsight, at the time it appeared both credible and desirable to many people in Britain. After all, Italy already possessed Somaliland, Eritrea and Libya. Moreover, her high birth-rate generated an extra half a million people each year, an increase that Mussolini intended to maintain by restricting women to their traditional domestic role. But as Italy lacked the resources to employ this surplus population at home, it followed that she must colonise the sparsely inhabited territory of northern Africa.

To those who accepted the pretensions of fascist Italy as a dynamic, virile, modernising force such ambitions could only be regarded as legitimate. Mussolini cultivated such expectations by his visit to Tripoli in 1926 where he proclaimed that in the 'Napoleonic Year of Fascism' it was Italy's destiny to recover the territory of the former Roman Empire and to draw lesser states – Greece, Yugoslavia, Spain – into her sphere of influence. These far-fetched ambitions won endorsement from some surprising sources. The former suffragette, Christabel Pankhurst, now a campaigner for Second Adventism, hailed the new Roman Empire which she believed 'is about to become the dominant factor in international affairs'.[26] Like other observers, Pankhurst accepted at face value the fascist claim that Mussolini had succeeded where his predecessors had failed in uniting his people, and confidently expected the proclamation of the new Italian empire. That this development entailed the spread of dictatorship was taken merely as symptomatic of the return to the conditions prevailing before the first Coming of Christ to earth.[27]

If such confident predictions appear absurd in the light of Italy's performance during the Second World War and in the context of a historiographical tradition that paints Mussolini as a mere buffoon, it is important not to dismiss them simply because we know the end of the story. By the mid-1920s

Mussolini loomed impressively over the European stage by virtue of occupying a key strategic and diplomatic position. He had momentum at a time when other great powers – notably France and Britain – seemed to be in decline; the United States remained immured in isolation; and Germany and Russia were absorbed by their internal controversies. 'He is the greatest figure of the age,' Rothermere enthused in 1928; 'Mussolini will probably dominate the history of the twentieth century as Napoleon dominated that of the early nineteenth.'[28] In retrospect such hyperbole only underlines the heroic inability of the *Daily Mail* to understand the present or to predict the future; but in the 1920s its propaganda conferred a measure of respectability on the fascist regime, and compounded the impression of unity, strength and aggression that Mussolini was so anxious to convey. It suggested that Britain's national interests lay in distancing herself from the divided and Socialistic French in order to cement a friendship with virile, anti-Communist Italy. By the 1930s this had become part of the consensus on the right of politics, not merely the view of an extreme fringe.

Inevitably, however, British views about Italian fascism began to polarise. To the immense irritation of Mussolini's supporters, the liberal press, especially the *Daily Chronicle* and the *Daily News*, regularly carried hostile reports on political conditions in Italy which the pro-fascists saw as an attempt to sow discord between the two countries.[29] On the other hand, their incorrect predictions about the fall of the fascist regime discredited them, and perceptions of Italy's value to Britain as an ally encouraged mainstream politicians, as opposed merely to right-wing ideologues, to keep on the right side of Mussolini. They made some clumsy attempts to reinterpret him for a British audience. On visiting Rome in January 1927 Winston Churchill swallowed uncritically the regime's propaganda about the improvements achieved under fascism, and informed the press: 'I could not help being charmed by Signor Mussolini's gentle and simple bearing and by his calm, detached poise in spite of so many burdens and dangers.'[30] The Foreign Secretary, Austen Chamberlain, observed that 'Mussolini would not be a fascist if he were an Englishman in England', which may have been an oblique way of suggesting that those who sympathised with him should feel safe within the Conservative Party. Churchill chose to put it less subtly when he admitted: 'If I had been an Italian I am sure that I should have been wholeheartedly with you from start to finish in your triumphant struggle against the bestial appetites and perversions of Leninism.'[31]

Churchill's response to Italian fascism was striking since, as a former Conservative who had spent the years from 1904 to 1923 as a Liberal, he was not naturally associated with the pro-fascist sections of Conservatism. The obvious explanation for his enthusiastic view lay in his extreme reaction to the revolution in Russia and in his return to the Conservative camp as an outspoken champion of anti-Bolshevism. Not that this carried conviction with all Tories, many of whom continued to regard him as an opportunist, a free-trader and a Radical. At the time of his visit to Rome Churchill was Chancellor of the Exchequer under Stanley Baldwin. Although they had defeated the first Labour government in 1924 and seen off the General Strike of 1926 with unexpected ease, Conservatives felt unhappy about their inability to make large inroads into unemployment in the later 1920s. Churchill was well aware that the economic costs of the nine-day General Strike had been huge, and he knew how lucky the Baldwin government had been when the TUC called it off unexpectedly. It was against this background that he assessed the relevance of the Italian experience in 1927. Although he emphasised that 'we have not had to fight this danger [Communism] in the same deadly form', the General Strike had left him highly appreciative that 'Italy has provided the necessary antidote to the Russian poison. Hereafter, no great nation will be unprovided with an ultimate means of protection against cancerous growths.'[32] Allowing for Churchill's fondness for lurid language, these remarks merit serious consideration. Though not a fascist by any means, he had evidently concluded that fascist *methods* for countering Communism would remain a valid option, even in Britain, if the challenge posed by the left were to reappear in a second, and better organised, general strike.

In the early stages of Mussolini's regime even Rothermere had conceded that his methods were 'not suited to a country like our own', but he had qualified this by saying that 'if our northern cities became Bolshevik we would need them.'[33] In 1927, when celebrating 'Mussolini's Five Years in Power', he asserted that the tendencies that had created a crisis in Italy in 1920–1 were currently at work in Britain; a conservative government in Italy had attempted to appease the Socialist clamour by a policy of concessions and surrender, but 'the only result was to hasten the arrival of disorder.' This, of course, was exactly the pattern Rothermere detected in Britain. In the intervening period he had become severely disillusioned with Baldwin and agitated by the General Strike; refusing to be reassured by the swift resolution of the strike, he condemned the Baldwin administration for allowing it to arise in the first place and for 'the feebleness which tries to placate opposition by being more Socialist than the Socialists'.[34]

While Rothermere was undoubtedly using fascists and fascism as a stick with which to beat the conventional Tory leaders, his unrelenting campaigns against them during the inter-war period reflected more than simply his imperialism and his enthusiasm for protective tariffs. Rothermere's diagnosis of post-war political and social problems was essentially a fascist one in that it encompassed not just anti-Bolshevism but a profound rejection of the parliamentary system and a sense of moral crisis from which the country had to be saved. 'I am proud that the *Daily Mail* was the first newspaper in England ... to give the public a right estimate of the soundness and durability of [Mussolini's] work,' he boasted in 1928.[35] His repeated visits to Italy in these years made him all the more concerned to correct what he saw as a misunderstanding of Mussolini in Britain, and prepared the way for his explicit adoption of the fascist cause under Oswald Mosley in 1934.

By 1929 British perspectives on fascism were increasingly influenced by the mounting economic-political crisis facing the country. Since the end of the war Britain's economic growth had been modest and she had largely failed to recover her pre-1914 export markets. As chancellor Churchill had taken a crucial decision in 1925 to return to the gold standard, but the effect was to overvalue sterling, and thus make exports expensive. Although conventional wisdom held that the new value of the pound could be maintained by reducing manufacturing costs, especially wages, one by-product of the General Strike was to deter most employers from attempting the extensive cuts that they thought desirable. As a result unemployment remained stubbornly high at around 10–11 per cent during 1927–9, and the Baldwin government increasingly appeared unable to lead the country out of the depression. This focus on unemployment contributed to its defeat by Labour in 1929, a development which angered and alarmed the right-wing critics of Conservative policy. In these circumstances the British apologists for fascism naturally focused on the economic dimensions of Italian fascism and on the regime's ability to live with the working class. Though he had been expelled from the Socialist Party, Mussolini had not lost sight of the causes that originally led him to Socialism.[36] Despite the suppression of normal trade union activity, Italian fascists were anxious to dispel the idea that their movement was anti-labour; they simply claimed to be anxious to prevent class conflict dividing the nation and to harness patriotic labour to the national cause.

The corporatist element thus assumed considerable importance in the fascist rationale, both in terms of its practical policy and as a symbol of the fascists' desire to exalt the state. In the parliamentary system, so the argument ran, it had proved almost impossible to control the forces of labour and capital, a point well taken by those on the right in Britain. But by granting full and formal representation to every interest, including labour, the state was freer to act impartially and to regulate the economy in the national interest. Among other things this encompassed imposing checks on profiteering, instituting minimum wages and funding a welfare system – policies which helped to explain why organised labour had ceased to be hostile to fascism.[37] According to Lord Sydenham, corporate representation allowed the sectional interests to make their contribution but not to embarrass the government or provoke controversy; and the political parties similarly lost their capacity to obstruct and divide under this system.[38] This, he claimed, was not a dictatorship but 'the greatest step in national reconstruction ever known'. The implication, as Sydenham did not hesitate to spell out, was that it would be mistaken to assume that the British would never tolerate this system as a practical way of combining patriotism with progressive reforms. Though such a drastic departure was, as yet, scarcely entertained by British politicians, the manifest inability of the Baldwin government to handle the economic depression and consequently to stave off the further advance of the Labour Party in 1929, forced many Conservatives to consider seriously their party's commitment to conventional parliamentary politics.

Even so, the question for disillusioned right-wingers in Britain in the 1920s was how to reconcile fascist-style autocracy with the British tradition. For some, the key to this lay in the relationship between fascism and monarchy. As the historian Sir Charles Petrie put it, an unqualified democracy was essentially a 'fair-weather system only, impossible in a time of storm and stress'; consequently 'the case for a dictatorship in times of crisis can hardly be overstated.'[39] But to move from democracy to dictatorship, so the argument ran, did not imply displacing the monarchy, for, as Italy demonstrated, the two worked satisfactorily in conjunction. In a remarkable travesty of Italian history, Petrie described how Victor Emmanuel had skilfully handled the post-war political crisis by inviting Mussolini first to join a government and then to form one of his own; this reflected public opinion and achieved a transition from a parliamentary to a fascist system without bloodshed.[40] Subsequently, 'under the Fascist regime King Victor Emmanuel III is working in the closest and most whole-hearted cooperation with Signor Mussolini'; this was possible, in Petrie's view, because monarchy and fascism represented the interests of the nation as a whole rather than the sectional interests associated with the political parties. In the same way, when the time came to terminate the dictatorship, Petrie reassuringly suggested, the monarchy was there to supervise the change.

For anti-democrats in Britain the obvious message in all this was that when firm government was required, as it plainly was during the 1920s and more especially after the political-economic crisis of 1931, it could be safely undertaken as a temporary expedient under the aegis of the Crown. The Italian model seemed to suggest that a move away from the parliamentary tradition need not involve a total discontinuity, for the central role played by the monarchy would soften the alien qualities of a fascist system.

FOUR

Boy Scout Fascism

'Each nation interprets [fascism] in its own way, and ours is essentially British.'

Brigadier General Blakeney, *Nineteenth Century*,
January 1925, 140

Britain's first fascist organisation emerged in May 1923, only six months after Mussolini's coup, inspired in part by his success as well as by fears of left-wing subversion in Britain. Historians have found it hard to take seriously the 'British Fascisti', as the organisation was initially known, regarding it as a movement for Boy Scouts who had never grown up. This impression may have been inspired by Brigadier General Robert Blakeney, one of the leaders, who characterised the British Fascists as the adult manifestation of the Boy Scout Movement: 'both uphold the same lofty ideals of brotherhood, service and duty,' he wrote.[1] Many members undoubtedly joined in the hope of finding something mildly adventurous, but had only a superficial grasp of its politics, as is suggested by a typical escapade in March 1925 when a group of British Fascists kidnapped Harry Pollitt, the Communist leader, on a train in Liverpool. They apparently intended to punish him by forcing him to spend a weekend in North Wales, which seems a far cry from the castor-oil treatment usually applied to the opponents of Mussolini. One might well conclude from such episodes that the British Fascists represented a rather English, dilettante expression of fascism.

In fact, the most influential figure in the British Fascists up to 1926 was no dilettante. Brigadier General Blakeney, who gave the new movement its organisation and its paramilitary structure, had been the general manager of the Egyptian State Railways until 1923. But its founder, Miss Rotha Lintorn-Orman, was more of an eccentric. The twenty-eight-year-old granddaughter of Field Marshal Sir John Lintorn Simmons was widely known as the 'Man-woman'. She had joined the 'Girl Scouts' in 1909 and even established her own troop in Bournemouth. Like many upper-middle-class girls Rotha Lintorn-Orman had served with distinction during the war and found the experience liberating. After working in Serbia with the Scottish

Women's Hospital Corps, for which she was decorated, she became Commandant at the British Red Cross motor school with responsibility for the training of ambulance drivers. In the process she realised the value of a uniform in winning new opportunities for women, especially after the war when attitudes towards women's employment became markedly hostile. The political views of her military family and her own experience of disciplined, patriotic organisations pointed Lintorn-Orman towards semi-military forms of political participation after 1918. The British Fascists also attracted other more conventional women including Viscountess Downe (a lady-in-waiting to Queen Mary), Lady Sydenham of Combe, Lady Menzies of Menzies, Baroness Zouche of Haryneworth and Nesta Webster. Despite the reputation of fascism for anti-feminism, many of these women played an active role and promoted the formation of women's units.

Much less is known about a second element in the British Fascists, namely the working-class and middle-class 'toughs' who engaged in regular confrontations with the Communists in Hyde Park. One of the earliest recruits was William Joyce, later notorious as 'Lord Haw-Haw', who joined in December 1923, aged seventeen. Born into a Southern Irish Loyalist family, Joyce became an ardent Conservative and Unionist who 'reviled everyone who held anti-British views'. As a teenager he hung around the local barracks of the Black and Tans and Lenaboy Castle, the headquarters of the Royal Irish Constabulary; his later claims to have been a British agent may have been fantasy, though he probably passed information to the Black and Tans.[2] After his family settled in Dulwich in 1923 Joyce joined the Junior Imperial League, the youth organisation of the Conservative Party, but he felt betrayed by the British establishment for abandoning the Union with Ireland. Increasingly consumed with hatred towards Catholics, Communists and Jews, he saw fascism as the best means of prosecuting his crusade against his and the nation's enemies.

More typical among the leadership of the British Fascists were men from military and naval backgrounds, including Brigadier General Sir Ormonde Winter (Deputy Chief of Police and Deputy Director of Intelligence in Ireland 1920–2), Brigadier General T. Erskine Tulloch, Colonel Sir Charles Burn MP, and Admiral John Armstrong. The new organisation also recruited many aristocratic and landed figures, notably Lord Garvagh, the first President, the Earl of Glasgow, Lord Ernest Hamilton (son of the Duke of Abercorn), the Marquis of Ailesbury, Lord de Clifford, Earl Temple of Stowe and Sir Arthur Hardinge, a former ambassador to Spain.

From these names it is immediately obvious that the British Fascists never attracted a politician of the first rank to provide the inspiring leader that all fascist movements required. The peers were largely obscure figures, disgruntled about falling land values, collapsing agricultural prices, high taxation and death duties. Already susceptible to the Radical Right critique of liberal democracy before 1914, such men felt now impelled to take some action. The retired military figures reflected a wider resentment among men who failed to find a satisfying role in a post-war Britain whose governments seemed bent on running down the armed forces and pandering to the organised working class. In addition to the professional soldiers, the organisation drew upon a reservoir of several hundred thousand ex-officers who had briefly risen to officer status as a result of wartime needs but were now suffering acutely from their inability to find employment commensurate with their new social standing.[3]

Hampered by uncertainty about how best to apply the fascist model to British conditions and by the lack of a dominant leader, the British Fascisti suffered from a series of disagreements and tactical reappraisals throughout the 1920s. As early as 1924 the organisation changed its name to the British Fascists, rather than *Fascisti*, in the hope of deflecting accusations of alien influence; nor did members wear a uniform until 1927 when they adopted the blue shirt and beret. In 1924 sixty members broke away to form the more militant National Fascisti, and in 1926 the General Strike provoked another and more serious split. Finally, in 1928 several former members, led by Arnold Leese, established the Imperial Fascist League, which was highly anti-Semitic and adopted a more explicit fascist ideology. These divisions inevitably created confusion about the different groups, and complicated life for the British Fascists who were anxious to distinguish themselves from the National Fascisti, a small organisation of extremists who wore black shirts and used the Roman *fasces*, or bundles of rods, to underline their links with Italian fascism.

Militantly anti-Semitic and more narrowly focused on street-fighting, the National Fascisti never disguised the fact that their aim was to 'smash the reds and pinks'.[4] Their leaders certainly had a taste for the melodramatic: 'comrades, under the shadow of your banners, it is beautiful to live, but if it is necessary it is still more beautiful to die.'[5] They also showed a talent for publicity, as they demonstrated in October 1925 when four armed members were despatched to hijack a delivery van en route to Euston Station carrying 8,000 copies of the *Daily Herald*. The van was crashed and abandoned. Although the perpetrators, who pleaded that they intended to draw attention to the subversive character of the newspaper, were easily caught, Sir Archibald Bodkin, the Director of Public Prosecutions, claimed he had insufficient evidence to charge them with larceny, choosing to prosecute them for causing a public nuisance instead. Such treatment led left-wing politicians to complain about the reluctance of the authorities to apply the law fairly to the extreme right, though many activists in the labour movement regarded the fascists as too ridiculous to constitute a serious threat.[6]

It is a comment on the National Fascisti that their best-known recruit was Valerie Arkell-Smith, a transvestite who spent many years masquerading as 'Sir Victor Barker', 'Colonel Ivor Barker' and 'Captain Barker'.[7] Born in Jersey in 1895 Valerie Arkell-Smith had been taught fencing, boxing and cricket by her father. During the war she joined the Voluntary Aid Detachments, drove ambulances in France and worked at a remount depot for horses in Bristol. There her colleagues called her 'Barker' and treated her as a man, which suited her very well.[8] Later she married Harold Arkell-Smith and had a son, but by 1923 she had left him and gone to live with a Miss Hayward. The pair disappeared to Brighton, appropriately enough, where they stayed at the Grand Hotel with Valerie posing as Sir Victor Barker. They married at St Peter's Church and lived in Hove where 'Sir Victor' worked as an actor.[9] Later she parted from her 'wife' and lived with another woman as man and wife in Rupert Street in Soho. By way of justification for her role, Valerie was later to claim that a uniform was essential for a woman as a means of obtaining employment.

It was while in London in 1926 that she accidentally came into contact with the National Fascisti when she returned another member's letter which had been delivered to her by mistake and was invited to join: 'Why not?' she wrote later, 'the role would help me in my pose as a man.'[10] As Captain Barker, Valerie was allowed to live at National Fascisti headquarters in Earl's Court where she became private secretary to its leader, Colonel Rippon-Seymour. She also taught fencing and boxing to the young recruits, and delivered lectures on 'Life', advising them to avoid getting mixed up with women. 'I quite enjoyed the life and was always ready to join in any of the *fracas* the young men had with the Communists,' she recalled. 'I used to go out with the boys to Hyde Park and there we had many rows with the Reds.'[11]

Though apprehensive that her sex would be discovered by the police, Valerie encountered no problems with the fascists: 'I am quite certain that they never for one moment suspected my sex ... believe me one pair of trousers makes a wonderful difference to matters of this kind.'[12] She left the National Fascisti in 1927, lived with a third woman as Colonel Barker in 1928, and by 1929 was working as a floor superintendent at the Regent Palace Hotel in Piccadilly where she reluctantly donned women's clothes – 'these horrid things'. This proved her undoing as it was there that she was served with a warrant committing her to prison for contempt of court in connection with bankruptcy proceedings. This led to the discovery of her sex at Wandsworth and consequent transfer to Holloway Prison.[13]

Subsequently Valerie Arkell-Smith was prosecuted for making false statements on a marriage register in a case that inevitably publicised the fact that she and Miss Hayward had lived together as man and wife. From a great height the prosecution counsel, Sir Ernest Wild, declared that she had 'profaned the House of God . . . outraged the decencies of nature, and broken the laws of man'.[14]

Coming as it did shortly after the ban on the famous lesbian novel, *The Well of Loneliness*, by Radclyffe Hall, the case generated enormous and unwelcome notoriety for Valerie Arkell-Smith and for the fascists in general. The young Diana Mitford relished an invitation from Lady Evelyn Guinness to stay at Climping in Sussex, 'the place formerly hallowed by the presence of Colonel Barker'. But not everyone shared her girlish delight: 'I soon discovered, however, that one must not mention Colonel Barker . . . her name was taboo and Lady Evelyn preferred to forget that she had ever existed.'[15] Such notoriety made the fascists look ridiculous, especially in view of their professed belief in the maintenance of traditional gender roles, and it probably deterred respectable people who were otherwise sympathetic to their ideas.

The example of Valerie Arkell-Smith may suggest that the early fascists do not deserve to be taken seriously. Historians have often regarded the British Fascists as rather confused and superficial, as having little grasp of fascist ideology and as essentially a movement of Conservatives inspired by fears about the empire, Bolshevism and the trade unions. This certainly reflects some contemporary opinion. According to Arnold Leese, 'there was no Fascism, as I understood it, in the organisation which was merely Conservatism with Knobs on.'[16] However, Leese disparaged the British Fascists by way of justifying his own rival, the Imperial Fascist League. His own views were so extreme that he condemned Mosley's British Union of Fascists for being insufficiently hostile towards Jews; and he discounted Italy because its fascism was not originally anti-Semitic. This is a reminder that fascist movements have varied in character over time and from one society to another. The fascist programme also took time to develop; in the early 1920s even Hitler simply relied upon what Ian Kershaw has called 'the standard repertoire of nationalist and *volkisch* speakers' so that his message could not readily be distinguished from traditional Pan-German propaganda.[17] According to Blakeney, the British Fascists 'did not consider that Italian methods pure and simple will ever do in this country, for the simple reason that the population is only apathetic and not communistic as in Italy'.[18] However, by the 1930s they had adopted uniforms, the corporate state and anti-Semitism.

Consequently, to disregard the British Fascists because of their common ground with contemporary Conservatism may be to miss the most important thing about them. As the case of William Joyce shows, the British Fascists were able to recruit from disillusioned Conservatives looking for a livelier form of political activity. As one recruit who admitted to being a Conservative put it, he had joined the fascists because of the 'crusted, stick-in-the-mud people in the Conservative Party'.[19] To assume that British fascism failed because mainstream Conservatives refused to take it seriously is to ignore the traffic of ideas and personnel between the two movements during the 1920s. Some distinctively fascist ideas, such as replacing parliamentary politics with a more authoritarian form of government involving a greater role for the monarchy and with a corporate system to allow the national interest to be reflected properly, made an appeal to disillusioned Conservatives. Conversely, many of the opinions expressed in the *Fascist Bulletin* under the editorship of Brigadier Blakeney certainly spoke to current Conservative concerns in ways that were not distinctively fascist. He criticised the politicians for the return to the gold standard in 1925, for committing Britain to costly debt payments to the United States, and for being too generous to Germany over reparations. He took them to task for failing to recognise the threat of external and domestic subversion: 'Do people realise sufficiently that, for the first time in our history, the revolutionary spirit is being backed by a first-class European power whose immediate and declared object is to smash up the British Empire by causing civil war in our midst, and that this power disposes of far greater funds for the purpose than all our patriotic societies put together?'[20]

Yet these comments lacked the shrill and embittered tone typical of the relentless attacks on Stanley Baldwin and the Tory leaders in right-wing publications such as the *National Review*, *Saturday Review*, *English Review* and *The Patriot* at this time. Nor did Blakeney advocate the corporate state or disparage parliamentary democracy, as many writers in the ostensibly Conservative journals were doing. At this stage the British Fascists took pains to emphasise their loyalty to the Crown and to the constitution. This may have been partly tactical, of course. As the Organising Secretary, Captain Robert Smith, put it: 'We are not linked to the Italian Fascists but use the name to denote citizens joining to defend the state. We are not violent like the National Fascisti and we do not wear uniforms.'[21] The British Fascists defined their programme in terms of a lengthy catalogue of principles and policies: upholding the King and the constitution, promoting class friendship, improving the conditions of life for the poor, protecting patriotic citizens from trade unions and promoting non-political unions, eliminating strikes, amending the parliamentary franchise to restrict it to those 'really qualified to vote', promoting Empire Free Trade and settlement in the colonies, development schemes for agriculture, forestry and smallholdings, preferential treatment for ex-servicemen, the gradual purification of the British race, restrictions on alien immigration, taxes on aliens and the withdrawal of licences from aliens who abused their privileges.[22] There is little in this list that would have looked out of place in the literature of Conservative candidates at this time, though the fascists were more explicit about matters such as restricting the vote and controlling aliens, for example. On this evidence the British Fascists and the Conservatives occupied overlapping positions on a broad spectrum rather than two wholly distinct positions.

Of course, for a new movement there were tactical reasons for emphasising the common ground, and fascists recognised that their reputation for violence could alienate potential recruits from the conventional right of politics. Much of the momentum behind fascism in the 1920s derived from a widespread fear of Communist subversion which, in an emergency, would require organised physical resistance of the kind that conventional politics seemed reluctant to offer. 'The task will be very formidable', wrote Blakeney, 'as street fighting against the swarms from the slums, supported at strategic points by trained groups armed with the devilish weapons of modern warfare, will be no child's play.'[23] If this seems unduly blood-curdling, it evidently reflected a recognised need in the early to mid-1920s. In effect the British Fascists appropriated typical Conservative language about the need to defend the British constitution as a means of justifying the paramilitary structure that was an integral part of their organisation from the outset. At the local level members were formed into units of seven men under a Leader and included an Adjutant, Signals Officer and Propaganda Officer; three units comprised a troop and several troops made up companies. The companies were part of a district controlled by the County Commanders and Area Commanders. At the top the organisation was run by an Executive Council and the nine-strong Fascist Grand Council. This hierarchy was further complicated by the separate women's units and cadet units for those under sixteen. The men were also subdivided into flying squads of 'young, active, unmarried men ready to go anywhere', a second line of older men who provided reserves, guards or garrisons, and technical units able to operate essential machinery.[24]

The spirit engendered by this system is reflected in a meeting of Brighton's British Fascists in March 1926 where the speaker emphasised that the movement was 'educational and evolutionary' and not to be confused with the 'Blackshirt Brigade', by which he presumably meant Mussolini's Blackshirts; he also dwelt fondly on the martial role of the 'young, virile and efficient' branch members:

> Suppose that there should be a Revolution next May ... we do not intend to wait until the time arrives and then say 'what can we do?' Instead of being an unorganised mob flocking to the support of the Government in time of crisis we shall be an organised body of men and women ready to do our utmost for the purposes of retaining Great Britain's integrity.[25]

The calculated ambiguity in this approach is readily comprehensible. Reluctant to admit that they intended to make a radical departure from conventional right-wing politics, the British Fascists pandered to thousands of dissident Tories who felt frustrated by the government's relaxed approach and wanted the reassurance that in an emergency someone would be ready to act decisively against the threat from the left.

Contrary to traditional assumptions a number of mainstream politicians took the British Fascists very seriously and sympathetically.[26] One of the first members of the Fascist Grand Council in 1923 was the Tory MP for Torquay, Colonel Sir Charles Burn; other supportive MPs included Patrick Hannon (Birmingham Moseley 1921–50), Robert Bower (Cleveland, 1931–45) and Sir Burton Chadwick (Wallasey, 1922–31). Some politicians had fascist connections throughout the inter-war period. As a student at Oxford in 1925 the romantic-reactionary Alan Lennox-Boyd (Mid-Bedford 1931–60) was attracted to the British Fascists because he felt they put the state above all else and upheld patriotism and law and order; as an MP in the 1930s he was linked with the British Union of Fascists as a member of the January Club.[27]

An insight into their thinking may be gleaned from a thoughtful and appreciative assessment of a British Fascist demonstration held in Trafalgar Square in November 1924 by Sir John Gilmour who was then Secretary of State for Scotland in Baldwin's government. 'Careful discipline has been inculcated by efficient organisation,' he noted; 'if such an assembly had taken place in Manchester or Glasgow there would have been a first-class riot.'[28] Although Gilmour was not entirely comfortable with the idea of an unofficial police force and thought that 'these amateurs' would eventually have to be protected by the professionals, he also recognised that 'the Fascisti, in theory at least, respond to a public need, namely some force which can help to check disorder; but their very existence is almost a provocation.' After weighing the advantages and drawbacks of private armies Gilmour reached some stark conclusions; as he saw it, the left already employed physical force as well as constitutional weapons, and 'I do not doubt that many are already considering the best method of forcing a conflict with the troops.'

The problem, he believed, was that 'the state at the present juncture can hardly take prophylactic measures; it must wait until the first serious assault is delivered and at the outset it will probably be unprepared . . . That the forces of the Crown may require substantial help in the future I do not doubt.'[29]

The equanimity with which a cabinet minister contemplated the militarist activities of the British Fascists is a caution against seeing the fascist movement as marginalised or eccentric. To Gilmour it was neither absurdly pretentious nor simply a danger to be suppressed. He might well have adopted a different view – especially if he had chosen to have regard for the legal position. Under the Unlawful Drilling Act of 1819 anyone who trained or drilled men in private forces was liable to up to seven years penal servitude, while those who attended for drilling could be fined at the discretion of the courts and imprisoned for up to two years. In addition the Defence of the Realm Act (Regulation 9E) empowered the Secretary of State for War or the Army Council to prohibit drilling in any specified area and to try offenders summarily.[30] However, by the inter-war period the 1819 Act was regarded as a dead letter, the authorities taking refuge in the view that as there was no real definition of unlawful drilling it had been considered undesirable to take proceedings.[31] It is worth noting that Sir John Gilmour later served as Home Secretary in 1934 at precisely the point when the violence meted out by Sir Oswald Mosley's fascist stewards at the notorious Olympia Rally forced the government to consider taking steps to check the operation of privately trained armies. His advice was to remain calm and do nothing.[32].

The Home Secretary from 1924 to 1929 was William Joynson-Hicks who, though not a member of any fascist organisation, played a central part in maintaining the connection between Conservatism and fascism. Since the early 1900s Joynson-Hicks had established himself as an unapologetic anti-Semite, and he used his term at the Home Office to further this by his control over the naturalisation and immigration of aliens. He was also well-disposed to fascist paramilitaries during the General Strike. Well before 1926 Joynson-Hicks was interrogated by George Lansbury and other Labour MPs as to whether he was aware that the fascist societies met regularly to drill and arm their members. In response Joynson-Hicks and his under-secretary, Godfrey Locker-Lampson, blandly insisted that they had no information on the subject.[33] The government's steadfast refusal to curtail private drilling exacerbated the feeling on the left that the law was not being applied in an even-handed manner as between fascists and Communists.

While ministers such as Gilmour, Joynson-Hicks and Locker-Lampson turned a blind eye to British Fascist activities, some backbenchers felt able to show their support more explicitly. Notable among them was Patrick Hannon who was extremely active in anti-Bolshevik movements including the Comrades of the Great War, an organisation for ex-servicemen, and as Director of the British Commonwealth Union (BCU) from 1918 to 1928.[34] The BCU sought to promote the interest of industrialists at home and in the empire. Many businessmen deemed such tactics necessary after the war because they saw Conservative politicians as being too susceptible to left-wing pressure. The BCU pursued its aim not simply by lobbying quietly but by funding an assortment of anti-Bolsheviks, including patriotic trade unionists and the Pankhursts' Women's Party, to campaign against strikes and to stand in parliamentary elections.[35] Throughout the 1920s and 1930s Hannon also collaborated with right-wing rebels such as Sir Henry Page Croft, Lord Lloyd and Lord Beaverbrook in trying to pressurise the Conservative leaders into adopting protectionism for British domestic and empire markets; he even schemed to replace Baldwin as party leader and supported Beaverbrook when he ran his own candidates against official Conservative ones.

His record made Hannon's politics especially ambiguous. He remained a Birmingham MP down to 1950 and clearly succeeded in covering his tracks later in life. Between the wars he operated as a conventional, if disloyal, Tory politician by harnessing a phalanx of right-wing movements both to protect the Conservative Party and to help shift it in what he thought to be the right direction. Yet his appointments diary shows that in December 1924 he sat on the Fascist Grand Council; he attended British Fascist meetings and dinners in Birmingham early in 1925; and he booked a House of Commons Committee room for a fascist conference in May.[36] When Hannon took the chair at a lively and crowded meeting at Birmingham Town Hall in May 1925, he emphasised British Fascist aims in terms readily accept-able to fellow Tories – loyalty to the Throne, empire, parliament and free speech; he also added 'the rights of enterprise', a good example of how recruits to a new movement are inclined to make it the repository for their own principles and causes.[37] The fascist speakers were subjected to a good deal of heckling by the Birmingham audience, and when questions were invited Hannon insisted that one questioner should remove his hat or he would close the meeting, a threat which provoked 'considerable hubbub'. But evidently the local fascists had not yet organised enough stewards since control was only regained when the organist struck up the National Anthem; the audience joined in, while the hecklers sang the 'Red Flag', and other patriotic tunes were played until order had been restored.[38]

Patrick Hannon's strategy in the 1920s was potentially a dangerous one; in Germany extreme right-wingers who felt confident of their ability to harness fascism to support and revive Conservatism lived to regret their mistake. Nonetheless, his involvement helps to make sense of the links between fascists and Conservatives during the 1920s. They shared the same disgust at the limp-wristed attitude of the Tory leadership towards the left, and the fascists played a distinctive role as suppliers of stewards for Conservative meetings which were otherwise vulnerable to disruption by Communists and Socialists. Political violence was such a long-standing tradition in Britain that all parties tried to equip themselves with stewards to keep order. In October 1924 the eighteen-year-old William Joyce acted as a fascist steward for Jack Lazarus, the Conservative candidate in Lambeth North, where he had made himself unpopular with the Communists. 'At the conclusion of the meeting there was the usual attempt to rush the platform, seize the Union Jack etc. and it was in the course of the ensuing mêlée that Joyce . . . was slashed across the face with a razor.'[39] Joyce, who lost so much blood that his life was in danger, emerged with a livid scar stretching from his ear to the corner of his mouth.

For the extreme right such attacks confirmed fears that Britain had been penetrated by a subversive and violent organisation and prompted politicians such as Hannon to involve themselves with the British Fascists. His colleague, Oliver Locker-Lampson, who represented the Birmingham Handsworth constituency, collaborated with them when he organised a series of 'Clear Out The Reds' rallies designed to protest about Russian and Communist subversion. At his request some six hundred fascist stewards turned out for an Albert Hall rally in July 1926 attended by two MPs, Henry Page Croft and Colonel John Gretton.[40] In October that year no fewer than 1,500 fascists appeared at the Albert Hall where they carried Union Jacks, formed a guard of honour, conducted Locker-Lampson and the other speakers down the gangway, and ejected anyone who disturbed the meeting.[41] They offered the same service to the Industrial Peace Union, an organisation led by the right-wing trade union leader, Havelock Wilson, which was a natural target for left-wing disruption; the British Fascists claimed that once the Communists saw the interruptors being ejected from Wilson's meeting they sneaked out quietly.[42] This may have been sheer bravado but it underlines the importance they attached to being able to demonstrate the effectiveness of their methods in the build-up to the next crisis.

Hannon was by no means an exception in maintaining a footing in two rival political organisations. Dorothy, Viscountess Downe served for eight years as President of the Conservative Women's Association in Scarborough and later held other party positions. But at the same time she was County Commander of North Yorkshire for the British Fascists, and in 1934 she joined the British Union of Fascists. Her prominence at fascist functions in

Yorkshire during 1926 and 1927 suggests that Lady Downe found nothing embarrassing in her role.[43] The explanation lies partly in the fact that the Conservatives had nothing like the formal and centralised approach to dual membership adopted by the Labour Party. The Labour Party annual conference repeatedly rejected applications for affiliation from the Communist Party, and its National Executive Committee issued strict instructions to local parties about the expulsion of Communist infiltrators. But in the absence of formal procedures the Conservatives essentially relied upon their constituency associations to handle membership problems. Inevitably this meant that as local associations were so heavily dependent on influential local patrons they were reluctant to take action in cases of dual membership. In the case of the British Fascists it was easy to turn a blind eye because they did not run their own candidates and even claimed to be a non-party, patriotic organisation which respected the British constitution; consequently, Conservatives could reasonably regard them as allies who supplied the party with stewards for its meetings and might, in some future crisis, fulfil an even more vital function for the state.

The relationship between the two organisations at local level was highlighted by an incident at Islington in October 1925 where the local branch of the British Fascists rented rooms in the South Islington Conservative and Unionist Club. This came to light only when a fascist member was wounded by a shot fired accidentally from a revolver.[44] Such minor incidents underline the point that many fascists routinely carried small arms and often possessed no firearms certificate. Reports of the local activities of the British Fascists also suggest that they offered very similar social programmes to the Conservative Associations including dinners, dances, bazaars, whist drives, garden parties, football teams and carol-singing patronised by the titled members; this must have made it easy for members to maintain a footing in both organisations or to move at will between them. In Stamford Arnold Leese enrolled eighty fascists during 1924–5, a substantial number for a small town, but he felt that 'very few of these meant business'.[45] This is consistent with the view that fascist branches had a high turnover as members moved back and forth between them and the Conservative associations, or, like Leese himself, moved on in search of something more militant.

The British Fascists' strategy of extending their influence at local level by cooperating with like-minded movements was complemented at the national level by their efforts to demonstrate links with the British establishment. This is evident from the importance they attached to the monarchy. Indeed, the relationship between fascists and the monarchy is a crucial aspect of the wider evolution of fascism between the wars, though it has attracted relatively little attention. For the British Fascists their dedication to the royal family represented more than simply a reflection of their ultra-patriotism. Like all fascist movements they venerated the idea of leadership, yet they had no real leader of any stature. Moreover, like many British people, they misunderstood the constitutional role of the monarchy, attributing more political influence to it than it really possessed. The war had helped foster an exaggerated perception of the monarchy in Britain because many ordinary people, feeling frustrated by the lack of decisive military and naval battles and lacking confidence in the politicians, looked to King George V to intervene and bang their heads together. One youthful middle-class diarist wrote in 1916: 'We wish the King would turn all the Government out and give orders himself, and really beat the Germans properly.'[46] Since fascists took a dim view of parliamentary politicians, they were even more disposed to exaggerate the actual – and potential – role of the King.

The British Fascists themselves enjoyed some connections with the royal family through prominent members including Colonel Sir Charles Burn, who had been Aide-de-Camp to the King, and Viscountess Downe who was a lady-in-waiting to Queen Mary. During the 1920s they made repeated, if clumsy, overtures designed to dramatise the relationship with the monarchy, particularly in connection with Armistice Day. In November 1925 they exchanged telegrams with the King, his formal reply stating: 'The King sincerely thanks the members of the British Fascists for their loyal message on Armistice Day.'[47] Similar exchanges also took place when the fascists offered congratulations on royal birthdays and condolences on royal deaths. The British Fascists even attempted to hijack Armistice Day as 'Fascist Sunday'. For example, in November 1926 they organised a demonstration in Hyde Park followed by a march to the Cenotaph, the laying of wreaths on the tomb of the Unknown Warrior and the consecration of British Fascist colours by the Reverend A. W. Gough, the Prebendary of St Paul's; finally they marched off to the Embankment to sing the National Anthem.[48] Again in 1927 some six hundred fascists laid wreaths at the Cenotaph before marching to Westminster Abbey where, they claimed, the western transept was reserved for them.[49] But what the British Fascists most wanted was permission from the Lord Chamberlain to march past Buckingham Palace where the King would accept a salute from them. In pressing for this Captain Robert Smith emphasised that the members were ex-servicemen and had been volunteers in the recent national emergency – a reference to the General Strike – and their aims were to 'uphold His Majesty's throne and the Constitution'.[50] However, the King was advised to decline this request. Nor did the fascists meet with success when Lintorn-Orman sought permission to use the Royal Crown on their publications. Several requests were also made, via the Home Office, to use a photograph of the King on the front page of their journal, the *British Lion*.[51] Since the royal photograph was commonly reproduced it is not clear that permission was really needed, but no doubt the point was to enable the organisation to say that it enjoyed official approval for its use.

By fostering their royal connections the British Fascists no doubt hoped to gain respectability and counter accusations that fascism was an alien or unduly violent movement. To some extent the same purpose was served by promoting a female membership. However, women's participation proved to be more complicated. For some fascist sympathisers the prominence of women in its ranks, especially in the shape of Rotha Lintorn-Orman, was a major cause for their reservations about the organisation. After all, many 1920s fascists professed to regard women's entry into politics as a central cause of the degeneration of democracy and they regarded unmarried women as highly abnormal. Lintorn-Orman herself fuelled their suspicions by her predilection for dressing up in men's clothes and her enthusiasm for teaching women to undertake unfeminine jobs such as changing tyres. However, Blakeney managed to reconcile Lintorn-Orman's role with traditionalist attitudes by emphasising that in the national emergency for which they were preparing 'the women Fascists will have to organise dressing stations and canteens for the fighting units.'[52] In any case, the anti-feminists could not entirely dictate the role of the female members because many women had experience in earlier right-wing organisations such as the Primrose League which had brought women into politics to uphold moral values, Christianity and the family against the threat of subversion and irreligion posed by Socialism. Consequently Lintorn-Orman found little difficulty in establishing a discrete role for female fascists as organisers of Fascist Children's Clubs. 'Women especially', she said, 'should make it their task and duty to prevent the spirit of the Red menace to influence the future citizens of the Empire.'[53]

However, this was not always as genteel an activity as it sounds. In the East End of London all-women meetings designed to promote the children's clubs attracted physical attacks from the left. At one such gathering in Silvertown in 1927 Lintorn-Orman was struck in the face when the local Communists encouraged the two hundred children present to hurl missiles at her platform.[54] In fact this was part of the attraction; many female fascists who received training in public speaking, first aid and ju-jitsu wanted to enjoy the more adventurous side of the movement. In London women aged between eighteen and forty, physically fit and at least five feet five inches in height, could join the fascist street patrols, which was a guarantee of excitement. However, the pattern and character of fascist activity varied a good deal from one area to another, and the boisterous behaviour of the East End was not always typical. At the more decorous end of the fascist spectrum Viscountess Downe and Captain Coates (North Yorkshire County Commander) presided over a gathering at the Harrogate Spa Hydro in 1926: 'Viscountess Downe carried all before her in a brief and charming speech in which she said that Fascist women must do their best to get back to the old idea of grit and independence. The Communist danger, she said, came from youths and girls under 23, who had never worked and never intended to.'[55] In Harrogate, at least, there was no heckling or dissent.

Despite the traditionalist tone of 1920s fascism, female fascists were clearly not a marginal element confined to the social side of the activities or to work with children. Most of the British fascist organisations enjoyed a high female membership and managed to accommodate women who adopted feminist attitudes; even Lintorn-Orman supported universal suffrage at the age of twenty-five.[56] The movement attracted strong-minded, patriotic women, like Lintorn-Orman, who came from conventional backgrounds but had been liberated by wartime experience in the Women's Auxiliary Army, the Women's Royal Naval Service, the Women's Royal Air Force, the Women's Police, the Women's Land Army or the Voluntary Aid Detachments. This left them politically aware and emboldened by the realisation that the uniform could be a weapon in attaining participation for women on a more equal footing with men. It was galling to find that the end of the war had triggered a reaction against women's work which threatened to deprive them of the opportunity for uniformed service. This obstructionism led the former suffragette, Mary Allen, to attempt to extend wartime police work by forming the Women's Auxiliary Service in 1923, and her colleague, Flora Drummond, to establish the Women's Guild of Empire in 1918. Lintorn-Orman's initiative in 1923 can be seen in the same context. Though not at first in command of the British Fascists, she acted as President of the Women's Units, and in 1926 she was instrumental in resisting the moves by Blakeney and others to merge the organisation with the government's anti-strike organisation; the Brigadier was forced to withdraw, leaving her in control up to her death in 1935.

The British Fascists probably reached their peak in activity and influence during 1925 and 1926. Although their membership was small, by the summer of 1925 they were drawing audiences of 2,000 at Birmingham and 5,000 in London's Hyde Park.[57] While few of these people were committed fascists, they were symptomatic of the growing relevance and urgency of fascist propaganda in the period leading up to the General Strike. At this time the movement seems to have been very active along the south coast, in the south-east, in London, in Scotland and in most major urban centres including Birmingham, Liverpool and Newcastle. This probably reflects two distinct social patterns; in residential areas and seaside resorts the movement appealed to respectable people of reactionary inclinations who felt politically marginalised, whilst central Scotland, Tyneside and Merseyside, which enjoyed a reputation for Socialist and Communist activity, offered a challenge to fascist missionaries who aspired to mobilise the non-Socialist working classes there.

From July 1925 onwards fascism gathered momentum from the rising tide of alarmist propaganda about Communist-inspired disruption; this was supposedly to be conducted under cover of a general strike and would involve attacks on railways, telegraph and telephone lines, gas, water, electricity and sewage services.[58] In September the government announced the creation of the Organisation for the Maintenance of Supplies (OMS), a semi-official body designed to raise volunteers to sustain essential services during the strike; this offered a fresh opportunity to the British Fascists, but it also introduced competition. While keen to protect their country during the immediate emergency, the fascists insisted on maintaining their distinctive long-term role in organising against civil war; they were anxious to offer their services to the OMS, 'but *as Fascists* and without losing our identity on joining their ranks'.[59] After some hesitation Joynson-Hicks, the Home Secretary, ruled that they must sever their connection with the British Fascists before joining the OMS or becoming Special Constables, which seemed to contradict the assurance he had previously given to Blakeney in July 1925.[60] Blakeney accepted the government's view that it could not collaborate officially with the British Fascists while they maintained their semi-military organisation; he was therefore willing to reorganise the movement along civil lines and even to change the name of the organisation.[61] However, Lintorn-Orman and others felt that this was calculated to dilute fascist principles and that three-quarters of the members wanted to maintain their independence. As a result, shortly before the General Strike Blakeney, the Earl of Glasgow, Lord Ernest Hamilton and Admiral Armstrong resigned in order to cooperate with the official system as the 'British Loyalists'.

In the event many fascists participated in the OMS and Specials as individuals, while the British Fascists organised their own 'Q Divisions' of men who were available to undertake anti-strike duties.[62] During the strike Colonel Rippon-Seymour of the National Fascisti repeatedly telephoned the Home Office with offers to place a body of his members at the disposal of the Home Secretary, perhaps hoping that in the emergency Joynson-Hicks would be more flexible. But he was fobbed off with advice about serving as Special Constables, and his requests for an interview with the Home Secretary were turned down.[63] However, official rebuffs did not stop the British Fascists offering their services to any business requiring lorry drivers and other volunteers, and during the strike Lintorn-Orman's London home became the headquarters from which vans and motor cars were constantly despatched.[64] To some extent this was a face-saving exercise designed to prevent the British Fascists being swallowed up by the official machine, but it also offered members the opportunity they ardently sought and enabled fascism to win some kudos from association with the patriotic cause. Aware that the emergency offered excellent opportunities to publicise their movement, they distributed fascist newspapers and propaganda throughout the West End and East End of London. They particularly targeted Shapurji Saklatvala, the Communist MP for North Battersea, for encouraging the troops not to fire on strikers; Saklatvala was cited as proof that by allowing the entry of aliens and coloured people Britain had opened herself to subversion.

Although the General Strike was an enormous stimulus for fascists in Britain, there are good grounds for thinking that after 1926 the movement entered a decline. However, this view is qualified by the unreliability of the evidence about membership. According to the Organising Secretary of the British Fascists, A. K. Hewlett, they had 400 'organising centres' by May 1925; by the end of the year they claimed to have 800 branches each containing from 200 to 500 members; and in May 1926 the membership figure was put at 150,000.[65] These figures are generally regarded as absurd exaggerations; but one should be equally cautious about the very small figures suggested by official sources which tend to relate to later periods rather than to 1925–6 when the high level of activity and formation of new branches and women's units indicates an organisation running into some thousands at least.

Symptoms of decline are, however, unmistakable. In June 1926 the journal *Fascist Bulletin* became the *British Lion*, but it was published fortnightly not weekly; it became monthly in 1927 and thereafter appeared increasingly erratically. The organisation had lost key personnel and suffered acutely from a lack of effective leadership. After taking over as leader in 1926 Lintorn-Orman steadily succumbed to the influence of alcohol. Her mother complained that the fascists were battening on to her for her money, encouraging her dependency on drink and drugs, and that 'drunken orgies and undesirable practices take place at her town residence'.[66] This is not to say the claims were true, but they created a damaging picture of Lintorn-Orman as a sad, eccentric figure, and of the British Fascists as a disreputable movement of marginal significance. Opponents claimed that the movement was becoming defunct because the collapse of the General Strike had made it irrelevant, but the fascists comforted themselves with the belief that 'history is repeating itself'; the General Strike represented an abortive attempt at revolution but a better organised one would surely follow.[67] Certainly the aftermath of the strike saw widespread disillusionment with the Baldwin government which the fascists tried to exploit by urging the need to follow up the strike by expelling undesirable aliens, imposing severe penalties for the preaching of sedition and for receiving foreign money, and by reforming 'political' trade unions.[68]

However, by the later 1920s the British Fascists increasingly fell between two stools. To some contemporaries they presented themselves essentially as an adjunct to the Conservative Party. On the other hand, opponents who regarded party political connections as bogus and opportunistic, suspected the fascists of wanting to dispense altogether with conventional parliamentary institutions.[69] Officially the British Fascists continued to insist that they were not offering an alternative to democracy; as Lintorn-Orman told the Home Secretary, when they said 'we are prepared to meet force with force', they merely referred to their role in protecting constitutional speakers and assisting the government in the event of a breakdown of law and order.[70] However, these protestations were undermined by their continual involvement with street violence, if only on a minor scale. The pattern of their activities as revealed in the press centred around demonstrations, usually comprising 200 to 500 people, in Trafalgar Square or in Hyde Park culminating in a march to Marble Arch. The Communists often set up rival meetings a hundred yards away and the two sides exchanged insults, sang the Red Flag and the National Anthem, and sometimes attempted to overrun their opponents' platform. At this stage the police would intervene and make a handful of arrests.[71] During 1927 reports began to appear in the press about 'Fascist Secret Arms Dumps'. Allegedly these included small arms, machine-guns and artillery secreted away in various parts of the country and at the disposal of a secret grand council comprising highly placed army, navy and air force officers who were preparing for the next general strike.[72] Lintorn-Orman routinely denied the charges, but it is obvious why such rumours gained credibility in the aftermath of the General Strike; many fascists did carry arms, they boasted many former officers among their members and eagerly contemplated another general strike.

In any case, while the British Fascists themselves maintained a relatively respectable front, the National Fascisti felt less inhibited; unconcerned about conforming to British traditions, they had always worn black shirts and berets. In March 1927 they attracted fresh notoriety when an aggrieved deputation from their Croydon Branch arrived at the headquarters in Kensington, armed with heavy sticks, and demanding to see the balance sheets because they suspected the officials of misappropriating funds.

Colonel Rippon-Seymour appeared dramatically at the top of the stairs flourishing a sword and a revolver. 'If you enter the room I will shoot,' he was reported as saying.[73] Although the colonel managed to hold off the deputation until the arrival of the police, this led to an investigation of the arms held at headquarters. It transpired that the revolver belonged to the secretary, 'Captain Victor Barker'. As a result Rippon-Seymour was convicted at the Old Bailey for common assault on Charles Eyres, the deputation leader, and for unlawful possession of a gun. Valerie Arkell-Smith's lawyers got her off the charge of possessing a revolver with a forged firearms certificate, and the search to which she was subjected before entering the court failed to reveal that she was a woman.[74] However embarrassing such publicity may have been, the British Fascists could hardly afford to disarm their members or dispense with their paramilitary structures because this would merely have accelerated the loss of membership. The logic seemed to point towards a more militant and explicitly fascist strategy rather than to any further compromise with convention.

By the autumn of 1928 frustration over the stagnation of the existing fascist organisations had resulted in the formation of the Imperial Fascist League, a small but significant step towards the more militant movements of the 1930s. Though founded by Brigadier General Erskine Tulloch, the IFL was dominated by Arnold Spencer Leese, an experienced veterinary surgeon who had spent the years from 1906 to 1912 investigating the diseases of camels at the invitation of the Government of India; he subsequently worked for the East Africa Government's veterinary department and became a Captain in the Royal Veterinary Corps during the war. A world expert on his subject, Leese published *A Treatise on the One-Humped Camel in Health and Disease* in 1928. He seems to have been a solitary individual, and, to judge from his autobiography, the closest relationship in his life was with his bull-terrier. Leese's prolonged imperial service had left him very detached from British life, but after the war he practised for a few years at Stamford in Lincolnshire, where he joined the British Fascists and was even elected as a local councillor. However, this experience only deepened his contempt for democracy. Canvassing among the ignorant Stamford voters 'impressed upon me what utter humbug the democratic vote really is'.[75] Given his bleak outlook on his fellow men it is not surprising that Leese also took a dim view of the British Fascists. He attempted to persuade them to change their name 'as I thought the initials were simply asking for it'. By 1927 he had left the organisation and retired to Guildford where he was to devote his life and much of his money to the Imperial Fascist League.

From 1926 onwards Leese appears to have been strongly influenced by Arthur Kitson and H. H. Beamish, leading figures in The Britons, who fostered in him an obsessive hatred for the Jews. He professed to having been shocked by his own ignorance and by the absence of debate about the Jewish conspiracy: 'I determined to break that silence and to make knowledge public property,' he wrote.[76] Leese had become so alienated that he sincerely believed that the British aristocracy had been corrupted by Jews as a result of repeated marriages with wealthy Jewesses designed to restore the tottering finances of landed families.[77] He also condemned the Church because he felt it had become warped by dubious Judaic doctrines including pacifism, internationalism and the brotherhood of man. As a result, under Leese's influence the IFL was more fanatical and ideologically strict than the other fascist organisations; deriding Italian fascism as subject to Jewish influence, it looked more to the German Nazis for a model. Decked out in fascist black and gold, the leading members wore a full-dress uniform comprising black shirt, khaki breeches and puttees, black boots, beret and cummerbund; they gave the Roman salute and adopted an armband comprising a swastika superimposed upon the Union Jack.[78] Members also took to using the 'PJ' (Perish Judah) greeting in their correspondence, and enthusiastically distributed sticky labels bearing anti-Semitic slogans such as: 'Scratch a Bolshie and find a Jew', 'Money spent with Jews never returns to Gentile pockets', and 'Britons! Do not allow Jews to tamper with white girls'.[79]

By comparison with the British Fascists the IFL offered an uncompromising version of fascism. Each week its journal, *The Fascist*, explained the virtues of the corporate state, and it unhesitatingly pronounced democracy to be a failed system which had fallen under the thumb of international financiers.[80] The prospect of a general election in 1929 provoked Leese to derision: 'The theory is that if you multiply ignorance any number of times you will get wisdom. The fact is that foresight and statesmanship are incompatible with the popular vote for obvious reasons; the average citizen votes for his own immediate advantage . . . so the contest becomes a rivalry in the art of bribery.'[81] He advocated a complete boycott of the election. Leese's own contribution to the debate over unemployment was a mixture of fascist economics, xenophobia and racism. He blamed the inability of the Baldwin government to reduce unemployment on the Bank of England which had penalised British industry by raising the bank rate to $5\frac{1}{2}$ per cent. The Bank, he argued, had been forced to act by heavy speculation among financiers in New York: 'What sort of sovereignty over our own national credit does this stupid system give us ?'[82] Leese despised American society because it included a large proportion of citizens of 'inferior racial stock' who caused crime and disorder and made politics even more degenerate than in Britain.[83] But Britain, too, suffered from excessive numbers of 'undesirables', that is, naturalised aliens. Leese proposed to deal with them by drawing a distinction between 'British Citizens', who, alone, would be entitled to full rights such as voting and serving in government, and 'British Subjects'; the first group would be confined to people of 'pure British blood or when of foreign origin . . . only white European races with a strong preference for the Nordic.'[84] A convinced eugenicist, Leese also aimed to increase the birth rate among the middle classes and to check procreation among the unfit which, he believed, went against the laws of nature.

Anxious to demonstrate its role as a fighting force, the Imperial Fascist League appointed L. H. Sherrard as Commander General of the Fascist Legions. But this grandiose title scarcely seemed consistent with the minimal support it commanded. The organisers never claimed to have more than 1,000 to 2,500 members, but even this was taken to be a wild exaggeration by the authorities who put the active membership at a few hundreds confined largely to London.[85] Perennially strapped for cash, the organisation was often unable to hire halls for meetings, but got round the problem by holding debates with the better-endowed League of Nations Union.[86] Admittedly the IFL proved to be a durable movement, lasting up to the Second World War, but this is largely because it was sustained by the fanaticism of Leese as Director General. Though it attracted men from other fascist organisations including Blakeney, Erskine Tulloch and Beamish, it lacked a figure of the first rank. In the 1930s it was eclipsed by the British Union of Fascists and by the charismatic Oswald Mosley whom Leese professed to regard as a mere adventurer.

The alien character of the IFL probably explains its failure to attract more than a small band of fanatics. However, 1930 saw the formation of a much more authentically English expression of fascism in the English Mistery whose members included William Sanderson, Rolf Gardiner, Anthony Ludovici, Viscount Lymington and Lieutenant Colonel Graham Seton-Hutchison who later joined the British Union of Fascists and founded the National Workers' Movement (later National Socialist Workers' Party) in 1933. English Mistery and its successor, English Array, are a warning against seeing fascism as an aberration or an importation in Britain. In some ways these organisations represented a logical development from the Edwardian Radical Right and from late-Victorian ideas about revitalising rural life. Looking back to a healthier rural society, English Mistery aspired to revive the aristocracy and the monarchy; it aimed to recover the purity of the English community by banning miscegenation and to restore national unity by rejecting liberal democracy which it blamed for dividing the country. English Mistery occupied the intellectual ground where fascism met the back-to-the-land tradition; deploring the disruption inflicted on society since the industrial revolution, it sought to recapture the original spirit of the British race. It regarded Jews as rootless, nomadic people who merely weakened the people's attachment to their land and traditional values.

The most prominent figure in English Mistery was Viscount Lymington who represented Basingstoke as a Conservative MP from 1929 to 1934; he eventually resigned his seat, claiming that principles were incompatible with party politics: 'Real national unity can only come about by a change in values which sets personal responsibility and service to the Crown before all other conflicting interests.'[87] After a split in the organisation Lymington went on to found the English Array, which had very similar ideas, in 1936. Flourishing the red rose, the flag of St George, its 'Marshal' and its 'Musters', English Array was Gothic in style and frankly reactionary in inspiration. It regarded the decline of the feudal system as the greatest misfortune to befall the English people; it saw the land and agriculture as the foundation of society, advocated a secure hierarchy stretching from peasant to king, rejected the modern, centralised state, dismissed democracy as a fraud, and excluded women from membership. Members subscribed to an elaborate creed:

> I have faith in the surviving stock of my own people. I have love for them and for the English soil from which they have sprung. I have hope that through the regeneration of that stock and of its soil . . . I hate the system of democracy which is in effect a tyranny that dupes men by allowing them to agitate in Hyde Park while it refuses them the right to be responsible for their own family.[88]

Resembling a Boy Scout troop as much as a political party, English Array organised its members into 'Musters'; they met at camps where they carted chalk, turned compost heaps, cut weeds, built fences and heard lectures from Anthony Ludovici. Influenced by Lymington and Ludovici, English Array shared many ideas in common with other fascist organisations, including its analysis of international finance, the need for selective breeding and racial purity, and its repudiation of parliamentary politics; this is why collaboration with Mosley's British Union of Fascists was seen as a possibility.[89] Unlike some fascist groups the Array had no aspirations to be a modernising movement. Its overriding aim was to return to agricultural self-sufficiency and to promote the consumption of unpasteurised milk and fresh vegetables instead of the tinned milk and canned food increasingly inflicted on the people of England. For both the Mistery and the Array the demise of parliamentary politics implied a revival of traditional monarchical authority in Britain. Members pledged: 'I will strive to restore the King to his rightful position as the mirror of his people's virtues, as their protector from private interests, and as their supreme executor of Government. For he alone can guarantee permanence.'[90] Not surprisingly, Lymington was keen to support Edward VIII against the cabinet during the abdication crisis in 1936.

Although none of them achieved a very large following, the emergence of the British Fascists, the National Fascisti, the Imperial Fascist League and the English Mistery reminds us that, well before the appearance of Mosley's much better-known organisation in 1932, Britain had already generated an extensive range of experiments with fascist movements. Before dismissing them for their eccentricity and lack of success, it is worth putting the British experience into perspective. Even the German Nazis, with much greater advantages, had made only a marginal impact on the German electorate during the 1920s, although their membership was very much larger. In the Reichstag elections of May 1928 their support stood at just 2.6 per cent, and if anything they appeared to be losing ground. Nor had the Nazis really managed to distinguish themselves from their rivals on the right of German politics in terms of ideology and programme; they were distinctive more for their dynamic and youthful image than their ideas.[91] Yet under the stimulus of an economic crisis which seemed to be beyond the powers of conventional politicians, the Nazis surged to 18 per cent of the poll in 1930; and, as a result, a movement that had been divided, extremist and marginal suddenly became central to German politics. Like the fascists in Britain, the German Nazis had adopted a dual strategy by presenting themselves as a virile fighting force ready to respond to a national emergency while also insisting on their intention to acquire power by constitutional means; when the opportunity to do so arose in the early 1930s, what had appeared highly improbable to most Germans quickly became an accomplished fact.

In this light there was nothing very eccentric about the British fascists, and their failure to make a decisive breakthrough by the end of the 1920s cannot be taken as proof that they were too extreme to be acceptable in British society. The support shown for the main elements in the fascist critique by public figures, including those who never described themselves as fascists, suggests that there was little really alien in their ideas. In September 1929 when the Duke of Northumberland published a sweeping attack on democracy in the *Morning Post*, the IFL composed an editorial pointing out that he had expressed the case in the terms used by fascists: would he therefore consider joining them?[92] In fact the Duke's journal, *The Patriot*, already publicised National Fascisti branch meetings during the late 1920s.[93] One Socialist journalist who investigated fascist activities considered them to be 'amateurish, rather muddle-headed people', but recognised that they still represented a real danger because of the response among disgruntled Conservatives. 'If they once began to turn their attention towards Fascism and its ideas they would find in the British Fascists an organisation ready to their hand.'[94] What has to be explained, then, is not only why some Conservatives felt the attraction of fascism during the 1920s, but also, why, despite this, the majority kept their distance from the fascist movement.

FIVE

Boiled Shirt Fascism

'The Conservative Party has been ... very much demoralised by its long sojourn at the waters of Babylon or, shall we say, its long diet of the flesh-pots of Egypt.'

The Patriot, 26 October 1922

On Saturday 14 December 1918 twenty-one million people went to the polls, most of them for the first time. Coming close on the declaration of peace, the election had been a competition to make Germany pay the costs of the war: 'We will squeeze Germany like a lemon,' Sir Eric Geddes reportedly promised, 'we will squeeze her until you can hear the pips squeak.' The politicians were kept in suspense until after Christmas because the counting of the votes was delayed so as to allow time for men still in France and Flanders to send in their ballots by post. But when the boxes were opened any fears the Conservatives had about the dangers of a new mass electorate had been exploded, for they had won 383 seats, giving them a dominant position in the triumphant Lloyd George Coalition. They could hardly have known that this marked the start of over twenty years of almost uninterrupted power. Yet throughout the period from 1918 to 1939 Conservatives behaved more as though they were in opposition; the party was racked by divisions and controversies fought between their leaders and many of their supporters in parliament and in the country. In 1916 they had felt obliged to serve in Asquith's coalition; the 1918 victory trapped them in Lloyd George's government until 1922; in 1931 they joined a coalition for a third time led by Ramsay MacDonald. Not surprisingly many Tories felt their party was perennially ensnared by the machinations of clever Liberal and Labour politicians, and betrayed by weak Tory leaders forever compromising their principles in a search of a few votes from dissident Liberals. The resulting sense of betrayal among many right-wing Conservatives left them vulnerable to the appeal of the more extremist organisations throughout the inter-war period.

Disillusionment with the Tory leaders manifested itself in August 1917 when a rebel MP, Sir Henry Page Croft, formed a breakaway group called the National Party. Imperialist, protectionist, xenophobic and anti-Semitic, the National Party demanded the elimination of German and Jewish influences in Britain which it accused of sabotaging the national effort in peace as they had done in wartime.[1] It represented a halfway stage between the militant ideas of the pre-war Radical Right and the fascist movements of the inter-war years. Though Page Croft was easily written off as marginal and as an extremist, his views were largely mainstream Conservative ones at the time and his candidates attracted many Tory votes at by-elections. The National Party ran twenty-five candidates in 1918 of whom two, Page Croft and Sir Richard Cooper, were elected. Significantly neither man was opposed by his Conservative association, and Page Croft himself managed to remain as the member for Bournemouth until 1940. Since National Party views were not regarded as unduly extreme, the party acted as a useful safety valve for right-wing Conservatism which might otherwise have been driven further to the right. The disappearance of the National Party in 1922 simply signified that most rebels calculated they could free Conservatism from the coalition and restore it to its true principles by working within the party.

Another breakaway movement, the Anti-Waste League, emerged in 1920 under the patronage of Lords Rothermere and Beaverbrook, voicing the anger of taxpayers at the retention of high wartime income tax and the extravagance of the 'Homes for Heroes' programme. Like the National Party, Anti-Waste ran candidates and took seats from Conservatives at by-elections where it tapped the bottled-up resentment among many middle-class people after the war. The fashionable view held that middle-class voters were being neglected amid the concern for manual workers who had improved their wages and gained the protection of the trade unions.[2] In a shrill and embittered piece on 'The Crushing of the Middle Classes', the *English Review* warned that 'between the two governing and opposing extremes of capital and labour, the centre or great middle class is in for a bad time.' Saddled with a huge National Debt the government was keeping taxes high and subsidising houses, pensions, food and railways:

> Labour can refuse to pay taxes under £250 a year, we cannot. We are not organised ... In politics we do not count – we are the taxpayers ... We are the brains of the country, its impulse, and registration, we who scrape together somehow from £500 to £2,000 a year, which is the price of the nation's genius ... Yet to whom shall we turn?[3]

This frustration and anger could easily have become the seedbed for fascism. The sense of grievance was especially keen among the 200,000 ex-officers who had been demobilised by 1920. Their role in the war had given them status, but this only made their adaptation to civilian life more uncomfortable.[4] Although unemployed, these men were excluded from the grant of free unemployment insurance enjoyed by other workers. Some were reduced to taking menial jobs as commercial travellers or junior clerks on salaries lower than their army pay. Unable to occupy a secure place in the middle class, they often turned their irritation towards women or manual workers who appeared to them to be cosseted and protected by governments and trade unions. Though their natural political expression was Conservatism, they felt let down and consequently some were later attracted towards fascism. In the event, 1920s governments did just enough to blunt the grievance felt by ordinary taxpayers. When respectable figures including Lord Salisbury, Lord Selborne, the Duke of Northumberland and Page Croft lent their support to the Anti-Waste campaign, the government backed down; by 1922 Lloyd George had slashed income tax and adopted a policy of financial retrenchment. These initial skirmishes convinced the right-wing critics that it would be premature for them to quit the party.

In fact, the success achieved by Northumberland, Page Croft and others on the far right against an apparently entrenched government buoyed by a fresh mandate, puts a question mark over the traditional assumption that inter-war fascism failed because British Conservatism refused to adopt its ideas; it is just as plausible to argue that it failed because Conservatism *was* susceptible to pressure from the extreme right. Some aspects of fascism, notably its anti-Semitism, its anti-Communism and its protectionist-imperial programme, were obviously compatible with orthodox Conservatism. Although attempts by Conservative governments to suppress fascist paramilitary organisation would have created controversy, they evidently appreciated that they might need physical force in the future as a counter to the advance of the left. With hindsight it is tempting to argue that British Conservatives simply did not need fascism because the left never posed a serious threat to their hold on power. Yet this ignores contemporary perceptions and the electoral arithmetic of the 1920s. Dominated by a trade union movement influenced by syndicalist ideas, the persistence of mass unemployment and the General Strike of 1926, the 1920s appeared to contemporary Conservatives to be a very dangerous decade, more so than the 1930s when Labour had been tamed and the National Government seemed entrenched in power. In the elections of 1922, 1923 and 1929 Conservatives won a bare 38 per cent of the vote, historically a low share; on this basis they could hope to win a majority of seats only if the other two parties divided the vote evenly. This helps to explain why Conservatives felt so insecure in the 1920s and were consequently loath to ignore the dire warnings issued by the fascist movement.

Aristocratic Conservatives were especially susceptible to the appeal of fascism because of their acute realisation that their class had lost its accustomed role after the war as political power passed to an industrial plutocracy, in effect a 'new aristocracy, whose power and mobility are based solely on wealth'.[5] The immediate cause of their dismay lay in what appeared to be an attempt to devalue the British peerage by Lloyd George's sale of extraordinary numbers of titles to men from backgrounds in finance or industry rather than from the traditional landed class. Between 1916 and 1922 some 90 new peerages were conferred; between January 1921 and June 1922 alone 26 new peers, 74 baronets and 294 knights appeared, mostly after large sums of money had changed hands. This spoils system was unmistakable evidence of the moral rot and of the alien conspiracy afflicting postwar government.

Perhaps the most indefatigable propagandist of conspiracy theory was Alan Ian Percy, the eighth Duke of Northumberland. After an army career in the Boer War and Egypt, the Duke had entered the Intelligence Department at the War Office in 1918 before retiring to devote himself to his political polemics.[6] He used his wealth, derived from land and coal, to subsidise the *Morning Post*, a newspaper that took pride in its role as champion of the British Empire and of the Southern Loyalists in Ireland. In 1922 Northumberland obtained another platform for his views by founding a weekly journal, *The Patriot*, to alert the people to 'movements threatening the safety and welfare of the British Empire' which he believed were ignored or concealed by most of the press.[7] A classic example of an extreme reactionary and obsessive anti-Semite, the Duke was officially a Conservative, though his views reflected much common ground with fascism; his early death in 1930 probably saved him from a formal involvement with fascism.

Obsessed by the 'vein of treachery' which he detected running through all post-war governments, the Duke lamented that many Englishmen were simply too relaxed to see the enemy plotting against them: 'we believe there are two classes in conspiracy – the initiates and the dupes,' he wrote.[8] To awaken their fellow countrymen the *Morning Post* ran a series on 'Our Bolshevik Moles', while in 1922 *The Patriot* published articles entitled 'The German-Bolshevik Conspiracy', 'Our Foes and How to Fight Them', 'Making Ready for Revolution', 'Revolutionary Portraits', 'The Communist Plot and How to End It'. In his analysis of the origins of Bolshevism and of the Jewish-Bolshevik conspiracy the Duke revealed how far his ideas had been influenced by *The Protocols of the Elders of Zion*.[9] For him the Russian Revolution represented the fulfilment of the French Revolution of 1789 which had set Europe on the disastrous path to democracy; it had proved fatal to good government, to liberty, to law and order, to respect for authority and to religion, and culminated in 'a state of chaos from which a new world tyranny will arise'. Depicting European history as a grand cycle of growth and decay, the Duke argued that society was now heading back into absolutism.

According to Northumberland, Britain was threatened by Pan-Germanism and revolutionary Socialism which were linked by 'the influence of international finance controlled by various great German-Jewish banking firms and their connections in other countries'; the German Jews who controlled finance and industry in Germany were using their position to influence the policies of British government too.[10] To highlight the dangers *The Patriot* published extracts from *The Protocols*, alerted readers to the growth of Zionism and publicised attempts by the Board of Deputies of British Jews to pressurise the government in 1923 over immigration: 'the swarming ranks of an alien Jewry are to pour into Great Britain.'[11] The inconsistency in a thesis that linked Bolshevism and international finance in a single conspiracy was generally ignored by its advocates, but some propagandists simply resolved the difficulty by arguing that the two forces were working towards similar objectives: 'Both aim at the enslavement of the country to foreign control, the one in Moscow, the other in New York. Both aim at the destruction of British industries and the elimination of this country as a serious competitive power in the world's markets.'[12] Such claims seemed plausible enough to those who believed that Britain was throwing away the opportunity presented by the Great War to overthrow free trade in favour of protectionism:

> When have our International Financiers ever been known to sacrifice an opportunity for placing British credit at the service of foreign powers, when the profits have been sufficiently tempting, for fear of injuring British trade and industry? We have built up German and American industry by loans from London bankers. Is not the Bank of England as much an international bank as any other in the world?[13]

In the 1930s this protectionist-xenophobic rhetoric was to give fascism in Britain much of its anti-capitalist character. More immediately it fuelled the immense frustration among Conservatives at the failure to use their position of power to protect domestic and imperial markets with tariffs. They won one concession from the coalition in the shape of the 1921 Safeguarding of Industries Act which gave protection to a limited range of goods formerly imported from Germany. But beyond that nothing was achieved. Although Baldwin fought the election in 1923 on a protectionist programme, his emphatic defeat led him to abandon the idea even when he returned to office in 1924. To the advocates of conspiracy theory his capitulation merely corroborated their claims: 'What power is it that compels every government, as soon as it is elected, to abandon its constructive programme, to break its promises to the electors, and to follow the same course as its predecessors of doing nothing?'[14]

Dramatic proof of the alien forces operating within Britain appeared on 8 June 1922, when Field Marshal Sir Henry Wilson, former Chief of the Imperial General Staff and now an MP, was assassinated by the IRA on his doorstep in Eaton Square. For the Duke of Northumberland it went without saying that the Bolsheviks were involved with the 'Irish murder gang' and that Wilson's death showed that the tentacles of a violent conspiracy extended into the heart of the West End.[15] Even the imminent war between Britain and Turkey in the autumn of 1922 was interpreted as the outcome of a plot by Lenin.[16] Faced with such evidence, the critics demanded to know why successive governments had allowed subversive organisations such as the Communist Party to operate freely in Britain. Before 1914, so the argument ran, toleration of such activity was understandable, 'but today when a revolution is within measurable distance, it is treason to the community'.[17]

Strictly speaking, after 1918 any immediate threat was posed not by Communism but by the Labour Party. Whatever their party's propaganda machine claimed, by no means all Conservatives equated Labour with Communism and subversion. During the war leading Tories such as Lord Milner had recognised the patriotism shown by the working class and the unions; and by the 1920s there was no doubt of the loyalty of leading Labour figures such as Arthur Henderson, J. H. Thomas and Ramsay MacDonald to the parliamentary system and the monarchy. On the other hand, many Conservatives argued that in Labour they faced an opponent different in kind from their old Liberal enemy. The close links between the party and the trade unions were regarded as unconstitutional because they placed MPs in thrall to external organisations; and the financial support of the unions was seen as a new form of corruption, more extensive than the old because Labour now contested a majority of constituencies. Increasingly, too, Conservative candidates and organisers complained about the disruption of their meetings by 'Socialist rowdies [who] are doing their best to prevent freedom of speech in this country'.[18]

After the 1922 election when Labour clearly emerged as the second largest party – and thus as the alternative government – it proved very tempting to portray it as extremist and alien. This was a tactical ploy designed to drive ex-Liberal voters into the Conservative camp; but some Tories genuinely believed that the Labour movement represented a threat to society, political institutions and the empire. Lord Sydenham, Nesta Webster and the Duke of Northumberland, who were obsessed with conspiracy theory, depicted Labour as a vehicle for Jewish, German and Bolshevik influence, however respectable and moderate its leading figures might appear. British Socialism was 'still intellectually the slave of the Bolshevist. And English Socialism, deriving its animating principles from Moscow, is the master and driving force of the Labour Party in the House of Commons today.'[19] In a debate with H. M. Hyndman in June 1921, Northumberland insisted that Labour's loose federal structure enabled it to shelter subversives so that, once in power, the party would become a tool of those who sought to overthrow the monarchy, the House of Lords and capitalism; already they took Lenin's money to fund strikes and the *Daily Herald*.[20] Labour Party representation at international meetings of Socialists also appeared to corroborate the charge that the Labour leaders had 'placed themselves under the orders of a foreign Socialist executive committee . . . Labour's parliamentary representatives have become puppets pulled by a foreign string . . . like marionettes controlled by a Hidden Hand. Mr Ramsay MacDonald will be but the prancing figurehead of the show.'[21]

These increasingly hysterical warnings about international conspiracies encircling Britain ran continuously through the decade. They generated a phenomenon which was later described by the *News Chronicle* as 'Boiled-Shirt Fascism' to denote respectable fascist sympathisers who maintained a footing within conventional politics, even though they despised it, hoping to rejuvenate Conservatism, but kept open the extra-parliamentary alternative. Their first major success came on 19 October 1922 when discontent over the coalition's Irish and Indian policies, the honours scandal, the exclusion of many rising Tories from cabinet office and the realisation that public opinion had turned against Lloyd George led the Conservative MPs, meeting at the Carlton Club, to insist on fighting the next election as an independent party. This decision spelled the end of coalitionism until 1931 and restored a wholly Conservative government under the former leader, Andrew Bonar Law, for the first time since 1905.

However, although the rejection of Lloyd George lanced the boil, it did little to mitigate the underlying discontent among traditionalist Tories who continued to feel that they were working against the tide. Many landed and aristocratic figures continued to see Britain being swamped by 'plutocrats' of non-British origin, such as Sir Ernest Cassel and Sir Edgar Speyer who had used their wealth to gain a footing in society and were condemned as 'a danger to national life'.[22] Then there was the invasion of rich American hostesses, including Nancy Astor and Emerald Cunard, to say nothing of Thelma Furness, the American mistress of the Prince of Wales. This dilution of the aristocratic dominance in society would not have mattered so much had they

not felt marginalised within the Conservative Party. The most signal indication that peers were no longer political assets came in 1923 when Bonar Law
resigned as prime minister and the obvious successor, Lord Curzon, was
rejected in favour of the bourgeois Stanley Baldwin. The peers repeatedly
demanded that their leaders redeem the pledge they had made back in 1911
to restore the powers of the House of Lords that had been abolished by the
Liberals in the Parliament Act. The emasculation of the Lords was widely
thought to have left Britain with single-chamber government, a dangerous
situation if a Socialist government came to power.[23] However, although bills
were introduced and the party conference passed resolutions each year,
nothing was done to reform the upper house. The party leaders had no wish
to provoke the Labour Party, which had very little representation in the upper
house; and by 1927 they had effectively abandoned any plan for reform.

This insulting attitude towards the House of Lords exacerbated the
economic grievances of many peers as landowners. Many of them had been
complaining about declining agricultural profits since the 1870s, but after
1918 they suffered from sharply falling commodity prices, dwindling rents
and massive sales of land. After the rash expansion of wartime, the 1920s
saw a reduction in the area of cultivated land. 'How are we to save Britain's
premier industry which is so vital for the preservation of our racial instincts
and for the health and stability of our country?' demanded Sir Henry Page
Croft.[24] A classic case of the alienated peer was David Mitford, who became
the second Lord Redesdale in 1916. He inherited £17,000 but considered
himself terribly poor. Redesdale vociferously condemned the parliamentary
politicians for his misfortunes and easily succumbed to fascism in the 1930s.
To such men the government appeared far more concerned about appeasing
agricultural labourers, farmers and the National Farmers Union than helping
the landowners who commanded few votes. It neither offered subsidies to
maintain agricultural profitability nor the tariffs to exclude cheap imported
food from abroad. This situation led a number of frustrated aristocrats to
settle abroad. The Earl of Glasgow was financially crippled by his estates
but economised by retiring to France until 1930. Others escaped to Africa,
notably to the 'White Highlands' of Kenya or to Rhodesia, where they sought
to recreate a feudal lifestyle free from the mass democracy that had blighted
their lives in Britain. Among the Kenyan émigrés were Lord William Scott
(son of the Duke of Buccleuch), Lord Erroll, the Marquis of Graham (later
the seventh Duke of Montrose) and Viscount Lymington (later eighth Earl
of Portsmouth). All of these men became involved with fascist organisations
or developed pro-Nazi sympathies; Glasgow had joined the British Fascisti
in 1923 while Lymington was prominent in English Mistery, English Array
and other extremist groups in the 1930s.

Despite this, the aristocratic critics caused far less trouble to the Conservative leaders in the 1920s than the press barons, notably Lord Beaverbrook, owner of the *Daily Express*, and the megalomaniac proprietor of the *Daily Mail*, Lord Rothermere. In April 1923 Rothermere boasted to his ally: 'if Bonar [Law] places himself in my hands I will hand him down to posterity at the end of three years as one of the most successful prime ministers in history, and if there is a general election I will get him returned again.'[25] But no prime minister could risk accepting the support of the press barons without pledging himself to their programme: tariffs to protect industry and agriculture, no concessions to nationalists in India or Egypt, and a restoration of the power of the landed class. As ill-health released Bonar Law from the pressure to concede these demands in 1923, it was left to his successor to meet the charge of betrayal for the remainder of the decade: 'The Conservative Party is completely fed up with all this running away . . . It has deserted too many Allies, betrayed too many friends, broken too many pledges in the sacred cause of coalitionism. It looks to Mr Stanley Baldwin to stop the rot.'[26] The member for Bewdley since 1908, Baldwin came from a family of ironmasters and was thus a much more bourgeois figure than the traditional Conservative leaders. After a slow start, he had obtained office in 1917, became President of the Board of Trade in 1921, and emerged unexpectedly as prime minister in 1923. It was his courage in voicing the Conservatives' outrage towards the coalition in 1922 and his declaration that there was 'no more important duty at present than to preserve the Tory party' that made him the obvious leader.[27]

But those who anticipated an aggressive and traditionalist Conservatism from Baldwin had misjudged their man. Baldwin's forte was his skill in reassuring middle-of-the-road opinion; he cultivated an image of himself as a relaxed, pipe-smoking countryman – which soon had his Tory critics deriding him as an amateur pig-breeder. He redefined patriotism in terms of a sentimental, almost mystical reverence for the sights and sounds of the English countryside, which sounded suspect to those brought up on a diet of rabid, xenophobic rhetoric. However, Baldwin proved to be a shrewd leader. Recognising how far the terms of political competition had changed in ways unfavourable to his party, he took pains to appeal to people beyond the ranks of the party faithful: to former Liberals, to women voters and to working men. Faced with a Labour Party now threatening to mobilise the working-class majority of voters, he saw that Conservatism must become more inclusive. Whereas Victorian Conservatism had championed traditional masculine values and causes, under Baldwin the party offered a more domestic and feminised image; but this left Conservatives vulnerable to fascists who disparaged them as feminised and thus as weak.

In particular Baldwin tried to avoid confrontation with the unions and was more relaxed about the rise of Labour than most of his colleagues. Despite party propaganda designed to portray Labour as unfit to govern, he frankly accepted it as the alternative government. More than any other modern Tory leader Baldwin sought to educate his own party. He actually urged his followers to learn from Labour; speaking in Newcastle in October 1924 he expressed his pleasure at the entry of working men into party politics, claiming, 'the ladder is being set up amongst us which may serve them no less effectively than the ladder that exists today in the Labour Party.'[28] How repugnant such sentiments were on the far right may be judged by comparing this with the reactionary comments of the Duke of Northumberland about working-class entry into politics: 'We now draw our statesmen, not from any hereditary class or great interest of the country, but just as they come up; if they are eloquent and plausible no question is asked of their knowledge and character, or even if they are of British blood.'[29]

It was, however, in external affairs that Baldwin's attempts to drag his party into the twentieth century caused the most protracted controversy. He was prepared to draw a line under the long and emotive link with Ireland, and to make concessions to demands for participation in government in several parts of the empire. He felt that Conservatives should try to avoid a repetition of the bitter divisions between them and the Liberals during the late-Victorian and Edwardian period over Irish and imperial questions. Since Labour was not actually bent on dismembering the empire, it seemed feasible to adopt a bipartisan approach by offering judicious instalments of reform to nationalist movements at regular intervals. Inevitably, for Tories already alarmed at evidence of subversion within the empire, all this seemed further proof that demoralisation had penetrated to the heart of their own party. Even Baldwin's most sycophantic advocate, the historian Arthur Bryant, failed to convince extreme right-wing critics of his soundness. 'I wish he had gone abroad a bit more,' commented Major Francis Yeats-Brown. 'You say he was only 47 when war broke out. I feel he has been too physically comfortable to understand what Europe feels, and what our distressed areas feel.'[30] In a revealing response Bryant conceded Yeats-Brown's charge: 'It touches the vital point that marks the misunderstanding in the post-war democratic world between rulers and ruled. Only where the physical suffering has been so acute that it has engendered revolution has that division ended.'[31]

To men from a military-imperial background Baldwin appeared effete, compromising and altogether too liberal to be a credible leader of the right. As a symbol of the generation of men who had not fought, he became the natural target for the complaint that the younger generation was being denied the reward for the sacrifice it had made in the trenches. This deeply held conviction was strongly reflected in the Conservative journals which expressed the confusion and despair among young, politically aware men. 'Were some great man to appear tomorrow,' declared one 'Would-Be Young Conservative', 'some man who had the strength to start a party, I for one would follow that man to the end.'[32] The youthful critics disparaged the Tory Party as quiescent – 'all obesity and watch chains' – intent on excluding youth from parliament, and unsympathetic towards their own behaviour: 'it is being extensively asserted by the old women of both sexes that the Youth of this country is immoral.'[33] Above all, they deplored the peace settlement as the work of the old men who 'have betrayed the youth who died for what is called liberty'.[34] In the hands of a politician like Oswald Mosley, who had fought in the war and was the epitome of virile leadership, these sentiments proved to be a powerful recruiting weapon for fascism.

However, despite this discontent on the right of politics, comparatively few of the critics felt compelled to make a formal change of allegiance at this stage. Much of the explanation lies in Baldwin's tactical skill in foiling his critics by keeping them in hope of a real Conservative administration. Only seven months after becoming prime minister in May 1923 he called a fresh general election in order to seek a mandate to introduce tariffs. In so doing he was putting at risk a four-year term of office for the sake of a major programme ardently desired by Conservative imperialists. This made Baldwin appear a more resolute leader than he really was. However, the initiative rapidly unravelled when the Conservatives lost 88 seats in the ensuing election in December, though they remained the largest party. Even worse, Labour unexpectedly emerged as a prospective government for the first time. 'Believe me,' Lord Rothermere telegraphed Lord Beaverbrook, 'even two months Labour Government will shake economic structure to its foundations with loss probably fifty per cent advertisement revenue for long period.'[35] In this way, Baldwin's misjudgement immediately destroyed his newly won popularity, and during December 1923 Conservatives were busily holding meetings to consider replacing him.[36]

Meanwhile, as Labour was a long way short of a majority, it remained uncertain who would form the new government. The cabinet discussed the constitutional precedents and decided to remain in office, meet the new parliament in January 1924, and thus put the onus on the Liberal and Labour parties to vote them out. Although Baldwin met Asquith, the Liberal leader, and Ramsay MacDonald to discuss a coalition, this was a remote possibility because, having fought the election to defend free trade, the other parties would have found it embarrassing to keep the Conservatives in power. In any case, few Conservatives were keen to stomach this solution. 'A coalition is unthinkable,' wrote the right-wing MP, Sir Frederick Banbury, 'we have just escaped from one and we cannot renew it.'[37] But if Banbury thought coalition bad, he saw a 'Socialist' government as worse, and suggested inviting Asquith to support a limited Conservative programme, or even offering Conservative support for a limited Liberal one. It was all to no avail. When parliament met in the New Year the Liberals and Labour voted Baldwin out of office and King George V invited MacDonald to form a minority administration.

As historians have usually seen the first Labour government as a damp squib it is easy to overlook the shock waves its arrival sent through the British establishment at the time. MacDonald filled his cabinet largely with patriotic, right-wing Labour figures, a number of former Liberal ministers (Richard Haldane and Charles Trevelyan) and several Conservative recruits including Lord Chelmsford and Lord Parmoor. Despite this the change of government provoked a mood of rising hysteria in some quarters. Nesta Webster warned that 'the installation of a moderate subversive government has always been the prelude to bloody revolution', citing the regime of Alexander Kerensky in Russia in 1917 as the most recent example. The Duke of Northumberland reminded his readers that the new ministers were mere puppets and that their first moves would be to corrupt the police and the army; the best outcome would be a civil war from which the patriots would emerge victorious.[38] At a meeting organised by the National Citizens Union in January to protest at the formation of the new government, Sir Frederick Banbury personally offered to lead a battalion of the Coldstream Guards into the chamber of the House of Commons in order to save the British constitution.[39] Such a reaction appears bizarre in the light of the reverential attitude of most Labour leaders for the parliamentary system and the prime minister's anxiety to make his administration conform to normal expectations. But it underlines the extent to which some Conservatives relished the prospect of the crisis created by a Labour government and saw advantages in a violent confrontation with Socialism. A militarist element now began to enter their political calculations, as was indicated in October when Page Croft launched an appeal to raise a 'platoon' in each constituency comprising forty men drawn from the 400,000 ex-officers: 'if they could not raise forty recruits for the cause of country and empire, they are not the men I take them for.'[40]

In the event the nine-month Labour government proved to be a shocking anti-climax. While *The Patriot* regaled its readers with regular pieces on 'Recognising the Reds', 'Is History About to Repeat Itself?' and 'Socialism – Then Revolution', Leo Maxse felt compelled to admit that after Philip Snowden's budget 'there is not even an instalment [of Socialism]'.[41] Deflated by the cautious conduct of MacDonald's colleagues, the far right was obliged to let the conventional leaders take the initiative. Baldwin adopted the characteristically relaxed view that Labour should be allowed a short period in office; as Neville Chamberlain observed, ' it would be too weak to do much harm, but not too weak to get discredited.'[42] Consequently the Opposition made little attempt to defeat the government, and Baldwin devoted himself to making speeches in the country with a view to rallying his disillusioned followers.

In September 1924, however, MacDonald lost a major division in the Commons and resigned, whereupon the King granted yet another dissolution leading to an October election from which the Conservatives emerged with 412 seats, a gain of 155 over 1923. Though a Conservative resurgence was always on the cards, some of its supporters were prepared to take no chances to secure victory. Early on the morning of Saturday 25 October, Jimmy Thomas, the Labour Colonial Secretary, woke up his colleague, Snowden, with the words: 'Get up, you lazy devil! We're bunkered.'[43] A hysterical headline in that morning's *Daily Mail* proclaimed 'Civil War Plot By Socialists ... Moscow Order To Our Reds. Great Plot Disclosed Yesterday'.

It transpired that a letter, dated 15 September, from one Grigori Zinoviev, the President of the Communist International, ordering the unleashing of the class war in Britain, had fallen into the newspaper's hands. For several months Opposition politicians had been attacking the government over its treaty with the Soviet Union and over its decision to abandon the prosecution of J. R. Campbell, a Communist editor, under the Incitement to Mutiny Act. By focusing attention on Labour's supposed weakness towards subversive movements these issues lent credibility to the Zinoviev Letter when it surfaced in the last week of the election campaign.[44] The *Daily Mail* used the Campbell case to corroborate its claim that the prime minister had failed to stand up for his country: 'Now we see why Mr MacDonald has done obeisance throughout the campaign to the Red Flag with its associations of murder and crime ... he is a stalking horse for the Reds as Kerensky was.'[45] It referred in detail to the letter's instructions for organising treasonable and terrorist activities: 'It enjoins them to undermine the loyalty of our soldiers and sailors ... Everything is to be made ready for a great outbreak of the abominable "class war" which is civil war of the most savage kind.'[46] To make matters worse, the prime minister remained silent for twenty-four hours and allowed the *Mail* to accuse him of concealing the letter for a month in the hope that he would never have to publish it.[47] At the time it was not recognised that the Zinoviev Letter was a forgery by a group of White Russian émigrés which had been planted on the Foreign Office by British Intelligence and the Conservative Central Office. Its release four days before polling dominated the election and was regarded by the Labour Party as the chief cause of its defeat.

However, its significance has probably been misunderstood. While the London journalists and party leaders excited themselves over the Zinoviev Letter, reactions at the grass roots were more phlegmatic. The Labour vote actually increased from 4.4 to 5.4 million; and the withdrawal of many Liberal candidates made it almost inevitable that many middle-class voters who had been alienated by protectionism in 1923 would rally to the Conservatives once again. Essentially the Zinoviev Letter helped to justify the alarmism of the extreme right at a time when it was otherwise beginning to lose credibility. By collaborating with the *Daily Mail* over the timely release of the letter Baldwin may have gained some short-term advantage, but in the longer run this only exacerbated his problems with his own followers.

In the event Baldwin's respite following his overwhelming victory in 1924 proved remarkably brief. The goodwill began to dissipate almost as soon as his new appointments were announced. A few right-wing figures entered the cabinet, including L. S. Amery, Lord Salisbury and Sir William Joynson-Hicks; but Baldwin drew the line at Sir George Lloyd and the Duke of Northumberland. Instead the cabinet was dominated by comparatively liberal men, including Sir Samuel Hoare, Edward Wood and Sir Arthur Steel-Maitland, and the 'careerists' – Lord Curzon, Lord Birkenhead and Austen Chamberlain – who were still associated with Lloyd George. Above all Tory protectionists and imperialists were disappointed to discover that tariff reform was not on the agenda and they reacted angrily to the appointment of a prominent free-trader and former Liberal, Winston Churchill, as Chancellor of the Exchequer.

Since 1923 Churchill had endeavoured to put his Liberal and coalitionist past behind him and worked his passage back into Conservative affections by employing some violently anti-Socialist rhetoric. Yet he continued to be regarded as a traitor and an opportunist. '[Churchill] now occupies a post where he can inflict considerable injury on British interests at home and abroad,' complained Leo Maxse, 'and we shall be agreeably surprised if he does not succeed in doing so.'[48] The critics correctly saw Churchill's appointment as the clearest possible indication that Baldwin had abandoned protectionism. This antagonised Rothermere who took the government's programme as a personal insult because he had convinced himself, as usual, that he had been responsible for returning Baldwin to office. 'I believe [the Zinoviev] Letter altered the situation to the extent of something like 100 seats. It was the culminating blow,' he told Beaverbrook. By the end of 1924 the two proprietors had decided to use their newspapers to force the government to abandon free trade. 'Go ahead,' urged Rothermere, 'you will eventually unship Baldwin.'[49]

Baldwin's only real concession to his right-wing critics in 1924 lay in the appointment of Sir William Joynson-Hicks as Home Secretary. Ever since his brief period in 1908–10 as the member for North West Manchester, a constituency with a substantial Jewish population, Joynson-Hicks had specialised in insulting the Jewish community. He had made it clear that he simply did not want the votes of a community that organised itself for political purposes; and he was invariably prominent in attacking Liberal ministers such as Herbert Samuel and Edwin Montagu who were Jews.[50] During the 1924 election campaign the Conservatives' emphasis on Russian subversion had involved a good deal of propaganda about 'aliens', a term which was used as code for 'Jews'. As the new Home Secretary Joynson-Hicks immediately promised to meet the expectations that had been aroused by curtailing 'alien' immigration and deporting 'undesirables'. He instructed immigration officers not to give them the benefit of the doubt when they attemped to enter the country and he accused his critics of wanting to flood England with the 'alien refuse of the world'. He had non-naturalised Jews deported for petty offences and delayed consideration of their applications for naturalisation for years.

In fact the Home Office had been excluding applications by Russian Jews for naturalisation for several years; but after 1924 Joynson-Hicks raised the hurdle by increasing the residency requirement from five to ten years, and to fifteen years for Russians.[51] Brushing aside the accusations of anti-Semitism which were levelled against him even by members of his own party, Joynson-Hicks frankly admitted that he regarded aliens who lived in their own communities, married within them and spoke their own language as unsuitable to be British residents. His views and his policy tacitly endorsed the fascist thesis that Britain needed to be more vigilant in defending herself from infiltration by alien subversives. Though the most prominent anti-Semite in government, Joynson-Hicks was by no means eccentric, and the readiness of the prime minister to promote him offered some reassurance that the goals of the extreme right could be attained by working within the framework of official Conservatism.

To his opponents Baldwin's greatest failing was his reluctance to stand up for Britain's external interests. Their sensitivity was partly a reflection of their experience of administering the empire, their careers in the army and above all their connections with Ireland. Deeply affected by the bloody civil war that broke out between the Irish Republican forces and the British government's notorious Black and Tans after the war, they were outraged when the Tory leaders capitulated in the agreement to end the Union with Ireland in 1920. At a stroke this made their party's name – 'Conservative and Unionist Party' – seem redundant. For years afterwards the Duke of Northumberland agitated on behalf of the 'Southern Loyalists' who had been left to their fate in the Irish Free State, and he continually used the IRA as evidence for his thesis that reformist movements were easily manipulated by violent and subversive extremists.[52] He believed that Britain's retreat from Ireland had left the country available as a base from which her enemies could plot the disruption of the mainland.

Moreover, weakness in Ireland was seen as 'the first Act in a greater tragedy' because it stimulated nationalism in Egypt and India. The Conservative government had inherited a policy of reform from Lloyd George which involved expanding the Indian electorate and extending power to elected regional assemblies. While Baldwin believed this would strengthen the pro-British sections of Indian society, his critics argued that concessions simply provoked agitations organised by what Lord Sydenham described as 'a class of partly denationalised Indians'.[53] Many British imperialists refused to accept that Gandhi and the Congress could in any way be representative of Indian opinion. Faced with nationalist pressure in Egypt, the government also felt bound to live up to the promises made during the war, and in 1922 Britain conceded a limited form of independence which kept control of foreign policy and the Suez Canal in British hands. Leo Maxse vainly complained that the promises had been made 'in the orgy of sentimentalism and self-determination that engulfed our government after the Armistice', and he insisted that power was being handed to 'a class whose only claim to government is that they [have] mastered western catchwords long since exploded'.[54] The deep division between Baldwin and many of his own supporters over Egypt was reflected in the disenchantment of Sir George Lloyd, a former MP who believed that Britain had betrayed her own interests by its concessions. Lloyd's appointment as High Commissioner for Egypt in 1925 ought to have reassured the imperialists, but he found himself frustrated in his attempt to recover British influence in domestic affairs and he blamed the Foreign Office for refusing to support him because it tacitly contemplated a complete withdrawal of British forces from the country.[55] In Lloyd's view, the Conservative government had effectively abandoned Conservative principles in favour of Liberalism.

Meanwhile, in Europe the principle of nationality was largely disregarded by Baldwin's critics. Despite the enthusiasm with which Conservatives had embraced Britain's cause in 1914, they refused to accept that national self-determination had been a worthwhile objective; Britain had fought not for the rights of Poles or Czechs, but to maintain her own empire. They were especially scornful about the moral principles introduced into the peace settlement by President Woodrow Wilson, and in particular they never subscribed to the programme of disarmament or to the League of Nations to which all post-war governments were ostensibly committed. This was by no means the view of a reactionary minority but typical of mainstream Conservatism in the 1920s. It was best articulated by L. S. Amery, who served as Colonial Secretary from 1924 to 1929. Amery regarded it as quite unrealistic to think that the League could maintain peace. 'Leagues of peace, disarmament etc. are all fudge,' he recalled, while Woodrow Wilson was 'stupider than I imagined'.[56] Amery took the same disparaging view of Lord Robert and Lord Hugh Cecil – the chief Tory advocates of the League – whom the Duke of Northumberland derided as the 'Maggots of Conservatism'. For the Duke, the League represented yet another symptom of the power of international finance based in the United States in collaboration with German-Jewish interests. Maxse denounced 'the cranks who believe in it and the Plutocratic Pacifism and International Financiers who have put up the money for it'.[57] Essentially, these critics feared that before long sympathy for the aspirations to self-determination among Africans and Asians would encourage the League to start meddling with the British Empire, and that Britain's sensitivity to Germany's sense of grievance would result in the return of the territories that Britain had acquired as League of Nations mandates.

Within Baldwin's cabinet the positive case for empire was advanced by Amery who energetically promoted schemes of emigration and imperial economic development. But little money was available to support Amery's ideas, and the grand vision of a cohesive empire united by imperial preference continued to be frustrated by political caution reinforced by a luke-warm public. Baldwin's ministers preferred to focus on domestic priorities, including widows' pensions, local government reform and equal franchise for women, for which it had no mandate in the critics' view. 'The Conservative Party in the House of Commons could pull this Government up at any moment,' complained Maxse, '[but] they have not the gump-tion to object.'[58] After their victory in 1924 this feebleness seemed inex-plicable. Baldwin enjoyed a massive popular mandate to govern, but chose to run away from Britain's enemies at home and abroad. It was against this background of discontent that many Conservatives viewed the approach of a general strike during 1925 as the decisive test of Baldwin's leadership.

SIX

The General Strike:
The Fascist Crisis Denied

'Constitutional Government is fighting for its life; if we failed, it would be revolution.'

Neville Chamberlain to Ida Chamberlain,
8 May 1926

Shortly before midnight on 3 May 1926 the Manchester express train bound for Euston left London Road Station with barely twenty passengers on board. It was the last such train to depart for several days. It got as far as Rugby where the drivers changed, and a few minutes later four pickets took up positions in the drive leading to the station. Britain's first General Strike had begun. For fascists the strike seemed certain to precipitate the crisis they had so often predicted and to create the chaos in which they would intervene to save the country.

The industrial and political crisis engendered by the General Strike had been eight years in the making. Like many other workers the coal miners had appreciated the experience of wartime when their industry had been operated by the government; subsequently their union advocated state ownership as the best means of maintaining the national wage settlements they had won. In 1919 when they demanded a six-hour day, a 30 per cent wage increase and nationalisation, Lloyd George managed to bury the issue by appointing the Sankey Commission to consider the future organisation of the industry; but he ignored its recommendations and in 1920 coal was decontrolled. Although coal output had increased greatly, poor investment and fragmented ownership had left the industry increasingly inefficient. Sustained by wartime demand, it proved unable to recover its export markets after 1918 because other countries had exploited their own reserves more effectively. In this situation a clash between miners seeking higher wages and owners determined to reduce costs was inevitable.

However, this coming clash was far more serious than a normal industrial dispute, because in 1921 a 'Triple Alliance' of miners, railwaymen and transport workers unions threatened a sympathetic strike which would have paralysed the whole economy. 'There is a general feeling that revolution may be closing upon us,' one minister's wife wrote in her diary.[1] To meet it, the government made preparations to use the troops in an attempt to keep industry going, and from that time onwards it possessed an emergency organisation for handling sympathetic strikes. In the event the other unions backed down, leaving the miners alone and obliged to accept cuts in wages. The collapse of the Triple Alliance on 'Black Friday' led the miners' leaders, Herbert Smith and A. J. Cook, to rethink, but not abandon, their strategy for harnessing the full strength of the union movement. The creation of a thirty-member General Council for the TUC made coordinated industrial action possible for the first time. During 1924, when several of the more right-wing union leaders temporarily left to serve in the Labour government, it was agreed that the TUC would lead a future general strike. The miners judged that this arrangement would make another betrayal impossible.

By this time the union movement had good reason to think it would need an overall defensive strategy. After peaking at 8.4 million in 1920, membership commenced a steady decline down to 1934, a reflection of the protracted economic depression which undermined the unions' bargaining strength. It was not merely miners' wages but those of most workers that were now under threat. In 1925 the Chancellor, Winston Churchill, had at last decided that the pound could 'look the dollar in the face', in effect restoring it to its pre-war level. This revaluation of the currency effectively made British exports more expensive by about 10 per cent. The only obvious means of maintaining sterling at this unrealistically high level lay in cutting the costs of industry. The unions could hardly fail to notice the consensus among employers, economists and politicians by 1925 that wages must fall if unemployment were to be reduced. In these circumstances a general strike was a defensive weapon to fend off the anticipated attack on working–class living standards. Its motivation was essentially material rather than political.

However, in the aftermath of the Zinoviev Letter few politicians were willing to accept so reassuring an interpretation. 'The Socialist Party fights with two weapons,' commented Sir John Gilmour, the new Secretary of State for Scotland in November 1924; 'having been defeated in the political field they can bring the alternative of industrial warfare into play.'[2] Consequently during the summer of 1925 the prospect of a general strike appeared to pose a political as much as an industrial challenge with external as well as internal implications. Wilfred Ashley MP pointed to the high level of activity by Communists among trade unions and he argued that the Bolshevik regime in Russia regarded its own survival as conditional upon its ability to inspire revolution in other European countries.[3] According to the Duke of Northumberland, who was himself a coal owner and had vigorously defended his interests at the Sankey Commission, 'the miners are just pawns in the game' and their wages merely offered a pretext for a crisis: 'The Third International [plans] to organise revolution in Britain by getting control of trade unions and manipulating the mass of workers. The role of the Parliamentary Labour Party is to camouflage this design until the time is ripe for action for a revolutionary strike on a gigantic scale.'[4]

To some extent the government itself endorsed the Duke's thesis in October 1925 by instigating prosecutions against twelve leading Communist Party members for seditious libel and incitement to mutiny. They received sentences of six and twelve months. Though this fell short of the suppression of the Communist Party that the Duke desired, it reflected the authorities' intention to curtail an organisation they believed to be fomenting mass industrial unrest. According to intelligence reports in 1926, the General Strike was financed partly by the transfer of funds from the Soviet Union amounting to £380,000. The government rejected claims that money on this scale could have been contributions by Russian trade unions and their members.[5] Subsequent investigation of the Communist Party revealed that it had received £61,500 from Russia in 1920–2, and was allocated further substantial sums by the Communist International during 1925, 1927 and 1928. The funds were transferred via the Narodny Bank where several clerks held the money in special accounts before passing it on to the British Communist Party.[6]

This interpretation of the General Strike as a subversive movement was not simply a delusion of right-wing fanatics, for it was to some extent endorsed by the Labour Party leadership. During their nine months in office in 1924 Labour ministers had not hesitated to use the Emergency Powers Act and arrange for troops to move essential supplies during strikes by tram workers and dockers. 'I only wish it had been a Tory government in office,' commented Ernest Bevin of the Transport and General Workers Union; 'we would not have been frightened by *their* threats.'[7] The attitude of Labour politicians was undoubtedly coloured by the circumstances of the party's loss of office in 1924. They recognised the force of the claim that the Russian Bolsheviks were pleased to see Labour being discredited by an ineffectual period in office because this would encourage the proletariat to reject parliamentary methods. A purely parliamentary strategy seemed ineffective now that the Conservatives enjoyed a huge parliamentary majority, and for a time this strengthened those who argued that the movement must look beyond parliament to direct action in order to defend the interests of working men and women.

As a result the Labour leaders showed a notable lack of sympathy with the miners during the period leading up to the General Strike. Ramsay

MacDonald was embarrassed when Baldwin granted a subsidy to the coal industry because he appeared to have backed down to the strike threat after ignoring the demands for intervention made by Labour MPs. During 1925 Snowden and MacDonald had publicly warned that Communists were gaining influence in the trade unions but were keeping their revolutionary aims in the background.[8] At the party conference at Liverpool in that year proposals to allow unions to send Communist Party members as delegates to local Labour parties and to the conference were rejected by crushing majorities; but the debate only served to corroborate claims that Communist subversion was a serious problem. The effect was to leave the right-wing interpretation of the General Strike largely unchallenged.

Both Labour and Conservative politicians recognised that even though the objects behind the General Strike were essentially material ones, the method now being adopted had major political implications. A general strike was, after all, a key element in the thinking of syndicalists who sought to overthrow parliamentary government by using a complete stoppage of work designed to paralyse the economy, thus enabling them to replace the system with some form of workers' control. These ideas had been in circulation before the war, especially in South Wales, and had influenced A. J. Cook, but were firmly repudiated by most union leaders. Consequently, the adoption of the syndicalist weapon by the TUC in the 1920s suggested an ideological shift among the unions. In fact, despite the patronising treatment they received from Ramsay MacDonald, the union leaders were ardent parliamentarians, and felt uncomfortable about the strategy to which they were committed. They evidently hoped that the mere threat of a general strike would be sufficient to force the government and the employers into a compromise as it appeared to have done in 1925 when Baldwin offered the subsidy. Their lack of ideological commitment was underlined by the failure to lay detailed plans for the strike. Failing a retreat by the government, they anticipated that the outbreak of a general strike would have such a devastating impact in terms of lost production that within a short time the authorities would back down and force the coal owners into a deal. In the process the government would lose credibility and probably be forced into holding a fresh general election. To this extent the strike was certainly political, if not in the usual sense. Whether the unions miscalculated about the political ramifications remains speculative; the General Strike proved too brief for the political effects to develop as they expected. But MacDonald's pessimism about the political implications for his party was probably misplaced in that he failed to appreciate how solidly the strike was supported by working-class communities or how vulnerable the British government was to a shutdown of the economy.

The crisis reached a climax at the end of June 1925 when the coal owners insisted that in view of their declining competitiveness in foreign markets and the fact that wages represented 70 per cent of their costs, they must return to an eight-hour day and abandon the national wage agreements. On appealing to the TUC's General Council for support, Smith and Cook won a promise to place an embargo on coal movements by the railwaymen in July. In this situation the government intervened. Baldwin offered a temporary subsidy to the industry to maintain current wages and hours pending an investigation by a Royal Commission under Herbert Samuel. 'Thank God!' wrote the King on hearing the news, 'there will be no strike now.'[9] For the TUC 'Red Friday', as this episode became known, appeared to validate their expectation that the threat of a general strike would be sufficient to achieve their aims. However, in March when the Samuel Commission reported, it, too, recommended wage reductions and an end to the subsidy which had cost £23 million, more than twice the sum expected in 1925. By this time Baldwin's options had narrowed significantly; his cabinet and his parliamentary followers would not tolerate a further retreat. Thus, although the General Council continued to negotiate with the government, at the end of April 1926 it decided to initiate the plans for a general strike. Its bluff was finally called on 3 May when the compositors working on the *Daily Mail* refused to set an anti-strike editorial and stopped work, provoking the government into abandoning the talks. On 4 May the strike began.

During the intervening months the political temperature had steadily risen as a result of the relaxed approach to the crisis on the part of the government. While the right-wing journals condemned Baldwin's subsidy out of hand as 'surrender', the British Fascists prepared to put some backbone into the civil power.[10] Cuthbert Headlam, a Tory member from County Durham, conceded that it looked as though Baldwin had been intimidated by the miners; and he recognised the force of the demand for 'strong measures' in the party: 'It would be no exaggeration to say that the future of constitutional government in this country may be at stake during the coming months.'[11] The loyalist Headlam may have been influenced by the apocalyptic warnings emanating from the extremists. The Duke of Northumberland contemptuously dismissed Baldwin's policy as one of 'drift[ing] helplessly towards the abyss, hoping until the last moment that something will turn up to avert the inevitable catastrophe'.[12] He warned that if a Socialist government came to power as a result of a general strike, it would not be able to proceed to a gradual programme of nationalisation but would be overtaken by violent revolution on the one hand and reaction on the other.

It was understandable that contemporaries interpreted the grant of a subsidy as evidence that the government was not prepared to handle the emergency. However, the cabinet papers make it clear that this was far from being the case. Baldwin's chief object was to avoid a general strike altogether by winning a breathing space in which either Samuel would produce a solution or the unions themselves would back away from industrial action. Though the government appeared to be acting precipitately in terminating negotiations on 3 May, its preparations were as complete as they could reasonably be; it also had some reason to think that the unions were less resolute for the strike than they appeared. Indeed, elaborate plans had been made to maintain law and order during a general strike and to ensure the movement of essential supplies. During the strike the cabinet's Supply and Transport Committee was to meet daily under the Home Secretary, Sir William Joynson-Hicks. Detailed supervision was delegated to eleven regions, each under a civil commissioner subject to the overall charge of the Chief Civil Commissioner, Sir William Mitchell-Thompson, and his deputy, J. C. C. Davidson. However, as the government wished to avoid being provocative, it kept quiet about its preparations and consequently exposed itself to criticism for excessive complacency.

In one respect, however, the authorities felt obliged to indicate how seriously they were treating the crisis. Though expecting to rely upon the police, the special constabulary and the armed forces during a general strike, they anticipated the need for thousands of volunteers to help to operate basic services, especially transport. This was politically awkward because any public appeal for volunteers by the government threatened to antagonise the unions and make the strike appear inevitable. The result was a compromise designed to obscure the situation. In September 1925 it emerged that a semi-private body known as the Organisation for the Maintenance of Supplies (OMS) had been established to recruit volunteers. Under the presidency of Lord Hardinge of Penshurst, the OMS was run by General Sir John McCalmont. Each of the 85,000 volunteers were required to sign an undertaking: 'I hereby enrol myself as a member of the OMS and undertake, when called upon by the OMS on the occurrence of an emergency, to offer myself for duty in maintaining and protecting essential services.' They received coloured cards: yellow for a 'worker', white for a 'driver', pink for a 'messenger' and blue for 'protection'.[13] On the outbreak of the emergency the OMS was to disband and hand its register of recruits and all other material over to the government, while its agents were to approach the local authorities to ascertain which duties or services they were to perform.[14]

The cabinet's embarrassment was reflected in the stance adopted in October 1925 by Joynson-Hicks who tried to imply that the OMS was really nothing to do with him and that it had taken the initiative in preparing for the emergency.[15] The reason for dissembling on the part of the Home Secretary is obvious. On the one hand he was reluctant to provoke the left by launching anything that could be represented as a strike-breaking machine. On the other hand, the prospect of a general strike was enormously stimulating to the extreme right, especially amongst the fascist organisations who expected it to precipitate a historic crisis for parliamentary government with which they alone were equipped to deal. The OMS had immediately been hailed by the *Daily Mail* as the 'Defence Against the Reds', while the Communist Party issued a statement describing its formation as 'the most definite step towards organised Fascism yet made in this country'. Even the Liberal *Westminster Gazette* observed that 'it will please the newspapers which want the Mussolini touch.'[16] Ramsay MacDonald, who feared that the strike would polarise opinion leading to violence between left and right, attacked Joynson-Hicks for sponsoring stunts designed to justify the OMS and creating an impression of an inevitable clash between rival forces. 'Communism would have been, to all intents and purposes, dead in this country,' he claimed, 'had its activities not been a political asset to the Tory Party.'[17]

In the face of these inflammatory statements Lord Hardinge and Joynson-Hicks took pains to emphasise the unofficial nature of the OMS: 'the association is non-party and has no political aims.'[18] Its distance from the government was underlined by its reliance on appeals to the public for funds. However, this was not wholly convincing once it emerged that the Council of the OMS was dominated by right-wing Conservatives including Lord Falkland, Lord Scarborough, Sir James Rennell Rodd and Sir Martin Archer Shee, as well as Lord Jellicoe, Admiral Alexander Duff and other retired officers.[19] The enthusiasm shown by the British Fascisti in enrolling their members as Special Constables also fuelled suspicions that the authorities were creating a strike-breaking force. According to Brigadier General Blakeney, the Home Secretary agreed in July 1925 to accept British Fascisti members into the OMS and the Specials. But a conference between the Home Office and the OMS concluded: 'the absorption into the Special Constabulary of units organised by an outside body with any sort of political flavour would give rise to questions of some delicacy'; and in October Joynson-Hicks insisted that the recruits should sever their connections with fascist organisations.[20] However, the effect was purely nominal: although fascists would not be permitted to enrol as a body as the British Fascisti intended, they could not be prevented from joining as individuals.[21] With notable understatement the organisers admitted the difficulty of maintaining control over 'an organisation like the OMS which naturally appeals to the adventurous spirit'. They therefore agreed to apply the same principle in admitting recruits strictly on an individual basis.[22] Even so, several local authorities and chief constables, including those in Liverpool and Buckinghamshire, quickly informed the Home Office that they did not want Specials who had bypassed the usual vetting procedures, and declined to make use of the OMS volunteers. 'There would be any amount of trouble', warned Liverpool's chief constable, 'if they tried to start a branch [of the OMS] in Liverpool.'[23] In Manchester, too, the chief constable insisted that his Specials had no connection with the OMS.[24]

Perhaps as a result of these cautionary measures, the flurry of controversy in the press during October died down for several months, leading some critics to conclude that the government, under the benign influence of the prime minister, had retreated from the whole idea of a volunteer force. 'The word went forth to snub the efforts of the peers and parasites who are so anxious to maintain supplies,' scoffed the *Daily Herald*. But by February 1926 it admitted, 'the OMS has bobbed up again.'[25] Officially some 85,000 volunteers joined the OMS. Additionally there was a huge increase in the number of Special Constables: in London alone they increased from 10,000 to over 61,000 during the strike.[26] According to the *Morning Post*, recruitment of the British Fascisti as Specials was simply postponed for a short time; and in any case not all local authorities had qualms about enrolling fascists in their ranks. In Wolverhampton it had been agreed that fascist recruits should march with the police and be sworn in as Specials under their own fascist leaders; and during the strike the chief constable was reported as saying: 'I do not recognise any organisation. I am only prepared to have the assistance of loyal citizens. They are not coming to me as Fascists at all . . . I think it is far better that they should be under proper control than remain on their own.'[27] In one south coast town 75 per cent of Specials were reportedly fascists.[28]

Although the authorities managed to deprive the fascist organisations of some of the prestige and respectability they had hoped for in responding to the national crisis, there were clearly limits to their ability to control things once the strike got under way. The British Fascists enrolled their men in 'Q Divisions', a quasi-military force available to police meetings and suppress disorder, and during the strike cars conveying men to danger points were constantly despatched from Miss Lintorn-Orman's home in Elm Park Gardens in Acton.[29] Colonel Rippon-Seymour of the National Fascisti badgered the Home Secretary to accept his men officially into the Special Constabulary rather than disbanding: 'We won't do that; we want to serve as a body,' he insisted.[30] When the *British Gazette* encouraged people to raise Union Jacks not Red Flags, Rippon-Seymour promptly suggested to

Baldwin that the Red Flag should be made illegal. But officials refused to be drawn into giving the fascists any official encouragement: 'we shall have these people interfering with Railway signalmen and other harmless necessary people, if they attempt to lower all red flags.'[31]

In the event the General Strike lasted only nine days, from 4 to 12 May, and ended amid a welter of self-congratulation on the tolerant and peaceful manner in which it had been conducted. 'Our dear old country can be well proud of itself,' wrote the King in his diary, 'as during the last nine days there has been a strike in which four million men have been affected; not a shot has been fired and no one killed; it shows what a wonderful people we are.'[32] The famous football match played between strikers and policemen at Plymouth provoked one bemused French observer to remark: 'The English are not a nation, they are a circus.'[33] Higher up the social scale opinion became sharply polarised. Hugh Gaitskell, then an Oxford undergraduate, borrowed an elderly Morris to transport copies of the *British Worker* and announced, 'Henceforth my future is with the working class', to his shocked aunt. 'I do not know what England is coming to,' she replied in tones reminiscent of Lady Bracknell; 'when I was a girl the working classes were neither seen nor heard!'[34] In the argumentative Mitford family, Jessica denounced her mother as a class enemy. 'I'm *not* an enemy of the working class,' retorted Lady Redesdale angrily, 'I think some of them are perfectly sweet.'[35]

It is, however, fair to note that Baldwin went some way to restraining the extremists on both sides. Characteristically he left it to the Transport and Supply Committee to run the country during the strike; he overruled the Home Secretary when he wanted to close down the *Daily Herald*, resisted the temptation to interfere with union funds, and determined that no movement of troops would take place before the strike began.[36] When it was suggested that Baldwin might make Churchill editor of the *British Gazette* he promptly agreed: 'Yes, it will keep him busy and stop him doing worse things.' But he refused to allow the excitable Churchill to take over the BBC during the strike.[37] In any case the cabinet machinery was strictly designed to maintain essential services and supplies rather than to break the strike, a distinction that seems to have been recognised by the strikers and helps to account for their passive response to the food convoys. In many areas the local strike committees or 'Councils of Action' themselves issued permits to allow the transport of food and sometimes cooperated with the civil commissioners.

Even so, things could easily have got out of hand. Tuesday 4 May, the first day of the strike, passed off without any real signs of disorder, partly because people appreciated having the day off work and no hardships had yet arisen. But on the following day the first serious incidents occurred, notably at Leeds where some 5,000 men threw lumps of coal at trams, smashing windows and injuring some of the passengers. In the ensuing struggle the police drew their truncheons to keep strikers away from the other trams.[38] By Thursday 6 May it was clear that the main clashes would arise in connection either with trams and buses or with food supplies at the docks. In Newcastle the pickets targeted and overturned carts of potatoes. Although the police were able to guard the unloading of ships, it proved difficult to distribute the food in the districts beyond the city boundaries.[39] In London the fighting occurred chiefly in the East End because of the docks and south of the river around the Elephant and Castle where many trams and buses converged. On 6 May a mob attacked a bus at the Elephant and Castle, removed the volunteer driver and set fire to his vehicle. Other buses in the vicinity received similar treatment.[40] The pattern was repeated in Glasgow the following day when men attacked trams and a depot in which they believed volunteers were waiting to drive the vehicles. In the general disorder stones were thrown and shop windows broken.[41] Again police used truncheons to disperse the crowds, and eighty-nine people were later charged with riotous conduct and a breach of the peace. But the targets were often specific rather than random. For example, each night strikers from Gateshead and County Durham crossed the High Level Bridge over the Tyne to stone the windows of the *Newcastle Evening Chronicle*. It required a mounted force and several busloads of police to disperse them.[42] By Saturday 8 May the situation had deteriorated to the point where the unions were now cancelling permits to move supplies, while the government was making more use of troops. Having mobilised large numbers of volunteers and Specials, the authorities declared themselves satisfied that they had maintained control.

However, the strike remained very solid, and it spread as more men abandoned work. One of the most serious riots occurred on 9 May at Preston where 5,000 people attacked a police station intending to release a man who had been arrested for throwing a missile at a bus. After two hours of fighting, three baton charges and reinforcements, the crowd was dispersed, though only eight arrests were made.[43] On Monday 10 May the strike entered its second week with no real sign of a return to work except in Birmingham. Indeed, on the 11th the TUC called out a second line of workers in engineering and shipbuilding, and the loss of power forced other men to abandon work.[44] There was little more the authorities could now do other than to increase the use of force against the crowds. But although riots took place in half a dozen northern towns, there was no general challenge to law and order. Most regions reported that they had enrolled as many volunteers as were required. On Wednesday 12 May the level of violence increased, but this proved to be the last day of the strike. A TUC deputation arrived at

10 Downing Street where they informed the prime minister that they had decided to call the strike off. 'All I can say in answer to this is that I thank God for your decision,' was Baldwin's response.[45] When the news reached the provinces it had little effect at first because many workers assumed that the government must have backed down. However, once the union instructions came through the men quickly returned to work except in the coalfield where the angry miners stayed out for six months.

The traditional explanation for the failure of the General Strike is that the government was well-prepared and the unions ill-prepared; but this is a considerable oversimplification. In reality a good deal of improvisation took place on both sides, and much of the volunteering effort was laughably amateurish. One youth arrived at Waterloo Station offering his services to Southern Railways who gave him a can of oil with instructions to walk the line oiling the points. Three days later he sent a message: 'Have arrived at Brighton. Send more oil.'[46] Despite their efforts to keep the recruitment of volunteers under control, the authorities were troubled by reports about enthusiasts, fascist and otherwise, opening offices on their own initiative and calling for volunteers. In the circumstances it must have been difficult to be certain what was an official organisation and what was not. Anyone who had experience in the police or army, or even with horses, could muscle in on the action. In Newcastle, for example, the chief constable used twenty mounted police and 'about fifteen private gentlemen in police uniform' to disperse the crowds, but he made a point of not informing the Watch Committee about them.[47]

A number of women also participated. Viscountess Astor MP and many other society ladies went to work in Hyde Park, preparing food for the police and volunteers and taking care to have themselves photographed wearing masculine trench coats and military-style armbands. Some former suffragettes also set up anti-strike organisations, notably Flora Drummond whose Women's Guild of Empire was already at work battling with Communism in the coalfields, and Mary Allen, a wartime policewoman, who established the Women's Auxiliary Service. Ever since the war Allen had taken to wearing a uniform that resembled that of the Metropolitan Police and had gone about making enquiries about suspects and keeping dossiers on them. Though she had been prosecuted in 1921, for wearing a uniform to which she was not entitled, the authorities felt it pointless to proceed against her as she did no great mischief.[48] The Women's Auxiliary Service disseminated anti-strike propaganda and organised entertainments for women in the East End with a view to keeping them away from strike activities. Mary Allen and Emmeline Pankhurst felt convinced that the General Strike would never have taken place if the miners' wives had been properly consulted.[49] This may have been wishful thinking, but it underlines the widespread desire to participate in the national emergency with or without official sanction.

In their Cotswold backwater the Mitford family threw themselves into the struggle. 'There was a thrilling feeling of crisis in the air,' wrote Jessica.[50] The Mitford sisters crept about the country lanes around Swinbrook vainly expecting armed Bolsheviks to spring from every hedge. They organised a canteen to cater to 'scabbing lorry drivers' as Jessica put it. But although they attracted little custom, the girls quickly proved unequal to the task. 'Oh darling, you know I don't know how to take things from the oven,' complained Nancy, 'besides I do so hate getting up early.'[51]

Many of the upper-class volunteers were too dilettante to make an effective contribution to breaking the strike, especially university students who happily seized the opportunity to skip lectures. Alan Lennox-Boyd reportedly turned up at Paddington Station to work as a guard, resplendent in top hat, tailcoat and white trousers. But once the strike was safely over the role of such amateur volunteers was enthusiastically hailed: 'when the call came there was no hesitation among the youth of Oxford, Cambridge or any other university . . . [who discharged] any duties cast on them with an efficiency that aroused the envy of many so-called "skilled" men.'[52] This was largely a delusion. Boyish dreams about driving steam engines remained, for the most part, fantasies. During the strike a mere 3 per cent of freight trains actually ran. In London the number of trains running rose from 4 per cent at the start to just 12 per cent by the end. Even this was achieved at the cost of many accidents. Driving lorries and buses proved to be more practical, though it exposed the volunteers to physical assault from angry strikers. Enough vehicles were in operation to keep supplies moving but only with the assistance of troops. The official reports issued daily by the authorities focused on successful food convoys and the dispersal of violent crowds, but largely ignored the loss of power which left most of British industry crippled. As a result, during the nine days some £400 million of trade was lost. Nothing done by the volunteers could reduce this damage to the economy; indeed, by maintaining food supplies they made it easier for the strikers to stay out.

Rather more significant in winning the strike may have been the use of troops. This, however, was a risky tactic that could have exploded in the government's face. Troops were most conspicuous in London where the authorities relied on a garrison comprising two regiments of cavalry and seven battalions of Grenadier, Scots and Welsh Guards, reinforced by four battalions of infantry, two companies of Royal Engineers, twenty-three tanks and forty-four armoured cars. In addition naval ratings were stationed at Victoria, Waterloo and Paddington. The army used Hyde Park as its major concentration point, and kept three columns of tactical lorries at the Tower, Chelsea and Wellington Barracks to be ready to move to the disturbed areas at short notice.[53] The question was how best to make use of this formidable force. The restraining influence exercised by King George V doubtless strengthened Baldwin's own predilection for caution. Kept in touch with hourly reports on the situation, he urged his ministers to avoid anything likely to drive the striking men to desperate measures. In particular he was offended by Churchill's announcement in the *British Gazette* on 8 May that the troops would enjoy government backing 'in any action they find it necessary to take in an honest endeavour to aid the Civil Power'. The King immediately protested to the War Office about this as it seemed calculated to encourage soldiers to risk violence.[54]

In the early stages the army discreetly concentrated its forces but avoided intervention. After three days during which the London docks had remained closed and no food or other supplies had left the Port of London, flour began to run short in the capital and the south-east. Consequently supplies were landed at the Victoria and Albert Dock under cover of darkness on 7 May and escorted by troops in convoy through the East End. This first convoy comprised one hundred lorries escorted by a battalion of Grenadier Guards, twelve Peerless armoured cars and eight Rolls-Royces. It was watched by large crowds, but 'they were not however aggressive and there was a considerable amount of cheering'.[55] As the East End was by far the most disturbed part of London, and its proximity to the docks made it a key area, the authorities decided to station troops at Victoria Park in Bethnal Green; from there they could move quickly to any part of the docks north of the river. On Saturday 8 May 'the inhabitants woke up . . . to find a large military camp in being in their midst. There is no doubt that the sudden arrival of so large a force . . . had a profound effect.'[56] By the 10th the East End was reported to be 'absolutely quiet, the entire population being cowed by the display of force made during the past few days'.[57] For the remainder of the strike these methods were employed to convey flour and petrol from Silvertown and Hackney Wick, and meat from the depot at Poplar. Troops and armoured cars were mobilised at Tilbury to stop violence against the police and drivers, but subsequently the drivers there refused to move without a military escort.[58] As a War Office report concluded, 'once such a protection has been given it is almost impossible to withdraw it as the workers think they are being abandoned.'[59]

Essentially the troops proved to be useful only because both sides in the dispute exercised restraint. For their part the strikers drew a distinction between the OMS volunteers, whom they disliked as strike-breakers, and the soldiers and police who were often drawn from their own communities and were simply seen to be doing their job. The military authorities recognised that they were not facing a planned campaign against the troops or against property, and that the workers largely followed union instructions not to go armed.[60] As a result, relations between the strikers and the troops appear to have been surprisingly good. For example in the Northern Division the commissioner reported from Newcastle:

> at the moment the attitude towards the troops and naval men is friendly, but it should be borne in mind that the Council of Action has advised the strikers to fraternise with the troops. Police are of the opinion that the troops and naval men will remain loyal, but it should be remembered that the bulk of the recruits for local requirements come from the surrounding colliery districts.[61]

For this reason soldiers were employed only when the civil authorities felt really hard pressed. They were always conscious of treading a narrow line between success and disaster. Since the strikers had no inhibitions about attacking the volunteers and the Specials, it was essential to keep the soldiers quite separate from them. Also, everything depended upon the moral effect of the presence of the troops and their equipment, for once they were driven to use force relations were likely to deteriorate swiftly. The authorities recognised that if troops were employed in very small numbers they would be a tempting target: a platoon, officially a body of 40–50 men but in practice consisting only of 20–25, was the minimum for guard duty, and a company, officially comprising 200 men but in fact consisting of 100–120, was the minimum for conducting an operation.[62] They recognised that tanks and armoured cars achieved the greatest effect, but a dangerous situation always developed when a vehicle broke down, forcing the crew to dismount and attend to it. Then the strikers ceased to be intimidated and 'the confidence and hostility of the crowds was always most marked'.[63] It was noticed that if soldiers advanced with bayonets fixed they 'can clear any crowd'; but they could not risk going any further in applying force for fear of provoking a passive crowd to violence: 'one young soldier, with one shot, can upset the whole apple-cart.'[64] These qualifications indicate that the authorities had clearly recognised the limitations of the use of military force in support of the state. This had major implications for the role which had been confidently anticipated by the fascists before the outbreak of the strike. The fascist contribution was not really necessary and was counter-productive to the extent that it threatened to provoke violence where the regular troops, judiciously used, were able to manage things.

The unexpected end to the crisis came as a huge relief and won Baldwin some fulsome compliments in unusual quarters. The *English Review* admitted that his restraint had been justified: '[the strike] has proven that England still has men who can govern.' Even the Duke of Northumberland commended the 'vigour and resourcefulness' shown by the government: 'The British people have, as in 1914, risen to meet a supreme emergency and set an example which will have far-reaching effects.'[65] Perhaps influenced by contemporary reactions, historians have largely designated the General Strike as a failure and correspondingly as a triumph for the authorities. In fact, both the government and its right-wing critics knew perfectly well that though the sudden end of the strike had given them a short-term victory, it had been a close-run thing. The loss of production and especially the fall in exports after a mere nine-day strike was not something that could have been sustained for long. Moreover, the TUC's decision to call it off created a misleading impression of weakness at the grass roots. Even the government's own privately compiled reports accepted that after nine days support for the strike remained solid; despite some scattered reports of a return to work among railwaymen and tram drivers, there was no reason for doubting that the General Strike could have been maintained for a longer period if the General Council had not backed down. It was indicative of the high morale among workers that they reacted with pleasure to the news of the end of the strike because they assumed that this meant they had won.[66] For their part the authorities appreciated that while they had been lucky that the unions had not prepared for the strike, they could not count on this in the future.

Once the initial euphoria had subsided, the war between the conventional parliamentarians and their critics on the far right quickly resumed: had the government learned the lessons after its earlier lethargy and timidity? With hindsight we know that 1926 proved to be the first and last general strike, but at the time there seemed no grounds for such optimism. The pessimistic view gained credibility from the determination of the coal miners to remain on strike for the next six months. This itself went some way to dissipating the prestige Baldwin had won in his own party; but it also proved damaging to him by fostering a sense of grievance among working-class communities which undermined the government's electoral position. For several months the government became preoccupied with the miners' strike which was believed to be financed by Moscow with a view to paralysing British industry – a view privately endorsed by British intelligence.[67] 'Frankly the country has been disappointed and disheartened by the anaemic attitude of Downing Street in the face of so gross and gratuitous an outrage,' commented the *National Review*.[68] Noting that the Poor Law authorities in England and Wales were spending £230,000 per week, and those in Scotland £25,000, to support the wives and families of coal miners, they argued that no relief should be granted if a husband refused to accept the available work.[69]

Regardless of the outcome, the strike had lent credibility to the extreme right because it offered proof that Britain had become the target of alien subversion, and it encouraged fascists to maintain their self-appointed role as patriots organised to combat the nation's enemies on the streets. Nor was this interpretation confined to the fascist fringe, for it crystallised the thinking of some mainstream politicians. Churchill, for example, drew the conclusion that a successful general strike 'would have subverted the representative and parliamentary institutions under which we have lived and grown since the great Civil War of the seventeenth century'.[70] The General Strike had deepened his existing apprehension about the rise of the Labour movement:

> The great fear which has always beset every democratic or working-class leader has been that of being undermined or overbid by someone more extreme than he. It seems that a continued progression to the Left, a sort of inevitable landslide into the abyss, was the characteristic of all revolutions.[71]

Though Churchill recognised that a Conservative government had, belatedly, managed to confront the crisis, he questioned whether the same resolution would be shown if a general strike coincided with a Labour government. In such circumstances he concluded that a fascist-style coup might be the only antidote to syndicalism: 'no great nation will be unprovided with an ultimate means of protection against cancerous growths, and every responsible labour leader in every country ought to feel his feet more firmly placed in resisting levelling and reckless doctrines.'

On the other hand, there was no disputing that the official handling of the strike had made the dire prophecies of the fascists appear exaggerated and left them looking irrelevant. Contrary to their claims, the government had learned some lessons, notably that it was best to rely on the police and the troops, and that volunteers could be more trouble than they were worth. In the aftermath the Supply and Transport Committee concluded: 'as regards the provision of general volunteer labour or Special Constables, the services of the OMS had been of no appreciable value ... [and were] not of such importance as to justify the Government's encouraging them to maintain their organisation.' Joynson-Hicks conveyed the news to Lord Hardinge: 'there is no need for any recruiting machinery in normal times.'[72] While this could be seen as evidence that the politicians had reverted to their habitual complacency, the official rejection of the volunteer system had a deflating effect on the fascist organisations in the later 1920s; by cutting them off from the official system the politicians deprived them of some of the respectability and prestige they desired.

However, the government spoke with two voices. While doing something to dampen fascist pretensions in the aftermath of the crisis, Joynson-Hicks offered them further encouragement by warning: 'Don't think for a moment that all emergency is over . . . I am convinced that [the General Strike] will be tried again.'[73] Special Branch reported several initiatives by the Communist Party during 1927 to launch quasi-military formations of workers. In South Wales a Workers' Defence Corps was organised involving drilling and marching with a view to protecting meetings, demonstrations and picketing. The Labour League of Ex-Servicemen was also trained in the use of force to protect speakers and combat fascism.[74] In fact the intelligence services did not regard these organisations as a significant threat, perhaps because they appreciated that the mainstream trade unions were in full retreat from the idea of a general strike. However, such activities raised the stakes, and the publicity given to them by the *Morning Post* helped to justify the accumulation of arms and military training among the fascists.

Joynson-Hicks' remarks about the next general strike certainly lent some plausibility to the right-wing critique of government policy during 1925. The crowning folly was held to be Baldwin's attempt to avert the strike rather than to resist it at all costs. During the crisis Sir John Simon, barrister and former minister, had famously pronounced general strikes illegal, though subsequent discussion suggested that this claim was unlikely to be upheld by the courts. Simon argued that the General Strike was not a dispute between workers and employers because there was no industrial issue between the TUC and the government; the object, then, was not to pressurise an employer but to force the government to act. However, other opinion held that sympathetic strikes were included in the scope of the Trades Disputes Act. In any case, provided the means used were legal, it mattered not whether the aims were unconstitutional; the fact that the strike coerced a government was merely incidental. This advice appeared to leave the General Strike as a genuine trade dispute and to that extent it could not be held to constitute a criminal conspiracy.[76]

However, this verdict simply encouraged both the far right and Conservatives generally to demand sweeping legislative action to correct the legal position. Proposals included placing a ban on all sympathetic strikes, making it a criminal offence to incite a general strike, banning strikes in all public and utility services, abolishing the political levy collected by the unions, ending picketing, and making trade unions liable for the costs of industrial action.[77] This threatened a return to the situation following the

Taff Vale Judgement in 1902 when one union was made to pay for a strike. This had proved controversial enough at a time when the Labour Party was barely off the drawing board. In 1926 it would have been seen as an attempt to destroy the trade union movement. Baldwin was not prepared to contemplate such a thing, but the hostile majority within the cabinet forced him to retreat from his earlier position. The resulting Trades Disputes and Trade Union Act of 1927 proscribed sympathetic strikes, banned civil servants from joining unions and, most controversially, modified the system of collecting the political levy by trade unions by requiring members to indicate that they wished to pay rather than putting the onus on them to say they did not. A blatantly partisan measure, it reduced the income of the Labour Party by about a third in the later 1920s. It was exactly the kind of measure Baldwin had vetoed before 1926. In fact the Act played into the hands of MacDonald in that it presented the unions with a symbol of Tory repression and gave them a motive for swallowing their doubts and uniting to return the Labour Party to office at the next election.

Indeed, the longer-term implications of 1926 were such as to undermine Baldwin far more than his opponents on the left and or the right. To appreciate this it is necessary to remember that the original aim of the General Strike had been to resist *general* reductions in working men's wages. Contrary to expectations, while miners' wages fell substantially, most wages were maintained; in fact, in real terms they gained in value between 1926 and 1930 because prices were falling. This trend had dire implications for government economic strategy, which was based on substantially lowering the costs of industry in order to maintain the pound at its new high level. In the absence of significant reductions in wages, British manufacturers found it impossible to recover export markets, leaving unemployment at a fairly high level during the later 1920s. Consequently, by 1929 when Baldwin's term was running out, he found himself weakened and sliding towards another election defeat. The concatenation of a second Labour government and a new round of industrial militancy encouraged Baldwin's right-wing critics to anticipate a renewed and much greater crisis in which fascism would at last find its historic opportunity to rescue the country from the hands of the limp-wristed liberal parliamentary politicians.

SEVEN

'Boneless Wonders': The Crisis of 1929–31

'Tom Mosley is a cad and a wrong 'un, and they will find it out.'

Stanley Baldwin at dinner with Sir Philip Sassoon
after the 1929 general election

In the spring of 1924 the eighteen-year-old Viscount Ennismore was thrown out of his London home by his father, the Earl of Listowel. His offence, for which he was later pardoned, was to have joined the Fabian Society.[1] If the young Viscount was not typical, he was by no means unusual, for between the First World War and 1930 many men and women from upper and upper-middle-class backgrounds repudiated their Conservative family traditions to join the Labour Party.[2] This embarrassing phenomenon extended into the highest echelons of Conservatism. Lady Cynthia, who was the daughter of Lord Curzon, though better known as the first wife of Sir Oswald Mosley, switched to Labour in 1924, becoming the MP for Stoke in 1929. During the general election of December 1923 the Labour Party produced a new platform speaker in the shape of twenty-four-year-old Oliver Baldwin, son of the outgoing Tory prime minister, Stanley Baldwin, whose conversion attracted 'a mass of correspondence, most of it abusive and some of it indecent'.[3] In 1929 Baldwin gained Dudley for Labour thereby ensuring a seat in parliament opposite his father who had become Leader of the Opposition. These shifts did not always entail rifts in the family, for two generations sometimes made the same migration as, for example, did Earl 'Buck' de la Warr and his mother Muriel, Lord Parmoor and his son Stafford Cripps, and the former MP Arthur Strauss and his son George. Other prominent ex-Tory recruits to Labour included Susan Lawrence, John Sankey, John Strachey, son of St Loe Strachey of *The Spectator*, Hugh Dalton, Hugh Gaitskell, Clement Attlee and Frances, Countess of Warwick; Lord Chelmsford served as First Lord of the Admiralty in the 1924 Labour government without actually joining the party.

Against this background Oswald Mosley's conversion to Socialism in the 1920s hardly deserves to be singled out as the act of a traitor to his class. It is also a caution against portraying his later fascism in terms of an authoritarian personality. Both as a Socialist and as a fascist the young Mosley was reacting to certain experiences and dilemmas that moulded his politics as they did those of others of his generation and background. Born in 1896, Mosley sprang from a Staffordshire gentry family that was already conscious of its loss of both political influence and material resources. Like many such people the Mosleys succumbed to the temptation to blame urbanisation, industrialisation and the liberal bourgeoisie for their misfortunes. As Robert Skidelsky observed, this background made Mosley part of the establishment but also explains his alienation from it.[4]

After being educated at Winchester, Mosley arrived at Sandhurst in January 1914, aged seventeen. By October he had joined the 16th Queen's Light Dragoons and served subsequently in the Royal Flying Corps, a glamorous but extremely dangerous form of war service. The war unquestionably accelerated Mosley's entry into politics. Like many idealistic youths who served as junior officers, he was deeply impressed with the effect of war in binding together men otherwise divided by class and opinion. Harold Macmillan and Anthony Eden emerged similarly impressed by the suffering endured by their fellow men for their country and convinced that the state owed them a duty not to let them down in times of hardship and unemployment. Mosley was, therefore, far from unusual in adopting a critical attitude towards his party leaders during the 1920s; indeed he personified the dissatisfaction among younger Tories with the older generation who were held to have bungled the peace settlement and failed to respond to social and economic problems at home. He looked for someone with enough vision to unify a society drifting steadily back towards its pre-war divisions. Mosley's temperament and personality, notably his impatience and arrogance, may have made him quicker to take the risk of challenging those in authority than most young politicians; but he was essentially a product of his time.

On demobilisation Mosley found himself a flat in Grosvenor Square. As a young, handsome man with a limp and a fine war record he became a prized guest for the leading hostesses – Nancy Astor, Lady Colefax, Emerald Cunard and Mrs Ronnie Greville – and succumbed to the temptations to lead a playboy's life. But the hostesses also brought him into contact with leading politicians of all parties who were keen to promote his political career. Despite his Conservative family background, Mosley 'knew little of Conservative sentiment and cared less', but was content to become adopted as the Coalitionist Conservative candidate for Harrow in September 1918. Campaigning under red posters and rosettes, he fought the election on an interventionist programme, which included minimum wages, state control of transport and electricity, state-financed smallholdings and slum clearance, protection for British industry, imperial preference and the exclusion of undesirable aliens. He cheerfully described his policy as 'Socialistic imperialism'.[5] In 1918 this was not unusual among Conservatives, but in view of the charges of opportunism later made against him it is worth noting that his 1918 programme informed his ideas for the rest of his career.

In the Commons Mosley quickly made his mark as an eloquent and independent-minded member. He showed his ambition in a maiden speech in February 1919 by attacking Winston Churchill on the grounds that he could not manage to administer the Ministries of War and Air simultaneously. His voting record in support of feminist legislation led the Six Point Group, a new equal rights organisation, to single him out as one of the best members in 1922 and 1923.[6] At a time when 'fusion' of the old parties into a new one under Lloyd George was in vogue, Mosley's disregard for traditional loyalties did not seem eccentric; but as interest in fusion subsided, his detachment from his party became increasingly obvious. He emerged as an articulate spokesman for the younger generation: 'Beware lest old age steal back and rob you of the reward,' he declared in October 1919, 'lest old dead men with their old dead minds embalmed in the tombs of the past creep back to dominate your new age, cleansed in the blood of your generation.'[7] Such emotive language indicated that Mosley was rapidly honing his oratorical skills. A. J. Spender, editor of the *Westminster Gazette*, described him as 'the most polished literary speaker in the House of Commons, words flow from him in graceful, epigrammatic phrases that have a sting in them ... to listen to him is an education in the English language, also in the art of delicate but deadly repartee.'[8]

It was when Mosley was campaigning for Nancy Astor in November 1919 at her by-election in Plymouth that he met Lady Cynthia Curzon. 'Cimmie' assured her father that although Mosley was well-known for flirting with married women, he had given that up in order to focus on his political career. Lord Curzon was also reassured to hear that the trustees of Mosley's estate would allow him an annual income of £8,000–10,000, and eventually £20,000. By March 1920 they were engaged. They married on 11 May at the Chapel Royal and held a 'small' reception at the Foreign Office attended by King George V and Queen Mary, the King and Queen of Belgium, much of society and half the political establishment. After a honeymoon in Italy the couple returned to plunge into a glittering round of London functions and country-house parties. 'We rushed towards life with arms outstretched to embrace the sunshine,' Mosley recalled, 'and even the darkness, the light and shade which is the essence of exuberance, every varied enchantment of a glittering, wonderful world; a life rush to be consummated.'[9]

Despite Cimmie's assurances to Curzon, Mosley had been accustomed to having a mistress in Paris, and he still enjoyed the pursuit of married women at the salons of leading hostesses, a game he described as 'flushing the covers'.[10] He had nothing but contempt for middle-class notions of morality and did not remain faithful to Cimmie for long. Of course, serial philandering was widely accepted in upper-class circles provided the parties were discreet and avoided divorce. In 1933 Mosley confided to Robert Boothby that he had told Cimmie about his other women. '*All*, Tom?' Boothby enquired. 'Well,' came the reply, 'all except her step-mother and her sister.'[11] When he became a Labour MP, Mosley recognised how easily he would damage his prospects by having affairs with the wives of his new colleagues; he therefore confined his philandering to upper-class circles, coining the phrase: 'Vote Labour: Sleep Tory'.[12]

To most of his contemporaries Mosley appeared to have everything made. They were therefore all the quicker to resent his ambition, arrogance and growing disloyalty. After attacking the government for using the Black and Tans to suppress Republican violence in Ireland, Mosley was severely heckled by his colleagues, and in November 1920 he crossed the floor of the House of Commons to sit as an Independent member. For a time he associated with the Liberals, but he could never subscribe to their free-trade sentiments, and was dubious about their prospects of regaining office. By the spring of 1921 his thoughts had turned to cooperation with patriotic Labour; in a letter to Lord Robert Cecil he observed, 'the psychological moment for an understanding with moderate Labour has at length arrived!'[13] But Mosley was in no hurry, perhaps because in 1921 Labour must have seemed as far away from office as the Liberals.

More immediately he hoped to retain his seat at Harrow where the Conservative Association refused to tolerate his conduct. Confidently asserting that the war had obliterated the old issues and made the old parties irrelevant, Mosley stood as an Independent, winning with 66 per cent of the vote in 1922 and 60 per cent in 1923. Even allowing for the absence of either Liberal or Labour candidates, this was a remarkable achievement at a general election. But he was realistic enough to know that his position would not be viable in the long run. His attacks on the government inevitably brought him into close contact with Ramsay MacDonald, a relationship strengthened by Cimmie. In 1924 Mosley greeted the new Labour government by deriding the 'loud lamentations of panic-stricken plutocracy' on the Tory side: 'tonight the army of progress has struck its tents and is on the move.'[14] On 27 March he applied to join the Labour Party.

Though initially regarded with suspicion by some Labour politicians who resented their rapid rise, Oswald and Cimmie were welcomed ecstatically by the party's rank and file. One contemporary account caught the mood when they appeared at a Labour meeting:

There was a movement in the crowd, and a young man with the face of the ruling class in Great Britain, but the gait of a Douglas Fairbanks, thrust himself forward through the throng to the platform, followed by a lady in heavy, costly furs. There stood Oswald Mosley . . . the song 'For He's A Jolly Good Fellow' greeted the young man from two thousand throats . . . the elegant Lady in furs got up from her seat and said a few sympathetic words . . . 'Lady Cynthia Mosley' whispered in my ear one of the armleted stewards who stood near me, excited, and later, as though thinking he had not sufficiently impressed me, he added, 'Lord Curzon's daughter.' His whole face beamed proudly. All round the audience was still in uproar.[15]

No fewer than seventy constituencies invited Mosley to become their Labour candidate. Characteristically, he decided to contest the Birmingham Ladywood seat in the heart of a bastion of popular Toryism, currently held by Neville Chamberlain. 'A droller choice as Labour candidate for an industrial constituency than this debonair young sprig of the aristocracy could scarcely be conceived,' scoffed the *Birmingham Mail*.[16] As the heiress to an American fortune Cimmie was derided as 'the Dollar Princess'. However, many working-class voters, who were still susceptible to a title, glamour and wealth, felt flattered by the attentions of Mosley; at the 1924 election, he almost achieved a dramatic upset when Chamberlain scraped in by a mere 77 votes. This laid the foundations for Labour's breakthrough in Birmingham in 1929. Noting that after 1924 his opponent scuttled off to a safe seat at Edgbaston, Mosley claimed with some justification that he had broken the Chamberlainite hold on the city's politics.[17] He himself returned to parliament as the member for Smethwick in December 1926 and Cimmie was elected at Stoke in 1929.

From its position on the extreme right the *National Review* rudely invited the 'YMCA element' in the Conservative Party to follow the Mosleys by joining Labour. But it admitted that the departure of the young and virile only accentuated the dominance of the feeble and the complacent figures it deplored; the journal complained that after 1924 Baldwin became 'rattled by victory which he proceeded to fritter away . . . by loading his cabinet with careerists whom the Party hoped it had done with'.[18] During the three years following the General Strike discontent rapidly mounted over the government's inability to rescue agriculture from its headlong decline, its continued refusal to introduce tariffs, and its acquiescence in the policies of the Bank of England and the Federal

Reserve Bank of America which kept interest rates at punitively high levels.[19] For all of these failures the 'careerist' Churchill received much of the blame. Baldwin's critics were also provoked by 'this YMCA Foreign Policy' which meant supporting the League of Nations and failing to defend British interests against Soviet Russia, the appointment of the Simon Commission on India, the refusal to reform the House of Lords, and the grant of equal suffrage to women, for which he had no mandate.[20] This chorus of complaint about Baldwin's policies provoked a fresh crop of articles in the Conservative journals between 1927 and 1929 designed to celebrate the successes of the fascist regime in Italy, to explain the working of the corporate state, and to emphasise the decay of democracy in the West.

However, Baldwin resisted the pressure exerted from the right because he thought it would be electorally disastrous to alienate his working-class support or that of the Liberals who had swollen his majority in 1924. In the end his strategy was undermined by the sluggish performance of the British economy. The economic recovery of the mid-1920s had never been particularly strong, and by 1926 unemployment was rising again, fluctuating between one and one and a half million during the later 1920s. From 1926 onwards the government seemed to have lost the initiative, especially after 1928 when Lloyd George published the famous Liberal Yellow Book, *Britain's Industrial Future*, which offered a sweeping and yet very detailed Keynesian strategy designed to stimulate the economy and reduce unemployment by half a million within a year. Although the Conservatives, backed by the Treasury and most orthodox economists, poured scorn on his programme, Lloyd George succeeded in generating a Liberal revival and, more importantly, focusing political debate on the unemployment question during the run-up to the 1929 general election. This proved very helpful for Labour partly because Lloyd George recovered some of the support lost to the Conservatives in 1924 and because voters assumed, incorrectly as it turned out, that Lloyd George's proposals for tackling unemployment would be implemented by a Labour government. Conservative candidates also discovered that the General Strike had aroused great hostility towards them among working-class communities, and that the effect of this was prolonged by the 1927 Trades Disputes Act which undermined Baldwin's reputation for fairness.[21] This diagnosis was reflected at the general election held at the end of May 1929. Labour increased its poll from 33 per cent to 37 per cent and its seats from 151 to 288, not far short of an overall majority. This appeared to give the party a better chance of implementing a left-wing programme than in 1924, and was promptly dubbed 'A Marxian Victory' by *The Patriot*.

Yet once again the right had jumped to the wrong conclusion. The real flaw in MacDonald's second administration lay less in its appetite for Socialism than in its weakness for economic liberalism. Philip Snowden, the new Chancellor, worked on the same basic assumptions about the economy as his Conservative predecessors. He assumed that the solution to Britain's current difficulties would be found in the restoration of pre-1914 conditions, in particular in the return to the gold standard which had already been accomplished in 1925. The rationale for this lay in the belief that sterling must continue as the chief international currency and that the promotion of a higher level of world trade would inevitably benefit Britain by restoring her export markets and thus reducing unemployment. The flaw in all this was partly that Britain no longer wielded the influence over world trade that she had enjoyed before the war, and also that even when world trade recovered, Britain failed to capture her former share of it. Mosley and other critics on the right correctly characterised this as a Victorian liberal economic strategy in that it sought solutions in the international sphere. By contrast, the alternatives espoused by the protectionists, by the ILP, by Lloyd George and by J. M. Keynes regarded internationalism as futile, and they focused instead on restoring the domestic market for British goods whether by tariffs or by stimulating demand.

In this situation the new premier, Ramsay MacDonald, had neither a Socialist policy to implement nor the interventionist-cum-Keynesian programme advocated by the ILP during the 1920s. Consequently, his government drifted through 1929 and 1930, struggling to finance the costs of rising unemployment and a growing budgetary deficit. In the summer of 1929 unemployment had stood at 1.1 million, a problem but not a crisis; but by December 1930 it had risen to 2.5 million or 16 per cent. Critics on both left and right agreed that the government was simply not in control. 'Many of us are beginning to think that the supreme need is not so much for Governments of a particular colour', complained W. J. Brown, a Labour member, 'but for Governments that will govern, and not fiddle about while the country drifts steadily nearer to disaster.'[22] The mounting failure of MacDonald's administration seemed symptomatic of a wider collapse of parliamentary politics in the face of the economic depression. The *Saturday Review* noted that while a number of Labour politicians were losing faith in their leaders, Winston Churchill had repudiated his leader by refusing to serve in the shadow cabinet at the start of 1931; Britain now had a government without a majority, one Opposition leader (Baldwin) with a party but no policy, and another Opposition leader (Lloyd George) with a policy but no party: 'When the boneless wonders get to the top, the men with backbone have to assert themselves or perish.'[23] This mood of pessimism and frustration during 1930 and 1931 gave fresh credibility to the fascist critique of parliamentary democracy in Britain.

By this time MacDonald's government had begun to unravel. One of his mistakes had been to divide responsibility for unemployment between Snowden as Chancellor of the Exchequer and J. H. Thomas as Lord Privy Seal. However, Thomas made speeches and undertook foreign tours but enjoyed no real power. Oswald Mosley had been appointed one of his junior ministers as Chancellor of the Duchy of Lancaster. Inevitably he found this ineffectual role unbearable. As a result, in February 1930 Mosley produced his own comprehensive memorandum for tackling the economic depression, involving the introduction of tariffs to protect home markets, control of the banks to promote investment, development plans for agriculture and road-building to create jobs, and the rationalisation of basic industries. It represented a mixture of Keynesian-Lloyd Georgian ideas, ILP Socialism, and protectionist-imperialist views. Mosley's memorandum received some appreciative comments from the *Saturday Review* and the *National Review*: 'when it has shed some of the doctrinaire aspects necessarily given to it in order to placate the Socialists, it will be . . . a valuable contribution to the right understanding of some of our national problems.'[24] However, rejection of his memorandum by both the Treasury and the cabinet made his resignation in May almost inevitable. 'I perhaps misunderstood you when I came into the Labour Party,' he told MacDonald.[25]

Mosley's brief experience in office had quickly convinced him that the obstacles in the way of any bold programme were institutional as much as ideological. Consequently a large part of his memorandum outlined a scheme for reorganising the government on the basis that it faced a task comparable to that of fighting a war. Elaborating on this in a subsequent speech in the Commons, Mosley advocated creating an inner cabinet of five members some of whom should be recruited from industry and commerce for their expertise and knowledge.[26] He wanted to establish an Economic General Staff to allocate resources, set production targets and quotas, guarantee prices and offer subsidies to support producers in agriculture. The views of producers in each industry would be represented on a National Council of Representatives. The strategy that emerged from this machinery would eventually be presented to parliament having already been exposed to informed criticism. 'In this way it might be possible to clear of political controversy detailed questions which can only be discussed in a foolish and inadequate fashion.' In one sense this was an idealistic and naive approach, founded on a belief that by pooling brains and expertise the national interest would somehow emerge unimpeded by party-political divisions and sectional interests. Both the scheme itself and the exasperation with parties and parliament that underpinned it clearly prefigured the corporate state under fascism.

However, Mosley had acted too precipitately in leaving the government. Had he stayed in office after making his protest he would have carried much more influence later as the economy continued to deteriorate. Austen Chamberlain scoffed at the resignation as 'amazing and all to the good, but it would be a mistake to treat [it] too seriously. Master Mosley is thoroughly disliked and distrusted in all parts of the House and will have no following.'[27] In fact Mosley enjoyed a good deal of support in the press and among younger members of Chamberlain's own party. But when he put his case to a meeting of Labour MPs on 22 May he won only 29 votes against 210 who took the cabinet's side. At this stage his chief Labour supporters were W. J. Brown, John Strachey, Oliver Baldwin, Robert Forgan and Aneurin Bevan. In the debate on 28 May he defended his programme and attacked the government for clinging to its 'illusion' about the export trade: 'It is to the Home Market that we must look for the solution of our depression.'

Beside the picture of fumbling and indecisiveness offered by the prime minister, Mosley appeared increasingly convincing. But having already been rebuffed by the cabinet and the MPs, his only remaining option was an appeal to the party conference in the autumn of 1930. However dismayed they were at MacDonald's leadership, many ordinary members and trade unionists felt loath to break ranks at the behest of a comparative newcomer. Brown summed up their attitude: 'Who is Mosley anyway? He isn't really one of us! True we have drunk his wine and smoked his cigars . . . but he doesn't really belong.'[28] Well-founded rumours that Mosley was engaging in talks with sympathetic Tory MPs stirred suspicions still further. Yet Mosley's electrifying speech at the October conference attracted a huge ovation, only slightly marred by a delegate who was heard to shout 'The English Hitler'. His resolution was only narrowly defeated by 1,251,000 to 1,046,000 votes. He also won election to the Party's National Executive Committee in the constituency section, an unmistakable sign of his popularity. As Labour support continued to suffer in by-elections and MacDonald's credibility sagged, a prudent man would have sat tight and awaited his opportunity.

However, Mosley's behaviour was partly influenced by the realisation that the Conservatives were in just as fractious and demoralised a condition as Labour. Since losing the election in 1929 – the second defeat under his leadership – Baldwin had become the target of bitter and sustained attack over protectionism and the empire which almost drove him from the leadership by 1930. Convinced from experience that the voters' fear of higher food prices made tariffs impossible, Baldwin seemed unable to recognise the depth of support for protectionism amongst ordinary Conservatives. Lords Beaverbrook and Rothermere capitalised on this by using their newspapers to launch a major campaign for 'Empire Free Trade', in effect using tariffs to exclude foreign goods from the British and empire markets. They won the backing of several influential parliamentarians including L. S. Amery, Lord Lloyd, Sir Patrick Hannon, Sir Henry Page Croft and Colonel John Gretton as well as industrialists and farmers, and recruited large numbers of Conservative Party members in the constituencies.[29] Beaverbrook carried his campaign well beyond the usual propaganda, forming the United Empire Party in February 1930 which ran candidates against official Conservatives in several by-elections.[30]

The prospect of a disastrous split among rank and file party members put Baldwin's leadership in jeopardy and finally forced him into a series of compromises. By the summer of 1931 the Conservative Party had committed itself to the introduction of a comprehensive policy of tariffs; this was sufficient to keep Lloyd, Amery and Page Croft within the party, although Beaverbrook continued his campaign to oust Baldwin. In the absence of a credible alternative Baldwin survived as Tory leader by default. But the divisions caused by the Empire Free Trade campaign had put in doubt the party's ability to win the next election and another Conservative failure seemed likely to trigger a major political crisis. 'The plight this government is bringing England to should be enough to make you see how imperative it is that a strong man should take power into his own hands and out of the hands of these betrayers and scoundrels,' Lady Houston told Lord Lloyd. 'Of course Baldwin ought to do it; but Baldwin *cannot* be strong, he hasn't got it in him.'[31] But what alternative was there? One *English Review* writer argued that 'the opportunity for a coup d'état is rapidly approaching . . . if a nation has persistently proved itself unfit for liberty, history, and more particularly recent history, shows that armed force is the only cure.'[32] Such apocalyptic language was a sign of the excitable mood of the time, caused by a government apparently helplessly adrift and an opposition too demoralised and divided to offer alternative leadership;[33] but it also reflected the way the Italian example had lodged in the minds of anti-democrats since the early 1920s.

In this context Mosley's readiness to abandon the Labour Party becomes the more comprehensible. If both main parties were unable to rise to the occasion there was everything to gain by cutting adrift from the discredited parliamentarians and their organisations and making an independent appeal to the dissatisfied members of all existing parties. That this had been in Mosley's mind since he left the cabinet in May is suggested by various remarks he made in the intervening period. At a dinner at the Astors he talked with Frank Pakenham who recalled him saying: '"After Peel comes Disraeli. After Baldwin and MacDonald comes . . .?" And he left the question hanging in the air. "Who comes next?" I asked him. "Comes someone *very* different," he growled.'[34]

It was thus no great surprise when Mosley launched the New Party in February 1931. He enjoyed the backing of several Labour MPs – Cimmie, Oliver Baldwin, John Strachey, W. J. Brown and Robert Forgan – but only one Conservative, W. E. D. 'Bill' Allen. Another Tory, Lieutenant Colonel John Moore-Brabazon, was on the verge of joining. However, Mosley told Harold Nicolson that the main response came 'from the younger Conservative group and is distinctly fascist in character'.[35] Harold Macmillan confirmed that, like other young Tories, 'his heart is entirely with the New Party but . . . he feels he can help us better by remaining in the Conservative ranks . . . five years from now the New Party will have its great opportunity.'[36] Promising to field four hundred candidates at the next election, which was increasingly expected, Mosley and Cimmie toured the country addressing audiences of thousands of people.

Suddenly a by-election loomed at Ashton-under-Lyne, a seat held by Labour with a small majority and now experiencing 46 per cent unemployment. Though this was far too early for the New Party, it felt obliged to fight the election. In the event the seat fell to the Conservatives, while the New Party won 16 per cent of the vote. Ashton proved to be a significant turning-point for Mosley's career. On the positive side he emerged as a dominating leader capable of attracting 7,000 people to hear him speak and earning tributes from a grudging press for his 'astonishing power of platform appeal' as *The Times* put it.[37] Though the New Party's poll appears modest, this was not how it seemed to Beaverbrook. 'Mosley polled an immense vote. Remember that he had no newspapers backing him,' he insisted. 'I do not write that fellow down. He may peter out, but if he does as well next time, he will bring his pigs to market.'[38] Beaverbrook understood that Mosley had attracted votes from both the other parties, thus making the Conservatives' winning margin much smaller than it would have been; consequently he threatened to split the Tory vote at the general election and would be in a strong bargaining position.

On the other hand the by-election provoked a bitter display of tribalism on the Labour side. Instead of blaming the defeat on its own leaders, the movement turned its anger against Mosley. Damned as a traitor and a Judas, he was subjected to physical attack throughout the campaign. On the steps of Ashton Town Hall where he was buffeted by Labour supporters after the declaration, Mosley remarked bitterly to Strachey: 'That is the crowd that has prevented anyone from doing anything in England since the war.'[39] The violent attacks to which the New Party was subjected by left-wing groups accelerated the evolution of Mosley's political strategy. Well aware that the Conservatives employed fascist stewards to police their meetings, he quickly concluded that the New Party would have to provide its own if it were to get a hearing. Since Mosley's oratorical talent was the New Party's chief asset, it was essential to prevent the disruption of his meetings. Consequently the party began to train young recruits – known as 'Mosley's Biff Boys' – under the leadership of the England rugby captain, Peter Howard. Although the immediate purpose was to steward meetings, the long-term object was to be capable of intervening against the Communists in the chaotic or revolutionary situation that was expected to develop in the declining months of MacDonald's regime. 'I think that Tom [Mosley] at the bottom of his heart really wants a fascist movement,' wrote Harold Nicolson.[40] The New Party's only other immediate need was financial. Sir William Morris, later Lord Nuffield, donated £50,000 to support the fifty candidates that were to contest the next general election. Unfortunately for the New Party, that came much sooner than expected.

During the summer of 1931 MacDonald's government was overtaken by the collapse of European banks and by the withdrawal of capital from London. In order to save the pound from an emergency devaluation the government needed large credits which were unlikely to be forthcoming unless it corrected the budgetary deficit. Since Snowden and MacDonald were anxious to avoid a devaluation, they proposed to restore the confidence of the financial markets by balancing the budget. To this end they appointed the May Committee which estimated the deficit at £120 million and advised expenditure reductions amounting to £97 million, including a 10 per cent cut in the unemployment benefit. Initially the cabinet accepted the package. Subsequently, however, the rejection of the cuts by the TUC's General Council led some members, including Arthur Henderson, to reconsider. Eventually, at a meeting on 23 August, the ministers split 12–9 in favour of the proposals. Such an even split marked the end of the government and MacDonald lost no time in tendering his resignation as prime minister. Thus, in the space of two and a half years governments of both main parties had fallen because of their inability to handle the economic depression; this appeared to herald the crisis of parliamentary democracy that fascists had long predicted.

In this situation the natural response was for the Leader of the Opposition to be invited to form an alternative government. However, when King George V hastily returned from Balmoral on 23 August to consult with the leaders of the other parties, he found that Baldwin – characteristically – was in France and not immediately available. The King therefore interviewed

Sir Herbert Samuel who was acting as Liberal leader as Lloyd George was incapacitated by a serious operation. Samuel urged that since the necessary economic measures would be unpopular, they would be best implemented by a temporary coalition government under MacDonald. Samuel's clarity and level-headedness impressed the King, and consequently when Baldwin turned up he took the initiative by asking whether the Conservative leader would be prepared to serve in a National Government.[41] Though less than enthusiastic, Baldwin could not easily refuse what was, in effect, the King's proposal. As for MacDonald, he accepted the idea with alacrity, no doubt seeing it as a release from an increasingly impossible attempt to govern through his own party.

A new cabinet of ten was swiftly formed comprising four Conservative, four Labour and two Liberal members. Though traditionally regarded as the product of a conspiracy against Labour, the formation of this National Government is more accurately seen as unfavourable to the Conservatives. It was they who made the greatest sacrifice by throwing up the immediate prospect of office and all the jobs that went with it. They were also reluctant coalitionists because they remembered only too well their experience under Lloyd George before 1922. By agreeing to enter a coalition Baldwin inevitably antagonised those of his followers who had been hoping to force him out altogether. For a time it looked as though they had been trapped into becoming responsible for taking unpalatable measures instead of fighting an election independently.

However, Baldwin's tactical shrewdness had not deserted him. He had made it a condition of joining the National Government that once the immediate crisis had been resolved a dissolution of parliament would be granted. In a statement obviously designed to reassure fellow Tories, issued on 24 August, he insisted that 'no party will be called upon to sacrifice any of the principles in which it believes.' Conservatives naturally feared that their recent commitment to introduce protectionism was about to be scrapped in a government of free-trading Liberal and National Labour members. They preferred to hold a quick election while Labour was discredited which would give them, at last, a mandate for tariffs. In fact, during September opinion in the new government crystallised around the idea of a general election. Strictly speaking this was unnecessary since the National Government enjoyed a comfortable majority and two and a half years of its term still lay ahead of it, more than enough time to carry out the object for which it had been established. Yet there was an obvious advantage in getting an election out of the way quickly rather than allowing the Labour Party time to reunite and benefit from any reaction against the measures instituted by the National Government.

Baldwin's calculations also changed. After his initial reluctance over joining a National Government, he began to perceive how attractive a coalition could be by comparison with the prospect of returning to a purely Conservative government in which he would be subject to enormous pressure from his own right wing. A National Government on a long-term footing after a successful election would to some extent put him out of the firing line because no one could deny the need to make concessions to Liberal and Labour opinion; moreover, the inevitable revolts by Tory members against government policy would be more easily weathered as a result of the extra Liberal and Labour members elected as supporters of the National Government. From this perspective the National Government represented a device for keeping the Conservatives under control rather than a plot to exclude Labour from office. This rationale led the National Government to hold an election in October 1931; consequently, what had originally been envisaged as a temporary expedient turned into a long-term fixture.

During the summer Mosley's New Party made preparations for an election, seeking candidates for the twenty-five seats it proposed to contest and launching a journal, *Action*, under the editorship of Harold Nicolson, designed to overcome what it saw as a press boycott of its activities. However, the party was handicapped by the fact that Mosley was ill and then absent on the Riviera. The news of the formation of the National Government at the end of August brought him home. But the present turn of events proved awkward for the New Party. It would have suited Mosley better if the bulk of the Labour Party had joined the new government, leaving its working-class voters vulnerable to his appeal. As it was, by maintaining its independence, even under the incompetent leadership of Arthur Henderson, Labour queered the pitch for the New Party. Labour took the same line as the New Party in attacking the cuts in expenditure, while the National Government itself competed for the patriotic-imperialist vote to which New Party hoped to appeal. It was therefore difficult for the party to adopt a distinctive stance.

Mosley himself provoked Labour by continuing to pour ridicule on its record during the previous two years: 'It is really idle to talk about the recent crisis as a bankers' ramp,' he argued. 'The Labour Party again and again supported the Chancellor of the Exchequer. They did not walk out of the bankers' palace until it fell down around their ears.'[42] However justified, this was probably counter-productive with a party already angry and demoralised over the defection of its leader. The rhetoric also aroused suspicions that the New Party was angling to join the National Government in order to secure some seats for itself. Given the politicians' attitude towards Mosley this was never likely. In any case, at this stage Mosley calculated that the new cabinet would fail to resolve the economic crisis that had brought it to power, and consequently he felt inclined to maintain his independence.

Meanwhile the New Party used its journal, *Action*, to recruit a number of young, upper-class intellectuals and students. It also trained a body of 'stewards' under Edward 'Kid' Lewis, a former welterweight boxing champion from the East End, to combat Communist violence. Equipped with uniforms, flags and insignia, the stewards were effectively a paramilitary force. Their presence seemed fully justified when Mosley addressed a vast public meeting of 40,000 people in Glasgow. There he was heckled by five hundred Communists and his bodyguard was attacked with stones and razors. 'Tom says this forces us to be fascist,' commented an increasingly unhappy Nicolson afterwards.[43] The violence followed Mosley through the election campaign, whether his meetings were controlled by the police or by his own stewards.

The election, held on 27 October, produced a result that shocked most of the participants. For the first time free trade failed to work its magic with the voters. The various supporters of the National Government won 67 per cent of the vote and no fewer than 556 seats. Labour suffered a major loss of support, its vote falling from 8.4 million to 6.6 million despite the increase in the electorate of one million since 1929; it held a mere 52 seats. The New Party managed to fight just twenty-four constituencies. Cimmie withdrew from Stoke because of ill-health and Mosley stood there in her place. Though polling strongly, he came in third, being one of only two candidates to retain his deposit.

After this debacle the organisation of the New Party rapidly collapsed, the headquarters closed and by December *Action* had ceased publication. However, though depressed, Mosley recognised that the New Party had simply been a victim of the turn of events; it had not had time to capitalise properly on the crisis following the breakdown of the Labour government. His mind soon focused on the next stage. As the economic depression deteriorated, he reasoned, 'Communism will quickly supersede the woolly-headed and woolly-hearted Social Democrats of Labour, and Communism's inevitable and historic opponent will arise to take the place of a flabby conservatism.'[44] Alarmed at the implications of this, Nicolson begged him 'not to get muddled up with the fascist crowd . . . In England anything along those lines is doomed to failure and ridicule.'[45] Not that a move to fascism was inevitable even at this stage. All the troublemakers in British politics – Lloyd George, Beaverbrook, Lord Lloyd and Churchill – were keen to enlist him; and he even received overtures from both the main parties for his return.[46] But after his experience in two parties Mosley now preferred to run his own organisation. The only question was how far to go in the direction of fascism. 'Tom cannot keep his mind off shock troops [and] the roll of drums around

Westminster,' complained Harold Nicolson. 'He is a romantic. That is a great failing.'[47] Any doubts Mosley may have had about his next move were dispelled in January 1932 when, along with Bill Allen, he visited Rome to see fascism in operation. During the next nine months the remnants of the New Party were absorbed into the British Union of Fascists.

With the benefit of hindsight this enterprise is easily dismissed as doomed from the outset. The establishment of the National Government and its sweeping victory in 1931 is commonly assumed to have resolved Britain's political and economic crisis and to have been unchallengeable until 1940. However, inevitability is a dubious guide to historical understanding. In fact, both the political and the economic crises that had brought the National Government into being proved to be much more intractable than is usually recognised. Seen from the perspective of the extreme right, the National Government represented not a resolution but an intensification of the fundamental flaws in the British political system: 'Mr Baldwin and Mr MacDonald are really no more than Liberals of the right and left respectively.'[48] In effect the crisis of 1931 polarised politics by concentrating all the elements of a discredited Victorian liberalism into government, leaving fascism as its logical opponent. This diagnosis seemed to be corroborated by the personnel of the new administration. According to the *Saturday Review*, Macdonald was too tired, Baldwin too easy-going and Snowden too ill to hold high office.[49] The Liberal ministers – Sir John Simon, Herbert Samuel and Walter Runciman – were simply derided for their neglect of British national interests. All those Conservatives who might have inspired some confidence on the right – Amery, Page Croft, Lloyd and even Churchill – were firmly excluded from the government.

Moreover, in tackling the economic depression the National Government signally failed in its immediate object of saving the pound. In September 1931 it abandoned the gold standard and effectively devalued the currency. By March 1932 the value of the pound had fallen from $4.86 to $3.40. Although the government did embark on a sweeping programme of protectionism after some hesitation, the benefits for industry were marginal and were not apparent for several years. Above all, unemployment continued to rise for some time, reaching 21 per cent in 1931 and 22 per cent in 1932 before falling slightly to 20 per cent in 1933. Thus, for a period of two years there remained a real possibility that the National Government would fail just as the previous Conservative and Labour governments had done. Inevitably this suggested to many critics that the parliamentary system had practically exhausted its options. It was this situation that made 1932 such a propitious time to mount a fascist challenge to conventional politics.

EIGHT

'Hurrah for the Blackshirts!':
The British Union of Fascists 1932–4

'In cultivating the old women of the nation [the National Government] has lost the young men.'

Sir Oswald Mosley, *Morning Post*, 13 June 1934

In January 1932 Mosley travelled to Italy with Harold Nicolson, Bill Allen and Christopher Hobhouse in search of a fresh strategy after the collapse of the New Party. Cimmie, who never lost her hostility to fascism, kept reminding him in her letters to consider the condition of the workers under a fascist state, and Nicolson warned: 'if he gets entangled with the boys' brigade he will be edged gradually into becoming a revolutionary.'[1] But inevitably Mosley enjoyed himself enormously in Italy, admiring fascist achievements, including the reclaimed Pontine Marshes, and experiencing the usual interview with Mussolini who was 'charming and asked a lot of very good questions', but cautioned him against attempting a 'military stunt' in England.[2] He returned home brimming with confidence, brushing aside Nicolson and the offers still available to him to rework his passage in conventional party politics. Mosley had no taste for the long haul this would have involved, and he judged the parties to be incapable of rising to the economic and political challenges Britain now faced. In this he was partly correct; both Labour and the Conservatives had become too hidebound and bureaucratised; but, in the absence of a renewed crisis, they still retained enough support to survive.

By April Mosley had wound up the New Party and parted company with Nicolson, though two former MPs, Bill Allen and Robert Forgan, followed him into fascism. Originally a Labour member, Forgan was a genial Scottish doctor who served Mosley as deputy leader and Director of Organisation until October 1934. Though loyal, he failed to stop the petty corruption that bedevilled the new movement or to control its expenditure which was twice its income. As an Ulster Unionist and heir to the W. H. Allen publishing empire, Bill Allen came from the opposite end of the spectrum. A leading propagandist, Allen proved particularly useful because his commercial contacts abroad made him a natural medium for handling the foreign subsidies received from Italy.

Yet contemporaries found Mosley less than entirely convincing as a fascist leader. He remained an odd mixture of missionary and playboy. Admittedly he devoted part of the summer to writing his 40,000-word manifesto, *The Greater Britain*, which combined his New Party economic strategy with an explanation of the case for fascism. It was a cogent document, offering a far more considered approach to fascism than any of his Continental counterparts had done. However, Mosley had by no means renounced his hedonistic lifestyle. Even Mussolini criticised him for spending too much of the summer on the Riviera and in Venice: 'it's not a place for serious reformers to linger in villas or grand hotels for more than a few days,' he told Lord Lymington.[3]

Mosley, however, possessed sufficient energy to launch a new political movement and a new affair simultaneously. He had met the twenty-one-year-old Diana Mitford, the wife of Bryan Guinness, in the spring of 1932. Trapped in a boring marriage, Diana came to life in the glow of Mosley's glamour and excitement, and she rapidly surrendered herself to his overwhelming sense of political purpose. 'He was completely sure of himself and of his ideas,' she wrote. 'Lucid, logical, forceful and persuasive, he soon convinced me as he did thousands of others.'[4] Diana was not alone in seeing him at this time as a future prime minister. At her twenty-second birthday party in June Mosley declared his love for her. Initially their relationship conformed to the rules of upper-class conduct. With his own flat in Ebury Street, Mosley juggled wife and mistress easily enough, and the long-suffering Cimmie was fully accustomed to his 'little frolicsome ways'.[5] However, he and Diana considered their affair to be a grand passion not to be restricted even by the liberal rules of aristocratic society. They became reckless. By New Year 1933, Diana, disregarding warnings that entanglement with Mosley meant disaster, had agreed to leave her home to live in Eaton Square, only five minutes' walk from the Ebury Street flat; Mosley would announce his arrival by tapping on her window with his stick.

Before long the two fathers, Lord Redesdale and Walter Guinness (later Lord Moyne), had formed a deputation to tackle Mosley direct. 'Those two old men are coming to see me,' he told Randolph Churchill, who enquired: 'What are you going to do?' 'I suppose wear a balls protector,' Mosley replied.[6] While he refused to divorce Cimmie, Diana took what was, at the time, an outrageous step by seeking a divorce from the compliant Bryan, who even agreed to respect convention by offering false evidence of his own infidelity to save Diana from having to appear in court.[7] To some extent matters were resolved by Cimmie's death from peritonitis following an attack of appendicitis in April 1933; even so, Mosley did not marry Diana until

1936. But his refusal to respect convention severely damaged him; to his critics his blatant disregard for traditional morality seemed all of a piece with his egotism and his political opportunism.

Buoyed up by his love for Diana and exhilaration at the fresh political challenge, Mosley launched the British Union of Fascists on 1 October 1932 at his offices in Great George Street. Addressing just thirty-two founder members he proclaimed:

> 'We ask those who join us . . . to be prepared to sacrifice all, but to do so for no small or unworthy ends. We ask them to dedicate their lives to building in the country a movement of the modern age . . . In return we can only offer them the deep belief that they are fighting that a great land may live.'[8]

His immediate appeal consisted in his economic programme, a marriage of Keynesian ideas for stimulating domestic demand and a policy of economic autarky influenced by the example of the United States with its huge home market insulated from the fluctuations of the world economy. In *The Greater Britain* Mosley traced the cause of the current economic malaise partly to a failure to keep pace with changes in science and technology, which now swamped the market with goods, and to a political system 'designed by and for the nineteenth century'.[9] This protectionist-nationalist emphasis made an obvious appeal to frustrated Conservatives and to workers in depressed industries; Mosley easily outflanked his right-wing rivals by his relentless attacks on successive governments for promoting imports of foreign goods and on City financiers for damaging British manufacturing and agriculture by making loans to foreign countries: 'These are alien hands which too long have held their strangle grip on the life of this country, and dominate not only the Conservative Party but the Socialist Party as well.'[10]

For many of his followers Mosley's chief appeal lay in his radical social-economic programme. Reynall Bellamy recalled that he 'combined the patriotism of the Right with the social reforms of the Left. It was the message I had been waiting for.'[11] However, Mosley never concealed the fact that signing up to fascism also involved a rejection of Britain's traditional political system which was 'devised to turn a man into a windbag in the shortest possible time'. In a debate with Jimmy Maxton in January 1933 he frankly described fascism as a revolutionary creed, claiming that Britain could never fully recover from her economic malaise without adopting a new political system 'organised with the authority and power which a Fascist movement could obtain'.[12] Mosley recognised that it was this, rather than his economic policy, that posed the biggest obstacle to the BUF. In *The Greater Britain* he rehearsed the recent failures of British politics arising from a system almost calculated to prevent governments from governing, and he frankly advocated a more authoritarian state which would be above party and sectional interests.

Aware that this made fascism appear alien to British traditionalists, he attempted to place Britain in the wider context of fascist development: 'If our crisis had been among the first, instead of among the last, Fascism would have been a British invention. As it is, our task is not to invent Fascism but to find for it in Britain its highest expression and development.'[13] Under a fascist system, government departments would consult the relevant interests through a National Council of Corporations representing workers, employers and consumers, with a view to determining what the national interest required by way of output, wages, prices and profits in each industry. Local authorities would be replaced by executive officers, who would be fascist MPs, and would ensure that the national plan was implemented. Mosley frankly characterised this system as 'Modern Dictatorship', that is, the people would entrust power to a leadership which would carry out their will unimpeded by the traditional paraphernalia of parliamentary procedure and partisan squabbling. Although a parliament would still exist, it would not represent territorial constituencies but a range of occupational franchises including everyone from miners to housewives. From time to time it would meet to review the government's work and exercise the power to dismiss it by a vote of censure. In that event the King would send for new ministers – a significant enhancement of royal authority which went some way to mitigating the alien quality of the corporatist system and undoubtedly appealed to many people on the right at this time.[14]

While the BUF attracted recruits from the conventional parties and others with no previous political experience, it initially expected to gather the remnants of the earlier fascist organisations. The British Fascists were still operating under Miss Lintorn-Orman, now cheerily descending into alcoholism, who devoted herself to pestering the police with wildly inaccurate stories about Communist arms dumps and shipments of weapons from Russia.[15] Lintorn-Orman spurned Mosley, whom she regarded as a Socialist, but most of her members joined him, leaving her organisation with 'three old ladies and a couple of office boys' and fast approaching bankruptcy. The main catch from the British Fascists was Neil Francis-Hawkins, a former surgical instruments salesman and workaholic who became Director General of the BUF in 1936. An excellent administrator, Francis-Hawkins aspired to fill the movement with unmarried men like himself in the belief that they would devote more time to the cause.

Mosley faced greater resistance from the Imperial Fascist League, still led by Arnold Leese, who admitted to being completely outclassed in terms of money and publicity. Leese professed to regard the BUF as a disaster to fascist development in Britain and Mosley himself as an agent who had been planted to discredit the cause.[16] Allowing for Leese's obsession with conspiracies, his reaction did raise valid questions about the extent to which the BUF fitted into the existing pattern of Continental and British fascist movements. While Leese complained that it fell far short of the ideal, others, such as Forgan and Allen, saw the wisdom of putting some distance between the BUF and the other fascist movements, fearing that it would be handicapped by appearing too alien.

Continental developments proved to have a major impact on the fortunes of fascism in Britain. It was in January 1933, scarcely four months after the formation of the BUF, that Hitler became German Chancellor. His decision to abandon the Disarmament Convention, withdraw from the League of Nations and repudiate the Treaty of Versailles alarmed opinion in Britain, not least because it implied the return of Germany's colonies which Britain had acquired as mandated territories. The suppression of trade unions in Germany in May 1933 aroused the hostility of the Labour movement, fearful that Mosley would do the same if he got the chance. On the other hand, many leading politicians sympathised with Hitler. It was tempting to regard his regime as a German version of the National Government, a response to the failures of parties and parliament faced with the economic depression. They argued that he had been constitutionally appointed Chancellor, and that his regime brought some welcome stability to central Europe. Moreover, he genuinely wanted peace. It was not in Britain's interest to allow the despised French government to drag her into a conflict with the Nazis merely to uphold the Treaty of Versailles.

At this stage British fascists looked more to Italy and the corporate state for their model; it was only after 1936 that Germany loomed larger. The IFL was the organisation of British fascists most closely linked to the German Nazis in the early 1930s, largely because they regarded the Italians as soft towards the Jews. Despite the common ground between his movement and Continental fascism, Mosley was anxious to present the BUF as a British form of fascism. He was also anxious to distance himself from the British fascists of the 1920s who, he felt, wanted to 'make fascism the lackey of reaction'.[17] Mosley envisaged his movement as a progressive, modernising one capable of attracting working men and ex-Socialists by its social programme. Even unsympathetic contemporaries recognised this element. 'It is not surprising that Mosley should be the uncrowned King of Brighton,' commented the *Observer* in 1934; 'it is surprising that he has been able to build up a strong organisation in Manchester.'[18] Another distinctive feature of the BUF was the extent to which it recruited female members, gave them a major role in the movement's activities, and even adopted feminist ideas. As with Mosley's progressive policy for working men, this was consistent with his views as an MP in the 1920s.[19] A third feature of the BUF was that, despite its militarist style, its domestic programme did not depend on preparations for war, and its external policy was rooted in the maintenance of peace; here, too, Mosley continued to articulate the reactions of men of his own generation to the Great War and to the 'Old Gang' politicians whom he blamed for embroiling Britain in it. Finally, Leese correctly diagnosed that, initially at least, the BUF largely lacked the obsessive anti-Semitism that he considered the hallmark of fascism. Mosley undoubtedly shared the prejudices of his class and his era towards Jews, but they scarcely figured in his early writings and speeches as a fascist. Of course, the organisation attracted extreme anti-Semites and over time it increasingly treated Jews as a central target of its propaganda, as did fascists in Italy. But at first Leese derided Mosley's members as 'Kosher fascists' and even accused Cimmie of having Jewish blood.[20] Eventually this provoked a violent attack by the BUF on an IFL meeting in November 1933 when Leese was debagged and thrown into the street.

Although Mosley admired Nazism for the spiritual regeneration of German youth, his movement was much closer to Italian fascism. Mosley regularly visited Italy, adopted the idea of the corporate state, and was rewarded with funding by Mussolini for several years. The BUF also shared the relatively relaxed Italian view of race as a product of the interaction of historical, cultural and environmental factors; by contrast the IFL favoured the more rigid Nazi idea of race as biological, and deplored miscegenation as leading to racial degeneracy. In April 1933 Mosley and Cimmie took part in the celebrations surrounding the International Fascist Exhibition in Rome, where British fascists carried banners at the march past of the Italian contingents. The Mosleys appeared on the balcony of the Palazzo Venezia with Mussolini, a rare gesture of acquiescence in fascism by Cimmie.

By contrast, Mosley's visits to Germany were less frequent and he never got on as well with the Germans. He took pains to draw a distinction between his movement and Hitler's, saying 'their methods are German methods . . . If a Blackshirt Government came into power in this country they would continue to be different in character.'[21] When Mosley eventually met Hitler in April 1935, the Führer did not take to him, perhaps because Lady Maud Mosley, Oswald's mother, had gone on record describing Hitler as an enemy because 'people in this country would not join [the BUF] on account of the brutal methods in Germany'.[22] Ironically, Mosley's marriage to Diana took place in Germany in October 1936 in Goebbels's drawing room in Berlin.

Hitler sent them his photograph in a silver frame embossed with 'A.H.' and the German eagle.[23] This caused considerable embarrassment at home. In Huddersfield Leslie Grundy recalled how startled the local fascists were when someone entered the public house in which they were drinking claiming that Mosley had married a Mitford in Berlin with Hitler acting as the best man: 'All our members present were taken aback and confused.'[24] He regarded this as an error which damaged the movement at a time when Hitler was coming to be recognised as a national threat.

Yet despite his occasional misjudgements there is no doubt that Mosley was the BUF's chief asset; he quickly elevated it into a far more serious proposition than the earlier fascist organisations. His main weapon proved to be his masterly platform performances, which numbered about two hundred a year. In the early 1920s he had learnt to speak without notes by getting someone to read a *Times* editorial to him and making an immediate reply to each point in turn. By the 1930s he could hold an audience for an hour without notes, astonishing his supporters by his ability to summon facts and figures without hesitation.[25] His speeches followed a regular pattern, beginning with an examination of the problem, followed by an exposition of his solutions and proceeding to a well-rehearsed and impassioned climax; witnessing the performance at Manchester's Free Trade Hall in 1934 John Charnley was 'completely bowled over, fascinated, imbued with an inner feeling of spiritual uplift'.[26] By this time Mosley's speeches had lost much of their earlier humour, perhaps because he now spurned the parliamentary tradition which treated politics as an entertainment or a game. But he was still a master of sarcasm and repartee when he chose to be; indeed, he sometimes instructed his stewards to leave the hecklers alone so that he could exercise his wit on them.

Much of his impact depended upon sheer physical presence. As a Labour MP Mosley had played up to the admiring young women in his audiences by smiling at them, caressing his moustache with one hand while slapping his trouser leg with the other, and being rewarded with cries of 'Oh Valentino!'[27] Nicolson described him in the New Party 'striding up and down the rather frail platform with great panther steps and gesticulating with a pointing, and occasionally stabbing index'.[28] A *Manchester Guardian* journalist noted: 'His disposition and face are those of a raider, a corsair . . . He has a lithe catlike figure . . . the moustache trim, the nose shapely, the teeth very white and perfect. The profile is aristocratic. The whole air is that of a soldier on parade.'[29] At the same meeting Mosley abruptly disconnected the microphone – 'I hate these machines' – an interesting reaction which underlined his old-fashioned approach to campaigning. For all his contempt for Victorianism, Mosley fully endorsed its belief in the power of platform oratory, and he never felt as comfortable with an age that increasingly relied on the more subdued radio broadcast. Consequently he was easily misled by enthusiastic mass rallies, interpreting each ephemeral triumph as a genuine upsurge of support.

As an orator Mosley was rivalled only by William Joyce who joined the BUF in 1933 aged twenty-seven. A child of Southern Irish Loyalists who was brought up as a staunch Conservative, Joyce felt personally betrayed by the British establishment; he also carried grudges over his rejection by the Civil Service and the Foreign Office which left him susceptible to any possible scapegoat for his personal misfortunes. This largely took the form of a violent and obsessive prejudice against Jews whom he blamed for the disfiguring scar across his face, which he had received when acting as a steward in the 1920s. Known to colleagues as 'the Mighty Atom', Joyce was paid £300 a year, becoming Director of Propaganda in 1934 with responsibility for research and training speakers. Soon he was deputising for Mosley at major rallies. 'You're a right bastard,' shouted one female heckler, to which he replied: 'Thank you, mother.' However, Joyce's rather fanatical oratory proved a mixed blessing, for his bitter and extravagant language alienated many people.

In November 1933 the BUF recruited an experienced journalist and skilled propagandist, A. K. Chesterton, who admired Mosley as a fellow officer and a leader of heroic qualities. Chesterton became editor of *The Blackshirt* and Director of Propaganda in 1937.[30] Alexander Raven Thompson, a thirty-four-year-old university-trained economist and philosopher, also joined at this time and became the chief theorist of the movement. Another prominent addition in 1934 was John Beckett, an impassioned and histrionic orator who acted as Director of Publicity. A patriotic Socialist and former Labour MP, Beckett's chief claim to fame was his attempt to steal the mace in the House of Commons in 1931. The combination of Chesterton, Beckett and Joyce accentuated the BUF's lurch towards anti-Semitism from 1935 onwards. The skills of Raven Thompson, Chesterton and Joyce in propaganda and ideology complemented the practical, organisational work done by Forgan, Allen and Francis-Hawkins.

Not surprisingly the leading personnel also included several military figures, notably Eric Piercy, an inspector in the Special Constabulary and ex-insurance agent, who commanded the Fascist Defence Force. There was also Ian Hope Dundas, a twenty-four-year-old former naval officer who liked to say the BUF created the same spirit as the Navy 'without the sea-sickness'; Dundas marched about headquarters with a bugler in tow. Like its predecessors the movement appealed to those with a military or imperial background, partly because it created a comforting sense of hierarchy, and partly because it gave expression to the social idealism generated by the war; some thought the BUF offered a kind of Socialism-for-soldiers with the advantage of proper leadership and discipline. This was especially important for those who had spent many years working in the colonies and been shocked by the extent of the social and political change they found on their return.

The most visible expression of the movement's militarism was its uniform, supposedly inspired by Mosley's fencing jacket. Officers wore a black shirt and trousers, while unit leaders and men wore a black shirt and grey trousers in addition to six badges and stripes to denote rank. Initially the Italian *fasces*, or bundle of rods, was used as the emblem, but in 1936 this was replaced with a flash of lightning in a circle, worn as an armband. Derided by opponents as the 'flash in the pan', this was interpreted as a flash of action in a circle of unity. 'We wear the Blackshirt as the universal symbol in the modern world of young men dedicated to the salvation of great nations from decadence and degeneration,' Mosley proclaimed. 'But we wear on every Blackshirt the Union Jack, and our Fascism is British through and through.'[31] Like many rank-and-file members, Louise Irving, a Birmingham schoolteacher, argued that the wearing of the simple black shirt 'eliminated all feelings of class distinction' in the movement.[32] Apart from its symbolic value the uniform also proved advantageous in enabling fascist stewards to identify each other in confused and violent situations.

Initially the Fascist Defence Force comprised three hundred men who lived a semi-military life at headquarters; many were unemployed men who appreciated the accommodation and pocket money of £1 a week. In August 1933 when the BUF acquired 'Black House', formerly Whitelands Teacher Training College, in King's Road, Chelsea, some 5,000 members could be accommodated. An elite section, known as 'I Squad', who wore breeches and leather boots, were paid £3 and trained to quell disorder against armed opponents. In effect Black House became a combination of barracks and social club. The daily routine was punctuated by Ian Dundas, whose bugle announced 'reveille' and 'lights out', and controlled by Eric Piercy, a physical fitness fanatic, who organised drill, fencing, boxing and ju-jitsu. This gave expression to the fascist conviction that young men should 'live like athletes' and that if Britain were to be saved from degeneracy her people 'must be led back to the playing field'. Headquarters also maintained thirty motor vehicles, including five vans specially equipped with wire mesh windows and plating at the sides for protection against missiles, each of which held twenty or so men of the Defence Force for rapid transportation to disorderly meetings.

But why was this paramilitary system necessary? Lady Ravensdale, the sister of Mosley's wife Cynthia, challenged him after a meeting at Farringdon Memorial Hall in October 1932 for 'glorying over his menials throwing two lads down the stairs'; she suggested his speeches were good enough to make strong-arm tactics irrelevant.[33] Yet Mosley always contended that, after his experience with the New Party, physical force was essential to prevent the left driving his movement off the streets; and like most fascists he still believed that on some future occasion he might have to save the British state from chaos and subversion. More immediately, the glamour and publicity engendered by paramilitary activity attracted spirited young recruits who could sustain the new movement until such time as the more staid politicians were ready to invite it to share power.

The problem was that as the BUF expanded, headquarters could not always control the activities of members who had been attracted by the opportunities for fighting and handling weapons. Reports reached the Home Office of local branches practising rifle-shooting, no doubt in the belief that one day their country might call upon their skills.[34] In public the BUF aimed to present an image of controlled and disciplined force in contrast to the 'rabble' of left-wing subversives. A typical display of force occurred at a meeting held in the town hall at Oxford in November 1933. Despite admission by ticket only, many anti-fascists managed to enter, and, according to the chief constable, the opposition was well-organised.[35] Some refused to stand for the National Anthem, and, after an hour, things became very disorderly with people throwing chairs and trying to mount the platform. The 120 stewards, half of whom were drawn from the colleges, lifted the objectors 'none too gently' and ejected them 'more vigorously than is usual'. Two aspects of this meeting were significant. First, though the violence provoked heated correspondence between the liberal historian, H. A. L. Fisher, and the Home Office, the disorder only lasted about ten minutes.[36] By and large, Mosley's methods worked to his satisfaction. Secondly, faced with complaints from Fisher about excessive violence and 'the use of private armies for the purpose of dominating public meetings', the police insisted they saw no brutality and that the complainants, having gone with intent to disrupt the meeting, had been surprised by the stewards. Sir John Gilmour, the Home Secretary, told Fisher that the organisers had acted within their rights.[37]

Even before this, anti-fascists had taken note of Mosley's boast in his debate with Maxton that he had the capability to meet a crisis not with words 'but with Fascist machine guns'.[38] Was this merely foolish bravado or symptomatic of something more sinister? Mosley, who always insisted on his respect for constitutional government, undoubtedly expected to obtain power initially through the electoral process; but his opponents naturally concluded that he would never tolerate an elected left-wing government, and he boasted of his ability to deny freedom of speech to Communists. But when opponents accused him of harbouring plans to overthrow the government, Mosley sued them. His first case in February 1933 was against *The Star* which had used his words in the Maxton debate. It was indicative of Mosley's respectability at this stage that the judge, Lord Chief Justice Stewart, heaped praise on his abilities, and the jury awarded him £5,000 damages.

Three years later Mosley had a less comfortable time when he brought an action for slander against John Marchbanks, general secretary of the National Union of Railwaymen, over similar accusations.[39] For the defence, D. N. Pritt produced a BUF document urging Blackshirts to mingle with members of the armed forces to seek new recruits and even promise them employment under a future fascist regime. He read a BUF advertisement: 'Lt-Col. A. G. Crocker, late of the Essex Regiment, has been appointed in charge of the Essex area. He will be glad to hear from comrades of the Regiment and from anyone interested in the Fascist Movement.'[40] Mosley freely acknowledged that ex-servicemen were joining his movement, but insisted that he refused to accept serving members of the forces. Pritt also quoted a good deal of damaging evidence about the weaponry recommended for Blackshirts including knives, knuckledusters, corrugated rubber truncheons filled with shot, potatoes stuck with razor blades and breastplates studded with pins. One Edward Bailey described his work in charge of the Reading Blackshirts in 1933, which involved drilling and instruction in the use of knuckledusters and batons. He quoted a Captain Kearswell, the administrative officer for the Oxford area, as saying of knuckledusters, 'these are the things you want. See that everyone of your defence force has one.'[41] In response Mosley consistently denied ever urging the use of any weapons apart from the rubber truncheons issued to stewards. When confronted with a specific example he simply claimed that the instructions had been disobeyed or that the weapons found had actually been confiscated from his opponents.[42] Pritt also resurrected Mosley's 1933 boast about putting machineguns on the streets if necessary. How long would it take him to acquire machine-guns, enquired Pritt. According to Mosley it would be 'only too easy'.[43] Clearly, by 1936 the opposition had had more opportunity to obtain evidence, and in any case attitudes towards the BUF had hardened. As a result Mosley received the insulting sum of one farthing in damages and the jury decided that each side should pay its own costs, which the judge interpreted as meaning that the action ought not to have been brought.[44]

Among the witnesses involved in the case was an ex-Grenadier guardsman who testified to the weaponry available both at BUF headquarters and in

Reading. This focused attention once more on attempts being made not only to recruit former servicemen but also to make use of fascists currently serving in the forces. Several months later a number of BUF members of the Territorial Army were required to resign by their commanding officers; the Director General commented that it would damage recruitment if the TA became known as 'a hotbed of Fascism'.[45] Subsequently, however, the War Office appears to have retreated, insisting that it had no objection to BUF members joining as long as they abstained from spreading political propaganda or wearing anything that suggested a political uniform. Evidently propaganda work had been going on in some regiments where it had caused discontent among the other men.[46] Since the War Office preferred to leave it to each local commanding officer to deal with any incidents, the extent of fascist penetration is difficult to estimate; but the authorities stopped short of any wholesale attempt to eradicate fascist influence in the TA.

Until recently it has been difficult to know what fascist activity was like at the local level. The large quantities of official material in the Public Record Office give a somewhat biased impression. When Special Branch and MI5 eventually took an interest in the movement their chief focus was on the street fighting between Blackshirts and Communists, and on disturbances at major rallies that provoked controversy in the press, questions in parliament and correspondence with the Home Office. As a result the traditional picture of fascism is heavily coloured by activities in London's East End culminating in the 'Battle of Cable Street' in 1936. But the only area for which local records of BUF organisation exist is Dorset – a valuable reminder of the importance of the rural dimension. Oral evidence and unpublished memoirs by surviving Blackshirts have also revealed much about provincial fascism, especially in Lancashire and Yorkshire.[47] These sources modify the heroic view of the BUF, as seen from London and the vantage point of the leadership.

In the Lancashire town of Nelson, Nellie Driver thought the fascist uniform rather silly; when one local member boarded a bus the passengers offered him money, believing him to be the conductor.[48] A Lancaster member recalled that good recruiting grounds were the Rotary Club (for small tradesmen) and the British Legion (for ex-soldiers). But the ex-servicemen were sometimes rather sad and ineffectual characters rather than brilliant leaders; one such sat in the Lancaster headquarters, 'didn't do any work, [but would] drink tea and talk about his big wartime experience, how he'd helped the Black and Tans in Ireland and things like that'.[49] Rank-and-file members cheerfully remembered the cranks and faddists in the branches – 'we seemed to attract them' – as well as 'dodgy' characters who sometimes absconded with the funds. Some suffered from alcoholism; Nellie Driver described a member who spent ten minutes in the pub for every five spent selling *The Blackshirt*. There were also lurid accounts from Stoke and Brixton where BUF branches allegedly functioned as brothels; in effect the members were using the headquarters as a convenient venue for sexual activity, and several women – but not apparently men – were expelled as a result. This was doubtless a symptom of the youthful nature of the membership rather than of unusual immorality.[50] Several rank-and-file members confirmed the official view that weapons were forbidden but admitted that some people carried them anyway. Arthur Fawcett, a nineteen-year-old Manchester member recalled: 'if you were going to a meeting at all and you knew it was going to be a rough-house then you would bandage your hands up to stop your knuckles getting knocked up.'[51]

Most importantly, local sources leave little room for traditional assumptions about the class composition of the BUF. In industrial towns members were drawn from unemployed men and women, factory hands and textile mill workers; and they came from a Labour family background as often as from a Conservative one. 'The story was that Mosley was a millionaire,' one member recalled, 'and all you had to do was join the BUF and you'd be looked after.'[52] Middle-class businessmen often supported the BUF financially, but preferred to be discreet about it, or were 'not interested enough to come onto the streets you know, that sort of thing'.[53]

Mosley focused his speaking tours on areas of declining industry, notably Lancashire and Yorkshire, where the working-class Conservative tradition offered potential recruits. In the cotton towns he campaigned for the recovery of Britain's export markets in India; in the Yorkshire woollen centres he denounced competition by low-wage Asian countries and the boycotting of British goods by Jews; and in mining districts such as Barnsley he condemned imports of coal from Poland while British workers remained unemployed.[54] By 1934 the BUF reportedly had 2,000 members in Leeds, including many from the residential districts, and other Yorkshire branches at Hull, York, Sheffield, Doncaster, Harrogate, Bradford, Rotherham, Huddersfield and Wakefield.[55] For a time Mosley even contemplated moving his national headquarters to Manchester.

These urban branches were usually modest affairs. In Lancaster the headquarters comprised two rooms above a shop. Similarly at Leytonstone in north-east London Leonard Wise remembered two rooms, one an office, the other used for meetings, tea and light refreshments; regular activities involved street sales of *The Blackshirt* and outdoor meetings held on Friday evenings, usually outside a pub, with the support of the BUF van containing a speaker and half a dozen stewards.[56] Manchester's headquarters offered a little more, according to two members, aged nineteen and twenty-three, notably a bar, a room for concerts and reading, and a gymnasium in the basement.[57] In Newcastle Robert Richard, the District Leader, who was himself in his twenties, took his members jogging round the city to distribute leaflets and chant 'Two–Four–Six–Eight – Whom-Do-We-Appreciate – MOSLEY'. In the summer the Geordie Blackshirts made forays into the pit villages of County Durham, and on Sundays they held regular meetings in Newcastle's Bigg Market. After a while these attracted the local Communists, according to Richard, and when the Blackshirt stewards formed a semicircle with their backs to the crowd to protect the speaker, opponents stuck pins into their backsides; the stewards then turned round sharply which gave the impression that they were about to attack, and a riot quickly developed.[58]

Contemporaries often commented on the predominantly youthful appearance of those who attended fascist meetings in the 1930s.[59] This was a source of pride and admiration for supporters of the movement. Sir Thomas Moore, the Tory MP for Ayr, enthused at the spectacle presented by the Blackshirts:

> around about were thousands, young, eager and virile . . . The men were fine examples of a healthy and intelligent mind in a healthy and well-made body; the girls straight-eyed, vivacious and comely, well matched with their male comrades. For the first time I realised that this was no passing whim . . . It is the rebellion of youth against age, of effort against inaction.[60]

This youthful constituency comprised two distinct social types, as the author, Naomi Mitchison, observed at the notorious Olympia rally in June 1934; one she described as 'real toughs with the nearest I have ever seen to the criminal face, and the other, nice, blond romantic-looking boys, not much over twenty, who want above all to be able to worship a leader'.[61] This latter type had been carried over from the New Party and was consolidated by means of the university fascist associations. By 1934 the BUF also had organisations in at least eleven major public schools including Winchester, Oundle, Haileybury, Mill Hill, Marlborough and Stowe.[62]

The explanation for the appeal of fascism to the young may have been partly a reflection of the uniform and the excitement offered by the BUF. Younger Conservatives had been searching since 1918 for a more vigorous alternative to the staid, bourgeois party leadership. In Leytonstone, for example, the Young Conservatives joined the BUF *en masse*, according to Leonard Wise.[63] For younger men and women, whether from a Tory or Labour background, the new organisation offered far greater scope to rise quickly to influential and challenging positions. In Nelson, for example, the

District Leader was aged eighteen. In Southport where John Charnley joined at twenty-three, he was soon invited to practise five-minute speeches on a soapbox, learning on the job.[64] This was reminiscent of the early ILP; but by the 1930s the Labour Party itself had grown too bureaucratised and hierarchical to allow new members to play an influential role. However, generalisations about youthful fascism do require some qualification because the movement experienced a high turnover of membership, a process which left scope for the age profile and the social composition to change over time. Young people often joined on a whim without a very clear idea of the ideology of the movement, and some of them were disappointed by the abandonment of the uniform in 1937. Also, the emphasis on the fascist 'peace' campaign in the later 1930s probably appealed more to middle-aged people who had experience of the previous war and was less inspiring to the young.

In addition to its youthfulness, the British Union of Fascists has traditionally been seen as predominantly an aggressively male movement concentrated in large conurbations. But local evidence increasingly reveals a far wider social range and some distinct regional variations. The movement was highly opportunistic in that it exploited issues which had local relevance, such as the presence of a Jewish community in Manchester, Leeds or the East End. What is less obvious is that from 1933 onwards Mosley devoted a high proportion of his time to speeches in market towns in agricultural counties. There he tapped into the traditional conservatism of a farming community which had been suffering from apparently intractable economic problems since the end of the war. A decade of falling prices had caused bankruptcies among farmers and extensive sales of land at low prices; even between 1929 and 1931 the price of wheat dropped by 50 per cent and that of beef by 30 per cent, driving many people to abandon cultivation.[65] As a result Mosley attracted large and enthusiastic audiences in market towns and won important activists through his agricultural policy; his 1933 campaign pulled in several disgruntled farmers and ex-Conservatives who had been forced out of the industry, including Reynall Bellamy, his Northern Organiser, Robert Saunders, R. N. Creasy, Jorian Jenks and Viscountess Downe.[66]

Agricultural propaganda also gave Mosley access to a Conservative audience through Lady Houston's *Saturday Review*.[67] In these articles he condemned the import of wheat and butter from Russia for leaving East Anglia derelict and thereby reducing the wheat acreage from 1.9 to 1.3 million between 1921 and 1930. He demanded to know why Britain imported beef from Argentina; and he heaped blame on the City of London financiers who made loans to Argentina to promote its exports, and on Tory governments for their reluctance to offend those financial interests. The

Conservatives, he argued at Appleby in Westmorland, had 'ceased to be the party of the countryside and had become the party of the City of London'.[68] According to Mosley Britain could expand its domestic market by £200 million – the value of imported food – money which presently went to fatten the income of foreigners. He aimed to double agricultural output under a three-year plan, and to establish an Agricultural Bank which would offer credit to farmers and help them meet the targets set by corporate planning.[69] In May 1934 he commenced another five-month tour of the agricultural districts involving four major meetings in every agricultural county from Cornwall to Essex and as far north as Northumberland and Westmorland.[70] He drew audiences of 1,000 at Grantham, 2,000 at Kendal and 3,000 at Dumfries, figures that few conventional politicians could command in such towns.[71]

In East Anglia, a region which enjoyed a tradition of rural rebellion, the BUF successfully exploited the farmers' sense of grievance over the payment of tithes to the Church of England. In 1933 the authorities began to punish farmers who refused to make payments by sending in the bailiffs to seize livestock and implements which were subsequently auctioned off as compensation. The BUF received legal advice to the effect that objectors could legally enter the land of a distrained farmer, with his consent, and obstruct the work of the bailiffs as long as they avoided violence.[72] In August 1933 groups of Blackshirts intervened at Ringshall, near Stowmarket, where they enjoyed the backing of local residents; and as a result the tithe owners decided to abandon their distraint action.[73] In a famous case at Wortham in Suffolk (near Diss) in February 1934 a body of thirty Blackshirts from Norfolk and Suffolk led by Dick Plathen intervened on behalf of a farmer facing a demand for £565. They felled trees to block the farm road, dug trenches and erected barbed wire to prevent access to livestock.[74] On this occasion the police arrested the protestors, apart from one Douglas Gunson who went on the run and was never caught. They were bound over after undertaking not to repeat their offences. In 1936 the Ecclesiastical Commissioners eventually abandoned their claim to the tithe in return for compensation. Almost regardless of the outcome, however, these escapades attracted favourable publicity and new members to the movement.

In some ways the most surprising aspect of the BUF was the extensive participation of women in its activities. Its counterparts in Germany and Italy, which enjoyed a reputation for extreme patriarchal attitudes, had effectively suppressed their feminist movements. In Britain pro-fascist writing by Anthony Ludovici in the 1920s had attributed the degenerate state of politics partly to female emancipation, and 1930s fascists such as

A. K. Chesterton continued to uphold such prejudices. In 1932 Mosley himself wrote: 'We want men who are men and women who are women.'[75] On the face of it the heady homoerotic atmosphere of Black House with its unmarried men, military barracks and public schoolboys was not attractive for women.

Yet in practice the movement became remarkably open to women. The Women's Section was established in March 1933 under Lady Maud Mosley who adopted a motherly role on behalf of the young women who seemed vulnerable to the predatory male Blackshirts.[76] She was succeeded by Lady Esther Makgill who used headquarters to run her own business and was sentenced to six months for embezzling funds; she in turn was followed by Mary Richardson, an ex-suffragette, and by Anne Brock-Griggs and Olga Shore who were responsible for the South and the North of the country respectively.[77] There was nothing eccentric in maintaining a separate organisation for female members; the Labour Party was organised along the same lines at this time. The women, who appeared prominently at fascist functions, have been estimated to comprise a quarter of the total membership.[78] They wore a black blouse, black beret and grey skirt – but no lipstick or other make-up.[79] When the *Sunday Dispatch* promoted a beauty contest for female Blackshirts in 1934 no one entered; Mosley explained: 'these were serious women dedicated to the cause of their country rather than aspirants to the Gaiety Theatre chorus.'[80]

Although the organisation obviously included many anti-feminist men, it seems clear that the female members of the BUF played a very active role. 'You weren't just a tea-maker, you know,' recalled Louise Irving of Birmingham. Nellie Driver conceded that in Nelson the women did make tea for the men returning from active duty, but they also received training in ju-jitsu so that they could throw people out of meetings; this was thought necessary if only because male Blackshirts could not decently manhandle female Communists.[81] By the inter-war period many conventional upper-class ladies had become accustomed to participation in political and electoral activity, and some of these recruits had been active Conservatives, including Viscountess Downe, Lady Clare Annesley, Lady Howard of Effingham and Lady Pearson, the sister of Henry Page Croft, who was thought to have a crush on Mosley. The movement also attracted adventurous young women, not least the racing driver 'Fabulous' Fay Taylour, the first woman to drive on a dirt track.

During the later 1930s these female members became increasingly prominent in the BUF's peace campaign.[82] They were also essential to the development of an electoral machine which was central to Mosley's long-term strategy. As doorstep canvassers the women presented a more reassuring image of fascism than that created by street violence and mass demonstrations.[83] Mosley himself had enough experience of Conservative politics to understand how great an asset women were at the constituency level. In November 1936 Norah Elam became the first BUF parliamentary candidate at Northampton; Anne Brock-Griggs stood at Limehouse in the London County Council elections and was parliamentary candidate for South Poplar, while Lady Pearson was adopted at Canterbury and Viscountess Downe in North Norfolk. The fascists boasted that 10 per cent of their candidates were female, a higher proportion than in any other party, and that this proved they were not trying to force women back into the home.

In explaining the motivation that led women into fascism it would be erroneous to dismiss them as being either misguided or manipulated. Many joined for reasons that had little to do with their gender; middle and upper-class women from Conservative backgrounds were reacting against conventional politics for the same reasons as men. Dorothy Downe, Norah Elam and Mercedes Barrington, for example, had worked for the Tory Party but simply grown disillusioned. In 1934 the Primrose League, which originally mobilised huge numbers of women for the Conservative cause, made urgent requests for guidance about fascism because of the drift of its members to the new movement.[84] However, several female fascists had once been active suffragettes, including Norah Elam (previously Mrs Dacre Fox), Mary Richardson, notorious for slashing the *Rokeby Venus* in 1914, Mercedes Barrington, and Mary Allen who had pioneered the women's police force during the war.

In fact, their migration to fascism was far less anomalous than it appears at first sight. For women who sought a great leader and had become alienated by conventional parties, the BUF seemed a natural successor to the Women's Social and Political Union (WSPU). 'I was first attracted to the Blackshirts because I saw in them the courage, the action, the loyalty, the gift of service, and the ability to serve which I had known in the suffragette movement,' explained Mary Richardson.[85] Several of Emmeline Pankhurst's colleagues regarded her movement as a forerunner of the inter-war dictatorships because of its insistence on total obedience to the Leader. During the war the suffragette leadership had adopted an extreme brand of patriotism and after 1918 Christabel Pankhurst repudiated votes for women along with the entire parliamentary system. Above all, the semi-military style of the WSPU had offered adventurous women the same challenge and satisfaction as the BUF.[86] Mary Allen had tried to recapture this by maintaining a women's police reserve in the 1920s. In some sense the ex-suffragette fascists still regarded themselves as feminists, and Norah Elam even suggested that fascism was a continuation of the Edwardian women's movement. However, they had become detached from the feminist movement which, like most fascists, they regarded as a symptom of a degraded political system; they derided Nancy Astor as 'this sorry specimen of feminine irresponsibility', and accused the 'professional spinster politicians' of selling out to the political parties.[87]

Despite this, the BUF couched much of its propaganda in distinctly feminist terms, and the movement claimed to offer a 'true feminism' by way of disparaging the other parties; some members argued that equality of the sexes was part of its attraction for them.[88] In contrast to its Continental counterparts, the movement was at pains to assert that fascism did not imply the return of women to a life of domesticity. As Alexander Raven Thompson and Anne Brock-Griggs explained, the corporate state would give women greater privileges than they enjoyed under democracy by ensuring proper representation for them as housewives.[89] Additionally, the corporate system would raise their status as workers, by ensuring that they enjoyed equal pay, by increasing remuneration in low-paid occupations, and by abolishing the marriage bar.[90] The rationale for all this lay not in promoting women's individual rights, but in serving the interests of the state by making full use of women's skills.

The same motive led fascists to uphold women's role as the mothers of a reborn and regenerated race, which meant trying to arrest the falling birthrate by means of maternity classes, more female doctors, better paid midwives, more maternity beds and home helps for recuperating mothers. But while Mosley regarded a higher birth-rate as desirable, he accepted the need to offer women better advice about birth control so that they could make the best use of modern scientific knowledge; the ignorance about birth control from which many poor people suffered was simply not in the national interest.[91] This amounted to a feminine expression of fascism, rather than feminism, but at a time when the main parties adopted a very equivocal attitude towards issues like equal pay and birth control, the BUF clearly managed to come to terms with a generation of women who took a measure of female emancipation for granted.

If there was a missing element in the wide range of support cultivated by the BUF it was the upper-class recruits who had been so prominent in the fascist organisations of the 1920s. This is the more striking in view of the sympathy shown for fascism in Germany and Italy at this level of society. The Mitfords were the best-known titled family of fascists, albeit an eccentric one, in the 1930s. Diana Mitford introduced Mosley to her nineteen-year-old sister, Unity, who was soon proudly flourishing her new black shirt: 'It's such fun.'[92] In the summer of 1933 the impetuous Unity declared her desire to visit Germany. 'But darling,' Lady Redesdale remonstrated, 'I thought you didn't like Abroad.'[93] However, Diana accompanied her to

Nuremberg which was decked out in flags to celebrate Hitler's coming to power: 'a feeling of excited triumph was in the air,' wrote Diana, 'and when Hitler appeared an almost electric shock passed through the multitude.'[94] When Unity eventually contrived to meet Hitler, he was delighted with her aristocratic credentials and Nordic beauty, though apparently confused that she was called 'Mitford' not 'Redesdale'; he patted her hand, saying 'Ah, poor child', in the belief that she was illegitimate.[95] As Jessica Mitford put it, 'Farve [Lord Redesdale] is one of Nature's Fascists. He'd simply *love* the Führer.'[96] This proved to be correct. The Redesdales were delighted and flattered by their visit to Germany where they were treated like royalty and ferried about by a chauffeur in a Mercedes-Benz. This, after all, offered a considerable contrast with their position at home where Lord Redesdale was financially embarrassed and politically marginalized.

By the mid-1930s, all over England, not to mention Scotland, obscure landed figures like the Redesdales admired Hitler, even if some of them disapproved of him as a lower-class demagogue. Those who stood out against the fashion, like the anti-fascist Tory MP, the Duchess of Atholl, found their position in society increasingly uncomfortable. One of Atholl's Scottish supporters commented on 'the increase in Fascism which one finds amongst the Army, landed and professional classes. It has nothing to do with Mosley, but has a stronghold in the Borders and east Lothian.'[97] Such remarks make it all the more striking that the growing sympathy for fascism in the upper classes was not, apparently, translated into formal support for the BUF. To some extent this reflected resentment towards Mosley personally on the grounds that he had betrayed his class by joining the Labour Party. Property owners were also doubtless alienated by the radical character of the BUF's social and economic programme. In 1934 an attempt to recruit Lord Guisborough, an influential figure in north Yorkshire, found him 'extremely sympathetic to Fascism . . . he is also on the point of resignation from the Conservative Party.' However, Guisborough was deterred by the extreme demagogic language used by William Joyce in Blackshirt propaganda, and by the mediocrity of *The Blackshirt* which seemed to be pitched at working-class readers.[98] 'We have a definite strata of our society predisposed to Fascism', Leigh Vaughan-Henry reported to Mosley, 'if we do not permit these errors of taste, insight, psychology and manner to injure us with it . . . we must have intelligence . . . if we are to have the type of consciousness and mental force capable of backing you in Government when the Corporate State becomes actual in this country.'[99] This correspondence underlined the dilemma facing the BUF: how to mobilise a mass movement while simultaneously cultivating upper-class reactionaries. For, however insulting Mosley may have been about the 'Old Gang' parties, he never lost sight of the fact that at some stage he would need a measure of support from within the establishment to lever him into power.

His own origins in the Staffordshire landed gentry left Mosley very alive to the difficulties involved in grafting traditional Toryism on to the urban street politics of the BUF. While the fascist machine offered the propertied classes an insurance against their fear of social breakdown, in the short term they could hardly help regarding it as rather vulgar. It was with this in mind that the January Club was established on New Year's Day 1934. Its secretary was Captain H. W. Luttman-Johnson, a Scots landowner and ex-cavalry officer in the Indian Army. The January Club operated reassuringly by means of dinners at expensive hotels where its members heard lectures on the corporate state. The chairman, Sir John Squire, claimed, disingenuously, that it was not a fascist organisation but was open to members of all parties who were 'for the most part in sympathy with the Fascist movement. They believed that the present democratic system of government in this country must be changed.'[100] In fact, the correspondence between Luttman-Johnson, Mosley, Forgan and Joyce leaves no doubt that the January Club was designed as a front organisation for the BUF.[101] Privately Luttman-Johnson, who briefly joined the BUF in 1933 and was interned as a fascist during the Second World War, acknowledged that the club had been formed to give Mosley an extra platform.[102]

The initial membership list of the January Club reflected the fascist sympathies of the right wing of Conservatism in the shape of current MPs including Alan Lennox-Boyd (Mid-Bedfordshire), Hugh Molson (Doncaster), Viscount Lymington (Basingstoke), Michael Beaumont (Aylesbury), Lord Erskine (Weston-super-Mare) and Sir Ernest Bennett (National Labour, Cardiff Central). Two others became MPs in 1935: Lord William Scott (Roxburgh and Selkirk) and Duncan Sandys (Norwood). Former MPs and candidates included Sir Warden Chilcott and Sir Fairfax Lucy.[103] Other January Club members were already involved with the BUF or other pro-fascist organisations including the Earl of Glasgow, General Sir Hubert Gough, George Pitt-Rivers, the Hon. F. J. Rennell-Rodd and John Beckett. The club also included many titled men including Lord Middleton, Earl Jellicoe, the Marquess of Tavistock, Lord Londonderry, and several pro-fascist journalists and writers such as Harold Goad, Sir Charles Petrie, Francis Yeats-Brown, G. Ward Price, Douglas Jerrold and Lord Rothermere. The club briefly attracted T. E. Lawrence who complained he could not afford to go into politics: 'I want your movement to hurry up,' he told the Secretary. Though Lawrence's views were fascist he declined to join, pleading that he was simply too tired.[104]

As the January Club did not aspire to be a party or to field candidates, membership could be represented as complementing rather than challenging the Conservative Party. Nonetheless, the MPs seem to have been remarkably unembarrassed to belong to a fascist organisation. Michael Beaumont, described by the *News Chronicle* as the first parliamentary convert to fascism, told the House of Commons in 1934: 'I am not a Fascist, but as an avowed anti-Democrat and an avowed admirer of Fascism in other countries, I am naturally interested in the movement.'[105] Several of the MPs took the precaution of qualifying their fascist sympathies by expressing their disapproval of Mosley himself. According to Reynell Bellamy, 'staunch Conservatives were heard to say that while not wanting Mosley in power, they would certainly like to see him and sufficient of his followers in parliament to startle the lethargic Baldwin into doing something.'[106]

In the light of such comment, how far did the January Club serve Mosley's strategy? Stage one had involved creating a quasi-military movement strong enough to resist the left. In stage two he intended to develop a more conventional political movement by building up an electoral machine. In the process Mosley hoped to get some fascists elected to parliament, but he never expected to win power outright; his opportunity would come after some further crisis involving collaboration with sympathetic right-wing MPs and peers, as had happened in Italy and Germany. The January Club was designed to foster an understanding of the corporate state among respectable politicians so that when the crisis arose the transition from parliamentary democracy would not seem too revolutionary.

However, as the January Club operated privately and did not aspire to become a mass movement, it is difficult to assess how widely its net was cast. It appears to have been confined to London's West End, though Charles Chenevix Trench reported a successful branch in Hull.[107] It identified many potential recruits among the younger Tory MPs including Harold Macmillan, John Boyd-Carpenter, Quintin Hogg and Derek Walker-Smith, 'the brightest of the Conservative *jeunes*', as Petrie put it.[108] Robert Forgan also urged Luttman-Johnson to 'be prepared to accept quite a number of small businessmen if we are to be successful in getting financial support for the movement'.[109] The club's meetings did attract representatives from several leading companies including Vickers, Morgan Grenfell, C. Handley Page, Siemens, London Assurance and Caxton Electric, though how much support was obtained is unclear.[110] Some members had misgivings precisely because the January Club seemed merely a front for the BUF. One told Luttman-Johnson that he would find it easier to secure recruits if 'the January Club were to divorce itself from the flavour of Tom Mosley'.[111] Perhaps to circumvent this objection Luttman-Johnson also formed the Windsor Club with a view to being more detached and thus open to a wider range of members. However, committed fascists regarded the Windsor Club with contempt because it banned uniforms from its meetings and appeared too willing to compromise with the existing social and political system.[112]

At all events, by the start of 1934 a discreet traffic of ideas and personnel had developed between fascism and the Conservative right wing. While some found the January Club a convenient and respectable halfway house, members of parliament lent Mosley their support in other ways. Henry Drummond Wolff was reported by Special Branch as donating £500 to the BUF, while Lieutenant Colonel Sir Thomas Moore, J. T. C. Moore-Brabazon, Patrick Donner and Earl Winterton spoke or wrote in its support.[113] In February 1934 Viscount Lymington, who ran a separate pro-fascist group, English Mistery, decided to quit as MP for Basingstoke, complaining that it had become impossible to campaign effectively for national defence or to save the British Empire.

Lymington's resignation highlighted the struggle that was being waged by the extreme right, in collaboration with fascists, to manoeuvre its men into safe Tory seats against the wishes of Conservative Central Office.[114] At Basingstoke they succeeded in replacing Lymington with Henry Drummond Wolff, a highly anti-Semitic and pro-Nazi figure who played an active role as intermediary between London and Berlin before the outbreak of war. After serving only one year as MP, Wolff resigned, ostensibly for health reasons.[115] However, he and Lymington managed to substitute another pro-fascist, Patrick Donner, currently a diehard opponent of the government's India policy. But before Donner's adoption the Basingstoke Conservative agent reported privately to Wolff: 'I met Mr Donner yesterday and I understand that he had a successful interview with Sir Oswald Moseley [sic].'[116] Though the meaning of this letter is not entirely clear, it implies that the candidate was being adopted with Mosley's approval or cooperation, an extraordinary proceeding, though entirely consistent with his aim of building up a body of parliamentary support to ease his eventual entry into power.

It is also apparent that although some pro-fascists were incurable backbench rebels, fascist sympathies were no bar to office: Lennox-Boyd, Donner, Moore-Brabazon and Lord Erskine all went on to hold government posts. Younger members such as Michael Beaumont and Lennox-Boyd clearly saw no need to hide their admiration for fascist regimes in Italy and Spain.[117] The explanation for their apparent recklessness in endorsing fascism is not hard to find. It reflected the politicians' low morale around 1934, their anger over the government's weakness in the face of nationalist pressure in India, and its susceptibility to pacifist opinion which, they felt, was inhibiting a major rearmament programme. They increasingly concluded that the National Government was a failure and that the voters had already begun to desert it.[118] Two seats were lost to the Labour Party at by-elections in

1932, two more in 1933 and four in 1934, the most dramatic of which was at East Fulham where a Conservative majority of 14,000 became a Labour one of 5,000. Although these setbacks were misleading – they did not herald a return to power by the Labour Party – at the time they caused deep gloom. Forced to contemplate another left-wing government, Conservatives felt they could hardly expect to get off as lightly as in 1924 and 1929; this time Labour would probably abolish the House of Lords and dismember the empire. 'It seems to me', wrote Cuthbert Headlam, 'that many of us might well fall in with a Fascist coup d'état, preferring a bourgeois revolution to a proletarian one.'[119]

At the same time several of the Conservative journals were effectively colluding with fascism not just by undermining confidence in the National Government but by disparaging parliamentary democracy in general. 'We see other great nations refusing to be handicapped by the Party machine,' wrote Sir Fairfax Lucy, advocating an alternative system based on indirect election and nomination by interest groups: 'whether we call this system Fascism or Corporatism or invent a new name or title, any organisation that takes up this work ... will have deserved well of its country and the empire.'[120] In the *English Review* Douglas Jerrold argued that Britain suffered from a weak state and liberal ideas when she needed a strong monarchical system; this left her at the mercy of free money and speculators. According to Jerrold the solution lay through an expansionist programme within a protectionist economy, a scheme which was close to Mosley's, though he chose to present it in terms of a revived Toryism.[121]

In 1932 the *Saturday Review* was bought by Lady Lucy Houston who used it as a vehicle for abusive propaganda against Baldwin whose tenure of office she denounced as 'the greatest disaster that has befallen Conservatism in modern times'.[122] So extreme were Houston's opinions that in 1933 she denied rumours that she was about to finance a new newspaper for Mosley, protesting that she was a militant patriot but not a fascist.[123] In fact her only disagreement with Mosley was personal rather than ideological. During 1934 Houston endorsed his speeches in editorials and printed articles by him accompanied by full-page photographs. Mosley used this opportunity to undermine parliamentary Conservatism: 'The function of modern Conservatism', he wrote, 'is merely to fit a weak brake on the runaway machine of liberal-Socialist ideas. Blackshirt policy scraps the whole machine and substitutes a new engine of modern design.'[124]

This pattern of support for the BUF in the Conservative journals culminated on 15 January 1934 when the *Daily Mail* published its notorious headline: 'Hurrah For The Blackshirts!', thus inaugurating six months in which it promoted the movement. There was nothing anomalous about this initiative. Lord Rothermere had been heaping praise on fascist dictatorship throughout the 1920s, and had offered to back Mosley in December 1931.[125] Yet Mosley was cautious about accepting his support because he understood that, like Lady Houston, Rothermere suffered from megalomania and intended to dictate terms for his support. In particular Rothermere wanted him to abandon the word 'fascist' in favour of 'Blackshirt', which he always used in his newspapers; he was not committed to the corporate state, and he intended to infiltrate his own United Empire Party candidates into the BUF. Consequently negotiations continued for some months until, according to Count Dino Grandi, the Italian ambassador, Mussolini intervened: 'a word from [him] was enough to put Rothermere quite suddenly beside Mosley.'[126] The ensuing relationship was not unlike that pertaining in several Continental countries where each side felt confident that it could use the other for its own purposes. Grandi noted that in Italy reactionaries like Rothermere had intended to harness fascism to defeat Socialism and democracy, thereby establishing themselves in power, but realised too late that they had opened the way to a real revolution in government rather than to a consolidation of the right wing.[127] The British experience differed only in the sense that Rothermere pulled out before things reached that stage.

Despite his reservations Mosley was correct in concluding that the risk was worth taking. Rothermere controlled a large slice of the press including the *Daily Mail*, *Sunday Dispatch* and *Evening News*, as well as several dozen provincial newspapers. He lauded the BUF as a modernising, virile, British movement, above party politics and above all as 'the Party of Youth'. 'The Blackshirt Movement', enthused the *Mail*, 'is the organised effort of the younger generation to break the stranglehold which senile politicians have so long maintained on our affairs.'[128] There followed a systematic campaign of promotion in which the *Sunday Dispatch* turned itself into a house journal for the BUF. Not content with regular features on 'What the Blackshirts Are Doing' and biographies of the leading personnel, it endeavoured to engage its readers' involvement in the movement. In April 1934 the newspaper offered free tickets to major rallies including the one at Olympia in June 1934, and £1 weekly prizes for readers' letters on 'Why I Like the Blackshirts'.[129] Winning entrants wrote: 'The Blackshirts place King and Country before personal motive. Up to the present, no party has done much good for the community', and 'I like the Blackshirts because they stand for Empire Unity, the re-establishment of British prestige and the reawakening in the British public of pride in the nation.' The *Sunday Dispatch* also carried frequent reports on female fascists along the lines of 'Girl Blackshirt Attacked' and 'Beauty Joins the Blackshirts', as well as pictures of women practising ju-jitsu, fencing and physical exercise.[130]

During the first six months of 1934 the Rothermere press made fascism so topical that even the hostile newspapers could not afford to ignore the subject. With a thousand new recruits turning up at the London head-quarters each week, a mood of boundless optimism soon took hold, and members began to talk about getting into power in twelve months.[131] Contemporaries quickly appreciated that the growth of the BUF posed a dire threat to the National Government, but they remained uncertain how to respond to it. 'For Democracy to suppress Fascism by force, or to attempt it, would be a confession of failure,' wrote Lady Houston; 'the wholesome and manly reaction of young Conservatives from official Conservatism is sweeping our youth into this form of protest.'[132] In a lengthy eulogy in the *Daily Mail* entitled 'The Blackshirts Have What the Conservatives Need', the Tory MP, Sir Thomas Moore, expressed what many were now thinking:

> There [is] little, if any, policy which could not be accepted by the most loyal followers of our present Conservative leaders . . . Why, therefore, the Blackshirts? The answer lies in one word – action . . . it is because the people believe that the Blackshirts will perform that the movement has made such strides in its appeal to the public. But if my analysis is correct surely there cannot be any fundamental difference of outlook between the Blackshirts and their parents the Conservatives . . . why should there not be concord and agreement between that old historic party . . . and this new virile offshoot?[133]

In view of Mosley's unconcealed intention of dispensing with parliamentary democracy, Moore's claim that there was nothing Conservatives could not accept in the BUF programme seems an overstatement, although, in the prevailing mood of 1934, less eccentric than it appears at first sight. The National Government had caused deep disillusionment among its own supporters by its insistence on forcing through reforms which seemed to put the Indian Empire in jeopardy. The right interpreted this as symptomatic of a wider malaise. In a debate on India at the party conference in October, Lord Ampthill warned: 'The Conservative Party is doomed and Parliamentary Government, as we know it, is on its last legs, unless something can be done to restore political aptitude and courage among those who try to lead the masses in our local organisations.'[134] Rather bizarrely, Baldwin himself appeared to endorse Moore's diagnosis when he declared: 'The policy of Fascism is what you may well call Ultramontane Conservatism. It takes many of the tenets of our own party and pushes them to a conclusion which, if given effect to, would, I believe, be disastrous to our country.'[135]

For a skilled politician this was an inept way of defending himself, for Baldwin was, in effect, conceding his critics' claim that Blackshirt aims were ultimately sound Conservative ones; this was almost calculated to lend credibility to the belief that fascism could be used to rejuvenate Conservatism and compel its practitioners to be true to its goals.

There was, however, one important flaw in all this. Mosley had consistently derided party politics as futile and portrayed fascism as an idealistic movement above petty squabbles. But he never cut himself off from them as decisively as he pretended, for he accepted that, given the necessity for an electoral strategy, he had at some stage to attract supporters from the other parties. Suddenly, in 1934 he seemed to be achieving this objective. But like a river that slows down as it picks up sediment, the BUF stood in danger of losing its momentum as thousands of middle-class ex-Conservatives threatened to turn it into a normal political party. 'Branches began to resemble Conservatives clubs,' complained one Blackshirt, 'for such members were only interested in social activities, not in taking our message on to the streets . . . these people were a pest.'[136] In the event, many of the recruits did not stay long, partly because the new movement proved to be rather too exciting for their taste. But Mosley never quite resolved the dilemma – how to retain the distinctive image of the BUF as a patriotic movement above the party bunfight while mobilising the conventional people required by an orthodox election machine.

For several months, however, the fascists enjoyed their triumph. In January Mosley travelled to Rome where Mussolini allegedly gave him £20,000.[137] In April at the first of three huge London demonstrations, the BUF packed between 8,000 and 9,000 people into the Albert Hall, its biggest indoor meeting so far. At the same time a new edition of *The Greater Britain* appeared. Mosley now claimed that his economic programme had been widely accepted and had been partly implemented by President Roosevelt as a way of reducing unemployment in America. 'Our great confidence has been justified to a greater extent than we could have dared to hope,' boasted Mosley. 'In this early period of Fascism in Britain we have advanced far more rapidly than any other Fascist movement in the world.'[138] At the start of 1934 the movement had claimed three hundred branches, and by June there were reportedly nearer five hundred, backed by a fast-rising membership of around 40,000.[139] Many of these were 'passive' members, but in view of the high proportion of inactive Conservative members and the Labour Party's reliance on a largely nominal membership of 'affiliated' trade unionists, this was far from unusual.

This expansion was underpinned by resources far beyond those enjoyed by fascist organisations in the 1920s and were sufficient to maintain a paid staff and a national machine capable of rivalling the other parties. Home Office estimates suggested that at its peak in 1934 the BUF spent £80,000 a year, and perhaps £40,000 in 1935; they estimated that £10,000 was derived from subscriptions and perhaps £5,000–10,000 from donations by Bill Allen.[140] For many years Mosley consistently denied that he received money from Italian fascist sources, but correspondence by Count Dino Grandi, the Italian ambassador, found in Mussolini's papers, suggests otherwise. In January 1934 Grandi wrote: 'Mosley has asked me to express his gratitude for your sending him a considerable sum which I have arranged to hand over to him today.'[141] In March he reported that Mussolini had been paying 3.5 million lire (£60,000) a year in monthly instalments of 300,000 lire. Special Branch eventually discovered how these funds had been transferred into a secret account, opened in July 1933, at the Charing Cross branch of the Westminster Bank at the suggestion of Bill Allen. Into this account poured the foreign subsidies, via a Swiss bank, in French, Swiss and German currency, the sums ranging from £9,500 in 1933 to £77,800 in 1934 and £86,000 in 1935, and falling to £43,300 in 1936 and £7,600 in 1937.[142] Money was usually withdrawn three to six times each month by Robert Forgan, Bill Allen, Ian Dundas and Major Tabor. The last withdrawal from the account was made in May 1937 when there was virtually nothing left.

Nor was this the only source. When under interrogation in the war Mosley claimed that he had spent £100,000 of his own money on the movement, and observers speculated that donations were made by Lord Nuffield, who had subsidised the New Party, Captain Gordon-Canning, the industrialist Wyndham Portal and Sir Alliot Verdon Roe, a famous pilot and the designer of the Avro aircraft. Mosley also had many friends on the Lancashire Cotton Exchange whose firms made donations.[143] According to William Joyce, Edward Barron, the son of the proprietor of the Carreras Tobacco Company, offered £100,000 provided the movement avoided anti-Semitism, but he 'rejected the offer with an impolite message'.[144] Mosley also hatched two abortive fund-raising schemes. The first was a joint venture with Rothermere involving the creation of New Epoch Products Ltd, to manufacture cigarettes which they planned to market through BUF branches; however, this folded when Rothermere withdrew his support.[145] Later Mosley contemplated establishing a network of radio stations, similar to Radio Luxembourg, based in the Channel Islands, Ireland and Germany. This was partly intended as a means of overcoming the press boycott of the movement at that time, but was also regarded as a lucrative venture; plans were, however, interrupted by the outbreak of war in 1939.

Buoyed by the backing of Rothermere's newspapers, sustained by generous funding, and emboldened by the low morale among government supporters,

Mosley posed a serious threat to the conventional politicians during the first half of 1934. At a conference called by the Home Office in November 1933, Sir Vernon Kell of MI5 had recognised the necessity for gathering more information about the fascists – providing he received enough funds to do it. However, his staff had been drastically reduced to thirty and MI5 focused largely on the activities of the Communists.[146] The Home Office itself admitted that the police had so far failed to get inside information about the movement.[147] In fact, regular surveillance of the BUF by Special Branch and MI5 did not begin until April 1934. They received detailed information about the internal divisions and the mood at BUF headquarters from Bill Allen, one of Mosley's closest colleagues, and Captain P. G. Taylor. Several others were believed to pass on information from time to time, including Joyce, probably because of his connection with Maxwell Knight, the eccentric MI5 officer known as 'M', who also ran agents in the British Communist Party.[148] Though apparently aware of this situation, Mosley was evidently untroubled by it. He probably judged that the Special Branch reports did the movement no great harm and may actually have had a reassuring effect insofar as they demonstrated that the fascists were not doing anything illegal.

Yet, while the politicians remained inert, the police were quicker to recognise the nature of the problem posed by the growth of fascism. At the start of 1934 Sir Hugh Trenchard, the Chief Commissioner of the Metropolitan Police, recommended a ban on fascist uniforms which he regarded as a major cause of disorder. Previously the police had seen some advantage in the uniform because it enabled them to identify offenders in a crowd, but this seemed increasingly outweighed by the provocative effect it had.[149] Trenchard also warned the Home Office that 'the BUF is to all intents and purposes a military formation', and, in view of the growth of similar movements abroad, it was 'a matter for urgent consideration whether action should not be taken to put a definite stop to movements of this kind while they are still comparatively small and easy to deal with'.[150]

In response the politicians pointed out that they had considered making the Communist Party illegal twenty years previously but that suppression of opinion was contrary to British tradition; in any case 'its proscription would result merely in driving the movement underground'; they would intervene only if threatened with civil strife or the kind of tyranny rampant on the Continent.[151] It was, of course, embarrassing to see the Blackshirts openly advertising their drilling in defiance of the prohibition on the use of arms and military exercises under the Act of 1819. However, this legislation was so little used that the officials felt uncertain whether military drill could be satisfactorily distinguished from gymnastic drill, and wondered whether to try a test case. Surprisingly, Trenchard himself considered drilling of little importance and insisted that the suppression of the uniform was the key issue.[152]

These inconclusive discussions were further complicated by the sudden emergence of the 'Rothermere Fascists' as Trenchard, showing more political nous than the politicians, quickly recognised. 'The Fascist movement has begun to attract a better class of recruits and its membership is increasing,' he noted. 'Should the movement expand to the dimensions which it has already attained in certain countries (a contingency which cannot be ruled out of consideration) it would probably be too late to deal effectively with the mischief.'[153] In fact, by the summer of 1934 that situation appeared to be fast approaching.

NINE

'Where Are the Bodies?':
The Politics of Violence 1934–7

'Had [Mosley] put his followers into blue pullovers instead of blackshirts much would have been forgiven him.'

Sir Charles Petrie, *Chapters of Life* (1950), 168

In the early evening of 7 June 1934, 1,100 Blackshirts, arrayed in five columns, began marching from their headquarters at Black House in the King's Road to Olympia for a rally at eight o'clock. Nine hundred other fascists made their own way there. Olympia was planned as the second of three triumphal events designed to capitalise on the BUF's popular breakthrough, which had begun with a successful Albert Hall meeting in April and was to culminate in a massive gathering at the White City in August. But as early as 6.30, when people began to arrive at Olympia, the 750 police on duty began to have difficulty managing the hostile crowd, 5,000 strong, that had gathered outside to obstruct entry and to jeer at those who arrived by cab or by motor car.

There was no shortage of targets, for Olympia was as much a society occasion as a political meeting. Months of propaganda in the Rothermere press had made the BUF fashionable, as well as a serious threat to the National Government, and much of the establishment, including as many as 150 MPs and scores of titled ladies and gentlemen, turned up to witness the spectacle.[1] As a result, the 12,000-strong audience was not finally seated until 8.30; ten minutes later fifty-six Blackshirts bearing fascist flags and Union Jacks marched down the central aisle followed by Mosley illuminated by four powerful spotlights. As usual at BUF meetings there were few platform formalities, and after the National Anthem Mosley began a speech designed to last for an hour and a quarter. In the event it took him until 10.50. Almost from the start he was interrupted from the gallery by people shouting 'Fascism Means Murder' and 'Down With Mosley'.

Accounts of the disorder that occurred sporadically for the next two hours varied greatly according to the bias of the observers. In such a large gathering it was impossible for anyone to see more than a small part of the proceedings; there were only seven Special Branch men in the hall and none in the gallery where the worst fighting occurred. The many hostile accounts emphasised not just the violence used by the fascists but the novelty of the techniques employed – the powerful loudspeakers, the spotlights and the behaviour of the one thousand Blackshirt stewards in keeping order. Powerful lights were focused upon each interruptor who was then seized by stewards and beaten before being violently ejected from the meeting. Storm Jameson, one of several writers and journalists present, claimed that even fascist supporters were:

> at a loss to know why [Mosley] held up his speech at each interruption for periods varying from three to six minutes when he could perfectly well have drowned them with a voice made unbearably loud by the amplifiers. Slowly we all understood that it was done to allow his Blackshirts to make a thorough mess of the interruptor . . . a solitary man or woman stood up, made or began to make a remark inaudible to all but his close neighbours, and was instantly set on by a dozen or more Blackshirts and kicked and pummelled unrestrainedly, before being ejected.[2]

The hostile verdict on the Blackshirts was repeated by observers from the left and right of politics. 'I witnessed scenes of great brutality such as I had never thought to see in England,' wrote the Reverend Dick Shepherd, while the MP, Geoffrey Lloyd, recalled: ' I saw things [at Olympia] that made my blood boil as an Englishman and as a Tory.'[3] Three other Conservative Members, T. J. O'Connor, W. J. Anstruther-Gray and J. Scrymgeour Wedderburn, left Olympia to deliver a letter to *The Times* denouncing the stewards' violent handling of hecklers as unnecessary: 'It will be a matter of surprise to us if there were no fatal injuries.'[4] However, such remarks have to be treated with some caution because MPs who were loyal to the government – and Lloyd was Baldwin's Parliamentary Private Secretary – were even more anxious than the Labour Party to discredit Mosley now that he appeared to be attracting so much support from them.

In its defence the BUF claimed that its methods at Olympia were justified because it faced, not traditional heckling, but a concerted attempt to disrupt the meeting which had been planned well in advance. It seems clear from Special Branch reports, and from articles in the *Daily Worker*, that this was true. The Communist Party had decided to make a spectacular show of opposition at Olympia. It encouraged members to apply for tickets and even equipped them with black shirts to help them gain entry. However, to observers inside the meeting their organisation was not always obvious; interruptions were often made by respectably dressed people whose intervention seemed spontaneous and who appeared to be acting as individuals though, in fact, they were surrounded by bodies of supporters. When one interruption had been dealt with the next would begin, so as to extend the disruption for as long as possible.[5] The Communists also arranged for the large counter-demonstration outside, and witnesses saw groups of armed youths making their way to Olympia looking for a fight. Much of the violence occurred after the meeting when stink bombs were thrown, motor cars were attacked and some Blackshirts were obliged to leave under police escort. In dealing with the crowd of about 5,000 anti-fascists the police arrested twenty-three people several of whom were carrying offensive weapons.

Communist disruption long predated the establishment of the BUF. Throughout the 1920s they had targeted Labour politicians as much as Conservative ones. In the debate on Olympia Clement Attlee wryly observed that his own meetings as an East End MP were regularly shouted down by Communists.[6] However, Communist tactics fluctuated opportunistically between attempts to discredit Labour and offers to cooperate with it. Following Hitler's appointment as German Chancellor in January 1933 the Communists began to promote united action against fascism with the Labour Party, the trade unions and the Co-operative Party. As a result, large-scale anti-fascist campaigns developed in areas such as Tyneside where hostile crowds of up to 10,000 people had attacked BUF meetings addressed by the former Labour MP, John Beckett, in May 1934. However, the Labour Party dismissed collaborative action as a ploy to accelerate Communist infiltration, and it argued that in Britain direct action by the left would merely stimulate fascism. In the event, although thousands of people turned out for anti-fascist campaigns, the Communist Party enjoyed little lasting success – to judge, at least, from its membership which fell from 9,000 in 1932 to around 5,000 by 1934.[7]

After experiencing violent attacks on the New Party in 1930 Mosley had consistently argued that he needed a Defence Force to ensure that he would not be driven off the streets by 'roughs' and 'Reds'. At a meeting at Manchester's Free Trade Hall in March 1933, where fighting had broken out between interruptors using chairs and fascists wielding rubber truncheons, the police had intervened to exclude the stewards. Since then Mosley had consistently refused to allow the police into his meetings. The problem was largely confined to major cities where the fascists provoked the opposition by holding military-style musters. After a mass rally at Manchester's Belle Vue in October 1933 and a similar one at Bristol's Colston Hall in March 1934, hundreds of uniformed Blackshirts marched off to their headquarters, thus presenting an irresistible target for the hostile crowds waiting outside. Although critics increasingly condemned the paramilitary style as a major cause of disorder, the pageantry and spectacle created by uniforms, banners and marching represented a key part of the BUF's tactics at this stage; it attracted working-class activists and was intended to create an impression of strength for the benefit of middle-class sympathisers. Well before Olympia the BUF had attracted admiration in some quarters for its ability to control public meetings; at Belle Vue, for example, Mosley had employed exactly the same techniques as at Olympia, involving spotlights on hecklers followed by violent attacks by the stewards. Mosley knew quite well that morale would suffer if the Defence Force was not vigorously used, and several fascists privately acknowledged that they relied on the Communists even in quiet areas of the country; one West Country member noted: 'Now that we have active opposition in Exeter I think we shall make great progress there.'[8]

This raises the question of Mosley's motives in 1934. Did he intend to impress the members of the political establishment who had flocked to Olympia with a striking demonstration of his powers? This could explain his refusal to allow police inside the building and what looks like an over-reaction to the interruptions and the use of spotlights when his loudspeakers would have enabled him to continue his speech. However, Mosley claimed that the lights were controlled by the newsreel companies who wanted to highlight any dramatic action. Also, there is no evidence that the BUF made any special arrangements for Olympia, apart from having 1,000 stewards. Rightly or wrongly, Mosley regarded his speeches as the movement's major asset, and by June 1934 he was keen to make the most of his opportunity to get his message across to the influential people whom he had deliberately invited to the meeting. On this basis he would not have wanted Olympia to turn into a violent and disorderly affair. The alternative, and most likely, explanation is simply that Olympia was too large a venue to be manageable. At normal meetings Mosley enjoyed exercising his powers of repartee with the hecklers, so much so that he often instructed the stewards to leave them alone. But at Olympia this was impossible in view of the size of the audience and the systematic nature of the interruption. It was noticed that the stewards became frustrated, lost their temper and thus increasingly resorted to violence as the evening progressed.

Opponents of the BUF also overlooked the fact that it had the law on its side as far as indoor meetings were concerned. Although heckling was a recognised tradition in Britain, many politicians had been outraged during the Edwardian period by the systematic disruption organised by the Women's Social and Political Union, whose methods were now copied by the

Communists. As a result, in 1908 Lord Robert Cecil had introduced the Public Meetings Bill which made it an offence to create disorder at a meeting so as to prevent the transaction of the business. It allowed the organisers to use their own stewards to keep order as long as they used reasonable force; they were not obliged to admit the police unless actual disorder occurred.[9] Although not invoked against the suffragettes, the Act remained in force, thereby giving the advantage to organisations like the BUF that preferred to rely on their own stewards rather than the police.

The fascists also claimed in their defence that the critics greatly exaggerated the violence that occurred at Olympia. Deriding Geoffrey Lloyd as 'Mr Baldwin's little private jackal', Mosley demanded to know: 'where are the bodies?'[10] The initial police reports appeared to corroborate this scepticism. One merely recorded that thirty people had been ejected 'with a certain amount of violence', and at Hammersmith Police Station it was noted that the rally passed off 'without any serious violence'.[11] In the light of accounts describing people being set upon by groups of fascists, knocked to the ground and beaten until bloody and semi-conscious, this sounds like understatement of a remarkable order. It is, however, explicable. It is now thought that about fifty people were ejected from the meeting, some of whom received hospital treatment, though not for any length of time. In an audience of 12,000 these casualties were not very extensive as seen from the perspective of the London police who were quite accustomed to outbreaks of political violence.

By contrast, received impressions about Olympia are heavily coloured by selective quotation from a few hostile MPs and newspapers. In fact, not everyone was shocked. A *Daily Express* reporter noticed that while some women screamed, 'others, of bolder spirit, were standing on chairs watching the fighting through opera glasses and laughing with excitement'.[12] Many of the MPs present contradicted Lloyd, demanded evidence of the injuries treated in hospital and dismissed press accounts as exaggeration. 'I saw no undue brutality,' declared T. F. Howard. Earl Winterton pronounced himself relaxed about the injuries sustained as they had been inflicted 'in the good old-fashioned way by the use of a fist'. And F. A. Macquisten scoffed that 'almost a score of people got black eyes and that sort of thing. Why, they would get more than that in the Cowcaddens in Glasgow on a Saturday night!'[13] Such remarks remind us that many inter-war politicians had grown up in an era when violence was a routine part of local politics in Britain. All parties employed what they euphemistically called 'stewards', and even after 1918 candidates retained boxers for protection or to intimidate the opposition in places like the East End. The pride expressed by Mosley and his followers in the Blackshirts' readiness to fight was part of this long-standing tradition of violence, albeit one that was passing away by the 1930s.

According to received opinion, the British Union of Fascists reached its peak in the summer of 1934; but Olympia burst the bubble, sending the movement into a prolonged decline for the rest of the decade. The explanation is that respectable opinion suddenly woke up to the real nature of fascism and recoiled from its brutality, while the authorities intervened firmly to suppress its militarist techniques. According to the *News Chronicle* the 150 MPs present at Olympia were unanimous in condemning the behaviour of the Blackshirts there.[14] Even fascist sympathisers like Sir Charles Petrie argued retrospectively that Mosley had failed not because of his ideas and aims but because his methods made his movement appear too much like a foreign conspiracy. 'At this stage in our political evolution we certainly have no need of private armies marching about in exotic costumes and under exotic names,' pronounced the *Morning Post*, a newspaper otherwise sympathetic to fascist ideas.[15]

However, these comments created a misleading impression. Reactions to Olympia, even in the immediate situation, were far more complicated. Readers of the *Morning Post* insisted that the fascists had been the *victims*, not the perpetrators, of violence: 'I was disgusted at the unsporting and thoroughly un-British-like behaviour of the mob under the Red Flag,' wrote one female correspondent; and in the *National Review* Captain Luttman-Johnson testified to 'the fine bearing of the young Blackshirt men and women under extreme provocation'.[16] The Conservative weekly journals were very relaxed about Olympia, and several Tory MPs, including Sir Nicholas Grattan-Doyle and Patrick Donner, publicly contradicted Geoffrey Lloyd, congratulating the BUF on giving the 'Reds' an object lesson: 'without freedom of speech there can be no democracy,' insisted Donner. After inviting Mosley to speak at an *English Review* lunch Douglas Jerrold commented: 'cries of Fascist brutality hurt no one but Sir Oswald Mosley, and do not hurt him very much for few people believe them.'[17] To some extent this was corroborated by Special Branch who warned that the press had not accurately reflected popular reactions to Olympia:

> so far from causing widespread indignation . . . it provided an unprecedented fillip to recruitment. For the next two days people of different classes queued up from morning until night at the National Headquarters at Chelsea. A working man among the recruits remarked on the mixture of ex-officers, public schoolboys and working men, and the general admiration in the queue for the organisation of the Blackshirts and their determination to preserve the right of free speech.[18]

The truth is that while the violence alienated some people, it also added to the appeal of the BUF among the young and militant anti-Communists, with the result that the organisation experienced a major turnover of membership during 1934–5.

Within a few days of Olympia MPs began to put pressure on the government to get a grip on the situation. Amid alarmist claims that the BUF had acquired machine-guns, armoured cars and an air defence force, a succession of backbenchers demanded to know why no action had been taken to check the emergence of private armies.[19] On 14 June Isaac Foot, a West Country Liberal and enthusiast for temperance, the League of Nations and individual rights, initiated a parliamentary debate on Olympia. Accusing Mosley of using 'strange methods that are new to our politics', he highlighted his threat to suppress the Communist Party if he came to power.[20] Foot must have been dismayed, however, when the House of Commons failed to express the unanimous rejection of fascism and its alien methods that he desired. From the outset members interrupted to accuse him of sympathy for 'your friends the Communists'. Far from turning on the issue of free speech in the sense that Foot intended, the debate rapidly polarised into an argument about Fascism and Communism.

Moreover, as the House was dominated by supporters of the National Government, the discussion seemed increasingly to reflect the differences between two schools of Conservatism; more than any other event the argument over Olympia crystallised the dilemma facing those Conservatives who were disgusted by Baldwinism but still felt nervous about fascism. Slightly more of the National Government backbenchers spoke in defence of fascist methods in the debate than against them. This was the more striking since many of the prominent pro-fascists such as Colonel T. C. Moore, J. T. C. Moore-Brabazon, Alan Lennox-Boyd, Patrick Hannon and Henry Drummond Wolff did not even speak in the debate. Brushing aside suggestions that Mosley's methods posed a threat to freedom of speech, they ventilated their disgust at being the victims of left-wing disruption for years: 'It is a rotten business, and we do not get the right of free speech,' complained F. A. Macquisten. 'There is no doubt that what Sir Oswald Mosley said is true; he does get quietness . . . If the Fascist movement goes on . . . we shall ultimately get free speech everywhere.'[21] Several members insisted that hecklers had no right of interruption and could legitimately be required to leave their opponents' meetings. These reactions help to explain why the BUF was pleased by the outcome of Olympia; by resurrecting the threat posed by the extreme left it propelled the movement to the centre of right-wing politics.

Yet the most intriguing aspect of the Olympia debate consisted in the explanations offered by MPs for the rise of fascism and its implications. Michael Beaumont, who had been outed as a fascist by the *News Chronicle*, observed that 'up and down the country a large number of respectable, reasonable and intelligent people are joining this movement.' H. K. Hales described the BUF as 'something that has captured the imagination of the youth of both sexes and increased the number of its adherents from a few hundreds to about a quarter of a million [An Hon. Member: Where do you get the numbers from?]' Several speakers made a point of distinguishing between Mosley and his followers. 'I do admire the tens of thousands of young men who have joined the Blackshirt movement,' declared T. F. Howard. 'They are among the best element in this country.'[22] These members regarded the BUF as meeting the need for a livelier and more virile expression of Conservatism, similar to, but more successfully than, the smaller organisations of the 1920s. However, others recognised that under Mosley fascism had become a more ambitious movement and enjoyed greater potential.

Much of the accumulated resentment felt towards Baldwin now burst out. According to Macquisten, Mosley was 'stealing a great deal of the thunder of the Conservative Party by declaring he is going to do all the things they said they would do but have not yet done. That is very awkward for the Conservative Party but this is a matter on which Hon. Members had better talk to the Conservative leaders.' Several members were clearly more exercised by the electoral significance of fascism than by the law-and-order problem. 'In my division young men are going over to the Blackshirt movement in shoals,' reported Howard, while Hales warned: 'if it continues to make progress it will have a big effect on the next election.'[23] Many of these Conservatives represented vulnerable seats won unexpectedly in 1931 which were lost in 1935 even in the absence of fascist intervention; in 1934, when Mosley was threatening to run at least a hundred candidates, they naturally feared that he would split the government's vote and let Labour back into office. From this perspective political logic pointed more to an accommodation with fascism than an attempt to suppress its organisation and methods.

Such calculations doubtless underlay the cautious response of the Home Secretary, Sir John Gilmour, to the debate. The fond belief that the authorities stepped in, once alerted to the threat posed by fascism to freedom of speech, is a myth. Gilmour, after all, had been favourably impressed by the smaller-scale military formations of the British Fascists in the 1920s. He now impaled himself firmly on the fence, backing away from any suggestion of legislation to curb drilling or uniforms, and even from an enquiry into existing laws and regulations: 'the worst thing we could do for democracy and for this House is to appear as if we were being stampeded.' He reiterated that fascist stewards were fully justified in ejecting anyone who disturbed their meetings, contenting himself with expressing the hope that in future they would allow the police to help.[24]

But Gilmour's ministerial platitudes succeeded in misleading the House as to the government's intentions; Cuthbert Headlam understood that they would legislate after consulting the party leaders, whereas Earl Winterton congratulated him for his undertaking to abstain from intervention.[25] In fact, at a meeting just before the debate ministers had agreed merely to watch the situation but to hint at the possibility of action.[26] When Gilmour invited his colleagues to consider whether it was desirable to tackle the wearing of uniforms, military drilling and police powers to control meetings, reactions were as inconclusive as ever. The Attorney General, Sir Thomas Inskip, catalogued the objections to doing anything. Drilling, he thought, might be stopped under the 1819 Act but as it was so old he would be reluctant to use it; he did not know how a political uniform might be defined, whether it would include armlets, sashes and badges, and how this would affect the Boy Scouts and the Salvation Army.[27]

There was, however, a suggestion that the Opposition leaders should be consulted about legislation. Yet consensus proved surprisingly elusive. The parliamentary debate had made it clear that intervention to restrict fascist activity would antagonise some Conservatives; Beaumont had specifically warned against trying to suppress the BUF. But with Mosley's next major rally at the While City now looming, the anti-fascist Tory members, Vyvyan Adams and Anstruther-Gray, wanted to know how Gilmour was going to handle it. Consultations with Lloyd George and Sir Herbert Samuel produced no result; they thought it impractical to eliminate private armies and hoped that they would die a natural death, a particularly feeble response from the official leaders of Liberalism.[28] Meanwhile the Labour Party was typically confused. On 26 June Clement Attlee and Walter Citrine waited on the Home Secretary to introduce a deputation from the TUC and the Labour Party. Citrine made no secret of the fact that they were finding it increasingly difficult to restrain the younger elements in their organisations who felt angry at the apathy of the union leaders and the inaction of the government. He cited a recent raid on the Blackshirt headquarters in Newcastle to support his claim that the left was already beginning to emulate the fascists.[29] On the other hand, Labour and the ILP strongly opposed giving the police extra powers to enter meetings, partly because of their belief that the law was not applied impartially as between left and right.[30]

Any prospect of agreement with Labour was further compromised by the Incitement to Disaffection Bill which was already making its way through parliament at this time. Designed to deter pacifists and Communists from seducing members of the armed forces from their duty by written word, it introduced punishments of up to two years in prison, or a fine of £200; even possession of literature was sufficient to convict for intent to commit an offence. The government's determination to deal with what was seen as a non-existent problem contrasted sharply with its reluctance to tackle the very tangible threat posed by fascist activity. Condemned by the National Council for Civil Liberties, the Bill was interpreted by Labour as proof of official bias against the working class and of ministers' desire to curtail the right of protest on the left.[31] One of the most embarrassing episodes at Olympia had been the entry of uniformed police into the outer corridors, where they rescued several hecklers who were being savagely beaten up by the stewards. Faced with blatant evidence of the disorder, however, the police had declined to enter the main hall; subsequently Gilmour claimed that it was not their duty to do so and that they had no authority to. This was shown to be incorrect shortly afterwards by a legal case (*Thomas v. Sawkins*) which arose from the entry of police into a Communist meeting in South Wales despite the protests of the organisers. Such cases appeared to corroborate claims that the police used the law selectively with the approval of ministers and the magistrates.

Given this lack of cross-party agreement, the cabinet was left to make up its own mind about how to deal with Mosley. Behind the scenes Sir Hugh Trenchard, Chief Commissioner of the Metropolitan Police, strongly reinforced the fears expressed by the Labour delegation. Both the BUF and the Communist Party had been 'delighted with the results of Olympia', he reported: 'each felt that it had given a great impulse to the movement.'[32] According to the police the fascists were busy throughout July opening new branches and holding meetings; but this had given a dangerous stimulus to anti-fascist activity. Trenchard instanced a meeting at Shoreditch Town Hall attended by a body of thirty Communists wearing khaki shirts and grey flannel trousers: 'they imitated exactly the Mosley tactics.'[33] By the end of July a Co-ordinating Committee for Anti-Fascist Activities had been established with the backing of the former Labour MP, John Strachey, Willie Gallagher, Ellen Wilkinson (currently a Labour MP), Fenner Brockway and Harry Pollitt. Its immediate task was to organise a counter-demonstration against Mosley's next major rally at the White City.

Trenchard, meanwhile, returned to his earlier theme by placing the BUF in the context of Continental fascist movements. During 1933 Hitler had effectively suppressed all political activity outside Nazi control, subjected his opponents to uncontrolled violence, and opened the first concentration camp at Dachau; at the end of June 1934 opinion outside Germany was horrified by the 'Night of the Long Knives' when the Chief of Staff, Ernst

Röhm, and leading SA members were arrested and executed. According to Trenchard:

> Superficially, at least, the BUF follow Nazi methods very closely. There is the same massing of banners, the same spotlight on the 'Leader', the same defence force, the same facile promises of relief from economic stress, the same kind of excessive simplification of thought wholly at variance with the complexities of life.[34]

He bluntly warned that once the fascists gained a share of power via a general election they would proceed to suppress all hostile opinion. Trenchard's diagnosis was now very similar to that advanced by John Strachey – that Britain was in danger of repeating the mistake the Germans had made in handling the Nazis.[35] However, despite this pressure, ministers felt tempted to follow the more sanguine view expressed by Cuthbert Headlam and several backbenchers who believed that too much controversy and attention merely advertised the fascists; it was wiser to let things take their course even if that meant allowing the stage armies of left and right to fight it out among themselves.[36]

What effects did Olympia have on fascist fortunes? On the one hand *The Blackshirt* flourished letters of congratulation from Tory MPs, though the only recruit was Commander Carlyon Bellairs, the former member for Maidstone. The Earl of Erroll became the BUF's representative in Kenya.[37] But by far the most notable recruit was J. F. C. Fuller, a choleric Major-General and distinguished military reformer who had been placed on the retirement list at fifty-five in 1933. In retrospect 'Boney' Fuller attributed his conversion to fascism to the frustration of his proposals for the mechanisation of the British army by a complacent military establishment. Although this may have been one factor, it overlooked the fact that Fuller's obsessive anti-Semitism, his paranoia about the League of Nations and contempt for democracy already predisposed him to fascism; a frank admirer of strong leaders, he believed in the corporate state as a means of removing power from the ignorant masses.[38] Fuller thus welcomed Mosley's conduct at Olympia and he became a key figure in BUF organisation as well as a parliamentary candidate.

On the other hand, the, admittedly unreliable, evidence about BUF membership points to a significant decline after Olympia, from a peak of 40,000–50,000 in 1934 to as few as 5,000 in 1935, followed by a revival to over 15,000 in 1936 and over 22,000 by 1939.[39] These Special Branch figures were an indication of the trends rather than a precise estimate, especially as the security services were not well-informed about fascist activity outside

London. The only surviving list of paying branch members is in Dorset which records 29 names in July 1935, a total which seems consistent with the view that this was the low point.[40] Interestingly, sales of *The Blackshirt* were 22,000 at this time, five times as many as the supposed membership.[41] This seems to indicate a substantial number of passive members who allowed their membership to lapse during 1935. Whether this was simply due to Olympia remains unclear.

During 1935 the movement became consumed with debate about its strategy and organisation, and Mosley was caught out when the National Government decided to hold an early general election in November of that year. This decision was determined largely by ministers' confidence in the economic recovery which had led to a small fall in unemployment and the restoration of the financial cuts made in 1931. Influenced by the experience of the New Party in 1931, Mosley felt chary about risking an embarrassing defeat for his candidates. At a specially called meeting at the Porchester Hall in October he announced that despite having 472 branches the BUF was not ready for a general election; fascists were free to vote for the 'Old Gang' parties but Mosley himself would abstain.[42] During the three weeks of the campaign the movement distributed fascist propaganda and Mosley continued to hold meetings, presumably hoping to benefit from the heightened public awareness engendered by the election but without the costs and risks. The BUF claimed that as it had existed for only three years it needed time to perfect its organisation, and the decisive struggle would come at the next election. However, its abstention could only be interpreted as a sign of weakness, and it inevitably killed some of the momentum until 1936 when fresh anti-Semitic and pro-peace campaigns reinvigorated the movement.

Much the most obvious explanation for the BUF's loss of 'respectable' middle-class support lay in the reactions of the media. After allowing Mosley to defend his action at Olympia, the BBC banned him for the next thirty-four years. One month after the rally Lord Rothermere decided to withdraw the support of his newspapers from the BUF. In Southport John Charnley recalled that recruitment fell off when the *Daily Mail* stopped promoting the movement, though he felt that many of the new recruits were opportunists or 'milk and water [fascists] who could not stand the pace and fell away when the going got tough'.[43] An internal BUF memorandum even suggested that Rothermere had harmed the cause by introducing 'a flood of paper members and induced some of the old active members to rest on their laurels'. General Fuller thought the Rothermere recruits had not been utilised properly, presumably because the organisation had been too focused on street politics to involve new members in the kind of activities they were accustomed to.[44] However, Fuller argued that hostility by the newspapers was actually advantageous in the early stages of a new movement because it 'puts enthusiasts on their mettle and keeps out the jellyfish'.[45]

The reason for Rothermere's decision is not entirely clear. Were the eyes of Rothermere and his readers opened when the violence displayed at Olympia showed them that the movement was more extreme than they had realised? This is not entirely plausible since the methods used were not new, and had even been commended by his newspapers, at least initially: 'when the necessity is forced on them, the Blackshirts are able and willing to meet violence with violence,' pronounced the *Sunday Dispatch*.[46] To some extent the British fascists were now discredited by association with the brutality of their Continental counterparts; Olympia was closely followed by the 'Night of the Long Knives', the notorious massacre of the Brownshirts by Hitler's SS on 30 June. But how far this influenced Rothermere must be doubtful, as he continued to write enthusiastically about Hitler right up to 1939.[47] In his letter to Mosley, Rothermere offered an alternative explanation when he said that he could not support anti-Semitism, though as his newspapers had already refuted such charges this seems inconsistent.[48] According to Reynall Bellamy, Rothermere told Mosley he had to pull out because of objections from his advertisers; catering firms such as Joe Lyons threatened to withdraw their full-page advertisements for swiss rolls and other comestibles if he continued to support Mosley.[49] This claim appears more credible in that Rothermere was sensitive to economic pressure; under stiff competition from the (anti-Mosley) *Daily Express*, the *Daily Mail* was losing circulation in an over-crowded middlebrow market.

Rothermere's vulnerability to such pressure underlines the point that his original support for the BUF had been conditional; he had attempted to make the movement sound less alien by dropping the word 'fascist' and referring only to the 'Blackshirts'.[50] Also, as a businessman he disliked the idea of the corporate state. In time he began to appreciate that, despite his backing for the organisation, he could not expect to dictate policy to Mosley. Essentially Rothermere had intended to use Mosley as another weapon against Baldwin, hoping to destroy the current Tory leadership and shift the party to the right, as he and the other press barons had been doing since the early 1920s. However, as the return of a Labour government would be even worse than Baldwin, he was always likely to withdraw at some stage. In 1934, with Labour winning by-elections and National Government supporters fearful of a split in their vote, it was time for a tactical retreat. This was underlined by the friendly exchange of letters between the two men in July. 'You have a unique gift of personal appeal,' wrote Rothermere, 'and the assistance which I have rendered you was given in the hope that you would be prepared to ally yourself with the Conservative forces to defeat Socialism at the next and succeeding elections. I do not see why we should not come together on the foregoing lines.'[51] Ultimately, then, it was not so much the brutality of the fascists at Olympia or ideological disagreements that had complicated relations between the two, but Mosley's insistence on pursuing an electoral strategy.

Although Rothermere's newspapers stopped actively promoting the BUF after July 1934, their action during the previous six months had the lasting effect of making the fascists newsworthy. The *Daily Mail*, *The Times*, *Daily Telegraph* and *Morning Post* continued to carry reports of Mosley's speeches around the country. However, Special Branch reported that during August and September the rush of new recruits had dwindled and in several parts of the country the movement showed signs of receding. It did not attribute this to Olympia directly, but to the emergence of a more regular and physical opposition to the BUF.[52] The movement received very hostile treatment in the *News Chronicle*, *Daily Express*, *Daily Herald* and *Manchester Guardian* which invariably reported fascist activities in connection with violent disturbances. However, since public meetings were regarded as essential for the fascists' campaign, in addition to street sales of *The Blackshirt* and *Action*, Mosley had no choice but to press ahead with them regardless of how they were reported.

Whether he felt obliged to modify fascist tactics after Olympia seems doubtful. Special Branch claimed that at some meetings Mosley was made to look ridiculous by noisy heckling and interruptions and, because he could not use unlimited force, he abandoned his claims to keep control.[53] Yet this was more an expression of hope than a description of the pattern of events over the next two years. The evidence gathered by Special Branch was, like that of the national press, biased towards big set rallies in London; but in the provinces things were different. In July 1934 Mosley addressed enthusiastic meetings at Worcester, Swansea, Ipswich and Preston with no disorder.[54] By November he was boasting that since Olympia he had held twenty-five large indoor meetings with no police presence and had relied on the fascist Defence Force alone: 'we have, after a long struggle, established freedom of speech and impressed upon the Government some sense of duty to the public.'[55] This was not simply bravado. During 1934 and 1935 fascist meetings took place in many small and medium-sized provincial towns with minimal or no interruption, let alone violence.[56] In January 1935, for example, William Joyce arrived at the Corn Exchange in Dorchester. Before the meeting Blackshirts marched around the town carrying black-and-yellow banners and Union Jacks, then stood around the hall with their flags and banners displayed against the walls. For two hours Joyce addressed an audience of 150 people, some of whom had paid 1s. 6d. for their seats, without interruption.[57] This was how fascism operated across much of provincial England, especially during the later 1930s as it developed its 'peace' campaign; this is easily forgotten because the official sources for the period tend to be dominated by reports of disorderly scenes in London and a handful of big cities.

Even in populous areas Mosley usually continued to employ the same stewarding methods at his indoor meetings. In October 1935 he addressed nine hundred people at the Porchester Hall in London where he was supported by one hundred stewards who removed five people on his specific instructions.[58] The previous July it required three hundred policemen to escort him into his meeting at the Town Hall in West Ham. Drowned out at first by booing, shouting and jeering, he used his stewards to remove the most vocal interruptors and was then heard in peace until he referred to the Jews. Renewed disturbances at this point led to a further fifteen removals, but the meeting ended peacefully with thirty minutes devoted to answering questions. Faced with complaints from the local Labour MP that they had stood by while interruptors were violently handled, the police insisted that they were not stewards, and that anyone who refused to leave when asked was a trespasser and could legitimately be removed.[59]

The only qualification to this pattern arose where an individual chief constable adopted a different policy. For example, in May 1935 Mosley travelled to Newcastle-upon-Tyne for a rally at the city hall. When the stewards threatened to eject interruptors the police entered the building and allowed them to remain; after attempting to speak for half an hour Mosley abandoned the meeting, but this was a rare retreat.[60] Sir Hugh Trenchard also dealt firmly with the prospective BUF rally at the White City, which held 80,000–90,000 people, in August 1934. Aware that the Communists planned another mass agitation, including strikes by transport workers to prevent Mosley getting there and by catering employees to cut off the usual food supplies, he intervened to insist that the owners allow police inside. He made it clear that they would permit heckling but intervene to stop any fighting and simply close the meeting if things became too disorderly.[61] Mosley decided to transfer the rally to Hyde Park and then postponed it to September. While these examples indicate how effectively resolute police action could cramp the fascists' style, they were exceptions; usually Mosley continued to police his own meetings as before.

Outdoor activities were another story. There, the chief constables adopted a more consistently interventionist policy, although this usually worked to the advantage of the BUF. For example, when the Dorset fascists wanted to hold a meeting they routinely notified the chief constable who simply acknowledged the request as a matter of course.[62] In Huddersfield the BUF conducted open-air meetings with permission of the police and experienced no disorder.[63] When the police banned a fascist meeting in the Market Place in Leicester in September 1934 for fear of disorder, William Joyce promptly asked the chief constable to say where they could hold a meeting. This was a shrewd way of ensuring that the police would accept responsibility for controlling any counter-demonstration.[64] The Leicester case produced an admission from the Home Office that chief constables had no legal right to ban meetings; in practice they tried to regulate the time and place of open-air meetings but were always open to challenge in the courts.[65] Hence their reluctance to intervene too often.

On some occasions the sheer size of anti-fascist counter-demonstrations in major cities including Sheffield, Hull, Leeds and Newcastle forced the BUF into retreat. Shortly after Olympia Mosley planned a rally on the town moor in Newcastle, for example, but cancelled it because of the opposition.[66] When his adjourned White City meeting eventually took place in Hyde Park in September the 3,000 fascists were surrounded by crowds estimated at between 60,000 and 150,000 and a cordon of 6,000 police. When Mosley appeared at Hull in July 1936 the Blackshirts were eventually forced to withdraw after an hour's fighting. According to the local police: 'The Fascists were not to blame as nothing was said or done to provoke the crowd. They did not interfere with anyone until bricks and other missiles were thrown and one of the party seriously injured.'[67]

These experiences indicate that Mosley was correct in thinking that the BUF had most to gain by promising to respect the law and by cooperating with the police. During the mid-1930s the police regularly protected open-air fascist meetings from hostile demonstrations, while leaving the Blackshirts to keep order at indoor gatherings by means of a judicious use of force. The conventional political parties calculated that they could live with this; Labour became more complacent about fascism after Rothermere withdrew his support, and the National Government took comfort from its success in retaining its majority at the 1935 general election. Consequently, for several years no steps were taken to check fascism, despite the controversy generated by Olympia.

Two conflicting explanations have been offered for this. Contemporaries such as John Strachey believed fascism had been checked by mobilising the working-class opposition, thereby demonstrating to the middle classes that fascism was far less strong than they had supposed. Strachey was correct at least to the extent that the Labour leaders' writ did not always run at local level where Labour members cooperated with ILP activists and

Communists. However, the cooperation was limited and sporadic; even Stafford Cripps thought it desirable to keep the membership separate from other left-wing organisations, and after its lively start, the anti-fascist campaign went into a decline during 1935.[68] An alternative explanation is that by abstaining from anti-fascist campaigns the Labour Party had the effect of reassuring the right wing of British politics that fears of some great Communist-fascist struggle were exaggerated; in effect, by reinforcing the liberal-democratic consensus, it helped to marginalise fascism. This seems valid at least to the extent that Labour leaders were loyal and orthodox supporters of the system, though this was not always acknowledged. But the explanation is not wholly convincing because many Tory politicians refused to conceal their dislike for the parliamentary system or their sympathy with fascism. Having stood on the sidelines through 1934, 1935 and most of 1936, the cabinet was eventually driven, reluctantly, to intervene against fascism by means of the Public Order Act which finally came into force in January 1937.

While it would be an exaggeration to suggest that the anti-fascist movement was the direct cause of the government's action, it did have an indirect effect by virtue of the pressure exerted on and by the police. During 1936 the BUF had discovered the value of anti-Semitism as an expedient for rejuvenating their movement, at least in the East End of London. However, they overreached themselves. As a result, by July the cabinet felt obliged to reconsider empowering the police to enter indoor meetings without invitation, and to prohibit outdoor meetings and marches which were likely to intimidate or cause a breach of the peace. Ministers feared that parliament was unlikely to agree to such a proposal because the habit of public meetings was 'so deeply engrained in English life that it appears ... to be impracticable'.[69] However, the reactions to Jew-baiting by the fascists in the East End created widespread disorder throughout the summer and autumn.

Although the police were as reluctant as the government to intervene against anti-Semitism, they recognised that the BUF had gained popularity in the East End, registering an additional 2,000 members in October.[70] Sir Philip Game of the Metropolitan Police pointed out that several leading fascists had decided to ignore Mosley's instructions to refrain from attacking Jews; convinced that they could not afford to back down, they intended to court prosecution for anti-Semitism.[71] To this end they made a practice of transferring their meetings from quiet areas to places where opposition was virtually guaranteed.[72] As a result things got out of control during 1936. Every month the police were obliged to attend hundreds of meetings in the East End, placing an intolerable strain on their resources. Even in November and December, when activities tailed off, there were still 500 meetings a month. In early December the fascists were briefly diverted by the Abdication crisis and then by the London County Council elections in the spring of 1937, but by then the cabinet had decided to intervene.

The climax of this phase came with the notorious 'Battle of Cable Street' on 4 October 1936, an episode that entered political mythology as the occasion when fascism was forced to retreat by counter-demonstrations. Strictly speaking, Cable Street involved another fight between the police and the anti-fascists rather than between fascists and anti-fascists. The police became convinced that it was highly undesirable for them to be forced into conflict with the working-class community in this way. Sir Philip Game, who warned that the BUF had become a much more dangerous movement during 1936, effectively admitted that the Metropolitan Police were unable to handle the situation. He therefore asked the cabinet to legislate for a ban on uniforms and on party political defence corps and to grant extra powers to prohibit marches.[73]

However, Game was not optimistic about the effectiveness of such measures. He thought a ban on uniforms would have only a marginal effect in removing 'some of its spectacular appeal to the young and foolish'. Restrictions on processions would have to be used sparingly because if the Communists defied them the police would become embroiled in even more clashes with working men. The best solution, Game insisted, would be the suppression of fascist organisation altogether. This the government refused to contemplate, and it therefore opted for the less controversial policy, as Game probably anticipated. It may have been significant that Game was dealing with a new Home Secretary, Sir John Simon, who replaced Gilmour in 1935. Though much derided in right-wing circles for his lawyerly indecision, Simon had impeccable liberal credentials, and was on record as opposing 'this dressing up in fancy uniforms and this aping of military organisation for political purposes'.[74] Under his skilful guidance the Public Order Bill was introduced into the Commons on 16 November and received the Royal Assent on 18 December.

The most widely known provision of the 1936 Act was the prohibition on the wearing of uniform in public places where it signified association with a political organisation. It also banned quasi-military organisations, that is, any in which the members were trained and equipped to enable them to usurp the functions of the police or the armed forces, or to use force to promote a political object. Chief constables received power to impose conditions on the route of processions and marches if they had grounds for anticipating disorder, and could apply to their local councils for a ban extending to three months. It became illegal for people at public meetings or in public places to carry offensive weapons and to use abusive, insulting or threatening language and behaviour. The punishment for offences committed under the Act were up to six months in prison, a fine of £100 or both.[75]

In view of this range of provisions there can be no simple verdict on the effectiveness of the Public Order Act. Contrary to expectations, it was by no means the uncomplicated anti-fascist measure it purported to be. In connection with public meetings, for example, the new law reaffirmed the right to use stewards to preserve order and to wear badges, which was not quite consistent with the ban on quasi-military organisation. The maintenance of the status quo was obvious at Mosley's meeting at Hornsey Town Hall on 25 January 1937 when stewards violently ejected four hecklers while the police remained outside and refused to intervene or even identify those responsible. The new Act even went further by adding to the provisions of the 1908 Public Meetings Act by empowering the police to require an interruptor to give his name and address if suspected of committing an offence. As this was calculated to deter hecklers and make a private prosecution easier, it clearly strengthened the already advantageous position enjoyed by the fascists.[76]

The restrictive powers in connection with marches were first exercised in June 1937 when the Metropolitan Police banned a fascist march from Limehouse to Trafalgar Square for six weeks and subsequently to the end of the year. However, this had only a limited effect, for the BUF simply routed the march outside the prohibited area. Some 110 fascist marches and 3,094 meetings took place in London during the first ten months of the new legislation.[77] Not only did these restrictions on marches fail to stem the expansion of the BUF in London, they were also used against left-wing marches; ministers had doubtless seen this as a valuable long-term advantage of passing the Public Order Act.

For its part the BUF adopted a policy of compliance with the law judiciously mingled with defiance. This was reflected in its response to the ban on quasi-military organisations which, interpreted literally, might have been designed to put an end to the organisation. However, this was not at all the object. Just before the Act came into force the BUF took the precaution of suspending all rankings and modifying any titles that appeared to flout the law. These changes were purely cosmetic: for example, 'Chief of Staff' became 'Director of Public Relations', 'Chief Contact Officer' became 'Contact Administrator', and 'London Command' became 'London Administration'. This was sufficient to make it difficult to prosecute the organisation without making any fundamental alteration to its operation.

Much more attention was devoted to the ban on uniforms. The Blackshirts themselves held contradictory opinions about it. Quite apart from its value as an aid to identification in a crowd, the uniform was regarded by many members as a symbol of the unifying purpose of fascism: 'the wearing of the simple black shirt eliminated all feelings of class distinction,' as Louise Irving put it.[78] However, by 1937 feelings had become more mixed. Reynall Bellamy regarded it essentially as a novelty which had helped to advertise the movement in its early stages but had now achieved its purpose.[79] Major-General Fuller went further, seeing uniform as something that alarmed people 'whose instincts are against violent change . . . It may appeal to the young and inexperienced, but if it remains unchecked it will lose more votes at the next election than anything else.'[80] If Fuller was correct, the uniform ban helped to promote the growth of a respectable fascist movement.

As early as September 1936 special instructions had been sent out from headquarters warning members to obey the law by not wearing uniform in public places.[81] Privately, however, they believed that the Public Order Act would be a dead letter in a year's time. This belief was based on the assumption that a badge or an armlet worn on a black shirt could not be defined as a uniform.[82] The BUF also took legal advice which indicated that an ordinary black shirt or a black polo sweater worn with civilian clothes would not fall foul of the new law.[83] Mosley deliberately appeared at his Hornsey meeting at the end of January in a black shirt, defying the government to prosecute him: 'neither they nor anybody else have yet been able to define what a political uniform is,' he scoffed.[84] In fact Mosley continued to wear what the fascists called 'undress' uniform without interference while the stewards at meetings wore armlets.

However, this was largely bravado, a necessary form of defiance by a great leader who could not afford to be browbeaten by the politicians he affected to despise. In fact the BUF's legal advice was unsound.[85] John Charnley was charged and fined £10, the magistrate ruling that the flash-and-circle armband was an unlawful uniform even when worn with civilian clothing.[86] During the first month of 1937 six people were convicted for wearing the uniform.[87] On the other hand, there are too many photographs of uniformed Blackshirts in public places during 1937 and 1938 to substantiate the claim that the uniform was completely discontinued.[88] It was scarcely feasible for the authorities to prosecute every offender; they simply hoped that the Act would have a deterrent effect, especially if the police took names and addresses of fascists wearing uniform with an added threat that prosecution might follow. Some were deterred. In Newcastle, Robert Richard recalled that, after some acts of defiance, the Blackshirts did mothball their uniforms in 1937, though they continued to wear them at headquarters.[89]

In fact, the ban on uniforms was not absolute; those who wished to wear them on ceremonial, anniversary or other special occasions could apply for permission to the local police who consulted the Home Office. During 1937 requests were considered from the Social Credit Party, the Greenshirts, the Woodcraft Folk, the Orange Order and the Peterborough Labour Male Voice Choir. Surprisingly the civil servants had failed to consider the implications of the Public Order Act for the marches and uniforms used by the Orange Order in Liverpool and by both Republicans and Unionists in Northern Ireland. Unwilling to stir up trouble, the Merseyside police claimed, somewhat implausibly, that Orange Order regalia was not clothing and thus not uniform.[90] Indeed, the local authorities were disposed to take a lenient view of requests to wear uniform, while the Home Office, safely aloof from the backlash, adopted a stricter line. Officials thought the Peterborough Male Voice Choir innocuous in itself, but wondered: 'what is to prevent the fascists from putting their members in uniform and claiming that they are all members of the "totalitarian choir"?' They were right to be cautious, for the BUF continued to probe the law. At Bognor the fascists asked to wear uniform in the Coronation Procession, which the police approved provided the marchers were local members and remained part of the main procession. East Grinstead members were granted permission to wear uniform for the fifth anniversary of the BUF as long as they avoided a public meeting. In December the BUF was allowed uniform at a dance held at the Seymour Hall in London on the basis that this was a private function. After a year the Home Office officials admitted that they 'had hoped that the passing of the Public Order Act would have so discouraged political organisations that they would give up altogether the maintenance of their uniforms'.[91]

Despite these qualifications, the ban on uniform was probably the most effective part of the Public Order Act, though it was clearly not very thoroughly enforced. In other respects, however, the legislation made no more than a marginal impact at most. As the campaign in the East End was to show, the police only occasionally invoked the proscription on insulting language and threatening speeches. The BUF made a calculated show of respect for the law, but maintained its military organisation, including its control over indoor meetings. The curtailment of some of its marches was a price well worth paying for embroiling the police with the anti-fascist demonstrators. If the Public Order Act had been introduced in 1934 it would almost certainly have made a greater impact; but by 1937 it was too late. By this time the BUF was moving on, outside the East End at least, to the 'peace' campaign, which was a more conventional and respectable affair, and focusing more on preparations for a general election expected around 1939–40.

TEN

'Drinking Tea With Treason':
Fascism and the Defence of Empire

'Our historic right to be in India is the same as the historic right of all our predecessors: the power of original conquest.'

Oswald Mosley, *The Greater Britain* (1932)

In September 1931 M. K. Gandhi attended a tea party at Buckingham Palace in connection with the Second Round Table Conference on Indian constitutional reform. King George V, who had initially refused to invite him, was reportedly affronted by the usual white cotton *khaddar* he wore. When Sir Samuel Hoare, the Secretary of State, introduced the Congress leader, 'the conversation began safely in a fog of platitudes about the weather'. But soon a chilly silence descended until the King blurted out: 'I tell you what it is, Mr Gandhi. I am to have none of your damned interference in my Empire.'[1] Never at a loss, Gandhi responded: 'I must not be drawn into a political discussion with Your Majesty when I am receiving Your Majesty's hospitality.' Questioned later by journalists on whether his dress was not rather scanty for the occasion, Gandhi cheerfully explained: 'The King was wearing enough for both of us.' The entire visit, by a man commonly regarded as a subversive agitator only recently released from gaol, encapsulates the anger and frustration of British imperialists anxious to preserve the empire from its enemies both abroad and at home; they believed the King could stop the rot if only he could be prised from the suffocating embrace of politicians like Samuel Hoare.

From an imperialist perspective the case for maintaining the Indian Raj seemed unanswerable in the 1920s. If the British quit, India would surely revert to the state of chaos in which they had found her in the eighteenth century. A society so deeply divided along lines of religion, caste, class and language could hardly remain a coherent political entity without the central control exercised by an external force. Imperialists believed that for most Indian peasant farmers the idea of a nation state was an irrelevance, and the grievances trumpeted by nationalist leaders reflected the interests of a handful of westernised lawyers, journalists and academics who commanded no influence among their fellow countrymen. This diagnosis was not wholly wrong. Founded back in 1885, the Indian National Congress had been restricted to educated, westernised men concentrated in Bombay, Madras and Calcutta, who had avoided taking up the social-economic issues that concerned ordinary Indians; they valued British rule as a unifying and modernising force in Indian society too strongly to wish to sweep it suddenly away.

Nonetheless, the imperialist analysis was deeply flawed. Although the Raj was ostensibly a military autocracy, it never possessed sufficient force to control such a vast country without a large measure of consent. As the British allowed some scope for criticising the government, notably through freedom of the press, and familiarised Indians with the ideas of liberal democracy, it proved impossible in the long run to maintain an unqualified autocracy in India. By the turn of the century many liberals considered British rule to be justified only if it led Indians gradually towards self-rule through wider participation in government. In this sense the imperialists were correct in seeing the real enemy within Britain itself. In practice the British never pursued a consistent strategy, but instead vacillated between periods of repression and phases of conciliation and reform. But for the critics even the slightest concession represented a danger because, if accepted, it became a lever for further reform, while if spurned by Indians it generated pressure for a more sweeping measure.

The First World War accelerated India's political evolution by generating economic grievances in the form of rising prices, food shortages and discontent over land revenue among small farmers. In this situation the new Secretary of State for India, Edwin Montagu, took a liberal and realistic view. At a time when millions of Indians had been mobilised to fight for the empire and a 'Home Rule' campaign had spread across the country, it would have been foolish to ignore the Indians' legitimate political aspirations. Accordingly in 1917 Montagu redefined British policy in terms of the development of self-governing institutions with a view to the eventual achievement of responsible government within the empire. The Montagu–Chelmsford Report of April 1918 proposed giving the vote to five million Indians, creating elective majorities in the provincial councils, and devolving powers over health, education, agriculture and public works to them. After ten years the new system was to be reviewed with a view to extending participation further.

Inevitably a severe reaction against the reforms soon developed in Britain. Post-war agitation in India, largely stimulated by economic discontent, was interpreted by many imperialists as proof of Bolshevik influence in the subcontinent. They therefore looked urgently for evidence of firm government and found it in Sir Michael O'Dwyer, the Lieutenant Governor of the Punjab. In March 1919 O'Dwyer imposed martial law after extensive disorder, looting and acts of violence towards Europeans in the towns of the Punjab. This culminated in the notorious action of General Reginald Dyer who banned public meetings in Amritsar and ordered his troops to fire on a gathering in the Jallianwallah Bagh, killing nearly four hundred in the process. Although Dyer was sacked for what became known as the 'Amritsar Massacre', in Britain he became a hero among imperialists who believed he had saved India from revolution by his timely intervention.[2] The *Morning Post*, the self-proclaimed champion of empire, launched a fund to support the former general, and eventually succeeded in driving Montagu from office.

In India Amritsar and its political backwash undermined the impact of Montagu's policy by making it embarrassing for Indians to cooperate with the new system. Moreover, another powerful factor was now at work. In 1915 Gandhi had returned to India after many years in South Africa where he had experimented with his techniques of non-violent action. At first neither the British nor his fellow Indians understood Gandhi because he placed little importance on the institutional approach to self-government; Gandhi believed that before Indians reached that goal they should gain greater awareness of and confidence in Indian culture, and distance themselves from western society. To this end he took up social and economic issues, including land revenue and self-sufficiency, rather than grand constitutional questions; and he demonstrated his ability to mobilise comparatively humble Indians who spoke the vernacular languages and had previously been uninvolved in political activity. From 1919 to 1922 he kept the country in continuous agitation. This involved a boycott of all things British including imported textiles which were consigned to huge bonfires. Gandhi's use of non-violence was not merely a technique to make it awkward for the authorities to repress the movement, it was also an expression of a philosophy designed to develop self-confidence and moral superiority among people hitherto unwilling to challenge the Raj.

Although many British imperialists professed to regard Gandhi's belief in non-violence, self-sufficiency and personal manual labour as absurd and fraudulent, they had no effective answer to his tactics. In any case, some British officials appreciated that he was a genuine moral leader as well as a politician; and although he had to be imprisoned from time to time, the total suppression of his movement would only create a vacuum filled by terrorists. By 1924 British claims that the Congress represented only a small westernised class had been overtaken by events. Non-Cooperation had generated a mass national movement enjoying the support of many Muslims, and a huge organisation financed by Indian businessmen. As a result, the nationalists could fight elections or organise agitations as they chose, and for the next twenty-five years they alternated between the two, to the confusion of the British authorities.

Against this background the maintenance of empire inevitably became a perennial concern for Conservative imperialists and for fascists during the 1920s. Empire offered tangible proof of their belief in the superiority of the English and of their fears about their deterioration as a ruling race. Although the outcome of the Great War had, in one sense, confirmed English superiority, the experience had also punctured the illusion in the eyes of the Indian and African soldiers who had witnessed the fact that, far from being a super-race, the British were no better than several other powers of the same order. For fascists imperial problems also offered striking confirmation of their analysis of British parliamentary politics as a failing system hopelessly mired in the liberal-conservative consensus. They were correct in the sense that all post-war governments regarded it as necessary to deal with the Indian National Congress rather than to ignore it or attempt to suppress it; this dictated judicious concessions designed to appease moderate nationalists and thus win their cooperation.

In the press resistance to this policy of imperial 'scuttle' was led by H. A. Gwynne of the *Morning Post*, by Lady Lucy Houston, and by the *English Review*, the *National Review*, the *Saturday Review* and *The Patriot*. These journals traced the origins of current British dilemmas to the Victorian educational policy which had established universities and, according to Lord Sydenham, was 'primarily responsible for the creation of a class of partly denationalised Indians into whose prentice hands Mr Montagu blindly committed the destinies of India'.[3] Sydenham condemned the British authorities for failing to combat seditious propaganda emanating from Berlin and Moscow and for allowing Gandhi, 'the sinister apostle of Hindu reaction', to tour the country freely spreading his ideas.

The extreme right saw India in a wider context. The first act of betrayal was the consent given by leading Conservative politicians to the creation of the Irish Free State in 1921. The Duke of Northumberland accused the coalition government of abandoning those Irishmen who had supported the Union with England to their fate as a minority in the South. In his view the violence employed by Sinn Fein marked it out as a revolutionary movement, not a nationalist one, and in the future Ireland would become a Bolshevik base from which to subvert English society.[4] The Duke was too obsessed with conspiracy theories to notice that after the civil war Ireland settled down as a conservative, Catholic, agrarian society posing no threat to anyone. However, the loss of Ireland had serious repercussions; in

Northumberland's words it was 'the first act in a greater tragedy – the dissolution of the British Empire'.[5] Northumberland, Sydenham and Lymington also claimed to detect the hand of Jews in this pattern of imperial disintegration. Hence the abuse heaped on Edwin Montagu and Lord Reading, formerly Rufus Isaacs. As Indian Viceroy from 1921 to 1926 Reading released Gandhi from gaol in 1924 before he had served his full sentence, a decision they interpreted as dangerous weakness.

For fascists the defence of the empire also seemed handicapped by the internal divisions within the ranks of Conservatism, not simply between liberals and imperialists but among the imperialists themselves. The different strands of imperialism were represented by Sir George Lloyd and Winston Churchill on the one hand and by L. S. Amery on the other. As Governor of Bombay from 1916 to 1923 Lloyd looked like a throwback to an earlier viceroy, Lord Curzon, in his enthusiasm for improvement in the shape of schemes for irrigation, agriculture and housing. He believed that Indian nationalism could be defeated by material improvement. In Bombay, which was close to Gandhi's home base, Lloyd had to weather the worst of the agitations of 1919–20, and it is fair to say that he was by no means a reactionary at this stage; he disapproved of Dyer's conduct at Amritsar and he wisely resisted the temptation to imprison Gandhi for as long as possible. Yet by the end of his term as governor in December 1923 Lloyd had moved sharply to the right. 'I am afraid Gandhi is really pretty wicked, as cunning as a fox and at heart bitterly anti-British,' he wrote.[6] Increasingly Lloyd felt he was being betrayed by politicians in London who chiefly wanted to avoid controversy by buying off opponents and shrank from the resolute action needed to maintain British control.

After Bombay, Lloyd briefly returned to the House of Commons, which he loathed, but finally received the peerage he desired and escaped to Egypt as High Commissioner in October 1925. However, Egypt proved even more frustrating because Britain had already conceded semi-independence in 1922. Although Britain still maintained troops in Egypt to protect the Suez Canal and retained control of foreign affairs, Lloyd was obliged to deal with an elected assembly and a vocal nationalist movement, a role that he found uncongenial. He felt handicapped by the Westminster government which he believed to be looking for an opportunity to withdraw entirely from Egypt. For its part, London considered Lloyd unrealistic in his ambition to restore British influence in domestic affairs and feared he was seeking an excuse to intervene.[7] The embarrassment of Lloyd's divergence from a Conservative government was barely resolved in 1929 when Baldwin lost office, leaving him to be sacked by the new Labour government. Baldwin pointedly failed to defend Lloyd at this stage, leaving Churchill to champion him.[8] By this time Lloyd had become a diehard imperialist, alienated by the parliamentary consensus that appeared to enjoy a stranglehold on imperial policy.

However, the imperial credentials of the Baldwin government were maintained by the more constructive and less embattled figure of L. S. Amery who served as Colonial Secretary from 1924 to 1929. A keen protectionist-imperialist, Amery had been influenced by Joseph Chamberlain's vision of reversing the process of national decline by the economic development of the empire. But Amery had concluded from the Boer War that it was futile for Britain to attempt to keep subject peoples within the empire against their will.[9] He disparaged Churchill's obsession with India as unrealistic and largely sentimental. Churchill, he complained, was 'a brilliant talker and military strategist who is frankly incapable of understanding finance or the meaning of empire development'.[10] By contrast, Amery was prepared to accept a measure of reform for India provided Britain concentrated on what he saw as more important – realising the material potential of the rest of Britain's possessions. In particular he looked to parts of Africa, notably Kenya and the Rhodesias, which might yield high returns from better investment and offered scope for emigration and settlement by British people. This would relieve unemployment, boost the market for British goods, promote imperial sentiment among the working class, and enable Britain to keep on level terms with the emerging superpowers.

Churchill never developed anything equivalent to this grand Chamberlainite vision of an imperial union, and was consequently never as convincing as an apostle of empire. As a stubborn free-trader he could not endorse the protectionist strategy which seemed essential if the economic advantages of empire were to be achieved; and as Chancellor he had obstructed the colonial investment that Amery desired. His sudden adoption of the Indian cause in 1930 looked too much like opportunism in a man who had only recently rejoined the party. During the 1920s, Amery succeeded in passing the Colonial Development Act, which was expected to build up the white population of Kenya, but he failed to secure the necessary investment. Ultimately plans for imperial emigration were wrecked by the international depression and collapsing agricultural prices which left many European planters bankrupt; by the 1930s more people were returning to Britain than were leaving for the colonies. As a result, after Baldwin's fall from power in 1929 Conservative imperialists felt disappointed and increasingly angered by the lack of progress towards an imperial tariff programme. It was this that gave extra momentum to the right-wing attack on constitutional reform in India during the 1930s.

Oswald Mosley largely endorsed the views of the Tory imperialists, though as an unelected politician he was less inhibited about asserting Britain's right to rule by virtue of conquest. He simply insisted that India owed everything to British rule, and that to hand her over to a small class who were 'either great capitalists or professional politicians in the pockets of the financiers' would lead to chaos and bloodshed. To fascists, already convinced that democracy had become a dangerous irrelevance in Europe, it seemed absurd to enfranchise 'some thirty million illiterates' in India: 'What folly to foist on India Western parliamentary institutions, which were never suitable to the East, at the very moment when they were breaking down at home.'[11] Consequently BUF propaganda disregarded Indian nationalism and claimed that the demand for reform had been generated by Soviet money: 'It is difficult to avoid the conclusion that Indian affairs are being handed over to the Third International.'[12] Mosley's immediate recipe for India was therefore to 'remain and govern', to maintain order and offer no surrender to the professional politicians and lawyers. The alternative, claimed William Joyce, 'is the destruction of our Empire. To lose the East is to lose all; for a nation which cowered before a Fakir [Gandhi] could never again play any part of the councils of Europe.'[13] Looking ahead, the BUF aimed at maintaining the princely states and applying the model of the corporate state which it considered far more suited to Indian traditions than Western-style democracy. Though an assembly would be permitted, only one-third would be elected; the Viceroy would choose his executive and have the right to reject any resolutions of the assembly.[14]

Apart from its moral and political significance, India occupied a central place in the BUF's strategy for developing a completely self-contained or autarkic empire based on the elimination of imports of food and raw materials from foreign countries which offered no market to Britain. Imperial territories were to enjoy direct representation in London where the development of their resources would be planned in the light of Britain's needs. India loomed especially large in this programme not least because during Gandhi's Civil Disobedience campaign in 1930–1 nationalists had picketed shops selling British cloth and boycotted imported cotton goods. As a result, merchants allowed their stocks to dwindle and cotton imports fell by nearly 60 per cent. Although trade recovered once Civil Disobedience had run out of steam, the campaign accelerated the long-term attrition of the market for British goods; indeed, during the 1930s India exported more to Britain than she imported. Mosley campaigned relentlessly in the distressed textile districts of Lancashire and Yorkshire, accusing British financiers of favouring the industrialisation of India because its cheap labour would fatten their profits. He argued that it was possible to restore the industry's markets and thus save thousands of jobs. To this end he proposed to exclude Japanese competition from India and the Crown Colonies, and to force Indians to reduce their tariffs against cotton imported from Lancashire.[15] By the 1930s so blatant an attempt to suppress Indian manufactures for the benefit of British would have provoked prolonged and violent boycotts. But it suited Mosley to adopt a bold stance and use declining industry as a stick with which to beat the National Government.

The fascists' thinking on India was closely connected with the importance they attached to the Crown. In common with many right-wingers they devoutly believed that the King shared their outrage at the cavalier treatment meted out to his empire. On this issue above all, they argued, he should be prepared to defy his ministers. Fascists also regarded royalty in India, in the shape of the princes, as the key to frustrating the government's reform programme. The 565 Indian princes ruled 40 per cent of the country and a quarter of its population. They epitomised the variety of the subcontinent, including as they did Muslims like the Nizam of Hyderabad, Hindus like the Maharaja of Mysore and Sikhs such as the Maharaja of Patiala. By keeping alive Indian traditions and pride they acted as a safety valve for the Raj. The British convinced themselves that the princes represented an effective bulwark against the rising tide of nationalism because it threatened them just as much as the imperial system. This, however, was a misunderstanding. Gandhi, whose father had been a *dewan* in a small princely state, shrewdly cautioned Congress against embroiling itself in agitations in princely territory as this merely played into British hands. In any case some princes had a keen appreciation of the strengths of the two sides. By steadily extending popular participation in their own territory, the British left the princes' autocratic rule looking increasingly anomalous. Fearful of being engulfed by a mass national movement, the shrewder princes accepted that if Congress was eventually going to inherit power, it would clearly be unwise to attach themselves irretrievably to the British.

However, for fascists of a romantic-reactionary outlook it was tempting to see the princes as an oriental expression of reverence for the idea of hereditary kingship. Lord Lymington, for example, emphasised that the princes were not merely decorative like the British Crown, they exercised real power, and as such they offered the best means of preserving authority and leadership from 'the present effort to foist an alien, bastard democracy on British India'.[16] Lymington also regarded the princes as significant for British domestic politics because they embodied the principle of hereditary kingship. 'This', he wrote, 'makes them not only the keystone of our Empire in India, but of the utmost importance for the re-creation of English Kingship which remains as a tradition in the hearts of Englishmen but which has been abandoned in the practice of English Government.'[17] Since the 1880s reactionaries had consoled themselves with the thought that the Raj remained the embodiment of autocratic government and was immune to the encroachment of democracy in Britain. Now the rise of Congress put this at risk and justified a last-ditch fight for princely power.

The culminating battle was fought over the Government of India Act of 1935, a characteristic product of consensus between Ramsay MacDonald and Stanley Baldwin. Imperialists and fascists found it especially galling that this reform was set in train by the much-maligned Baldwin administration. In 1926 Baldwin had appointed a liberal Tory, Edward Wood (Viscount Irwin), as Viceroy. The British were obliged to institute a review of the Montagu–Chelmsford reforms after ten years, but in 1928 Baldwin decided to anticipate this by appointing a commission of senior politicians under the Liberal, Sir John Simon; this triggered the evolution of a bipartisan reform which would survive his own fall from power. Baldwin's initiative revived interest in constitutional change in India and led Congress to adopt 'Dominion status' as its aim. By this time Dominion status implied full autonomy, even in foreign affairs, and voluntary membership of the Commonwealth. In 1929, under Gandhi's leadership Congress agreed that, failing a British offer of Dominion status, it would initiate a new campaign of Civil Disobedience in 1930.

The prospect of renewed agitation dismayed Irwin who regarded it as essential to do business with Gandhi. But this required a bold stroke before the Congress deadline ran out. Accordingly Irwin sailed for Britain in July 1929 to seek approval from all the party leaders for a promise of Dominion status as the goal of British policy in India. Baldwin, now in opposition, agreed without even consulting his colleagues. By October the Viceroy had returned to India to announce his new declaration in the hope of winning moderate nationalist opinion and forestalling the threatened agitation. However, his strategy began to unravel when MPs protested that Baldwin had tricked them; the new premier, Ramsay MacDonald, suggested that Irwin's proposal amounted to no more than Montagu's 1918 declaration; and in January 1930 Churchill resigned from the shadow cabinet to be free to oppose reform.

In a series of articles in the *Daily Telegraph* in March Lord Lloyd advanced the case for maintaining the status quo. He pointed to the mutual economic advantage arising from British rule; but he noted that whereas before the war Britain had supplied 63 per cent of India's imports, she now supplied only 48 per cent.[18] How Britain was to recover her former share Lloyd failed to explain. Beyond this he relied heavily on an archaic view of Indian society: the country laboured under the influence of Hinduism and the rigidity of the caste system, which discouraged enterprise and kept the country in a backward condition. Progress, according to Lloyd, would not be attained via the ballot box or extensions of the Montagu–Chelmsford system of devolved power.[19] This scepticism was widely shared, for example by hitherto loyalist backbenchers like the Duchess of Atholl who at this stage was not associated with the diehard group led by Lloyd and Churchill.[20] However, Baldwin went some way to defusing the attack by committing himself to an Empire Conference designed to develop the imperial market, which eventually met at Ottawa in 1932. Meanwhile Indian reform was postponed by the crisis in the autumn of 1931 when the National Government assumed power.

However, the emergence of opposition to Irwin's policy in Britain convinced Congress that the Viceroy's word was not enough. In order to avoid a breakaway by the Congress left wing, led by Nehru, Gandhi rejected the offer to attend a Round Table Conference in London and launched Civil Disobedience, a vast nationwide campaign which ran with some interruptions from the spring of 1930 to 1934. Yet Gandhi had no wish to prolong the agitation because he feared it would disintegrate into mere violence. For his part the Viceroy still hoped to win his consent to the new constitutional reforms. Both therefore remained open to a compromise. Although Irwin reluctantly allowed the provincial governments to tackle the agitation by arresting nationalist leaders and treating Congress as an illegal organisation, he knew that in London the Round Table Conference was making progress; by January 1931 it had approved a sweeping new scheme for a federal system incorporating British India and the princely states in a single national government. Consequently, Irwin took the risk of conducting negotiations with Gandhi while he was still in prison, to the fury of imperialists at home: 'You have the extraordinary spectacle of the Government of India drinking tea with treason and actually negotiating with sedition,' thundered Lloyd.[21] By March the two men had agreed a pact; Gandhi was released from gaol, he called off Civil Disobedience and agreed to attend the Round Table Conference.

To the diehards the details of Irwin's deal were less important than the demoralising psychological blow the British had suffered as a result of his handling of Gandhi. All over India district officers and police had been engulfed by the nationalist agitation, and no sooner had they been allowed to arrest the ringleaders than they came under instructions from New Delhi to release them again. Although Gandhi had called off Civil Disobedience, he reserved the right to reactivate it, and many activists did so on their own initiative. The critics also had a valid complaint that Irwin had elevated Gandhi's status by treating him as the representative of Indian opinion.

By August 1931 Gandhi had arrived in Britain where he attended the conference, was received at Buckingham Palace and even made a triumphant tour of the Lancashire cotton towns where he was treated more as a hero than as an enemy of the empire. Not surprisingly Lloyd felt convinced that Britain was repeating her mistakes over Ireland, as he told Baldwin:

> If [Gandhi] is the avowed head of revolution in India – not merely the protagonist for self-government under the Crown but for complete independence – then Edward [Irwin] had absolutely no moral or political right to negotiate with him on equal and intimate terms . . . We bought peace in Ireland by negotiation with the evil forces of assassination . . . If we repeat the performance in India, where next shall we be called upon to pay the bill?[22]

Churchill argued that all concessions were futile: 'The truth is that Gandhism and all it stands for will, sooner or later, have to be grappled with and finally crushed. It is no good trying to satisfy a tiger by feeding him with cat meat.'[23] Yet Churchill and Lloyd overlooked the implications of their uncompromising tactics: 'Do you think a democracy will stand for the necessary measures?' enquired Lord Middleton.[24] He was doubtless correct that a prolonged attempt to suppress a huge nationalist movement by force was too high a price for the British electorate to pay for the maintenance of the status quo. For the fascists, however, such calculations offered further proof of the flabbiness of democratic politics.

The National Government shocked its critics by drawing up a sweeping scheme based on the federal system outlined at the Round Table Conference, including an Indian electorate of over thirty millions, full self-government at the provincial level, and an elected parliament in which the princes were to be represented. 'The general idea may be right,' complained the Duke of Atholl, 'but it never was anticipated that it should be galloped at this pace . . . You cannot give nations complete control straight away, but it must be given in small homeopathic doses.'[25] Opposition to the scheme was so bitter that it was not passed until 1935. The parliamentary resistance was coordinated by the India Defence League which some eighty Tory MPs and many peers joined; the leading rebels included Lord Lloyd, Sir Henry Page Croft, Churchill, the Duchess of Atholl, Lord Lymington, Patrick Donner and Colonel John Gretton. Though overshadowed by Churchill, Lloyd and Page Croft were the most effective leaders because of their impeccable record of loyalty to the empire and to the party. It was Lloyd who led the attack at the Conservative annual conferences in 1932 and 1933 where he adopted an increasingly apocalyptic view of British policy, characterising it as the withdrawal of the Roman legions and the start of a general decline of British military power. Lloyd pointed bluntly to the connection between the Indian controversy and the alarming rise in the popularity of the BUF during 1934: 'You cannot be surprised if the Conservative Party will not look after the interests of this country as well as of India, that more and more people in this country will prefer a blackshirt to a White Paper.'[26]

Lloyd's views on empire, democracy, the depression and rearmament were so close to those expressed by Mosley that he was expected to end up in the fascist camp. He became the target of Douglas Jerrold of the *English Review*, Lady Houston of the *Saturday Review*, and of the perennial rebel, Lord Beaverbrook, who wanted him to start a new party. The eighty-three-year-old Lucy Houston was one of the most eccentric figures operating on the far right of politics in this period. In 1926 her husband, the steamship owner Sir Robert Houston, had died, leaving her six million pounds which she distributed lavishly to promote what she regarded as worthy causes; these included subsidies to *The Patriot* and the Boswell Publishing Company after the death of the Duke of Northumberland in 1930, and to the *National Review* now under Lady Milner. Houston's desire for a personal platform tempted her to buy a newspaper, but she made do with the *Saturday Review*, for which she paid £3,000.[27]

Her wealth, her volatility and her extreme opinions made Lady Houston a thorn in the side of the National Government for much of the decade. A favourite tactic was to accuse Ramsay MacDonald of being a traitor and invite him to prosecute her.[28] She sailed her yacht, *Liberty*, along the south coast bearing the message, 'TO HELL WITH RAMSAY MACDONALD', in letters six feet tall until the Admiralty moved her on.[29] An admirer of Mussolini – she named her dog Benito – Houston disparaged Baldwin as 'that bumbling old humbug' and Anthony Eden as 'that nancyfied nonentity'.[30] But she venerated George Lloyd as the 'Man of Destiny' whose work in Bombay and Egypt showed him capable of saving the empire. Houston always insisted she was a patriot not a fascist, but it seemed surprising that she did not take up Mosley. She had a weakness for swashbuckling politicians and sometimes talked about giving him £200,000; however, they fell out when she was lampooned in *The Blackshirt*.[31]

In 1933 Lady Houston thrust her money at Lloyd in a bid to persuade him to supplant Baldwin and MacDonald. 'I want you to put yourself forward,' she told him. 'I would gladly give £100,000 to see you p[rime] m[inister] . . . that would be the most patriotic thing I could possibly do for my country.'[32] However, Lloyd still wished to be a loyal Tory and he appreciated that if he accepted her offer Lady Houston would want to dictate terms. 'Of course I can't accept this money if I have to give an undertaking . . . to form a new party,' he told her.[33] However, he accepted £11,000 to finance his campaign against the India Bill. Lloyd did not intend to over-throw the National Government, but to counter what he saw as the left wing of the coalition which enjoyed undue influence over India and national defence.[34] Between October 1933 and summer 1934 he spent her money to hire offices, organise meetings, distribute propaganda and employ Duncan Sandys on behalf of the India Defence League. However, by June 1934 Lloyd admitted: 'I am afraid the meetings did not get the response that I had hoped for', and he stopped spending Houston's money.[35] At this point he seems to have broken with her.

Meanwhile, Lucy Houston occupied herself with other tactics to over-throw the India policy, including interventions in by-elections against government candidates and a scheme to buy an island in the Channel where she hoped to establish a radio station to broadcast anti-government propa-ganda. As she believed her telephone was tapped, she and her aides used false names when communicating.[36] But by far her most dramatic stunt was the famous Everest Flight of 1933. The idea of flying over the top of Mount Everest seems to have originated in the romantic mind of John Buchan.[37] The venture combined scientific, commercial and political motives in equal measure. A committee including Buchan, the Marquis of Clydesdale, Lord Semphill, Lord Peel, Lord Burnham of the *Daily Telegraph* and R. D. Blumenfeld of the *Daily Express*, was formed in the autumn of 1932 to promote the scheme 'with the object of increasing our prestige in India and the East generally and also making a flight in the international interest with British aircraft'.[38] The committee chose two Westland Wapiti biplanes for their ability to function at low temperatures and at high altitudes, and shipped them to Karachi where they were reassembled and flown to Purnea, fifty miles from the Nepalese border.[39]

The intriguing aspect of the Everest Flight was its political status. At the outset it enjoyed wholly respectable connections, winning cooperation from the Government of India, the Maharaja of Nepal and the Air Minister, Lord Londonderry.[40] John Buchan and the young Marquis of Clydesdale (the heir to the Duke of Hamilton) were loyal, mainstream Conservative MPs. In the 1920s Clydesdale became popular as a pilot and as Scottish middleweight boxing champion; in 1930, aged thirty, he had won a by-election at East Renfrewshire though he had not previously been seen as a politician. When the Everest Committee ran into financial difficulties Clydesdale turned to Lady Houston, who had donated £100,000 to support Britain's attempt to win the Schneider Cup in 1931 following the government's refusal to help; Britain was successful, using a 340 mph monoplane which prefigured the Spitfire of 1936.[41] Houston entertained doubts about the young Marquis's suitability, but when a more experienced pilot, Commander Fellowes, took command, she handed over the £15,000 required. 'What a lucky boy you were to catch me in the right mood to help you,' she told Clydesdale.[42]

With Lucy Houston's money the 'Houston-Everest Flight' as it became officially known, took on a much sharper political complexion. During 1932 and 1933 she had waged a vitriolic campaign against the government's Indian policy, denouncing Irwin as 'a dangerous sentimentalist and many think a traitor to his class'; Baldwin's external policies 'lean definitely towards a sloppy liberalism if not Socialism. He is prostituting Conservatism to Internationalism and surrender.'[43] Clearly, for Houston the attraction of the Everest Flight lay in offering a new stick with which to beat the government. 'The chief aim of the Marquis and myself in this Adventure', she wrote, 'was to show India that we are not the Degenerate Race that its Leaders represent Britain to be.'[44] This made things awkward for Clydesdale who was on friendly terms with MacDonald and had so far avoided joining the India rebels. However, in October 1932, before joining the expedition, he appeared before his constituents in Paisley to seek their permission; they would have no member for three months and he had no wish to cause a by-election. Though he suggested, uncontroversially, that the expedition aimed to foster British prestige in the world, Clydesdale adopted Houston's language: 'The success of this flight will have a great psychological effect in India . . . It will do much to dispel the fallacy that this country is under-going a phase of degeneration . . . It will show India that we are still a virile and active race and can overcome difficulties with energy and vigour.'[45]

In the event Clydesdale and his co-pilots successfully completed two flights in April 1933, clearing the summit by five hundred feet; on their return they were fêted by *The Times* and featured in a film, *Wings Over Everest*, by Gaumont-British in 1934. But the enterprise became diverted by the inevitable controversy between the committee and Houston who felt she was being denied her proper role; 'it is of course very difficult dealing with someone who is not quite normal,' one member explained.[46] The polit-ical impact was blunted partly because Clydesdale himself seems to have been reluctant to attack the government's Indian policy, to judge from his evasive replies to constituents later in 1933.[47] As a result Houston doubt-less felt angered at her failure to capitalise fully on her investment.

Clydesdale's caution reflected that of most MPs. The strength of the opposition to the India Bill lay largely outside parliament in the Conservative Party and the constituency organisations where rank-and-file views were highly reactionary. The Duchess of Atholl's local party chairman told her that democracy was unsuitable for nine-tenths of the white races, let alone for 'natives'. When standing in a by-election at Hitchin in June 1933, the Conservative candidate, Sir Arthur Wilson, insultingly repudiated Baldwin's letter of support in protest at his imperial policy, without apparently damaging his chances.[48] For several years the cabinet struggled to keep the lid on this discontent. In May 1933 the Junior Imperial League, the Conservative Women's organisation and the Grand Council of the Primrose League all expressed their opposition. In February the National Union of the Conservative Party approved its India policy by only 189 to 165 votes, and the 1934 party conference narrowly accepted it by 543 to 520. However, in parliament the rebels usually gathered only forty to fifty members into their lobby. This might have been enough to kill the legislation under a purely Conservative government, but with 554 members the National Government could withstand rebellion on this scale.

Why was the opposition to the India Bill such a failure? In part, as we have seen, because sound imperialists such as Amery refused to join them. The critics' claim that Britain was playing into the hands of Congress by establishing a new national legislature seemed less than convincing because the government had built into it major safeguards designed to prevent Congress winning a majority; for example, princely territory was allotted more representatives than its population merited and the princely representatives would be nominated not elected. According to Lord Irwin the parliament would be 'a very Tory Assembly'.[49] The government could plausibly claim to be consolidating Britain's position not sacrificing it. 'Personally I do not know that there is anything so terrible in [Dominion status],' Amery commented, 'if the attainment of the goal is postponed long enough.'[50] Party loyalty also remained strong in the House of Lords where, although many peers joined the India Defence League, only fifty to sixty actually voted against the government. The Duke of Atholl believed that upper-class Tories were instinctively reluctant to upset the government and split the party, whereas middle-class opinion was much more hostile to reform because it had investments in India and worried about the security of pensions under a future independent government.[51] Nor was Churchill's prominence in the campaign entirely helpful because of his tendency to turn the issue into a personal cause. Churchill also lacked both the skill and the inclination to cultivate fellow members. As Cuthbert Headlam observed in 1932, he had committed 'the unutterable folly of never coming into the House unless he was going to speak for an hour against the Government. The result is that he has lost all influence with the new members and has no kind of following.'[52] Sometimes he was heard in chilly silence, and sometimes laughed at. In a debate on 13 June 1934 Amery laid a trap by suggesting Churchill's motto was 'fiat justitia et ruant coeli'. When Churchill immediately demanded 'Translation', Amery replied: 'If I can trip up Sam [Hoare], the Government's bust.' Happy to see Churchill made to look a fool, the House dissolved in laughter.

Their weakness in parliament encouraged some of the India rebels to desperate measures. Viscount Lymington resigned as an MP in 1934. In May 1935 five members wrote to Baldwin threatening to resign the whip: the Duchess of Atholl, Sir Joseph Nall, Linton Thorp, Lieutenant Commander Astbury and A. J. K. Todd. The reasons given by the Duchess included not merely India, but the neglect of national defence, opposition to the milk marketing schemes, lack of protection against Japanese cotton, the amalgamation of small coalmines, and the threat to small shopkeepers by the big chain stores.[53] This catalogue underlined that for the rebels India was symptomatic of a wider rejection of the National Government. By focusing on India Churchill had not picked the best grievance. His son Randolph compounded the impression of disloyalty by intervening in a by-election at Wavertree in Liverpool in 1935 against an official Conservative candidate. By thus splitting the party's vote he handed the seat to Labour. Undeterred, Randolph promoted another rebel Tory, a former BUF member, Richard Findlay, at the Norwood by-election, though with less effect.[54]

If these were slightly desperate actions, the India rebels still had one effective shot in their locker. Though the odds were stacked against them in parliament, in India itself they enjoyed formidable allies. Lymington's resignation as an MP in February 1934 freed him to visit India as a representative of the India Defence League with a view to mobilising the princes. Their reaction was critical because the new federal government of India would only come into being if ratified by them. Yet they remained suspicious of the implications of entering the federation; most princes wanted India to remain an integral part of the empire and they preferred to be linked to the new government by treaties with the Crown. They were therefore natural allies for Lymington who visited influential rulers including the Maharaja of Patiala, the Maharaja of Mysore and the Nizam of Hyderabad, where he managed to undermine the British government's policy by spreading the idea that 'the Conservative Opposition has had the upper hand in England.'[55] By sowing doubts about the strength of the government at home Lymington encouraged the princes to reject the scheme. He discovered that eighty of the 104 members of the Chamber of Princes were unhappy about the British proposals, and learnt that the government had been pressurising the princes to accept the federal scheme against their will.[56] Lymington's visit boosted the princes' determination to resist official advice, and subsequently they declined to ratify the proposals with the result that the federal government of India never came into existence.

This was the rebels' one unequivocal victory over Baldwin and Hoare. Yet despite this, the Government of India Act, which was eventually passed in the summer of 1935, represented a decisive defeat for the imperial cause.

It gave Indians complete self-government at the provincial level. The elections to inaugurate the new system were not held until 1937. To the dismay of the British officials, who thought they had outflanked Congress by expanding the electorate, Congress won outright majorities in six of the eleven provinces and was the largest party in three others. It formed governments or joined coalitions in eight provinces. Although the provincial governors enjoyed the right to veto legislation it was a power they could not afford to use for fear of precipitating the resignation of their ministries and a return to agitation. At the same time the Indian Civil Service, the 'steel frame' on which administration of the country rested, was rapidly becoming Indianised; by 1939 it included 540 Indians as against 759 Britons. Thus, in both the political and administrative sense it is fair to say that India had to a large extent become self-governing before the Second World War. There was to be no repetition of the campaign waged by imperialists between 1931 and 1935 against Baldwin's policy. After 1945 the cause was championed by comparatively marginal groups such as the Monday Club, and even the return of Churchill to the premiership in 1951 failed to reinvigorate the imperial cause.

By the sheer vigour of their attack on Baldwin's India policy, Churchill and Lloyd had taken some of the wind out of Mosley's sails; and in the process they helped to keep some of the extremists attached to parliamentary politics when they might otherwise have been seduced by fascism. However, when Churchill abruptly dropped the issue in August 1935, he left the imperial field clear for the BUF once again. Admittedly, India was swiftly eclipsed by the growing fears of a war with Italy over Abyssinia and the announcement of a general election in the autumn. Mosley himself launched a fresh campaign for peace and cooperation with Mussolini. However, if empire enjoyed less prominence during the later 1930s, it continued to feature prominently in BUF propaganda, largely because the depression in Britain's textile-producing regions remained an unresolved problem as India continued on her path to economic self-sufficiency. By 1936 India was producing 85 per cent of her cotton cloth and 70 per cent of her steel consumption. As a result of the crisis of 1931 India had effectively won control of her own tariff policy which left her charging a general tariff of 25 per cent and 15 per cent on cotton imports from Britain. At the same time, after gaining control of her exchange rate policy she devalued the rupee.

These trends undermined British influence since the major British companies investing in India shared the same attitude as Indian manufacturers in welcoming tariffs and a lower exchange rate. Their stake in India's economy did nothing to strengthen the case for recovering British political control. This, of course, was exactly the charge levied against international capital by the fascists: that it lacked patriotism. With this in view, for the rest of the decade Mosley threw himself into campaigning in the depressed manufacturing towns of Lancashire and Yorkshire. However, he was rowing against the tide. In addition to recovering British control over tariff policy, Mosley advocated measures to force Indian mill-owners to pay higher wages.[57] Yet attempts to recover Britain's former markets in India at this stage would have required the virtual suppression of an indigenous industry whose leaders had linked their fortunes to the national movement. This was an unrealistic ambition in a society now organised for political action on a massive scale, and it served no purpose other than boosting the fascist movement in the north-west of England.

ELEVEN

Corporatism, Capitalism and the Economic Depression

'The joke was that so many on our side came from the same kind of Socialistic background as our most deadly enemies.'

Arthur Beavan, Cardiff BUF, in J. Christian (ed.),
Mosley's Blackshirts (1986), 56

All over Europe fascism seized its historic opportunity amid what it saw as the failure of liberal democracy to respond to the challenge of prolonged economic depression between the wars. Traditional explanations for the rise of the Nazis emphasise the turmoil caused by inflation and unemployment, their appeal to farmers angered by collapsing prices in the 1920s, and their ability to mobilise the votes of the centre and right-wing parties; they appeared to capitalise on the distress of the lower middle classes – a section of society alienated from conventional politics by the economic crisis and squeezed between big business on the one hand and the trade unions on the other. In the case of British fascism the less the underlying political culture served as an obstacle to the movement, the greater the need to consider the role of economic contingencies. How far was fascism affected by the timing of economic depression and by the extent and nature of its impact on British society? Did the conventional politicians manage economic problems so as to spare crucial sections of society from the material pressures that made them susceptible to fascism on the Continent, or were they simply lucky? Mosley himself felt convinced that the 'Old Gang' parties had miscalculated; they saw the economic crisis as a temporary phenomenon which would pass away as the slumps of the nineteenth century had done. He considered this improbable because traditional world markets had become largely closed to British exports and because modern technology was capable of generating far more goods than the market could absorb.[1]

Yet in a sense it was Mosley who miscalculated. Although many of those who responded to his appeal did so primarily because they were impressed by his economic programme, the depression in Britain never quite gave fascists the momentum they enjoyed elsewhere. This was partly because, although unemployment and poverty have traditionally loomed large in the historiography of the inter-war period, Britain's slump was a comparatively modest affair. At the worst point in early 1932 output in the United States had fallen by a massive 40 per cent and wages by 60 per cent. In Germany gross domestic product declined by 15.7 per cent between 1929 and 1932 and industrial production by 40.8 per cent. For Britain the equivalent figures were 5.8 per cent and 11.4 per cent. Over fifteen million Americans were out of work by 1932, and in Germany unemployment reached six million in 1933 compared with only 2.3 million in Britain. Not surprisingly, the political responses in the shape of Franklin Roosevelt's New Deal and Hitler's job-creation programmes were on a far greater scale than the modest investments undertaken by the National Government in the distressed areas. Consequently, by 1937 German unemployment had fallen to just 2.7 per cent, whereas in Britain it was still 7.7 per cent or 10.8 per cent among insured workers. In short, Britain escaped the worst of the economic fluctuations experienced by her rivals; she learned to live with a substantial, but steadier, rate of unemployment and never faced the devastating economic collapse that threatened the stability of society and the political system elsewhere.

Timing is also a relevant part of the explanation for the fortunes of the fascists. During the 1920s the fascist organisations had focused on political issues rather than the economy, and the economic-political crisis reached its peak around 1930–1 before the British Union of Fascists had even come into existence. Although Mosley's economic analysis was undoubtedly a powerful one and made a great impact during the early years of the life of the National Government, he enjoyed a comparatively brief opportunity. Unemployment attained very high levels during 1931, 1932 and 1933, but by 1934 it had begun a fall which continued until 1937, before rising again in 1938. Between 1932 and 1937 industrial output increased by 46 per cent and unemployment fell from three million to one and a half million. Admittedly this represented only a limited recovery, being concentrated in the building industry, motor cars, aircraft and electrical goods while the traditional heavy industries continued to shrink.

However, the general perception, from 1934 onwards, that Britain had come through the worst saved the National Government from being discredited; it forestalled any significant revival by the Labour Party because voters anticipated that its return to office might well bring back the economic crisis; and it emboldened the government to risk holding an early general election in November 1935. The more secure the grip of the National Government on the country's problems, the less the middle-class voters saw the need for the fascist alternative. Consequently the BUF

(*Above left*) Rotha Lintorn-Orman, founder of the British Fascisti, in 1923.
(*Above right*) Alan Ian Percy, 8th Duke of Northumberland and founder of *The Patriot*, pictured
by the *Saturday Review*, 7 April 1934. (*Below*) Sir Patrick Hannon MP (*centre right in light suit*),
an active supporter of the British Fascisti in the 1920s, at an Anglo–German conference in 1926.

(*Above left*) Arnold Leese, Director of the Imperial Fascist League and world authority on the diseases of camels.

(*Above*) Gerrard V. Wallop, Viscount Lymington MP (9th Earl of Portsmouth), a prominent figure in the English Mistery and English Array, pictured by the *Saturday Review*, 24 March 1934.

(*Left*) Food convoys, guarded by armoured cars, in the East India Dock Road during the General Strike, 1926.

FACING PAGE
(*Main image*) Viscount Rothermere launches the *Daily Mail*'s campaign for the British Union of Fascists, 15 January 1934.
(*Middle*) Oswald Mosley and BUF members with Italian fascists in Rome, April 1933.
(*Below*) Oswald Mosley with William Joyce ('Lord Haw-Haw', *far left*).

Hurrah for the Blackshirts

By VISCOUNT ROTHERMERE

BECAUSE Fascism comes from Italy, shortsighted people in this country think they show a sturdy national spirit by deriding it.

If their ancestors had been equally stupid, Britain would have had no banking system, no Roman law, nor even any football, since all of these are of Italian invention.

*　*　*

THE Socialists, especially, who jeer at the principles and uniform of the Blackshirts as being of foreign origin, forget that the founder and High Priest of their own creed was the German Jew Karl Marx.

Though the name and form of Fascism originated in Italy, that movement is not now peculiar to any nation. **It stands in every country for the Party of Youth.** It represents the effort of the young generation to put new life into out-of-date political systems.

That alone is enough to make it a factor of immense value in our national affairs.

Youth is a force that for generations has been allowed to run to waste in Britain. This country has been governed since far back in Victorian times by men in the middle sixties. When prosperity was general and the international horizon calm, that mattered little, but to cope with the grim problems of the present day the energy and vigour of younger men are needed. Being myself in the middle sixties I know how steadily the seventh decade stiffens one's prej

Under the control of these old British Governme real popularity a abroad. In the vital matter of air-defence this country has been allowed to sink from the f_____ to the lowest position among

While the leader reorganising their break the crushir crisis, our own ar dawdle. They a preparing British and Ceylon by the Southern Ireland

*　*　*

THE Blackshir organised eff generation to br which senile pol maintained on ot its organisation, is purely British, with Italian Fasc Navy has to do w

Such an effort v nation's realisatic shown by the ast Blackshirts are r the big industria reach me from th substantiate thes largest active me try. **A crusading to British politic** who would be v

similar movement in France or the United States have so far failed to realise the profound importance of the new national activity which is stirring all around them.

and disgusted by the incompetence of their elders in dealing with the depression that has followed on it. The other is made up of men too young to remember the war but ready to put all their ardour and energy at the service of a cause which offers them a vigorous constructive policy in place of the drift and indecision of the old political parties.

Blackshirts proclaim a fact which politicians dating from pre-war days will never face—that the new age requires new methods and new men. They base their contention on the simple truth that parliamentary, gov

alone. It can be justified by the gigantic revival of national strength and spirit which a similar process of

national affairs. But which of our older politicians, looking back on his own record, dare assert that they are on the wrong lines?

Government by one or other of the

views were an effective substitute in human affairs for action, the National Government would be the best that Britain has ever had. But the experience of the past two years has proved that these futile and time-wasting devices are no more than a screen for inertia and indecision.

*　*　*

THE huge majority obtained by the present Government at the general election of 1931 was the last vote of confidence that this nation will ever give to Old Gang politicians. Two years from now another general election will be almost due. The whole future of Britain will depend upon its issue.

A prolongation of the present regime may be regarded, in the country's present mood, as out of the question. There will be a pronounced swing either to Right or Left.

If the inflated, impulsive, and largely

At this next vital election Britain's survival as a Great Power will depend on the existence of a well-organised

ciples into our country.

*　*　*

THEY will find the loyalties and aims of the Blackshirts as British as

(*Above left*) Major–General J. F. C. Fuller, influential advocate of mechanised units for the army, who became a close advisor to Mosley and a BUF parliamentary candidate.
(*Above right*) Lady Lucy Houston, millionaire owner of the *Saturday Review* and sponsor of the 'Flight over Everest', 1933. (*Below, right to left*) Maud, Lady Mosley, Sir Charles Petrie and Sir John Squire at a January Club dinner at the Savoy.

(*Above*) Oswald Mosley inspects women fascists in the Limehouse Branch, 4 July 1937. (*Left*) Mosley basking in the admiration of his supporters during a march from Kentish Town to Trafalgar Square, 4 July 1937. (*Below*) Mosley speaking from the top of a loudspeaker van in London, July 1938.

(*Above*) Communists demonstrate against a BUF March, 4 July 1937. Notice the expressions on the faces of the police. (*Below, left to right*) Lord Redesdale, Lady Redesdale, their daughter Unity Mitford and Dr Fitz-Randolph of the German Embassy, at an Anglo–German Fellowship concert, December 1938.

(*Left*) Sir Archibald Henry Maule Ramsay MP, founder of the Right Club, who was interned under Regulation 17D 1940–44, with his wife at Lords for the Eton and Harrow match, July 1937.

(*Right*) Admiral Sir Barry Domvile, former chief of Naval Intelligence and founder of The Link, with Arthur Bryant, historian and R. A. Butler's go-between with the Nazis, in 1933.
(*Below*) Lord Mount Temple (*second from left*) at an Anglo–German Fellowship dinner, July 1936.

(*Above*) BUF Women's Drum Corps at the Earl's Court Peace Rally, 16 July 1939.

(*Below*) The scene at the BUF's Peace Rally at Earl's Court, 16 July 1939.

abruptly withdrew its candidates and abstained from contesting the 1935 election in which the government retained nearly 54 per cent of the vote. Although Mosley protested that he simply needed more time to build an electoral machine, what he really required was a renewed sense of economic crisis, of which there was no sign until the brief slump around 1938.

None of this made fascism impossible in Britain, but it certainly placed limits on the scope of its appeal to several sections of British society. The most obvious contrast with Germany's experience lay in the severe inflation around 1923 which destroyed the value of salaries and savings for millions of people. Britain, on the other hand, experienced protracted deflation, partly due to falling world prices but also to the deliberate policy of her governments which were keen to drive prices down and maintain the value of the pound. Although this deflationary policy proved damaging to industry and thus to employment, it had the effect of keeping wages and salaries buoyant throughout the inter-war period.[2] In fact, by 1929 wage rates in Britain were at their 1923 level, while prices had fallen by 6 per cent during the same period. Even in the worst of the depression from 1929 to 1932, money wages fell by only 4 per cent while wholesale prices dropped by 25 per cent and the official cost of living index fell by 12 per cent. Consequently, despite hardship in certain sectors, most families enjoyed rising real wages between the wars; by 1935 the value of wages in terms of what they would buy had increased by 17 per cent compared with 1924.

This is why the traditional pessimistic picture of inter-war Britain has been extensively revised in recent years. Far from being crushed by poverty, many British people in all classes enjoyed rising expectations and higher living standards. This was conspicuously in evidence in booming sales of consumer goods and minor luxuries including cosmetics, cheap fashionable clothes and women's magazines, as well as leisure activities such as the radio, cinema-going, dances and football pools. But by far the most striking manifestation of growing real income was the massive house-building programme and the marked trend towards home ownership; by 1939, 31 per cent of all homes were owner-occupied compared to only 10 per cent before the war. During the 1930s a semi-detached house could be purchased for as little as £400 and a deposit of £25. In this context the popularity of the National Government among people on modest incomes in both middle and working classes was quite soundly based, and the refusal of Baldwin to be stampeded by right-wing attacks into abandoning his 'liberal' policies seems entirely comprehensible. He was far more interested in the material interests of the non-political majority than in appeasing the vocal minority of ideologues on his right. The cheap money policy pursued by the Chancellor of the Exchequer, Neville Chamberlain, effectively kept interest rates low for homebuyers. He was also at pains to grant tax allowances in respect of dependent children so as to minimise the tax paid by families on small and medium incomes. For example, it has been calculated that in 1929 a man with two children earning £400 a year paid no income tax.[3] Taxes had been increased in the 1931 crisis, but by 1935 they had been lifted, leaving most middle and working-class people in a favourable situation if they were in employment.

Faced with such a strongly entrenched government the fascists modified their position. During the 1920s they had been obsessed with the threat of Bolshevism at home and abroad. However, by the 1930s it no longer seemed credible to portray Bolshevism as an enemy spreading inexorably across the world. At home Labour had turned out to be a toothless tiger, most unlikely to usher in a Socialist regime even if it ever returned to power. Consequently the BUF repositioned itself in the 1930s; by denouncing the failings of the capitalist system it went some way to occupying the space vacated on the *left* by the decline of Labour. This shift has not been widely recognised, perhaps because it seems so inconsistent with our assumptions about fascism as a phenomenon of the extreme right. It is, of course, true that the anti-capitalist rhetoric adopted by European fascist movements was limited and specific in nature; it amounted to a denunciation of finance capitalism rather than an intention to abolish private property generally. Moreover, despite their extreme language about the failings of capitalism, fascists did little to tackle the evil they had identified once they came to power.

How the British fascists would have behaved in office remains speculative; but it is undeniable that many Blackshirts were attracted to fascism by the same considerations that led others into Socialist organisations. A contemporary of William Joyce noticed that his hatred for Jews was equalled by his hatred for capitalists: 'he might easily have become a Communist agitator . . . he thinks the Nazi movement is a proletarian one which will free the world from the bonds of plutocratic capitalists.'[4] Like Mussolini, Mosley himself had come to fascism from a Socialist background and he carried much of his earlier creed with him in his positive view of state interventionism and his determination to use the resources of the state to improve the condition of the people. Among BUF leaders Alexander Raven Thompson was a former Socialist, John Beckett and Robert Forgan had been Labour MPs, and W. J. Leaper and John Scanlon had come from the ILP.[5] As a result, whereas the 1920s fascist organisations had been dominated by militant anti-Socialists, the BUF was disparaged by its fascist rivals as watered-down Socialism; and, to judge from the propaganda in *The Blackshirt* and *Action* it consciously positioned itself as a rival to the Labour Party for the support of those who suffered from the ravages of the capitalist system. According to Raven Thompson, Labour had little to offer workers in cotton textiles and similar declining industries. Instead of painting Labour as a tool of the Communists, the BUF merely derided its pretensions to Socialism. John Beckett claimed that he had found more sincere Socialist conviction in the BUF than he had ever seen in the Labour Party, and that his speeches 'were practically the same as those I had made in the ILP'.[6]

Although these claims cannot be taken literally, they underline the point that, like most growing movements, fascism extended for a considerable distance across the political spectrum. While Mosley made the corporate state sound very much part of the modernising mission of fascism, it could as easily accommodate the backward-looking approach associated with Viscount Lymington and English Array. It is, however, interesting that when Lymington resigned as a Tory MP, his local Labour Party invited him to become their candidate.[7] Lymington's brand of fascism was reflected in the writing of propagandists who presented fascism as a return to English medieval traditions. In 'Fascist Principles in the Middle Ages', for example, A. K. Chesterton explicitly linked the corporate state with the medieval guild system which he credited with checking exploitation and promoting economic stability; it fixed prices, regulated output and protected the interests of both workers and consumers.[8] This happy state of affairs, according to Chesterton, had been disrupted by the revolt against discipline, the decline of the Church, the rise of Liberalism and the growth of class conflict. Conversely, the survival of the medieval system would have limited the explosion of wealth and population, but would also have maintained 'a civilisation based upon spiritual values as opposed to commercial values'.

Like Socialism, fascism offered a Utopian solution to the problems afflicting contemporary society: moral regeneration, national unity in place of division, and material improvements by way of popular welfare schemes to be put in place by the corporate state. Ever since leaving the Labour Party in 1930, Mosley had pursued his vision of an autarkic Britain – a self-contained national economy that would be insulated from the shocks and vicissitudes of the world economy.[9] He accused the politicians of refusing to follow the example set by Italy and Germany, and of stubbornly looking into the past for economic salvation, a futile policy which left Britain perennially at the mercy of international slumps and the interests of foreigners.[10] As Raven Thompson put it, corporatism would replace destructive individualism with a community-led policy. Under the aegis of the corporate state a fascist regime would set targets, allocate resources, and control wages, prices and profits in the light of the national interest; this would enable it to deal with problems of overproduction and underconsumption. If necessary the corporate state would reduce the working week so as to spread the work available, and it would stimulate employment and the domestic market by funding schemes of reconstruction.[11] In 1933 the BUF rather cheekily welcomed J. M. Keynes for his 'conversion' to fascism, and commended President Roosevelt for adopting parts of its programme.[12]

According to Mosley, under a fascist regime Britain would only resort to foreign supplies of raw materials and foodstuffs that she was unable to supply herself. Assuming a 'natural balance of exchange' between Britain and her colonies, the empire would be developed as a self-contained unit based on the exchange of British manufactures for colonial food and raw materials.[13] According to BUF propaganda, the Conservatives could never follow this policy, despite their protectionist credentials, because they had fallen under the influence of the great financial interests who insisted on investing in and importing from foreign countries to the detriment of British producers and workers. The fascists even promised to intervene to curtail the freedom enjoyed by the Stock Exchange to manipulate shares so as to create fortunes for a handful of speculators, though this evidently did not deter Mosley himself from drawing income from a range of stocks and shares in foreign companies.[14] Ultimately this strategy was intended to isolate Britain from an international economy that she could no longer control and, at home, to resolve the conflicts between employees and owners over wages and prices.

From 1935 onwards the movement's anti-capitalist bias was underlined by the growing use of the term 'National Socialist' in BUF propaganda. Not all the BUF leaders were happy about this, but some of them saw it as an opportunity to capitalise on the termination of the link with Rothermere and the *Daily Mail* which, they believed, had swept too many Conservatives into the organisation; now that many of them had left, the BUF enjoyed greater freedom to sharpen its image as a critic of capitalism and of its Conservative allies. This seems to be reflected in the tone of the propaganda issued by Raven Thompson, William Joyce and A. K. Chesterton. In 1935 Chesterton, for example, wrote a piece on 'The Economics of Savagery' which stopped just short of advocating the abolition of capitalism.[15] In a characteristically vitriolic attack Joyce denounced the 'mean, narrow-souled, pig-eyed, comfortable employer of labour, who sees in Conservatism the hope of conserving the wealth which he has amassed', and he dismissed the Conservative Party as 'one loathsome, fetid, purulent, tumid mass of hypocrisy'.[16] This was strong language even by fascist standards, and it is hardly surprising that Mosley eventually concluded that Joyce had become a little too offensive to be an asset. Nonetheless, Mosley was clearly keen to maintain a sharp and distinctive appeal to working-class communities in areas like Lancashire and Yorkshire where he hoped to offer fascism as a patriotic successor to both the Socialist and the Tory tradition.

Thus the violent anti-capitalism of fascist propaganda reflected not simply the extravagant emotionalism of leaders like Joyce, but a deliberate intention to outflank Labour and to displace the trade unions as representatives of manual workers. To this end the BUF established the Fascist Union of British Workers (FUBW) whose aims were to fight the Means Test, resist wage reductions and protect the unemployed; in the long run it hoped the FUBW would play a role comparable to that of the TUC in relation to the Labour Party.[17] From 1936 onwards, *Action* devoted a weekly page to union affairs, chiefly aimed at discrediting the trade union leaders whom it depicted as self-seekers and placemen who invariably betrayed the men. Writing from his experience as a Labour MP, John Beckett mocked the unions for their extravagant expenditure on officials and bureaucracy and for financing the Labour Party despite the reluctance of many members to vote for it. It was no secret that under the corporate state the workers would lose the right to strike because it was inconsistent with the overriding aim of eliminating the chaos inherent in liberal society and of ensuring that the national interest took precedence over sectional concerns. However, Beckett argued, this would be no real loss because the corporate system would remove the causes of strikes and lockouts by giving the unions one-third representation in each corporation along with one-third for employers and for consumers.[18] The worker would thus participate in planning output, wages, prices and profits, and enjoy greater influence than he had at present.

Despite these efforts, the proletarian aspect of 1930s fascism has often been disregarded on the grounds that the territory was firmly occupied by Labour and the trade unions. This, however, is to overlook the fact that only a minority of the working class voted Labour at this time. In any case, the drastic shrinkage of union membership from 8.3 million in 1920 to 4.4 million in 1933 had left millions of workers outside the sphere of organised labour despite a modest recovery of membership after 1934. There was consequently huge scope for a radical movement to take advantage of disillusionment with Labour, even if the BUF was far from wholly successful in doing so.

Moreover, as detailed studies of local fascism have appeared it has become clear that rank-and-file members were often drawn from unemployed working-class people, especially in the North of England and in the East End of London. The BUF branches in the East End experienced a high turnover of membership precisely because of the unemployment, both seasonal and cyclical, afflicting manual workers there. When they picked up jobs, branch activity usually fell off for a while; this was inevitable because over half the total membership comprised skilled and unskilled manual workers.[19] In such communities the options for political involvement were limited: Conservative organisation hardly existed, the Liberals were in decline and Labour seemed to offer little real opportunity for representation, leaving a vacuum for the fascists. 'I suppose it would have been easy to have joined the Communist Party,' explained one East End fascist, 'but I found that the more patriotic party had a lot more appeal to me. And I think this probably was [the case] with a lot of members. You could have gone one way or the other.'[20] The fascist-Communist link worked at a practical as well an ideological level as Nellie Driver noticed in Nelson: 'Ex-Communists made the best active members. They were not nervous of street work, or of opposition. It was not unusual for Communists to come to our meetings with the intention of causing a riot, and then to stay behind to fill in an enrolment form for British Union membership.'[21]

The intimate relationship between fascism and the Labour movement emerges repeatedly from the accounts left by BUF members from various parts of Britain. Echoing the East London member, a Birmingham school-teacher, Louise Irving, concluded that Labour was useless at handling economic issues, and believed that Mosley's programme represented 'Socialism at a national level – a highly patriotic kind of Socialism'.[22] Arthur Beavan of Cardiff and John Charnley, who lived in Blackburn and Southport, both had Socialist fathers. Patrick O'Donegan, a Shoreditch cabinetmaker, remembered having a Labour father who disliked the Communists and admired Mosley. Arthur Fawcett of Salford had working-class Labour parents, but he detested Labour, and his two brothers became Tories. 'Dixie' Deans, a boxer who trained the young Blackshirts in Hoxton, had previously been in the National Unemployed Workers Movement.[23] The account left by another working-class member from Huddersfield, Leslie Grundy, illustrates the route that led to fascism. Unemployed during the 1920s, Grundy concluded that the decline of the local textile industry was beyond the ken of the politicians, and he was impressed by the power exerted by financial interests in destroying the Labour government in 1931.[24] George Hoggarth, an Essex farmworker, started from a pro-Labour and pro-union position, and, by implication, would have been active in Socialist organisations if it had seemed worthwhile; but he became sufficiently disillusioned with them to join the BUF.[25]

Such rank-and-file fascists were clearly far removed, socially, from the world of the January Club and the pro-fascist metropolitan intellectuals on the *National Review*. To a large extent the fascism of these latter groups reflected their hostility towards democracy and their concern with international and imperial questions rather than with the depression and unemployment. By contrast, the working-class recruits to fascism felt that Mosley spoke to their economic grievances, a function which might otherwise have been met by Labour or Socialist organisations; they seem to have felt, not so much that Socialism was wrong, but that it was too weak, unresponsive to their needs, or insufficiently patriotic. The left-wing fascism they espoused may not fit schematic views of fascism, but it reflected the reality of the rank-and-file movement in the 1930s.

At a time when the remedies offered by Conservative, Liberal and Labour politicians for the economic depression and the decline of manufacturing appeared decidedly woolly, the violence of the BUF's attacks on finance capitalism undoubtedly gave the movement a distinctive cutting edge, especially when associated with anti-Semitism. However, anti-capitalism was a mixed blessing in that it deterred orthodox Conservatives who were otherwise sympathetic. As long as the National Government kept alive hopes of a complete recovery from the slump by using more cautious and conventional methods, Conservatives felt unwilling to contemplate a more drastic and Socialistic alternative. This inevitably put constraints on the extent to which the BUF could exploit its potential support on the right and among the middle classes during the later 1930s; it also explains why the fascists took a close interest in the renewed drift towards depression in 1938, which, had it lasted longer, might have discredited the government and proved Mosley correct in his pessimistic analysis.

On the other hand, anti-capitalist rhetoric was by no means a total handicap because it tapped into a long-standing tradition of hostility within British Conservatism, one which became increasingly vocal and embittered after the war. This can be traced back to the late-Victorian era when many families suffered from declining land values and dwindling agricultural profitability, at a time when the 'new' commercial and financial wealth was encroaching on their political and social leadership. Titled men drew what now seems a remarkable distinction between different types of wealth. They regarded those whose fortunes were held in land as entitled to special status because they were self-evidently committed to their country; unlike financiers they could not easily move their wealth nor use it to promote the interests of foreign countries. Queen Victoria memorably voiced this sentiment when she rejected Gladstone's proposal to ennoble Lionel de Rothschild: 'She cannot imagine that one who owes his great wealth to speculations on the Stock Exchange and loans to foreign governments can fairly expect a British peerage.' The point is, however, that Rothschild eventually got his peerage, along with dozens of other 'plutocrats' as they were derisively known in traditional landed circles. The social and political advance of these men provoked claims that Britain was falling under what were variously described as cosmopolitan, alien or Jewish influences, and thereby losing her grip as a great imperial power.

For a time the First World War checked these fears and gave a reassuring boost to patriotism, but after 1918 the realisation that they were losing political influence made the traditional landed class increasingly paranoid. During the 1920s 'capitalism' was being blamed for causing 'flabbiness', undermining British traditions, and distracting the people with purely materialist ambitions.[26] Although almost all the post-1918 governments were either Conservative or Conservative-dominated, many on the right wing of politics regarded their economic strategy as fundamentally flawed. During wartime, when Britain had been obliged to abandon the gold standard, her pattern of trade had been severely disrupted. Faced with the loss of export markets and invisible earnings from abroad, most politicians, economists and businessmen believed it essential to attain the pre-war level of trade as quickly as possible and restore the pound sterling as the leading medium of exchange. In 1918 the return to the gold standard was pronounced by the Cunliffe Committee to be the overriding objective of British policy.

Endorsed by most politicians, this strategy reflected the Victorian, internationalist, free-trade thinking which was anathema to fascists and to right-wing Conservatives. However, they appeared to be going against the grain as the pound rose in value from $3.40 in February 1920 to $4.79 by 1924, close to the pre-war level. This emboldened the Baldwin government to return to gold at the old parity of $4.86 in 1925. As a result, not only did British exports become more expensive, but bank rate and interest rates were raised in order to defend the pound at its new high level by attracting and retaining foreign funds in Britain. This became a running grievance throughout the decade. In 1929 for example, the critics pointed to the confabulations between Montagu Norman of the Bank of England and his American opposite number, the President of the Federal Reserve Bank, which resulted in an agreement to raise interest rates from $4\frac{1}{2}$ to $5\frac{1}{2}$ per cent; this, they contended, was contrary to British interests because it deterred investment and prevented a fall in unemployment.[27] 'We seemed to have forgotten to be Tories in the real sense,' commented Lord Lymington. 'Instead we were conserving nineteenth-century Liberal ideals of laisser faire, of devil take the hindmost.'[28]

In addition to Lymington, vocal anti-capitalist Tories included Douglas Jerrold, Sir Charles Petrie and Francis Yeats-Brown, all of whom felt disgusted by Baldwin's liberal Conservatism. They traced the party's current malaise to the exodus of big business from Liberalism in the 1890s and 1900s; fearful of Socialism, business joined the Conservative camp where 'it soon acquired a dominant position'. Petrie argued that this actually undermined the Conservative Party by making it appear to the working classes as part of a capitalist conspiracy and by infecting Conservatism with its timidity. 'I am a Tory not a Conservative,' insisted Petrie, 'and when I criticise Conservatism it is because, under the influence of Whiggery and Big Business, it has departed from what I believe to be the basic principles of Toryism.'[29] During the 1920s and 1930s Conservatives who thought along these lines felt marginalised by the party machine and by Baldwin's determination to make Conservatism acceptable to Liberals. When Central Office took steps to prevent Douglas Jerrold becoming a parliamentary candidate, he reacted by acquiring control of the *English Review* in 1931 which he used as a platform for 'real Toryism as opposed to the plutocratic Conservatism represented by the official party under the then Mr Baldwin's uninspiring leadership'.[30] Petrie, Lymington, Arnold Lunn and Sir Arnold Wilson MP formed the core of the *English Review* group of anti-Baldwin Tories.

For these rebels there was no clearer proof of their diagnosis than the blindness of the Conservative Party and urban England generally towards the plight of agriculture, the bankruptcies among farmers and the government's perverse reliance on imported food supplies.[31] Quite simply, they regarded agriculture as the most crucial element in British society and considered it deserving of unqualified support and protection. In a typical manifesto entitled 'Folly and Fertility', Lymington insisted that if Britain became self-sufficient in food she could employ an extra half a million men on the land.[32] By 1938 his analysis reached a stark conclusion in a book, *Famine in England* in which he painted an alarming picture of the next war when the scarcity of food would lead to a breakdown of law and order. Gripped by the fascist obsession with moral and physical degeneracy, Lymington bemoaned the fashion for feeding a generation of Englishmen on tinned food, the loss of 250,000 agricultural labourers since 1921, the spread of suburban development and the deterioration of the urban population: 'in every great city there is a scum of sub-human people willing to take any chance of a breakdown in law and order.'[33] He attributed the current decline to the exploitation of the land during wartime, the impact of death duties and the ruinous land sales of the 1920s. In particular he blamed the influence of the banks when dealing with farmers faced with collapsing prices, and the large profits enjoyed by middlemen, especially the big chain stores and United Dairies.

Above all, though, Lymington and the other critics condemned British governments for their readiness to keep the home market open to imported food and for granting credits to competitors such as Russia and Argentina to export to Britain. Since the return to gold in 1925, he argued, British policy had steadily undermined domestic producers, a policy which merely 'made the world safe for banking'.[34] Russia and Argentina became the two favourite targets for fascist propaganda in the 1930s. The BUF highlighted investments by the City of London designed to expand textile production in Argentina, thereby accelerating the loss of the British market there and boosting Argentine imports produced with cheap labour.[35] Nor did Mosley shrink from criticism of Canada and Australia for promoting their manufacturing industries, which were relatively inefficient, to the detriment of British exports.[36] Unlike many Conservatives he remained sceptical about the value of the agreements on empire trade reached at Ottawa in 1932. Hopes of significantly boosting Britain's sales to the empire foundered on the determination of the Dominions to develop their own industry; in any case, as Mosley noted, Canada was now more inclined to buy extra goods from the United States than from Britain.

From this perspective the claims of the National Government to be restoring the country's agriculture and manufacturing seemed implausible and fraudulent. It was wedded to a system of finance capital which left Britain 'at the mercy of free money and speculators'.[37] For fascists the only effective remedy lay in a strategy of economic nationalism and expansion of the domestic market within punitively high tariff barriers. There was nothing objectionable in this approach for large numbers of Conservatives even though most of the landed and titled figures remained reluctant to align themselves openly with fascism. Mosley, however, was working to a long-term plan, and his confidence that they were being steadily converted to the philosophy of the corporate state was not wholly an illusion.

On the other hand, in the short to medium term the fascists suffered from the fact that the general improvement in living standards after 1933 discredited their pessimistic view and made the corporate state appear less an urgent necessity than a distant ideal. Consequently, during the mid and later 1930s the BUF targeted those sections of society that either failed to benefit from the general improvement or felt neglected; this included farmers, shopkeepers and a wide range of small businessmen, and textile workers, all of whom were portrayed by fascists as the victims of unfair competition by alien and cosmopolitan interests.

As we have already seen, the well-founded grievances of the agricultural community during the 1920s made it a natural focus for the BUF. Fascists were attracted to agriculture both because it was already part-way along the road to corporatism, and because it spoke to the romantic-nationalist strain in the movement; men like Lymington adopted the 'Save Our Soil' rhetoric, deploring the threat to the countryside posed by developers, suburbanisation and the break-up of traditional family farms.[38] The National Farmers' Union (NFU) had been established in 1908 to represent farmers – as opposed to labourers or landowners – to lobby MPs and to influence legislation; its membership rose from 76,000 in 1920 to 131,000 by 1939. Although the NFU occasionally backed parliamentary candidates, as it did four Conservatives in 1922, it purported to be politically neutral and sought the direct representation of its members in parliament.[39] Fascists were keen to point out that only the corporate state would guarantee this. Although governments had been happy to incorporate the NFU into the official system during wartime, they seemed reluctant to allow it much influence in normal times. For its part the union's leadership felt very uncertain about its policy and strategy; it resented all state regulation and interference on the one hand while demanding protection for the industry on the other. The NFU was damaged by the impression that it enjoyed an informal alliance with the Conservatives, though the union was, in fact, disapproved of by Baldwin who regarded it as narrow and selfish.[40] Politicians felt more sympathetic to the interests of consumers in keeping food prices low, and to the labourers in maintaining minimum wages. As a result, farmers felt politically marginalised, which only exacerbated their sense of grievance over their economic distress. In 1930 prices for potatoes and cereals were so low that some farmers claimed it would not be worth harvesting the crop, and they threatened to withdraw the employers' representatives from the district agricultural wages committees.[41] They regularly rebelled against their own leaders and against the political parties generally. Recognising that this discontented and volatile community was susceptible to fascist propaganda, the BUF engaged in a running battle with the NFU, which was anxious to make its collaboration with the government respectable, for the allegiance of rank-and-file farmers.

In theory the shift to a general policy of protectionism in 1932 should have resolved the problems of agriculture. However, Mosley's scepticism was proved justified by the agreements reached at Ottawa that year.[42] In general the tariffs were too low to give significant assistance to British producers. Moreover, the commitment to imperial preference meant conceding low tariffs on empire goods which consequently won a large share of the domestic market; British farmers needed even higher tariffs to exclude imports from outside the empire. However, the government's emphasis on low food prices and on promoting empire trade, left them with little alternative. In effect, after decades of controversy, it emerged that tariffs were not a solution for the weaknesses of British manufacturers or farmers.[43] They went some way to excluding foreign consumer goods, but made little impression on the traditional heavy industries that had shrunk so drastically since the war. This situation enabled the fascists to denounce the new protectionist policy as a failure caused by the timidity of MacDonald and Baldwin.

However, the National Government had not yet exhausted its options. It effectively adopted the Agricultural Marketing Act which had been drawn up by the previous Labour government. This led to the introduction of subsidies and to the establishment of a number of marketing boards for milk, potatoes, pigs, wheat, sugar and hops, which were to buy up farmers' output. The chief inspiration behind this programme was Walter Elliott who served as Minister for Agriculture from 1932 to 1935 and had an eye on the politics as much as the economics of farming. Elliott used the system of marketing boards to draw the NFU into a closer relationship with government by incorporating its representatives into the administration and giving them seats on the boards.[44] To some extent this enabled adjustments in agricultural policy to be implemented by private discussion between the interested parties and the ministry, effectively eliminating parliament from the process. The policy culminated in the appointment of Sir Reginald Dorman-Smith as Minister of Agriculture in January 1939, an appointment which the BUF described as 'the last move in the Conservative Party's little game with the farmers'.[45] It was certainly a singular appointment. The MP for Petersfield, Dorman-Smith had no previous ministerial experience, but he was a recent NFU President and also a member of Lord Lymington's English Array.[46] Taken together, the political and economic dimensions of the agricultural policy indicate how close it was possible to get to a corporatist strategy within the British parliamentary system; the policy underlines the importance attached to countering the fascist case by demonstrating that farmers' interests were not being neglected.

As a result of the subsidies and marketing boards, agricultural output increased by 16 per cent between 1931 and 1937 in return for an annual expenditure of between £30 and £40 million pounds. This was a modest boost to the industry, but it failed to reassure the whole of the farming community. Some critics complained that the government was trying to manipulate the NFU by introducing Conservative Central Office representatives into its organisation with a view to quashing farmers' protests.[47] Lymington, who had initially agreed to serve on the Milk Marketing Board, conceded that it had raised the retail price but not the wholesale prices of milk; he resigned in 1933 complaining that middlemen were still allowed to exploit the producers by getting them to sell below the guaranteed price.[48] This sounds impetuous on Lymington's part, but as farmers in several areas voted to reject the Board he was not wholly out of touch.[49]

In *Action* the BUF published a regular 'Farmer's Diary' containing detailed reports written by Jorian Jenks, a farmer who was the movement's adviser on agriculture. Each week a specific grievance was highlighted:

imports of Irish lamb, bacon, fruit, or sugar beet for example. The BUF persistently attacked Elliott for continuing to give subsidies on imported beef.[50] In 1935 it complained that milk producers were not receiving an economic price and demanded that the Marketing Board fix the price to cover costs and a profit.[51] In 1936 the Potato Marketing Board came under attack for advising farmers to be cautious over planting, even though potatoes were still being imported.[52] In 1937 the BUF targeted poultry breeders, arguing that for every egg laid in Britain another was dumped by foreign producers.[53] Mosley himself maintained his visits to farming districts during the later 1930s and apparently received invitations to speak from producer groups and even several county executives of the NFU.[54] It is significant that the two constituencies in which Mosley contemplated standing at the next general election were both agricultural – Evesham in Worcestershire and Ormskirk in Lancashire.[55] As a result of the war he was never put to the test, but the choice is an indication of the fascists' own assessment of their potential support.

By comparison with its concern for the farmers the government offered virtually no substantial support to small shopkeepers, a similarly disgruntled section of society. Admittedly, the BUF itself was slow to appreciate the potential at first; it may have been provoked by accusations that big business had forced Rothermere to abandon his backing for the BUF in 1934 by withdrawing its advertising. The multiple or chain stores offered an easy target for fascist propaganda because many of them were under foreign ownership and were responsible for huge imports of goods produced by cheap foreign labour. As a result the BUF regularly attacked Marks & Spencer and Montagu Burton as Jewish, Woolworths as American, Unilever as Jewish-Dutch, and the Vestey Meat Trust for dealing in Argentine beef, not to mention Sainsbury, Liptons, Boots and Timothy Whites, though they showed more caution towards the Co-operative Stores. All these combines were condemned for crushing small shopkeepers by means of bulk purchases, price-cutting, and bullying the producers into giving large discounts.[56] The BUF even characterised price-cutting in the retail trade as equivalent to blacklegging among workers or working for less than union rates, because it damaged the employment of other employees.[57]

This propaganda signified that the BUF entertained high expectations from small businessmen during the later 1930s. 'Shopkeepers have almost more to gain from corporate organisation than any other section of the community,' claimed Raven Thompson who, as the movement's chief ideologist, undertook to elaborate the fascist solution to the problems of the small man.[58] He accepted that the current weakness of purchasing power among consumers had exacerbated the rivalry between the Co-operatives, the multiple stores and the small shops, but he argued that fascism would remedy this partly by expanding domestic demand. But the BUF proposed to go much further in regulating the distributive trade by controlling competition and minimising the overlap between shops by restricting retailers to selling specific products. Under the corporate state a Distributive Trades Corporation would be established with the power to issue licences to prevent the growth of an excessive number of retail outlets in each area. Licences would be granted to the big combines only in large towns and only if they dealt in British goods. Combines deemed to be too alien would be closed down and their outlets redistributed to private traders or Co-operatives. A Co-operative Central Buying organisation would obtain the advantage of bulk purchase for small shopkeepers and support them against the threat of bankruptcy.[59]

The BUF campaign for small business was at its height during 1937–9 when *Action* ran several weekly columns for shopkeepers. It used these to attack the 'Sunday Trading Tricksters', that is, Jewish shopkeepers who had the choice of opening on Sundays under government legislation on Sunday Trading, while others had no option but to close and lose business.[60] This was complemented at the local level. In Dorset, for example, Ralph Jebb, the BUF's parliamentary candidate, conducted a personal canvass of local shopkeepers in 1937 and held special meetings for them.[61] In Bethnal Green, Hackney, Stoke Newington and other parts of East London the fascists exploited resentment by local grocers and hairdressers towards Jewish businesses, hoping to attract new recruits into the organisation.[62] The BUF had correctly calculated that a distinct constituency was open to its message. In most working-class communities there was a long-standing tradition of setting up small shops, often in the front room of family homes, as an insurance against the unemployment of the main breadwinner. A successful business exercised a perennial appeal, not only as a means to prosperity, but as a route of advance up the social scale. All too often, however, this proved to be an illusion, for a high proportion of small shops made negligible profits or ceased trading due to their customers' unpaid debts. Unsuccessful proprietors were naturally susceptible to propaganda that offered easy scapegoats for their failure, whether the big chain stores or small Jewish-owned shops.

East End shopkeepers must have found the attention paid to them by Mosley, who made regular appearances, very flattering. In a typical address to small traders in Bethnal Green in April 1938 he reminded them that although essentially individualists, they must combine to protect themselves; already they were the victims of the big Jews, but now the Sunday Trading legislation put them at the mercy of the small Jews too.[63] Mosley used the shopkeepers' dilemma to illustrate the wider case for a corporate state:

'Democracy spells ruin to the small independent trader who finds that his pleas are ignored by the Government, spurned by the press and laughed at by the Opposition.'[64] He rammed home his usual message that the Conservatives were too committed to non-intervention and high finance to be interested in saving the small man from being driven out of business; only the BUF would fight their case. In the long run the corporate state would grant them an occupational franchise and thereby save them from being swamped by the big battalions of voters as they were at present.

There is some evidence that the BUF made significant headway among newsagents at this time. In 1937 it challenged the legislation that stopped them employing juvenile labour, thus forcing up their costs and compelling them to impose a delivery charge on customers.[65] As a result of a BUF poster attacking Woolworths for paying low wages and imposing long hours and other criticism of multiple stores, W. H. Smith imposed a ban on all promotional material by the BUF. In retaliation the fascists organised sales of *Action* outside Woolworths stores and claimed to have increased its circulation as a result.[66] Such activity brought them to the attention of the trade newspaper, the *National Newsagent*, which encouraged its members to read *Action* and display its posters.[67] The general secretary of the Federation of Retail Newsagents endorsed BUF proposals for the distributive trades and demanded a statutory national agreement to end the 'chaos' in the trade.[68]

Several similar proprietors were targeted by the BUF, including small drapers, who were alleged, rather implausibly, to be suffering competition from department stores such as Debenham & Freebody, Harvey Nichols, Selfridges, and Marshall & Snellgrove.[69] In 1938 some four hundred taxi drivers attended BUF headquarters to hear an attack on the influx of alien drivers, many of whom were alleged to be using taxis as a supplementary income. As a result the taximen invited Mosley to address them. To rousing applause he proposed to abolish the private hire services, which were undercutting the regular drivers and depriving them of their livelihood, and to use the machinery of the corporate state to regulate their industry so as to eliminate the current chaotic conditions.[70] The BUF also took an interest in the low wages paid to clerks and hotel employees, and highlighted the ineffectiveness of union organisation in these sectors. In such cases the fascists not only claimed that the corporate system would raise inadequate wages, but pointed to social policy in Italy and Germany where the state gave additional support to men who were trying to maintain families on low incomes.[71]

It is difficult to assess the success of this campaigning, though an analysis of BUF membership in the East End found that 24 per cent were drawn from lower middle-class occupations and a further 14 per cent were self-employed people including shopkeepers.[72] This is a high proportion, and suggests that at local level British fascism did resemble the larger Continental movements in composition. The fact remains, however, that the movement was working comparatively narrow seams in British society. The prospect of launching a wider appeal revived during 1937 when the economy seemed poised to descend into another slump. Mosley forecast that by the autumn of 1937 prices would be rising faster than wages, thus giving the fascists the opportunity to foment industrial unrest: 'They must be prepared to use every weapon available in order to obtain control of an appreciable section of the working class, so that the party would be ready to strike hard in two years from now.'[73]

In view of the fascists' condemnation of strikes this was particularly cynical, though for a time it looked as though the economic recovery was indeed unravelling. In early 1938, when unemployment stood at 12.9 per cent, Mosley launched a new campaign in Lancashire. No less than 32 per cent of cotton weaving capacity and 24 per cent of spinning capacity remained unoccupied during the last two peacetime years. This underlined the fragility of the economic recovery and its reliance on the stimulus provided by rearmament. Unemployment was still at 11 per cent when the war broke out. However, the looming depression was soon swept away. The desperate demand for munitions workers during the Second World War rapidly restored full employment, and thereby disrupted Mosley's carefully calculated plan to appeal to the voters at the forthcoming general election as the one leader capable of rescuing Britain from a fresh round of social and economic collapse.

TWELVE

Anti-Semitism and the Reorganisation
of Fascism 1936–8

'I don't regard Jews as a class, I regard them as a privileged misfortune.'

William Joyce, speech at Chiswick, January 1934

In November 1936 the *Evening Standard* carried several lengthy reports by Dudley Barker on the dangerous situation in London's East End. 'An evening journey east of Aldgate', he wrote, 'is an astonishing experience.'[1] Hundreds of meetings were being held each month by both fascists and Communists, all attended by the police for fear of outbreaks of violence. Barker described open-air meetings where

> around the crowds are lines of police, almost shoulder to shoulder. Police cars patrol slowly by, and under the lamplight stand police horses ... Casting a wider circle still one finds small parties of Blackshirts parading the main streets, bickering here and there in a childish fashion with Jews ... shouting slogans that spell the letters of Sir Oswald Mosley's name and occasionally singing the unpleasant song with the refrain 'We've got to get rid of the Yids'.[2]

These gatherings were more or less under control, but 'leading down from the main streets are the deserted side-streets where the much-discussed terror by night is said to stalk, and where stories are told of safety-razor blades stuck in potatoes and apples, or the peaks of caps, of bits of piping, lengths of railing torn from the house fronts, and knuckledusters, knives and hobnailed boots used as weapons against the partisans who wander into opposition territories.'

As Barker recognised, anti-Semitism in the East End predated the Blackshirts by many years. By 1900, following years of persecution of the Jewish communities of eastern Europe, Britain's Jewish population had risen to 160,000; this represented about 0.3 per cent of the total population, though many people insisted it was much higher. Like the Irish before them, poor Jewish immigrants tended to concentrate in large urban districts, especially London's East End, Leeds and Manchester, thereby generating accusations about overcrowding and pressure on the Poor Law; subsequently they became the target of complaints about sweated labour and the undercutting of existing businesses. By the 1890s anti-immigrant propaganda had become an important element in populist Conservative campaigns in the East End and delivered a number of victories to Tory candidates in working-class constituencies there. In 1905 the Balfour government enacted the Aliens Act in an attempt to appease anti-immigrant opinion, but controversy continued through the Edwardian period over how strictly the legislation was implemented by the Liberal governments. Meanwhile, well-established Jewish families, now capitalising on their wealth to win entry to society and politics, attracted accusations of opportunism and disloyalty. The 'Court Jews' – Sir Ernest Cassel, Baron Maurice de Hirsch, the Rothschilds and the Sassoons – who became part of the Prince of Wales' circle, were the focus of such resentment. These attacks culminated in the controversy over the Boer War which some Radical and Socialist critics interpreted as an unnecessary war instigated by Jewish capitalists wielding influence behind the scenes to protect their interests in South Africa. Though relatively mild, such propaganda left the British susceptible to later conspiracy theories circulated in *The Protocols of the Elders of Zion*.

On the positive side, many Jews had clearly become integrated into British society and politics. Well-organised bodies of Jewish voters helped to deliver many urban seats to the Liberals, and Jews worked their way up through the trade unions and the Labour Party. Inevitably there was a downside to this progress, in that it fostered the belief among right-wing propagandists that the Jews were becoming a powerful and sinister element in Britain. Through his journal, *G.K.'s Weekly*, G. K. Chesterton pursued a vendetta against Jews whom he depicted as parasites and irritants embedded in Christian society.[3] In the *National Review* Leo Maxse portrayed them as a fifth column, a credible claim at a time of growing apprehension about spies and saboteurs planning the disruption of the country following the expected German invasion. These were not simply the obsessions of a few cranky intellectuals and frustrated politicians; they reached a popular audience through newspapers and novels such as *The Thirty-Nine Steps* and *Huntingtower* by John Buchan: 'Capital had no conscience and no fatherland', declared one of Buchan's characters, 'besides the Jew was behind it . . . Yes, sir, he is the man ruling the world just now.'[4]

The First World War initiated a prolonged period of increasingly hostile attitudes towards Jews, especially after 1917 when they were widely implicated in the Bolshevik Revolution. Amid mounting hysteria an Aliens Restriction Act passed through all its stages in one day in August 1914. It allowed the detention and deportation of undesirable aliens; in 1915 all male enemy aliens were interned. On the eve of the war Lord Rothschild had urged Britain to be neutral, and the *Daily Mail* led complaints that Jews were shirking the call-up and demanded their exclusion from official service. In fact, 41,500 Jews served in the British forces, representing 13.8 per cent of the Jewish population compared with a rate of 11.5 per cent in the general population. The real targets of press attacks were the non-naturalised Russian Jews who were not eligible to serve and in any case felt unhappy about fighting to support the hated Tsarist regime. Prominent Jews, including Sir Ernest Cassel and Sir Edgar Speyer, became the object of legal action challenging their right to be privy councillors; and Sir Alfred Mond sued for libel when a Conservative alleged that he was not fit to be a member of parliament. This attack on Jews in public life received support in the respectable press, notably from H. A. Gwynne and Wickham Steed, the editors respectively of the *Morning Post* and *The Times*, who initially endorsed the *Protocols* as authentic and wanted all Jews removed from official service.

Although the *Protocols* was widely accepted as a forgery in the 1920s, this did nothing to check the circulation of crude anti-Semitic material by H. H. Beamish's organisation, The Britons, the prolific author, Nesta Webster, the Duke of Northumberland's journal, *The Patriot*, and Arnold Leese's Imperial Fascist League. It was Leese who enjoyed the dubious distinction of being the first to advocate the extermination of the Jewish people, while Beamish advocated their removal to Madagascar. In such a climate it became feasible for Sir William Joynson-Hicks to rise to the Home Secretaryship in 1924, largely on the strength of his reputation as an unapologetic opponent of the Jewish community. In effect anti-Semitism was rife at all levels of British society and throughout the political system. Although this prejudice did not result in active discrimination except over immigration and naturalisation rights, it reflected a ubiquitous racist view of the supposed flaws and characteristics of Jewish people and an assumption that Jews were highly organised for sectional rather than national interests. However, the issue did not become prominent until 1933 when Hitler's assumption of power led immediately to boycotts of Jewish businesses in Germany, legislation designed to exclude Jews from the professions, and internment in concentration camps. As a result, some three to four hundred Jews escaped to Britain each month during 1933, and about one hundred in 1934. Edward Doran, the MP for North Tottenham, demanded the prohibition of this 'invasion of undesirable aliens', and, as unemployment was still very high, the government restricted the entry of refugees.[5] In fact, however, the costs to Britain were minimal because the Jewish community offered to bear the refugees' expenses, and by 1938 Jewish refugees themselves had created 250 businesses generating employment for around 250,000 people.[6]

At the time, however, the beneficial contribution made by highly educated and resourceful Jews was ignored amid a prevailing belief that the political and economic influence exercised by Jews was damaging to British inter-ests. 'We find the Jewish influence naked and unashamed,' wrote Alexander Raven Thompson in *Action* in 1936.[7] For most, though not all, fascists such exaggerated beliefs were simply axiomatic and they culminated in the charge that Jews were responsible for dragging Britain into war with Germany in 1939. Yet although many studies have been made of the Jewish community and anti-Semitism in Britain, scholars have been chary of attempting to assess the validity of contemporary claims about Jewish influence. Like all minorities and pressure groups, Jews experienced great difficulty in trading their political participation for real influence. For example, although urban Jews became an important element in Liberal electoral strategy, they failed to get the 1905 Aliens Act repealed when the party returned to power. Since 1858 Jews had been eligible for election to parliament, and by 1899 they returned nine MPs, mostly Liberals. Yet this comparatively easy acceptance into the system involved an unspoken obligation to abstain from promoting sectional interests too energetically; ambitious politicians could rise as indi-viduals by identifying themselves with their party rather than with their community. Thus, Rufus Isaacs (Lord Reading), Herbert Samuel and Edwin Montagu held a string of offices in the Edwardian Liberal governments, eventually reaching the cabinet, though all became targets of vitriolic anti-Semitic campaigns.[8]

By 1929 the number of Jewish MPs had risen to seventeen, and remained at sixteen in 1931 and 1935. However, Jews in all three parties continued to suffer from racial prejudice and disparagement of their patriotism by their opponents throughout the period. Though third-generation British, Edwin Montagu (Liberal) still found himself derided as an alien. Sir Philip Sassoon (Conservative) was told by David Kirkwood: 'You are no Briton. You are a foreigner.' In a notorious incident in the Commons in 1938 a Tory member, Sir Robert Bower, invited Emmanuel Shinwell (Labour), who was born in London and lived in Glasgow, to 'Go back to Poland'. An angry Shinwell crossed the floor and, finding Bower 'continuing to sit there grinning and silent. I thereupon clouted him on the face.' Although Bower was reproved by the Speaker, his remarks attracted some vituperative supporting corre-spondence; one lady told him: 'I am no very great admirer of Hitler, but in one thing he was right . . . The Jews. They are a creeping cancer in the soul of any country they fasten on to. Britain is being handed over to them and no one seems to care.'[9] Only a handful of Jews achieved ministerial office between the wars – Montagu, Samuel, Reading, Shinwell, Sassoon and Leslie Hore-Belisha – and it is worth noting that four of these were handicapped by being Liberals. To find the obsessive anti-Semite, William Joyce, heaping personal abuse on Hore-Belisha was unsurprising: 'his melon-like physiognomy expanded in a horrible Moroccan Jewish grin'; more telling were the remarks of the well-connected Chamberlainite MP, Sir Henry 'Chips' Channon, who described him as 'an oily man, half a Jew, an opportunist, with the Semitic flair for publicity'.[10]

The experience of Philip Sassoon, an ambitious, but less controversial figure, was perhaps a better indication of the difficulties. At the age of twenty-three he succeeded his father as Tory member for Hythe where he continued to spend lavishly on the constituency. He was extremely well-connected, serving on the staff of Sir John French and Sir Douglas Haig, becoming a friend of the Prince of Wales, and acting as parliamentary secretary to Lloyd George and later to Stanley Baldwin. Sassoon put his London and country houses at the disposal of his leaders and by 1931 he was entertaining the cabinet to lunch practically every week.[11] Catering one's way to the cabinet was still a perfectly acceptable method of advance, employed successfully by Lord Londonderry for example. Yet if Philip Sassoon always seemed close to positions of power, he obtained meagre returns for his efforts. He approached Lloyd George for a job without result;[12] and under Baldwin he was confined to an under-secretaryship at the Air Ministry before briefly serving as First Commissioner of Works in 1937. In fact Sassoon was used by the politicians rather than the other way round. Desperately anxious to win acceptance as an Englishman, he lacked a base in a party that tolerated Jews only insofar as they were useful.

Despite these obstacles, did Jews exert influence behind the scenes as the fascists claimed? Britain's commitment to the creation of a homeland for the Jews in Palestine can be traced to the memorandum put before the cabinet in 1915 by Herbert Samuel who became High Commissioner in Palestine in 1920. The cause enjoyed the backing of several influential figures, notably A. J. Balfour and his niece, Lady Blanche Dugdale, an indefatigable ally of the Zionist leader, Chaim Weizmann.[13] Other right-wing supporters included Lord Milner, L. S. Amery, Sir Mark Sykes and Joynson-Hicks, though their Zionism was not an indication of sympathy for Jews, but rather an attempt to shore up British influence in the Middle East.[14] In any case, Sassoon took no interest in Zionism and Montagu used his influence to oppose it.[15] Jewish MPs took up constituents' grievances with the Home Office, but were often inclined to let non-Jewish members voice their concerns in parliament. Their influence over immigration, naturalisation and refugees was fairly marginal, and even a well-organised pressure group like the Board of Deputies of British Jews made little impact on unsympathetic home secretaries.

However, most fascists devoutly believed that the real power exercised by Jews lay in the economic sphere where their role as financiers and company directors enabled them to ensure that British economic strategy favoured the City and foreign investment at the expense of manufacturing. It has been established that a high proportion of non-landed wealth in Britain was Jewish;[16] but how far its holders commanded any distinctive influence is obscure. There is no reason to believe that the undoubted bias in British policy in favour of finance was a reflection of Jewish interests as opposed to the general run of banking and commercial interests, not to mention the views of economists and politicians. In support of their claims, fascists repeatedly pointed to the pressure allegedly placed on Lord Rothermere by Jewish companies to withdraw advertising from his newspapers if he continued to promote the BUF. Similar cases were occasionally cited; the *North Manchester Guardian* received threats from advertisers in the Cheetham district of Manchester because it had printed letters supportive of Mosley.[17] However, such actions were defensive reactions to attacks on Jews, rather than evidence of effective influence. The same is true of the well-coordinated attempts to subject Nazi Germany to economic pressure after 1933. This originated in the United States, but in London, too, meetings of the Jewish textile trade were held to consider what steps to take, and Jewish merchants resolved to boycott German goods.[18] Winston Churchill was a notable supporter of such moves.[19] In the later 1930s fascists used such evidence to substantiate their claims that, as the Jewish community had been deprived of its stranglehold over the German economy, it was trying recover its position by mobilising Britain and America for war.[20]

In the context of inter-war attitudes the surprising thing about the British Union of Fascists is not that it was anti-Semitic, but that the connection should require any qualification. At one of his first BUF meetings in October 1932 at the Memorial Hall, Farringdon Street, Mosley responded to hecklers by referring to them as 'three warriors of the class war – all from Jerusalem'.[21] This was his first recorded anti-Semitic remark. It is indicative of the climate of the 1930s that he did not regard it as evidence of prejudice towards Jews; he was merely expressing commonly held assumptions that equated Communists with Jews. In the same way, when he condemned international financiers he argued that this was only incidentally critical of Jews. There is, in fact, some validity in Mosley's claim that his movement had not originally been anti-Semitic. He himself had never been obsessed with Jews in the manner of Sydenham, Northumberland, Webster, Beamish and Leese whose anti-Semitism had a *racial* quality; nor did he subscribe to the kind of conspiracy theory advanced in *The Protocols*. In 1931 one of his New Party candidates had been the Jewish boxer, Ted 'Kid' Lewis. Thus, when he wrote *The Greater Britain* in 1932 Mosley made no reference to the Jews, and he dismissed the Imperial Fascist League as 'one of those crank little societies . . . mad about the Jews'.[22] Of course, his moderation was to some extent a reflection of purely tactical considerations in that he recognised as early as 1933 that Hitler had 'made his greatest mistake in his attitude to the Jews'.[23] An internal BUF analysis of the movement's decline in 1934 argued that Mosley's original position on the Jewish issue had been sound and popular but that the movement had departed from this with 'very grave repercussions'.[24] The truth is that although Mosley fully shared the prejudices about Jews that were current in Britain at this time, he had not envisaged anti-Semitism as a central element of his movement in 1932. The conclusion seems inescapable that his subsequent use of the Jewish issue was at least partly political or opportunistic.

Certainly Mosley was not slow to sharpen his attitude, especially when the BUF began to attract several vocal and embittered anti-Semites, including William Joyce, A. K. Chesterton and Major-General Fuller, who regarded him as rather soft on the subject. Though Fuller attributed his own conversion to fascism to the issue of army reform, he said little on that subject; instead he wrote excitable diatribes about 'The Cancer of Europe' and denunciations of the League of Nations as 'a bastard and a pink Jewish-Bolshevik baby'. Fuller even revived the medieval idea of the Jews as agents of the Devil in a vast scheme to destroy Christianity.[25] In the *Fascist Quarterly* Chesterton mocked Jews for seeking respectability and then trying to dominate the host society: 'To go to a swimming pool anywhere near London or the large cities is as efficacious as baptism in the Jordan; one becomes positively anointed with Semitic grease,' he wrote.[26] It was the blatantly pro-Nazi Joyce, however, who posed the greatest challenge to Mosley's restrained view. At an after-dinner speech at the Park Lane Hotel a member of his audience was shocked by Joyce's face – 'luminous with hate' – on the subject of the Jews: 'never before in any country had I met a personality so terrifying in its dynamic force, so vituperative, so vitriolic . . . We listened in a kind of frozen hypnotism to this cold stabbing voice.'[27] In fact, on this occasion Joyce was being restrained for the benefit of his respectable and uncommitted audience.

The combination of Nazi anti-Semitism and the influx of virulent anti-Semites into his organisation left Mosley buffeted by forces beyond his control. According to *The Blackshirt* the Jewish issue was unknown to Italian fascism, and the BUF itself had initially forbidden Jew-baiting in any form.[28] But as Hitler's accession to power had led to the persecution of German

Jews, it was natural for Jews in Britain to see the BUF as part of the wider threat and to participate in anti-fascist campaigns, even in the face of warnings from the Board of Deputies to avoid doing so. Consequently, the fascists portrayed themselves not as the instigators, but as the victims of aggression by the Jewish community in league with Communist Party. Joyce regularly flourished figures showing that in 1934–5 20 per cent of the 293 people convicted of assaults on fascists were Jewish.[29]

During 1934 the BUF deliberately pushed the Jews to the centre of its propaganda effort. In November Mosley devoted almost an entire speech at the Albert Hall to arguing that his Blackshirts were compelled to defend themselves against violence and blackmail: 'Fascism has accepted the challenge of Jewry.'[30] The official BUF line now disparaged Jews as an anti-national element within British society. In July Mosley had told Rothermere that Jews were no longer admitted to the Union and that although racial and religious persecution would not be permitted under fascism, 'we shall require the Jews, like everyone else, to put the interest of Britain first.'[31] The BUF openly stated its intention of deporting those who failed to show a proper display of patriotism and allowing them to take their money with them only if it had been 'honestly earned'; even Jews who remained in Britain would be barred from becoming members of parliament or civil servants.[32]

While this growing emphasis on the Jews was to some extent simply a response to street-fighting with the left, it was also a more calculated move, a means, in effect, of arresting the decline of the movement. In the second half of 1934 many leading fascists privately accepted that the BUF had lost momentum, and Mosley concluded that the march to power would take longer than he had expected.[33] To some extent this was seen as a result of factors beyond their control. Rothermere had withdrawn his support; the novelty of the Blackshirts had worn off; and they had become the target of effective attack in the *News Chronicle* and the *Manchester Guardian*. The cause had also been damaged by association with Hitler and his regime: 'It is essential that if we are to overcome this, we take Italy as our model, rather than Germany for there is a very widespread admiration for Mussolini and the progress of Italy under Fascism.'[34] From this perspective the BUF's drift towards confrontation with the Jews merely compounded the mistake. While Joyce was keen to maintain attacks on Jews, others argued that this simply provoked opposition: 'What the big Jew yearns for is that Fascists will knock the little Jew on the head, so that non-Jew popular opinion will be shocked. Then they will spend millions to exploit the situation.'[35]

This debate over tactics led to prolonged jockeying for influence over Mosley within the leadership during 1935 and 1936. For a time Joyce appeared to be in particular favour with Mosley. However, this was resented by Robert Forgan who resigned in May 1935 to be replaced by F. M. Box, a former Conservative agent. But Box himself soon came unstuck. He attempted to get the expenditure under control, which was naturally unpopular at headquarters.[36] The organisation had been spending about £25,000 a year on salaries to sustain a much larger headquarters staff than was really justified. Box also failed to appreciate that Mosley, who suffered from an excess of vanity, liked to be told how well everything was going. Rather than flattering him Box offered a more realistic plan for a steady build-up of the organisation in the country. He also disliked Jew-baiting and violence, and he complained: 'It is a pity Rome is now dictating Mosley's policy.'[37] In effect, Box and Fuller wanted the BUF to develop more along the lines of a conventional political party, whereas Raven Thompson, Joyce, Francis-Hawkins, Chesterton and Beckett sought to maintain the ideological cutting edge of fascism and its aggressive public display. As a result Francis-Hawkins was reported by Special Branch to be steadily gaining influence during 1935; eventually Box quit, and by the start of 1936 Mosley had given Francis-Hawkins effective control of the organisation.[38]

However, this by no means resolved the underlying issue: what was the most appropriate strategy for fascism in Britain? Received opinion suggests that by the later 1930s the BUF had become dominated by anti-Semitism. Yet this is not entirely consistent with the fact that Joyce himself left the organisation, as did other extreme anti-Semites. Internal critics argued that *The Blackshirt* was increasingly seen as mediocre and off-putting, while the extreme language used by Joyce in BUF publications alienated a wider audience and undermined the movement's credibility.[39] Mosley himself gradually came to see Joyce in this light, though he did not dispense with him until 1937 after his anti-Semitism had failed to get him elected to the London County Council. However, Mosley's real intentions are far from clear. According to one leading historian he endorsed Francis-Hawkins' preference for concentrating on the Blackshirts and the show of military paraphernalia.[40] Yet this seems inconsistent with his decision to adopt an electoral strategy. Mosley had always envisaged acquiring his first foothold in power through normal parliamentary means, although he could not afford to make too much of this to a movement emotionally committed to anti-parliamentarianism. Seduced by Mussolini's mythical 'March on Rome', many leading Blackshirts eagerly awaited the opportunity for a physical coup. However, other fascists complained that this delusion had been spread to the branches and 'thus drives away those with any intelligence'.[41]

Major-General Fuller, who became increasingly influential with Mosley, warned that the movement must abandon its crude, aggressive image and stop talking about 'revolution' and 'dictatorship', language which might have been justified initially but now alienated the voters.[42] 'It must not be overlooked that this is an old country, very solid, stable and matter of fact,' wrote Fuller. 'Most of the Blackshirts are too young to realise this . . . In a revolutionary country they would be right, but in a conservative country they are wrong.'[43] Consequently, for Fuller the immediate objective was to steal the thunder of the National Government, attract its better elements, and win some seats in parliament; he pointed out that many of the 'Rothermere Fascists' had left because they had not been properly utilised. The implication was that the BUF must develop into something like a conventional party organisation and that the role of the Fascist Defence Force would be downgraded or at least become less conspicuous.

For all his platform braggadocio Mosley was sufficiently realistic, especially after 1934, and perhaps still sufficiently imbued with British political culture, to see the wisdom of Fuller's analysis. He never doubted that he would be able to seduce part of the political establishment into accepting the idea of the corporate state; but this was best accomplished gradually under cover of an electoral strategy which would allay some of the apprehension about radical change. This involved striking a difficult balance because Mosley could not risk disappointing his more enthusiastic and aggressive followers; he had to keep them with him but also stop them getting out of control for fear of ruining the more respectable side of his campaign. This was by no means eccentric, for many earlier political movements in Britain, from Chartism to the suffragettes, had operated 'physical force' and 'moral force' wings simultaneously; but the tactic required skill and luck if it were not to explode in the face of the leaders.

Unfortunately for Mosley several things went wrong during 1935. In June he was considering whether to stand for election in Evesham or in Ormskirk, and the print run for *The Blackshirt* was doubled to 24,000.[44] But his plans were put on hold when the prime minister decided to risk an early general election in the autumn – before the BUF was ready. The development of an election machine was also being hampered by dwindling resources. Privately, Count Grandi had begun to pour cold water on the British fascists during 1935. 'All this money, believe me, Duce, even on the best supposition, simply goes down the drain,' he wrote.[45] According to Special Branch, Mussolini reduced his monthly subsidies from £3,000 to £1,000 by 1936, leaving the organisation unable to finance a full-scale general election.[46] This led to further reductions of headquarters staff from 129 to 57, the dismissal of regional organisers, and to the sacking of Joyce and Beckett as paid speakers in 1937.

These setbacks inevitably meant a long-haul strategy rather than the quick dash to power that had briefly looked feasible in 1934. Once the 1935 election was out of the way, the movement could start preparing for a serious challenge around 1939-40. By January 1936 a complete reorganisation was under way under the direction of Francis-Hawkins. While the movement continued to publish *The Blackshirt* to cater to a working-class readership, it launched a new weekly, *Action*, supposedly for the more educated; initially *Action* read more like a normal newspaper, incorporating pages on sport, women and films, and was clearly designed to attract the uncommitted. Under the editorship of John Beckett, *Action* achieved a circulation of 26,000 while *The Blackshirt* sold 23,000.[47] Since 1935 the movement had also published the *Fascist Quarterly*, which carried lengthy articles comparable to those in the conventional journals; in 1937 it became the *British Union Quarterly*. The decision to drop the word 'fascist' from the name of the organisation at this time was a telling indication of the new strategy; though apparently well-received in rural districts, it caused more dissent among the urban members.[48]

The key aim of this reorganisation was to place a properly trained election agent in every district. According to Fuller, it had previously been too easy for people to become branch organisers without scrutiny, thus allowing rogues and Special Branch informers into the organisation.[49] District Officers were to become parliamentary candidates and to open an election fund to finance their campaigns; it was optimistically estimated that £300 would suffice for a campaign in a borough constituency and £400 in a county seat. Mosley urged that every ward should build up a small body of active workers backed by a much larger number who would simply make regular donations: 'You must keep in touch with these inactive members, not ignore them as we did in the early days.'[50] The active members were to receive a free uniform provided they undertook to devote a minimum of two nights a week to the BUF and to sell a quota of *Action* and *The Blackshirt*.[51] Additionally, each district was urged to equip itself with transport, loudspeakers and a brass band designed to make a big impression at outdoor meetings. Once each town had its band they were to take it out to the villages and expound the fascist programme for agriculture: 'this has proved again and again to be irresistible to farmers and farmworkers alike. You have to arouse the countryside.'[52] To judge from the records of the local BUF organisation in Dorset, the movement made some progress with this scheme; a parliamentary candidate was adopted, the election agent received some training, women speakers were coached, and the branches organised canvassing which 'will be done largely by women'.[53]

By the end of 1936 Mosley boasted one hundred fascist parliamentary candidates. These included some highly respectable names such as Vice

Admiral Powell in Portsmouth Central and Major-General Fuller who was to oppose Duff Cooper at St George's, Westminster. As the new Public Order Act was about to come into force this announcement was timely, for adoption of candidates went some way to discrediting accusations that the movement was aiming to acquire power through violence. Optimistic as ever, Mosley declared: 'I want the first impact of our MPs upon Parliament to be that of a disciplined, organised movement marching into that place, giving it the shock of its life. I don't want to go there with an ordinary, flabby Parliamentary Party of the old character.'[54] But Fuller complained: 'O.M., I am afraid, is no general . . . [he] will not see sense. He goes rampaging on talking of fighting 400 seats. This is all absurd.'[55] Fuller wanted him to build his cells quietly and concentrate on 'gutter electorates' in the East End before branching out.

The adoption of this longer-term electoral strategy did nothing to impede local campaigns against Jews during 1936 and 1937. To judge from its efforts in East Anglia, Lancashire and the East End, the BUF's tactics were to home in on immediate and relevant grievances, with the result that the movement assumed a slightly different character in each region of the country. This logic dictated that the importance it attached to the Jews varied. When John Charnley enquired at his local headquarters in Southport he was told that the movement was not anti-Semitic at all; but in complete contrast a Carlisle recruit described how members were required to march round a room chanting, 'The Yids, the Yids, we've gotta get rid of the Yids!'[56] In October 1935 Mosley had given John Beckett and A. K. Chesterton carte blanche to do whatever they could to consolidate the movement in the East End, which was tantamount to promoting anti-Semitism.[57] The resulting campaign was actually pioneered by 'Jock' Houston, an effective Cockney orator who was transferred to Manchester when he was found to have a criminal record; subsequently E. G. 'Mick' Clarke took over his role.

From its beginnings in Bethnal Green the attack on Jews quickly spread across the East End, and during 1936 regular complaints about Jew-baiting arrived on the Home Secretary's desk. The issue became significant in the three main areas of Jewish settlement, London with about 200,000, Manchester with 35,000 and Leeds with 30,000. Even so, there is some doubt about the effectiveness of anti-Semitism. In Yorkshire, for example, the period of rapid growth for the BUF in 1934 preceded the agitation against the Jews; when it reached its height in 1936–7 the membership was in steep decline.[58] Provocative fascist campaigns in the Jewish areas of Manchester and Leeds merely stimulated anti-fascism organisation. A BUF march to Holbeck Moor near Leeds in September 1936 clashed with a hostile demonstration of 20,000 people in which Mosley and many other fascists were attacked and injured by missiles.[59]

In response to complaints from local Jewish residents, the Manchester police attended all fascist meetings and kept notes. But they insisted that BUF meetings were 'conducted in a very orderly manner and without giving any cause for objection'; they argued that trouble only arose if Jews attended and interrupted the speakers.[60] At a meeting at Platt Fields in Manchester in June 1936 Jock Houston referred to Jews as the international enemy, dominating banks and commerce and fomenting war between Britain and Germany; he also attacked individual Jews by name. However, the Attorney General, Donald Somervell, told complainants that no criminal offence had been committed.[61] In any case the local constables present at the meeting insisted that 'Houston's speech was in no way provocative . . . [he] made no reference to the Jewish question at all.' The other speaker, they reported, 'did not make use of any offensive remarks at all other than the usual political statements that are made at all these meetings.'[62] These were revealing remarks, and only too typical of police constables' views; in effect anti-Semitic speeches were so routine as to be scarcely noticed. Many people simply discounted hostile comments because they seemed justified. One Home Office official, responding to abusive letters about Jews, noted: 'there is a considerable body of feeling in this country against the Jews, not because they are Jews, but because of the undesirable social and economic activities in which some Jews engage.'[63]

Left-wing accusations about police bias in favour of the fascists were actually corroborated privately by Blackshirts who saw them as friendly and noted that there was some common membership with the BUF. At one point the East End police became so friendly towards the fascists that the Home Office felt obliged to send in outsiders, known as 'Simon's Body Snatchers', to make arrests.[64] The explanation for the bias lay partly in the fact that the police compared the Blackshirts' behaviour at meetings and demonstrations favourably with that of the Communists. When Sir Percy Harris, a Bethnal Green MP, complained about the BUF, he was simply assured that the police regarded Blackshirt marches as manageable; they did nothing illegal, and, as for Jew-baiting: 'in this locality such speeches are fairly well received by the majority of the persons attending.'[65] Failing redress either through the police or through the courts, many Jews inevitably joined the Communist Party and other anti-fascist organisations despite advice from their own leaders to keep a low profile.

It must, however, be said that at the level of Chief Commissioner, the police showed much more concern about taking action against anti-Semitic propaganda. However, they were somewhat handicapped by the inadequacy of the law. In September 1936 a case was launched against Raven Thompson following a meeting of 800 people in Bethnal Green where he ignored cautions against using abusive language.[66] The dismissal of this case was a major deterrent to further prosecutions. Minor incidents involved less risk. A Blackshirt selling *Action* at the corner of Tottenham Court Road and Oxford Street in September attracted a hostile crowd when he shouted 'Down with the Jews'. Police then warned him, but as he ignored them he was arrested, charged and cautioned.[67]

Despite its small numbers the Imperial Fascist League was responsible for some of the worst attacks on Jews. Since 1934 the Board of Deputies had been pressing the Home Office to prosecute its leader, Arnold Leese; but officials judged it unwise to give him publicity.[68] They also felt that in cases involving the distribution of literature they could only prosecute for libel or causing a breach of the peace, which was not likely to be effective.[69] Eventually, however, the authorities decided to charge Leese and his printer, Walter Whitehead, with conspiracy to effect a public mischief by printing scandalous and libellous statements about Jews in *The Fascist* in July 1936. When the case was tried in September William Joyce sat in court taking copious notes. Leese pleaded not guilty, employing a variety of arguments: that ill-will between Jews and Gentiles already existed and that he was not trying to cause it, that the Jews were referred to as descendants of the Devil in St John's Gospel, and that, as they were not British subjects, the Jews were not protected by British law. 'This prosecution is not a criminal prosecution at all but a political prosecution,' he claimed; 'it is an attack not just on Leese and Whitehead, but is an attack on the British custom of Free Speech, and is an attack made because the people involved are Jews.'[70]

Although Leese was convicted of creating a public mischief, for which he received a six-month prison term, the prosecution met with limited success. He was acquitted of the charge of seditious libel, probably because the jury saw him as a man of honest convictions who did not deserve serious punishment. Also, as the officials had correctly foreseen, even a successful prosecution had little effect on the small groups of fanatics who peddled anti-Semitic propaganda. Although the IFL became dormant while Leese was in prison, he subsequently published *My Irrelevant Defence* in which he elaborated on his claims about the ritual murder of Christians by Jews. During the next three years neither he nor other equally extreme anti-Semites were prosecuted because the Director of Public Prosecutions had concluded that cases of seditious libel for attacks on Jews would fail, and because the politicians felt it a mistake to give publicity to otherwise insignificant organisations.

Mosley himself actually instructed his speakers to refrain from attacks on Jews on the grounds that they were likely to do more harm than good, but he was not in control of the movement in the East End. Apart from the BUF, the agitation there was stirred by the Imperial Fascist League, the National Socialist League and the National Workers Party (later National Socialist Workers Party), an extreme pro-Nazi group founded in 1933 by Lieutenant Colonel Graham Seton Hutchison, another disillusioned wartime soldier.[71] Joyce and the other leading figures regarded Mosley's advice as a retreat which would only damage morale. Far from moderating his language, Joyce was keen to court prosecutions of the leading BUF figures.[72] The action taken against Leese left him exulting in the thought that the movement had now entered a new phase of government persecution; the more fascists were arrested the more public sympathy they would win. According to Joyce, the fact that the Jews had manoeuvred the government into this tactic 'showed clearly that Britain is today under a hidden dictatorship far harsher than that in Germany and Italy'.[73]

It was this reckless attitude that swept the BUF into increasing confrontations in the East End culminating in the notorious 'Battle of Cable Street' on 4 October. When the fascists announced their intention of marching through the East End, some 77,000 people signed a petition within forty-eight hours demanding a ban on it. However, the Home Secretary told a deputation led by local mayors that he would not interfere as the government did not wish to infringe freedom of speech.[74] As a result the anti-fascists, adopting the slogan of the Spanish Republicans defending Madrid – 'They Shall Not Pass' – pushed ahead with elaborate plans to block Mosley's route. By 2.00 p.m. on 4 October 50,000 people had gathered to prevent the entry of the march into the East End, and something between 100,000 and 300,000 additional protesters waited on the route. Barricades were erected across Cable Street and the police endeavoured to clear a route by making repeated baton charges. Eventually at 3.40 p.m. Sir Philip Game told the 3,000 fascists to abandon their march and escorted them back to the Embankment.

In this way Cable Street went down in history as a decisive check to fascism. In reality it was nothing of the sort. Almost all the fighting took place between the police and the anti-fascist demonstrators. More importantly, Cable Street did nothing to dampen anti-Semitic agitation in the East End. In the immediate aftermath large and enthusiastic audiences turned out for BUF meetings in Stepney, Shoreditch, Bethnal Green and Stoke Newington, and by the autumn Special Branch had concluded that the movement had gained popularity and boosted its London membership by 2,000.[75] A defiant Mick Clarke warned: 'It is about time the British people of the East End knew that London's pogrom is not very far away now.

Mosley is coming every night of the week in future to rid East London and by God there is going to be a pogrom!'[76] While the fascists capitalised on the local organisation they had built up, their opponents could not easily repeat opposition on the scale of Cable Street. They held their hand, fearful that continued disorder at fascist meetings might encourage the government to use anti-fascism as an excuse for legislation designed to restrict their own street campaigns; in this the Communists were not far wrong.

However, for a time the agitation in the East End seemed to tail off. As always, the onset of winter weather reduced the number of meetings, though some five hundred still took place each month. In December the attention of the fascists was briefly diverted by the crisis over the abdication of Edward VIII; and in 1937 they focused on the Spanish Civil War and the need to avoid entangling Britain in foreign conflicts. By the spring Special Branch felt that BUF fortunes were at a low ebb and would fall even further if only the press would ignore them.

In the East End the movement decided to test its popularity by contesting the London County Council elections in March. Mick Clarke and Raven Thompson stood in North East Bethnal Green, Anne Brock-Griggs and Charles Wegg Prosser in Limehouse, and William Joyce and Jim Bailey in Shoreditch. During February and March the BUF held about 150 election meetings with an average attendance estimated at 1,400; as the rival parties kept away there was little heckling.[77] Anti-Semitism certainly formed a major part of their campaign; fascist propaganda accused Jews of corrupt influence in slum clearance schemes, poor hygiene, exploitation of labour, running cut-price shops, opening on Sundays, insurance frauds, drug trafficking, the white slave trade, lowering the tone of the area and devaluing British cultural life. More generally, the BUF adopted a distinctly populist stance for the local elections, trying to present itself as an anti-party movement by inviting the voters to return its candidates as 'watchdogs' who would 'keep a sharp look-out that no grafter of Right or Left takes advantage of the present rotten system to fill his pockets'.[78] It proposed to abolish rates and replace them with a universal property tax based on the services supplied and adjusted according to the wealth of each district; in other words there was to be an element of redistribution: 'it is a principle of National Socialism that the privileged owner shall be made to recognise his social obligations and assist those who are less fortunately situated.'[79]

On Polling Day the BUF practised all manner of infringements of electoral law designed to intimidate its opponents: chalking pavements outside polling stations, displaying sandwich boards in front of the doors, parking vans outside its rivals' headquarters, forcing rival vans on to the kerb, stopping rival vans by placing its own vehicles in front and behind them, and broadcasting the close of the poll at 8.30 when there was still half an hour to go.[80] It was as though the fascists were rehearsing for the kind of elections they planned to run when they got into power.

Mosley's hopes were high, and in Limehouse a victory was expected for Brock-Griggs and Wegg Prosser. In the event his candidates polled just 23 per cent in Bethnal Green, 16 per cent in Limehouse and 14 per cent in Shoreditch. Although the leaders professed themselves well-pleased, these results were clearly disappointing. The only mitigating factor was that as the local government electorate excluded non-ratepayers, it was less representative of young people who provided much of the BUF's support. Raven Thompson was reported 'rather bewildered at the result'. Joyce took his defeat badly. At the count in Shoreditch he treated his opponents to an abusive speech and promptly stalked off the platform; he decided his nomination as a candidate had been 'arranged by Hawkins in order to discredit him'.[81] The truth was that the campaign had exposed the fascists' inexperience; they had been misled by their election organisers who were easily impressed by enthusiastic meetings and kept telling Mosley how well they were doing.[82] The outcome of the LCC election accelerated Joyce's detachment from the BUF and led Mosley to dismiss him from his paid position. He and Beckett moved on to form the National Socialist League in April 1937, thereby making it easier for Mosley to refocus the movement on issues other than anti-Semitism.

By April 1937 things were getting back to normal in the East End according to Special Branch reports; disorderly meetings and anti-Semitic abuse was again the order of the day.[83] Yet in January the new Public Order Act, with its prohibitions against just such provocation, had come into force. However, in May when several East End MPs complained to Sir John Simon, the Home Secretary, about fascist intimidation of their constituents, he lamely replied that the use of the Public Order Act depended on its interpretation and on the view taken by the police of their duties under its provisions.[84] Eventually the Chief Commissioner insisted that anti-Semitic propaganda should no longer be ignored; speakers should be warned and then arrested if they persisted in using grossly abusive language.[85] The first prosecution over the use of insulting language towards Jews was against one Joseph Gough for a speech in the Birmingham Bull Ring in the summer. Gough, who refused to be bound over for six months, received a month in prison. In June Mick Clarke was arrested for a similar offence. However, in August the *News Chronicle* was still complaining that the police were too sluggish about using the new Act.[86] In July 1938 Clarke was again convicted for anti-Semitic remarks at a meeting at Stepney where he was quoted as referring to: 'You dirty rotten bastard Jews. Dirty Jews. You scum of the Earth.'[87] Despite this, Clarke's case involved a private prosecution that went ahead without police evidence. By this time most fascist speakers had become more circumspect in their language. In any case, by 1938 the BUF was concentrating more on its 'peace' campaign. The public response to this in the East End was more muted, even though Jews remained the indirect target for their alleged role in entangling Britain with Germany.

The significance of anti-Semitism in the wider explanation for the failure of fascism in Britain is problematical. It seems obvious that insofar as the BUF drifted into a more extreme position it eventually discredited itself with respectable opinion. Certainly anti-Semitism, in both Germany and Britain, complicated Mosley's long-term strategy by continually embroiling his followers in street violence when he wanted to build an election machine. The 1937 LCC elections suggested that while the systematic exploitation of prejudice against Jews could give the movement a solid base, it was not sufficient to make it more than a minority cause.

On the other hand, there is a case for saying that the BUF suffered by being insufficiently anti-Semitic, and that in the later 1930s it was outflanked by far more militant organisations at a time when the influx of Jewish refugees was pushing the issue up the agenda. In these years opinion in Britain began to polarise as a result of Nazi persecution of the Jews. Charles Wegg Prosser left the BUF because he deplored its anti-Semitism, and other right-wing groups suffered in the same way; the Anglo-German Fellowship, for example, was highly embarrassed by anti-Jewish laws in Germany and experienced a major loss of membership as a result.[88] Conversely Joyce, Beckett and Chesterton quit the movement in search of a more aggressive approach to the Jewish question, and although the leaders denied responsibility for anti-Semitic activities, there is evidence that rank-and-file Blackshirts operated as agents provocateurs in 1938–9; a favourite technique was to distribute sticky labels in public places bearing such slogans as 'Christ Was The First Fascist', and 'Any Jew Is Worth Two Englishmen'.[89] This rank-and-file activity could not be controlled, and, in any case, it was easy for members to act under the auspices of other extremist organisations.

During the last three years of peace a rash of such groups appeared in Britain. Even the British Fascists had adopted an anti-Semitic policy by this time. In 1936 H. H. Beamish returned from exile, though The Britons was now defunct. The Imperial Fascist League had made the Jews the focus of its campaigns. Leese revived the myth, last current in medieval times, about Jewish involvement in ritual murders of Christians, and he propagated Beamish's idea for expelling all Jews to Madagascar.[90] Several new organisations also appeared at this time. In April 1937 Joyce and Beckett formed the National Socialist League. They took only sixty BUF members with them, a dwindling band of fanatics operating out of a headquarters in

Vauxhall Bridge Road, addressing street-corner gatherings, exchanging insults with opponents and getting into fights. In his pale trench coat Joyce strutted about as though imitating Hitler; but his colourful rants against Jews, 'dribbling old prelates, verminous Bloomsburgians, myopic printers' hacks, and every sort of meddlesome old woman, male or otherwise', were delivered to small audiences who often told him to 'go and live in Germany if you like it so much'.[91] He appeared in court in November 1938 and May 1939 for minor assault but both cases were dismissed.

Joyce also became involved with a more sinister group, the Nordic League, which emerged later in 1937. For the first year it operated as a secret society using passwords for entry to meetings, and numbers, not names, for its officers, though intelligence agents turned up regularly to report its proceedings. But towards the end of 1938 the Nordic League went public with a campaign designed to traduce Jews as warmongers.[92] While most members were obscure individuals, the League attracted several prominent men including Joyce, Beamish, Fuller, Brigadier Blakeney and Lord Brocket (the former Conservative MP, A. R. N. Nall-Cain). Its leading figure was Captain Archibald Henry Maule Ramsay, currently Tory member for Peebles and South Midlothian. Dedicated to saving their race and their country and to friendship with 'our blood brothers' in Germany, Nordic Leaguers used the 'Perish Judah' greeting and enlivened their gatherings with Nazi marching songs and films with such titles as 'Secrets of the Abattoir', featuring the ritual slaughter of cattle by Jews. The League enjoyed links with a large number of small fascist and anti-Semitic societies but not with the BUF.

As Britain slipped towards war members of the League became totally gripped by conspiracy theory. In May 1939 Joyce regaled them with accounts of Neville Chamberlain taking lunch with Sir Philip Sassoon, while another speaker observed that the prime minister 'had of course received fresh instructions from his Jew boss.'[93] Captain Ramsay pandered to their fears by describing the 'hidden hand' that was manipulating the press, the BBC and the Conservative Party; passages from *The Protocols* were also read to show how its predictions were being fulfilled.[94] Although Ramsay praised Chamberlain, he warned that 'the invisible power behind the premier was forcing him the way he did not wish to go. He needed the backing of all patriotic loyalists in order to achieve his ends.'[95] Though regarded by MI5 as quite unbalanced, to Nordic League members Ramsay appeared an authoritative and credible figure; and his suggestion that it lay with them to save the premier from the evil forces surrounding him was no doubt an uplifting one for a beleaguered body of fanatics alarmed at the inexorable drift into war with Germany. Although the authorities had enough material to prosecute, they rightly felt that Ramsay and the League reached too small an audience to be really dangerous.

Yet another, and more popular, anti-Semitic organisation, The Link, also appeared in July 1937. Its founder, Admiral Sir Barry Domvile, was a distinguished if somewhat unhinged character who had served on the Committee of Imperial Defence from 1912 to 1914, seen active service during the war, and been Director of Naval Intelligence from 1927 to 1930. For several years Domvile had become increasingly obsessed with the notion of a Judeo-Masonic conspiracy which he described as 'Judmas'. He argued that Britain had been led astray from her natural allies into the orbit of the United States and the Jewish financiers who controlled its policy; and he rejoiced that since 1933 Hitler had upset 'the whole of the stage setting so admirably arranged by Judmas'.[96] Domvile and The Link were associated with the Anglo-German Fellowship, though uncomfortably so, for the latter was a more upper-class organisation and less hostile towards Jews, though otherwise equally enthusiastic about Nazi Germany.[97] The Link counted Professor A. P. Laurie, Lord Redesdale, Captain Ramsay and another MP, Sir John Smedley Cook, among its members, but it chiefly aimed to win a popular following. Large branches quickly appeared in Birmingham and Southend, and membership reached 2,000 by April 1938 and 4,300 by June 1939.[98] In the spring of 1939, as Domvile busily toured the branches, he reported: 'everywhere I go I am asked about the Jews and what we are going to do about them.'[99]

The modest success enjoyed by The Link is a reminder that in the late 1930s extreme anti-Semitism was by no means an eccentric or marginal phenomenon; indeed it moved sharply to the centre of the stage for a time. This was because the growing problem of Jewish refugees had become entangled with the threat of war. Up to 1938 only 30,000 refugees had entered Britain from Germany, the result of the Nuremberg Laws of 1935 which deprived Jews of citizenship rights and prohibited intermarriage. During 1938, however, many more people fled their homes as a result of the German annexation of Austria, the dismemberment of Czechoslovakia and the notorious *Kristallnacht* of 9 and 10 November, when the Nazis attacked thousands of Jews, burnt synagogues, looted shops and homes and had 20,000 arrested and forced into concentration camps. In December Jewish property was officially 'Aryanised', effectively excluding Jews from economic activity in Germany.

These events greatly increased the pressure on the British government to admit refugees from Nazi oppression, but, contrary to traditional belief, much of British society proved to be remarkably unmoved by the plight of the Jews. In fact the government's initial response was to tighten the existing entry requirements by introducing new visas; ministers consistently justified their caution on the grounds that any mass immigration would provoke hostility towards Jews. Such claims were especially hypocritical in view of the fact that Neville Chamberlain himself was using the journal, *Truth*, to spread anti-Semitic propaganda written by his agent, Sir Joseph Ball.[100] *Truth*'s small circulation made it insignificant, but the popular press was as keen as ever to exploit prejudice against aliens. A *Daily Mirror* headline in 1938 – 'Britain Becomes Dump For The Nazi Exiles' – was typical. The propagandists offered respectable reasons for ignoring the plight of the refugees. In his book, *The Case for Germany*, Professor Laurie blandly denied there was anything wrong in Germany and claimed that the Jews were protected by the police from ill-treatment. The Redesdales dismissed reports about the persecution of Jews as Communist-inspired and insisted that, in any case, 'the Jews had brought all this trouble on themselves'. As a staunch apologist for Germany, Diana Mosley simply considered the atrocities as necessary to the survival of the Nazi regime. The popular patriotic historian, Arthur Bryant, who was employed by Conservative Central Office and was close to Baldwin and Chamberlain, disseminated some of the most poisonous propaganda; among other things he blamed Jews for the moral decline of Germany: 'these prototypes in real life were to be seen in the innumerable night-clubs and vice-resorts which mocked the squalid poverty of the German capital.'[101]

In fact, by September 1939 the British government had admitted around 70,000 Jewish refugees, a small enough figure to exclude the majority of those trying to escape but large enough to fuel a virulent agitation by fascist propagandists during the remaining months of peace. By the spring of 1939 Mosley was reviving his movement on the basis of the simple claim that the country was being dragged into an alien quarrel by sinister financial interests: 'the jackals of Jewish finance are in full cry.'[102] Yet even Mosley was outflanked by more extremist organisations. One such group started a pro-fascist newspaper, *New Pioneer*, in December 1938 supported by John Beckett, A. K. Chesterton, Lord Lymington, Anthony Ludovici, Major-General Fuller and Rolf Gardiner. 'We still ask ourselves', wrote Chesterton, 'why what the Jews declare to be their wrongs should be expiated by the shedding of innocent British blood.'[103] As editor of *New Pioneer* Lymington argued that it was uncharitable to Britain's own struggling black-coated workers to admit the refugees, and that wealthy Jews should be responsible for finding a solution, preferably a national homeland.[104] The BUF competed by running scare stories in which it suggested: 'Refugees To Have Your Boys' Jobs', and 'there is still plenty of spare cash for the aliens, however little there may be for the starving British worker.'[105]

In fact, the refugees did not become a burden on state finances. The Baldwin Refugee Fund, which had been established in September 1938, had raised £522,000 by September 1939, partly by attracting private money from cinemas which offered 10 per cent of their takings. Another half a million pounds was raised voluntarily by Jewish organisations in this period, making a total of two million pounds since 1935. The outbreak of war by no means put an end to this final emotive phase of anti-Semitism; but complaints about the economic burden of the refugees were soon to be eclipsed by the impact of the war which created an urgent need for extra labour.

THIRTEEN

'Who is King here? Baldwin or I?'

On 22 January 1924 King George V wrote his diary entry for the day: 'Today 23 years ago dear Grandmama [Queen Victoria] died. I wonder what she would have thought of a Labour Government?'[1] A good deal less than her grandson did, no doubt. George V had ascended the throne as an insecure young man in 1910 to find himself in the middle of a first-class constitutional crisis between the Liberal government and the House of Lords. Yet his twenty-six-year reign proved to be a triumph. In a period when royal families were collapsing or being discredited all across Europe, he showed a capacity to adapt and to manoeuvre successfully around the danger points. He certainly possessed a clearer grasp of his role as a constitutional monarch above party politics than his grandmother ever had.

The outbreak of war in August 1914 spared the King from the perils of domestic controversy and allowed him to play his role as the symbol of the national and imperial cause. When victory came George V emerged as the indisputable focus of patriotic celebration, attracting emotional expressions of support for the monarchy even from left-wing politicians who might have been expected to endorse republicanism. In this respect British experience contrasted with that of Germany whose military defeat discredited the whole autocratic, imperial system that had precipitated the war; it was followed by the swift departure of the Kaiser and by an unstable period in which influential sections of German society refused to accept the legitimacy of the democratic Weimar Republic. In Italy, where victory seemed more like defeat, the monarchy survived but the incumbent lacked the capacity to unite the country or the judgement to sustain the parliamentary system. Both countries suffered from a dangerous vacuum at the top of society which left an opportunity for extremist movements and for authoritarian leaders.

Yet there was nothing inevitable about this outcome. For the British royal family the Great War and its aftermath was an alarming time, especially as

King George and Queen Mary fully shared the prejudices of the limited circle in which they moved. Distrusting foreigners on principle, they found it hard to endure the excessive sentimentality aroused by the League of Nations; [2] in the aftermath of the war they feared the spread of Bolshevism, the wave of industrial militancy and the threat to private property. But however reactionary his instincts, the King's conduct was invariably tempered by realism. For example, the Russian Revolution of 1917 raised the question whether he should offer sanctuary to his Romanov relations in Britain. When the government agreed to offer asylum without fully considering the drawbacks involved, George V intervened to say that he would prefer them to go to Switzerland or Denmark.[3] He was undoubtedly correct in thinking it wise to keep his distance from an oppressive regime whose downfall had been a cause for celebration by liberal opinion in Britain; the Romanov link would have played into the hands of those who hoped the Bolsheviks' success would inaugurate a wider overthrow of imperialism in the West.

During the 1920s the Crown also played its part in recognising the Labour Party in its new position as the alternative government. 'No question of Republicanism as a serious proposition ever finds a place in Labour discussions,' commented Jimmy Thomas, a leading trade unionist and MP.[4] Indeed, the party discussed the issue just once for fifteen minutes at its 1923 conference where it rejected a Republican resolution by 3.69 million votes to 0.38 million. J. R. Clynes confidently predicted: 'If Labour came to power tomorrow they would find the King prepared to accept their advice as readily as that of the Liberal or Tory parties.'[5] His confidence was put to the test in January 1924 when the King invited Ramsay MacDonald to form a government as the leader of the second largest party despite the fact that he had only 191 MPs. 'I had an hour's talk with [MacDonald],' recorded the King. 'He impressed me very much; he wishes to do the right thing.'[6] On meeting him the new Labour ministers felt flattered and moved by his simplicity and sincerity: 'I had expected to find him unbending,' wrote Clynes, 'instead he was kindness and sympathy itself.'[7] As a result, the Labour Party became integrated into the governmental system without the controversy that it might easily have engendered.

George V faced an equally sensitive situation in 1926 over the General Strike. Although the Crown was not directly involved, the King demonstrated his awareness of the threat to national unity. Though declining to intervene, he cautioned his ministers to avoid doing anything likely to drive the striking men to desperation. When Churchill used the *British Gazette* to claim that 'the Armed Forces of the Crown will receive the full support of the Government in aiding the civil power', the King immediately protested to the War Office. He also advised the cabinet to resist any temptation to legislate during the strike in order to interfere with the use of union funds; he pointed out that as the men had been very restrained, such provocative action would be counter-productive.[8] As a result the monarchy maintained its position as a symbol of patriotic sentiment above party controversy. However, on the extreme right of politics this record seemed more a betrayal of the monarchist tradition than a triumph. Sir Charles Petrie complained that since Victoria's time the politicians had exploited the development of the pomp and pageantry surrounding the royal family in order to obscure its loss of real influence.[9] Any reversal of the trend would require a very different man on the throne.

Moreover, the popularity enjoyed by George V between the wars made the Crown appear more secure than it really was. Beneath his public triumphs, George V was privately a bad-tempered and often frightening man; both he and Queen Mary were rather cold and distant figures who left the emotional scars of family life on all of their children. The eldest son, David, the future King Edward VIII, though in many ways the most normal, was prone to depression and suffered a prolonged state of adolescent rebellion against parental control. Albert, Duke of York was rather dim, shy, lacking in self-confidence and frightened of his father. Henry, Duke of Gloucester was even more dim-witted. George, Duke of Kent caused considerable worry because of his dissolute lifestyle, fondness for nightclubs and relationships with both men and women. Prince John, who suffered from epilepsy, was largely excluded from the family and died in 1919. It was not a promising bunch from which to recruit the future King.

Much the most important single step towards securing the future of the monarchy arose by accident when the Duke of York fell in love with Lady Elizabeth Bowes-Lyon and, undeterred by several refusals, persuaded her to marry him. Yet although the announcement of their engagement in January 1923 caused a considerable stir, little was done to inform the public about the event. However, an enterprising journalist on *The Star* broke with convention by calling at the London home of the Earl of Strathmore in Bruton Street to congratulate his daughter. 'How kind of you to come,' Lady Elizabeth greeted him, displaying the easy charm that was to become her hallmark, 'Bertie – you know everybody calls him Bertie – has gone out hunting.'[10] Making the most of his opportunity, the *Star*'s representative quizzed Lady Elizabeth about her ring, where the Duke had proposed and how many times, where the couple planned to live, and whether she had received congratulations from the prime minister – 'not yet!' He carefully described her dress and concluded, 'The bride is very petite and has a magnetic personality.'[11] Today this famous interview seems remarkably bland, but in 1923 it caused a considerable stir because royalty simply did not reveal itself to the newspapers or the public in such an informal way. According to the received account the King, who was extremely fond of his daughter-in-law, reproved her, and, as a result, the new Duchess of York never gave another interview for the remainder of her long life. However, the marriage between Prince Albert and Lady Elizabeth Bowes-Lyon endowed the British monarchy with a very necessary insurance. While the new couple proceeded to produce two daughters and to cultivate an image of tranquil domesticity, which pleased the press and entranced the general public, they also took some of the pressure off the more wayward heir to the throne who showed little sign of marrying and settling down.

The Prince of Wales felt that he had experienced a 'wretched childhood', deprived of his mother's love and subject to endless criticism from his father who repeatedly told him to smoke less, eat more and take less exercise. Not surprisingly, from an early age he developed doubts about his fitness to become king. Frustrated at being prevented from fighting in the war, he eventually managed to join a regiment in France, but was irritated at being moved away from the Front whenever an attack loomed. 'I feel I'm the only man here without a job,' he complained.[12] After 1918 the Prince increasingly realised that his father was unable to appreciate how far things had changed, but believed that he himself understood the ordinary British man much better. Convinced that the men who had fought in the Great War deserved a better life, he became critical of the politicians' failure to fulfil their obligations to them. The Prince may have been immature and opinionated, but war had awoken his social conscience.

During the 1920s the Prince of Wales grew increasingly resentful of the restrictions placed upon him both as heir to the throne and as a man. Lacking a focus in his life, he looked desperately for love and company to save him from depression. His need for a mother figure soon led to involvement with a number of unsuitable women, including Mrs Freda Dudley Ward, the wife of a member of parliament.[13] As he began to make visits to the provinces and the Dominions, he was immensely flattered by the warmth of his reception. With help from Winston Churchill he learnt to deliver speeches, and as a result his self-confidence began to grow. But so, too, did his resentment towards the stuffiness of the court and his disenchantment with his personal staff. As the decade wore on the Prince became determined to become king on his own terms without the restrictions and the formality that his father had accepted; his would be a modern, streamlined monarchy in touch with his people's needs.

Unfortunately the Prince of Wales picked up opinions as easily as he acquired married women friends. His sympathy was easily aroused and he acted on impulse, but his views were as likely to be progressive as reactionary. On a visit to Durham and Northumberland in 1929 when he saw the life endured by coal miners he dropped some remarks about their 'appalling' and 'perfectly damnable' living conditions.[14] Such incidents sowed the seeds of distrust between him and Stanley Baldwin which were to prove so fateful in 1936. On the other hand, during the General Strike he ventured out with the police and loaned his motor car and chauffeur to help transport copies of the *British Gazette*.[15] Long before he succeeded to the throne the Prince's congenital inability to endure a purely dignified role detached from partisan affairs had become obvious, and in the eyes of the politicians and the court he inevitably appeared as a loose cannon. After a conversation with him about the Blackshirts in May 1934 the Home Secretary noted: 'we agreed that, without knowing much about them, we both thought it quite a good movement except for Mosley.'[16] Early in 1935 Special Branch reported that the Prince met Mosley in the company of the society hostess, Lady Cunard, where he questioned him about the strength and policies of the fascist movement.[17]

Although the Prince of Wales was hardly a fascist, he was predisposed towards the movement because his own rebellion against the old men who controlled the court and the cabinet made him a natural part of the constituency to which fascism appealed; he, too, saw himself as a champion of the younger generation and vaguely sought a more modern way of doing things. As we have seen, their patriotism, imperialism and their yearning for leadership made British fascists of the 1920s enthusiastic monarchists. But as yet they had given little thought to the precise relationship between the monarchy and a fascist system. Yet this relationship was of crucial importance for the fortunes of the fascist movement in Britain.

At first sight the cult of leadership that characterised Continental fascist regimes appeared alien to the British tradition. But in the 1930s British fascists endeavoured to adapt this to British expectations by pointing to the King's traditional role in putting down over-mighty subjects and protecting his subjects; they liked to cite the action of Edward I in expelling the Jews for antisocial conduct. They argued that fascism and the monarchy performed the same function by representing the nation as a whole rather than sectional interests or classes.[18] As proof of the compatibility of monarchy and a fascist regime they pointed to Italy where the court of King Victor Emmanuel with its associated hierarchy continued in parallel with the system of fascist honours and titles. According to Arnold Leese, in a fascist state the prime minister would be appointed by the king, as Mussolini had been, and, when a vacancy occurred, the Fascist Grand Council would offer names of successors to the king; in this sense the king would be more than a figurehead in the political system.[19]

Leese's idea of an enhanced role for the Crown was far from eccentric in inter-war Britain. By the end of the 1920s Conservative opinion had become aroused by the decline in the powers of the Crown and refused to accept the change as irreversible. In his influential book, *Conservatism*, Lord Hugh Cecil suggested that as the British public had lost faith in the representative system, which was a nineteenth-century idea, it should be prepared for a return to greater monarchical power. J. H. Blaksley put the case more explicitly in 'The Tory Ideal':

> To Tories a monarchical revival would be a wholly acceptable reform. The nature of Kingship is such that a deeper authority resides in it than in any republican system, and the Nation's best safeguard against tyranny, whether of baron, priest, adventurer, profiteer, or trade union official, must exist in the freedom of the Monarch.[20]

These sentiments were, of course, echoed by both English Mistery and English Array who regarded the king as the embodiment of the accumulated wisdom of his people and as their ultimate protector. They made no apology for their mystical belief in the monarchy; for them the king was semi-divine, a mixture of the human and the sacred just like the maharajas of the Indian princely states.

These romantic notions received academic endorsement from the historian, Sir Charles Petrie, who considered that the coronation made the king God's representative on earth. For Petrie the monarchy was best understood as part of the feudal system, which was itself a form of society close to fascism: 'The Feudal State was essentially a Corporate State in which the individual counted for very little and the corporation for a great deal.'[21] Far from being a despot, the king had his place in this system like everyone else. Like Lord Lymington, Petrie believed that the British had erred in allowing their king to become separated from his people; they had acquired the habit of letting him out to visit hospitals, launch ships and perform other trivial functions.[22] English Array became almost paranoid about the King as a virtual prisoner of the court, and there is some evidence that they infiltrated their supporters into the royal household with a view to emancipating him.[23] Their object was to restore him as the real leader of his people rather than merely a figurehead.

With this in view, they convinced themselves that their opportunity would come when the despised National Government of Baldwin and MacDonald eventually discredited itself: 'If in some hour of crisis His Majesty saw fit to give his subjects a strong and personal lead from the Throne, we might expect the sudden discomfort of all those wire-pullers and adventurers who misrepresent alike the wishes of the King and of his people.'[24] Opponents of democracy like Petrie took great comfort from the royal intervention in 1931 when George V had taken the initiative in securing a new administration following the collapse of the Labour government. The National Government was *his* government in a way that was not true of any other administration. Petrie argued that people had been looking for a Mussolini figure when the King stepped into the breach; and although custom had narrowed his choice of ministers, 'the King has the right to choose whom he will as prime minister'.[25] He hoped that if members of the royal family – especially the Prince of Wales – realised how popular they were, they would be prepared to make intervention the norm not the exception; the King might, for example, revive the old practice of presiding at cabinet meetings which had been abandoned at the accession of George I.[26]

For fascists it was especially frustrating that royal intervention in 1931 had produced what they regarded as a Frankenstein monster comprising all the elements of a discredited liberalism. As long as the parliamentary system continued to be presided over by a popular figure like George V who remained determined to stick to his constitutional role, it would prove an uphill task for them to persuade the people that the existing system was really bankrupt. In effect the British monarchy acted as a safety valve for extreme nationalist and anti-democratic sentiment, diverting it away from politics when it might otherwise have been mobilised by the forces of the right. A popular monarchy limited the scope for a charismatic leader of the sort that fascist movements considered necessary. Paradoxically, while the monarchy hampered fascism, at the same time it helped to strengthen the fascist mindset by sustaining the faith in a great leader figure capable of saving his country from the self-interest and corruption of party politics. The frustrations of the 1930s, especially the failure to deflect the National Government from its reform policy in India, led many disillusioned right-wingers to claim that the King had been let down by his ministers.[27] They saw their best hope for the future in the heir to the throne. Douglas Jerrold, an unapologetic enemy of democracy, claimed: 'All that is left of our national pride and national determination is centred on Windsor not Westminster. The sovereign is not the titular but the real leader of the nation in 1935.'[28]

These effusions were a natural product of the celebrations surrounding the old King's Silver Jubilee in 1935. Would his successor be the means of breaking the stranglehold of the National Government at last? Such expectations were strikingly reflected in an extraordinary campaign run during the summer of 1936 by the *Saturday Review*, following George V's death in January of that year. Under Lucy Houston the journal had become steadily more antagonistic towards the National Government over the League of Nations, Indian policy and the war in Abyssinia. Lady Houston, who regarded the new King, Edward VIII, as a 'Prince Charming', ran a series of articles advocating Britain's need for a benevolent dictator.[29] In June she published a dramatic petition addressed to the King couched in extravagant language: 'We want to hail you as our man of destiny who will free us from our perplexity . . . and heal our wounded pride which has fallen so low. Italy has her Mussolini; he is *her* man of Destiny . . . We look to you, our beloved King, to be our Leader, the only leader we can trust to save us.'[30]

Sweeping aside conventional notions about the royal role, Houston insisted, 'Queen Victoria commanded her ministers and they obeyed – and you have the same absolute right . . . Summon these men, the greatest enemies England ever had, and give them your ultimatum. Cowards and poltroons that they are, they will crumble at your feet.'[31] Uninhibited in her language, Houston repeatedly asked: 'Will the King be a Dictator?'; she drew parallels with the 'strong men of Destiny in Italy and Germany', and claimed that 'the King is a man placed by Divine Right at the head of the Race to rule it and command it.'[32] The campaign attracted some striking endorsements of Houston's view. One reader simply urged that 'the best English counterpart to the regimes of Hitler and Mussolini is the principle of personal Government by the King'; another explained that 'I have tried Fascism but found it much too Socialistic . . . Besides, I want to see the King supreme, not Mosley . . . A Royal Autocracy is the only form of authoritarian government which could gain the support of all sections of the community.'[33]

In effect, the proprietor of a leading Conservative journal was advocating a royal coup against the elected government as the only alternative to the humiliations of parliamentary democracy. Houston's message and her extravagant language cannot but have been unsettling for the government, not least because the *Saturday Review*'s campaign formed the background to the abdication crisis that broke in the autumn of 1936. What effect, if any, the idea of a royal autocracy made on the new King himself remains speculative. He was, however, in personal contact with Houston during the abdication crisis, and the impression of popular support for him can only have fed his existing disregard for his constitutional role. From Baldwin's perspective, Houston's shrill championship of Edward VIII, however far-fetched, can only have intensified the reservations he already had about the new King.

It was not until the 1930s that the then Prince of Wales had begun to take an interest in foreign affairs. He shared many of the attitudes commonly held in upper-class circles: acute fear of Communism, hostility towards the French, and enthusiasm for Anglo-German friendship. Meeting the former

Austrian ambassador, Count Mensdorff, in November 1933, the Prince surprised him by expressing sympathy for the Nazis and for dictatorship: 'of course, it is the only thing to do,' he declared, 'we will have to come to it as we are in great danger from the Communists too.' In a similar vein he told Louis Ferdinand of Prussia that 'dictators were very popular these days and . . . we might want one in England before long.'[34] During 1935 when Italy invaded Abyssinia, he made it clear to Baldwin that he opposed the imposition of sanctions and that he supported the claims of both Italy and Germany to colonies.[35]

Though such views were routine in upper-class circles by the 1930s, the Prince's habit of dropping casual comments of this kind to important foreigners indicated his ignorance of, or disregard for, his position. Ministers were particularly irritated by his habit of making ill-judged public comments on international issues. In June 1935 he delivered a speech to the British Legion in which he urged that its members ought to pay a visit to Germany. While the Prince considered this an unremarkable expression of his interest in promoting Anglo-German friendship, his remarks upset the French and embarrassed the government at a time when they were negotiating with Germany for a naval agreement. The speech also drew criticism from the left-wing press, which in turn gave the BUF the opportunity to defend him and his right to express his opinions.[36] The cabinet agreed that the Prince should keep his views to himself or obtain the prior approval of the Foreign Secretary. But he showed his disregard for this advice by delivering a very pro-German speech to a party of German ex-servicemen which horrified his father. Completely unrepentant, the Prince told Sir Samuel Hoare a few days later: 'Don't you think that it is very stupid making a fuss about my speech? I cannot see why anyone should criticise it.'[37]

Paradoxically, the royal penchant for intervention would have been easier to manage if the Prince's views had been opposed to the government's policy. The difficulty lay in the fact that ministers also regarded Germany's grievances as justified, wished to retain the cooperation of Mussolini and intended to promote friendship with Germany. But by blundering into diplomatic affairs the Prince of Wales not only complicated Britain's ability to bargain with the Germans, but also aroused French suspicions about Britain's commitment to them. Leading Nazis, who became paranoid about criticism of their regime in the British press, were eager to cultivate pro-German opinion in influential circles. This led them to exaggerate the influence wielded by aristocratic figures in Britain and to regard the succession of the Prince of Wales as a key step to attaining their goal.[38] Their ambassador, Joachim von Ribbentrop, reported that the Prince had criticised the British Foreign Office for its one-sided approach towards Germany; and his speech to the British Legion in June 1935 was enthusiastically received by the Nazis. In a letter of congratulation Prince Henry of Reuss wrote: 'All of us know perfectly well that You in Your exposed position would never have taken a step which would not have been felt deeply by Yourself.'[39] Aware that his accession to the throne could not be long delayed, the Germans maintained a flow of flattering letters to the Prince, and they instructed von Ribbentrop to encourage him in his role as champion of Anglo–German friendship. They assumed that as King he would exercise even more influence over government policy; in this they were correct, at least in the sense that he had no intention of emulating his father's cautious respect for the cabinet's policy.

By the beginning of 1936 the waywardness of the heir to the throne and his refusal to accept advice had led his own staff to consult Baldwin, MacDonald and Sir John Simon about reining him in before it was too late.[40] However, time was running out. 'After I am dead the boy will ruin himself within twelve months,' the old King reportedly warned.[41] When George V eventually died on 20 January 1936 ministerial attention immediately focused on the bachelorhood of the new forty-one-year-old King, presumably on the assumption that he required a good woman to settle him. Back in 1931 he had met Mrs Wallis Simpson, then a thirty-five-year-old American woman currently on her second marriage to Ernest Simpson. By 1934 she and the Prince were set on marriage. The relationship had been ignored by the King and Queen, though they were extremely annoyed when their son had attempted to introduce Mrs Simpson to functions at Buckingham Palace, and they banned her from court. For his part the Prince always denied that she was his mistress, though they were reportedly seen in bed together.

Through the summer of 1936 tension about their relationship mounted as a result of extensive reporting in the foreign press about their holidays together. Eventually matters came to a head in late October when Mrs Simpson's divorce was heard; but although a decree nisi had been granted, she still had to wait six months before she became free to remarry. In an interview on 20 October the prime minister told the King: 'You have only one disadvantage. You are not married and you should be . . . You may think me Victorian but I believe I know how to interpret the minds of our own people.'[42] This was completely the wrong line to take and did nothing to improve matters. At this stage the crisis was accelerated by Edward's private secretary, Major Hardinge, who advised that the cabinet should tender formal advice to the King and suggested that Mrs Simpson be sent abroad. This prompted the King to summon Baldwin on 16 November.

After this meeting Edward went off to South Wales leaving Baldwin to hope that the visit would 'raise kingly thoughts in the mind of the King'.[43]

But after inspecting the Dowlais steel works in Glamorgan he confirmed the politicians' misgivings by expressing his feelings at the desperate conditions endured by the workers there: 'something must be done to meet the situation in South Wales, and I will do all I can to assist you.' When the newsreel companies reported sympathetically on the visit, their commentary – 'these men want work. New industries must be brought to the stricken areas of South Wales' – sounded like the King's own words. The embarrassment and anger felt by the politicians was underlined by Ramsay MacDonald's comment: 'These escapades . . . are an invasion into the field of politics and should be watched constitutionally.'[44] Yet Edward blithely ignored them, indeed he promptly planned a new trip to another depressed region, the North-East.

The determination of the prime minister to force the abdication of the new King in December 1936 was an extraordinary episode which has never been credibly explained. The received view of the abdication is that Baldwin and his ministers could not accept the idea of Mrs Simpson either as Queen or as the King's wife in a morganatic marriage, and that they were supported in this by the British public and the Commonwealth. The whole crisis has been viewed in terms of a very English obsession with morality and sex. However, moral considerations played only a limited part in the story. There is no doubt that Baldwin had taken offence at the lax morality of the Prince of Wales and genuinely regarded Wallis Simpson as unsuitable. However, like most politicians of the time he upheld the moral standards of upper or upper-middle-class England. When Baldwin confronted the King on 17 November he insisted, according to Duff Cooper's account, that 'while the country would never accept such a marriage, they would not object so strongly to his having a mistress. That [the King] thought, was the height of hypocrisy.'[45] Indeed, both Baldwin and Churchill, though on opposite sides on the issue, found it hard to understand the King's refusal to follow precedent by keeping Mrs Simpson as his mistress and simply being more discreet about it. The explanation is that Edward VIII was part of a younger generation whose ideas had been formed in the period since the Great War dominated by the ideal of romantic love leading to marriage and a life of domesticity. He had woken up, late in the day, to the realisation that he might not have to undertake a traditional arranged marriage to a foreign princess which would trap him for ever in the stuffy world of palace etiquette; a 'modern' marriage to Wallis Simpson was all of a piece with his ideas about the monarchy and life.

To recognise that the participants took different views about social and moral questions does not, however, begin to explain adequately the seriousness of the crisis surrounding the royal marriage in 1936 or the uncharacteristic speed and determination with which Baldwin pursued the abdication in late November and early December. A marriage to Mrs Simpson would undoubtedly have been unpopular in some quarters and generated embarrassing publicity for a time. However, that was already happening, and the damage to British prestige caused by the abdication was at least as great as the marriage would have been. The real problem lay in the fact that since coming to the throne Edward had confirmed all Baldwin's misgivings about him; he represented a threat to the government partly because of his readiness to embarrass them over social problems, but more because of his intention to act independently in foreign affairs. The politicians' view of him was exacerbated by his own private secretary, Alec Hardinge, who described him as 'entirely ignorant of the powers of a consti-tutional sovereign and of the lines on which a King's business should be carried on'.[46] Moreover, the indications are that his accession to the throne in 1936 heightened Edward's wilfulness. In a conversation with the pro-Nazi Duke of Saxe-Coburg he described an Anglo-German alliance as an urgent necessity. When the Duke enquired about arranging for Baldwin and Hitler to talk it over, he heatedly responded: 'Who is King here? Baldwin or I? I myself wish to talk to Hitler, and will do so here or in Germany. Tell him that please.'[47]

This account may well give an exaggerated impression of the King's outburst, but it authentically reflects his total lack of discretion; if the Germans wanted to believe him to be an English version of a National Socialist, he seemed willing to encourage them. For the British authorities royal intervention was especially unwelcome in 1936 because of Hitler's dramatic action in remilitarising the Rhineland. According to one account the King claimed: 'I sent for the prime minister and gave him a piece of my mind. I told the old so-and-so that I would abdicate if he made war. There was a frightful scene. But you needn't worry. There won't be a war.'[48] In fact, Edward was merely striking a pose because his government had no intention of resisting the German move into the Rhineland, but ministers were naturally anxious not to be seen letting down the French who felt understandably agitated at the threat to their strategic position posed by German remilitarisation. Inevitably the King's blatant disregard for his constitutional role generated a favourable view of him in Germany where he was seen as a leader not a mere cipher; at the height of the abdication crisis in December the *Anglo-German Review* fanned the flames by quoting Gustav Stresemann: 'You have a splendid King. Why don't you let him out of his cage?'[49]

As if the King's behaviour was not worrying enough, ministers also suspected that Mrs Simpson's supposed Nazi sympathies would lead her to leak confidential documents to the German government. During November and December she was kept under surveillance by Special Branch who watched her London home in Cumberland Terrace, though without discovering anything notable. But they accumulated quantities of salacious material supplied by credulous American sources. According to one famous story attributed to the FBI, von Ribbentrop sent Mrs Simpson seventeen carnations, an odd number which supposedly represented one for each occasion on which they had slept together. A Mrs Nettie M. Strickland of Annapolis in Maryland regaled Scotland Yard with accounts of Wallis Simpson's background in the Italian criminal underworld; she alleged that she was of largely Italian blood with a quarter American Indian, had 'the mouth of a prostitute', and constantly plied the King with alcohol which she often spiked with drugs.[50] Revealing the talents of a novelist Mrs Strickland claimed: 'Your King's life is in danger in her hands, she may drug him to make him marry her while he is unconscious or she may stab him with a dagger (all Italian women carry them).' Finally she warned that Simpson would organise wild parties at Buckingham Palace at which her Italian friends would drug the wine and then rob the Palace of its rare old paintings and gold plate while everyone slept.[51] There is nothing to indicate how Special Branch or indeed cabinet ministers reacted to such 'intelligence'; but while their own intelligence may have told them to treat it as absurd, it confirmed their prejudices about Mrs Simpson and gave expression to the kind of gossip that was otherwise confined to gentlemen's clubs.

Meanwhile speculation in the foreign press about the King and Mrs Simpson made it increasingly difficult to suppress the issue in Britain. On 27 October, when she was awarded a decree nisi at Ipswich, the American newspapers reported: 'King's Moll Renoed in Wolsey's Home Town'. Baldwin now accepted that before long the affair would become public knowledge in Britain, and his mind began to run on more radical solutions to the royal problem. His colleague, Duff Cooper, who discussed it with him on 16 November, noted: 'as we separated he said he was not at all sure that the Yorks would not prove the best solution. The King had many good qualities, but not those which best fitted him for his post, whereas the Duke of York would be just like his father.'[52] Baldwin's remarks indicate that he was thinking as much of the political dangers of governing with a loose cannon like Edward VIII as of the moral aspects. In this light Mrs Simpson was more of a godsend to Baldwin than the central issue, offering him a means of easing the King out on personal moral grounds without the necessity for opening up the underlying constitutional issue. Even so, Baldwin had embarked on a difficult and dangerous course. He took care to consult several elder statesmen and leading figures in other parties.[53] In particular he had to know how the Labour leader, Clement Attlee, would respond if the government resigned following the King's insistence on remaining on the throne and marrying Mrs Simpson. Utterly conventional in their attitude towards the British constitution, the Labour leaders agreed that the King's marriage was a public and political matter not a personal one, and they would therefore refuse to form an alternative administration.[54]

This apparent consensus among the parties denied the King an alternative government and made it inconceivable that parliament would enact legislation to allow him a morganatic marriage to Mrs Simpson. In this way Baldwin appeared to have manoeuvred Edward into a position in which he would either have to abandon Mrs Simpson or abdicate. His best course of action, suggested by Winston Churchill and Lord Lloyd, was to send Mrs Simpson abroad for a year and proceed with his coronation; after some triumphal imperial tours his position would then have been much stronger and the prime minister's weaker.[55] Appreciating this danger, Baldwin summoned his cabinet on 27 November with a view to speeding things up. Duff Cooper was puzzled by this sudden urgency on Baldwin's part.[56] But by now Baldwin had begun to realise that opposition to an enforced abdication was likely to be much stronger both among politicians and in the country than he had anticipated. The cabinet had been slow to appreciate that a 'King's Party' was forming. Esmond Harmsworth, the son of Lord Rothermere, was already in touch with the King and with Churchill. Meanwhile, Lord Beaverbrook, who had sailed to New York, immediately returned to Britain to see the King on 21 November.[57]

The leading figures in the King's Party were Churchill, Beaverbrook, Rothermere, Lord Lloyd, Walter Monckton, Oswald Mosley, Lady Houston, Duff Cooper and Sir Archibald Sinclair, the Liberal leader. Moreover, although the King made no attempt to appeal for support, he attracted spontaneous offers such as that from Viscount Lymington who wrote: 'in whatever way you wish to command it you have my service now and always. I am able to carry the rank and file and most farmers of North Hampshire.' Lymington's whiff-of-grapeshot language was echoed in many of the supportive letters sent to the King by people who saw the crisis as a good opportunity to change the government, including ex-servicemen who freely offered to fight for him if necessary.[58] At the same time it was reported that the 'Imperial Policy' group of MPs had declared itself ready to take up arms on behalf of the King.[59]

Evidently parliament was far from solidly behind Baldwin. On the evening of 4 December a group of MPs representing all parties wrote to the King promising support in any action he took; and on the 6th some forty Conservative MPs and peers, led by Sir Reginald Blaker, had been formed to resist abdication.[60] This is not entirely surprising, for those

Tories who had been trying for years to destroy Baldwin's leadership naturally saw this as their best opportunity to force his resignation. There were also indications that the Liberal leader, Sir Archibald Sinclair, had changed his mind about supporting Baldwin.[61] According to Lady Houston, the King visited her at Hampstead during the crisis and they exchanged letters. At one point she despatched a large parcel containing £250,000 which her chauffeur delivered to Fort Belvedere, though later in life the Duke of Windsor denied that she had given him money.[62] Her account seems plausible partly because Houston habitually threw cash at her causes in this eccentric fashion, and because of the Duke's obsession with his poverty. There can be no doubt that Houston would cheerfully have bankrolled the King's Party at an election.

These indications of support suggest that, contrary to the traditional view, a King's Party rapidly emerged in late November to early December 1936, and that if the King had been sufficiently determined to call Baldwin's bluff by risking the resignation of the government, a very dangerous situation would have developed. At the worst, a new minority government appointed by Edward VIII would have fought a highly divisive general election. However, there was an even worse alternative: that his administration would have governed *without* risking an election for the three years remaining of the life of the current parliament. Such a course of action had been urged before the crisis and was again advocated during the crisis. This helps to explain the alarmist mood detected by Duff Cooper during early December amongst politicians suddenly aware of the forces gathering behind the King. He reported that a number of junior ministers who had kept quiet in cabinet 'thought a *coup d'état* was not impossible. They suggested that the King might accept the Prime Minister's resignation and send for Winston [Churchill] to form a Government.'[63] Already the *Saturday Review* had suggested that the King could dismiss his ministers and live with the present parliament for three years, and the BUF leaders argued that he was entitled to choose his own ministers for a period from three to five years.[64] Several ministers anticipated that although a government led by Churchill would initially be defeated in the Commons, he might be tempted to hang on for a while, or that 'an attempt might be made to upset the Parliamentary system altogether. It had disappeared in other countries recently. Why not in this?' One Labour member was even heard to enquire: 'are we going to have a fascist monarchy?'[65]

It was widely assumed that in the event of Churchill forming an administration, Mosley would be included. This seems plausible especially as he would have been an asset to the government in an election campaign. According to John Beckett, Mosley, who was at the Adelphi Hotel in

Liverpool when the crisis became public, acted as though he was expecting the King to accept Baldwin's resignation and then invite him into office; carried away by the drama of the occasion, he eagerly contemplated fighting an election and broadcasting to the nation.[66] Mosley may have been deluding himself at this point, but he was surely correct in seeing constitutional deadlock of this kind as a vital precondition for the fascists' entry into office even at a time when they lacked significant popular support; in the event, December 1936 was the closest fascism came to obtaining a share of power in inter-war Britain.

The strength of Mosley's position was that his movement was to the fore in articulating popular sympathy for Edward VIII. There would have been little point in a King's ministry attempting to hold out against a parliamentary majority if his cause had not enjoyed support in the country. Ever since 1936 it has been widely accepted that the policy of the government reflected public opinion both in Britain and in the Commonwealth. This interpretation, however, originated with Baldwin, and it is now clear that he was highly disingenuous on the subject. Although the prime minister consulted others about the royal marriage he did so largely before 3 December, which was when ordinary people were first informed about what was happening; in any case, he merely took soundings from such individuals as Dominion prime ministers and Governors General who represented a narrow circle of people who shared his own attitude.

In fact, far from supporting the prime minister, public opinion suddenly began to rattle his windows in anger at his policy after 3 December. On that day 5,000 people attended a meeting of 'Defence of Freedom and Peace' at the Albert Hall. As this was not connected with the abdication issue, the platform party was startled when a mention of the King's name provoked spontaneous cheering and the singing of the National Anthem.[67] The next day crowds of mostly young men and women gathered outside Buckingham Palace to cheer the King and sing 'For He's A Jolly Good Fellow'. That evening people carrying banners proclaiming 'We Want Edward' and 'Long Live the King' marched through the West End to demonstrate at the Palace and in Downing Street where the cry went up to 'Flog Baldwin'. As the four policemen in Downing Street were unable to keep order, reinforcements were summoned to clear the street and the crowds moved into Whitehall and Trafalgar Square.[68] On Sunday 6 December the crowds again invaded Downing Street, while the cabinet was in session, to voice its opposition to abdication. Several ministers including Kingsley Wood, Samuel Hoare and Lord Zetland got booed and jeered, and as a result latecomers avoided Downing Street by entering through Birdcage Walk. When the Archbishop of Canterbury, who had adopted a censorious view of the King's behaviour, tried to leave, angry protesters surged round him and it was some time before he managed to reach his car and escape into Whitehall.[69] All day the crowds outside Buckingham Palace reduced traffic to single file, and, when moved on, they gathered at the Victoria Memorial to sing.

It did not go unnoticed that among the crowds milling about in Downing Street were many Blackshirts, and each day the BUF loudspeaker van passed up Whitehall and the Mall broadcasting: 'Stand by the King. That is the Message of Mosley in this time of crisis.'[70] According to Reynall Bellamy, when Edward became King 'The Movement rejoiced for it felt that with a member of the war generation, and a kindred spirit, on the Throne, there would be a close understanding of our hopes and aspirations.'[71] This sentiment reappeared not just in fascist recollections of the abdication, but in the thousands of letters that poured into Buckingham Palace from ordinary people who saw Edward as their spokesman because he had shared their suffering in the war. Jorian Jenks argued that the King 'clearly believed in many of the things we believed in: in Britain and her Empire; in the need for real action to relieve the desperate poverty of the poor; in avoiding another war . . . and consequently in not picking a quarrel with Germany.'[72] Within days the BUF had launched a campaign stretching from Dorset to Scotland. Its slogan 'Stand By The King' was chalked and painted in words three feet high on roads, pavements, buildings and hoardings, accompanied by the BUF symbol, a streak of lightning in a circle. In Newcastle-upon-Tyne the streets resounded with the chants of the young Blackshirts who regularly jogged around the city distributing leaflets: 'Two–Four–Six–Eight – The King – Must Not – Abdi-cate'.[73]

It seems clear that the abdication controversy stimulated fascism, if only briefly, both because it spoke to the fascists' need for patriotic leadership and because Edward VIII symbolised the rebellion of youth against a generation of discredited politicians. 'We all, of course, knew that as Prince of Wales the King had been a bit of a lad,' wrote a Huddersfield member.[74] The King's refusal to be coerced into a loveless marriage led working-class fascists to cherish him as an anti-establishment hero. 'The Establishment disliked him because he was unconventional and had too acute a social conscience,' commented Reynall Bellamy. Other fascists claimed that he 'took up the cause of the unemployed as the impotence of the politicians became apparent'; he 'became more and more a challenge to Baldwin and the establishment as a whole . . . The Labour Party were also jealous of his close involvement with [the] interests of the working class who honoured and respected the Prince.'[75] Not all fascists, however, took this view; there are indications that higher up the social scale pro-fascists were as conventional as non-fascists. Admiral Sir Barry Domvile, for example, took a poor view of 'the King's delinquencies', and after hearing his abdication speech wrote: 'A good riddance. Long Live King George VI.'[76]

Mosley himself swiftly capitalised on the opportunity to outflank the conventional politicians by championing the monarchist cause. His speech to a huge meeting in Victoria Park in Bethnal Green on 4 December was a fine example of his populist rhetoric: 'How would you like a committee of Bishops and old skirts in parliament to pick your girl for you?' Pointing to the closed ranks of the party politicians he boasted: 'In crisis I come when the politicians dare not come – I come to the people. My message is let the people speak. The King should not be forced to abdicate by a junta of politicians who have no mandate from the people.'[77] Gleefully anticipating a common Conservative–Labour front in an election campaign, William Joyce proclaimed: 'the great circle of bourgeois respectability will drive into the same foetid camp the apostles of commercial tyranny and the gentle disciples of Socialist Capitalism.'[78] According to the BUF 50,000 people heard Mosley in Victoria Park (compared with an estimate of 4,000 by the *Daily Express*) and it printed a four-page newspaper on the event. What is not in doubt is that the issue made Mosley and his movement newsworthy once again, and enabled him to reach a wider audience than he had done in 1934, when supported by the *Daily Mail*; overnight the abdication gave the BUF a distinctive and popular position. However, the crisis proved to be too brief to effect a significant improvement in the fortunes of the movement. Indeed, the eruption of support for the King by fascists and others may have been counter-productive in that it demonstrated how dangerous Edward VIII would have been on the throne, thereby strengthening Baldwin's resolve to force the issue to a conclusion as quickly as possible. In the long run the campaign probably consolidated the BUF's reputation as a radical, anti-establishment movement with working and lower-middle-class people, but also complicated its relations with respectable society.

However, the potential of Mosley's monarchist stance in 1936 is underlined by the vociferous expressions of support for the King from the popular press, in particular the *News Chronicle*, the *Daily Mirror*, the *Daily Express* and the *Daily Mail* which between them accounted for a large majority of newspaper readers. They rapidly placed Wallis Simpson before readers who had hitherto been hardly aware of her existence. Large photographs appeared alongside sympathetic and flattering accounts of 'The Story of Mrs Simpson' which built her up as an acceptable royal wife.[79] Each day brought dramatic reports of her journey across Europe as though fleeing from persecution. Editorially these newspapers threw Baldwin's argument back in his face. 'What would be the price for his people of the King's Abdication?'

asked the *Express*. In successive articles in the *Mail* Rothermere eulogised the King:

> His, after all, is a marvellous record . . . His popularity is no ephemeral growth but the result of a life of effort and devotion in the empire's cause . . . Abdication is out of the question . . . the effect on the Empire would be calamitous . . . The nation should be taken into the confidence of the King . . . he must not be harassed on a matter of such vital importance as this.[80]

On the constitutional issue the editors saw no great difficulty in distinguishing between a royal wife and a queen. The *News Chronicle* argued: 'It is for the King to say, like every other man, who shall be his partner for life. It is for Parliament to say who shall be Queen of this country and to regulate the succession to the throne.'[81] It advised that the King should marry Mrs Simpson as Duke of Cornwall, so that she would not be his consort, and leave it to parliament to enact the necessary legislation to make this possible.

The press also adopted a different view of the morality of the situation. Conceding that some people disapproved of divorce, the *Express* countered, 'but has it got to be gratified by the entire Empire giving up a splendid and hard-working King?' The objections to the marriage of a divorced person, the paper suggested, came from the Church, the West End and the aristocracy who saw royal marriage anachronistically as an act of high politics involving foreign powers: 'that day is now done . . . and with it has gone the duty of the King to accept the advice of his ministers on his marriage.'[82] A *News Chronicle* reader complained: 'Snobs are deploring the break with tradition. Some of us, however, can see, rather, a break with hypocrisy.' Editorially the paper noted:

> the days have gone by when the King of England could only marry into a royal house . . . He is a bachelor. A true love match – and a democratic one at that – would be popular. Now that kingship is no longer endowed with the qualities of semi-divinity, but in effect become a hereditary Presidency, the public is little disposed to interfere with the King's personal affairs.[83]

While many politicians disapproved of Mrs Simpson as a vulgar American and a divorcee, lower down the social scale these things were no drawback and even admirable. For many ordinary people Edward VIII was not challenging but conforming to moral standards by seeking to marry his sweetheart.

This view is corroborated by the readers' letters that poured in to the *Mail*, *Express*, *Mirror* and *News Chronicle* voicing hostility towards the cabinet's policy. 'We can afford to lose Ministers but not the King,' was a typical comment.[84] They recorded a rising tide of resentment at the exclusion of the public by the politicians. 'Mr Baldwin and his cabinet are not competent alone to decide the issue. Let the whole people decide by plebiscite if necessary.'[85] According to an *Express* reader 'the public have lost confidence in the political leaders . . . why not hold a ballot on the question?'[86] While Rothermere printed letters uniformly supportive of the King in the *Mail*, the *Express* reported that nine out of ten took this view; the fair-minded *News Chronicle* published correspondence reflecting both sides of the argument, but it noted that the majority believed the King should be able to choose his wife. Since the reader-ship of these newspapers incorporated millions of middle and working-class people, there is little foundation for the view that the prime minister was acting with the backing of the British public during the abdication crisis.

Despite this, public opinion proved insufficient to save the King, partly because events moved very fast, but essentially because the King himself lost the will to fight. There was a dangerous moment on 2 December when Edward made a request to broadcast to the nation; at first Sir John Reith seemed willing to comply, but he took the precaution of consulting Baldwin first.[87] Not surprisingly, ministers regarded this as an attempt to appeal over their heads; Baldwin condemned the broadcast as an unconstitutional act calculated to divide the nation.[88] But he was put on the defensive the following day when Churchill, speaking in the House of Commons, urged that no irrevocable step be taken without consultation with parliament. 'MPs on all sides, deeply impressed with Mr Churchill's suggestive words, greeted the request with prolonged cheers.'[89] In response Baldwin said little but promised to consider the question.

When the cabinet met the next day they took alarm at the collaboration between Churchill and the Rothermere–Beaverbrook press, so much so that Neville Chamberlain urged Baldwin to insist that the King make up his mind immediately whether he would abdicate or give up Mrs Simpson; ministers clearly feared that he would foil them by leaving the country.[90] Over dinner at Fort Belvedere on 5 December Churchill advised the King to play for time, and to that end he drafted a letter to the prime minister in which he claimed the King was under great strain, was 'near breaking point' and had suffered two blackouts in the course of their conversation. He pleaded with Baldwin for time and patience to allow him to recover 'out of kindness and chivalry'.[91] But the cabinet gave this short shrift. Neville

Chamberlain observed that Churchill's account of the King's health was at variance with that of the prime minister. Ministers suspected, correctly, that Churchill was advising the King to prevaricate on the grounds that he could not marry Mrs Simpson until her divorce became absolute next April. They now regretted that Baldwin had even agreed to allow the two men to meet; as Churchill was not a minister and was working against the cabinet it was 'utterly unconstitutional'.[92] The King, rather disingenuously, had claimed he had no one to talk to and that in any case he 'had no opinion of Mr Winston Churchill's judgement'.

Meanwhile Churchill had drafted a statement on behalf of the King for the Sunday newspapers, and on Monday 7 December Rothermere and Beaverbrook followed this up with more claims that the country could not dispense with him. However, weekend visits to their constituencies had left many MPs impressed with the views of their party officers who were hostile to Mrs Simpson, and when Churchill rose in the Commons at Question Time he was howled down. He stalked out of the Chamber snarling at Baldwin, 'You won't be satisfied until you've broken him, will you?'[93] Realising by now that the National Government might become a victim of Churchill's opportunism, its supporters had closed ranks against him. Then, on Tuesday 8 December Mrs Simpson issued a statement effectively renouncing any desire to become Queen which the *Express* and the *Mail* hailed as 'The End of the Crisis'.[94] This, however, made no impression on those in the government who were paranoid about Mrs Simpson. Sir Horace Wilson warned that she still intended to return and set up a 'court' of her own: 'It must not be assumed that she has abandoned hope of becoming Queen of England. It is known that she has limitless ambition, including a desire to interfere in politics. She has been in touch with the Nazi movement and has definite ideas as to dictatorship.'[95]

At this point, the crisis suddenly collapsed. Baldwin had presented his ultimatum and the King, unwilling to face the consequences of rejecting the advice of his ministers, had agreed to abdicate. 'Our cock won't fight', as Beaverbrook succinctly put it. In a conversation with one of his members Oswald Mosley remarked that 'he had no enthusiasm for the job and in any case you cannot continue fighting for a man who will not fight for himself.'[96] That night Baldwin sat down to an uncomfortable dinner with the Duke of York, the Duke of Gloucester and the King who was suddenly happy now that he could see his way to marriage with Wallis. By 9 December they were haggling over the details of the abdication and the financial settlement which Walter Monckton negotiated on the King's behalf. Next day he signed the Instrument of Abdication, and on the 11th was finally permitted to make his broadcast to the nation. For another three weeks

Lady Houston maintained her attack on the 'junta of politicians' and the 'conspiracy' that had driven Edward off the throne.[97] But the BUF promptly wound up its campaign; and even Churchill realised that he had blundered by taking up the royal cause.

Although the new King, George VI, and Queen Elizabeth, quickly succeeded in re-establishing the British monarchy, for years to come they felt uncertain of their position because of the continuing popularity of the new Duke and Duchess of Windsor who seemed likely to put everything in jeopardy by a visit to Britain or a newspaper interview. This is understandable. During the crisis people had gathered outside the Yorks' home shouting 'Edward is right. We want Edward', and much of the press comment on the indispensability of Edward VIII was hardly flattering for the alternative monarch. The letters arriving at the Palace and the subsequent surveys by Mass Observation indicated that George VI was resented by many people for usurping his brother's throne.[98] In many respects the Duke of York presented a sorry spectacle; his only assets were his wife and his children. It did nothing to improve his self-confidence that his brother kept telephoning to offer advice. In view of the power of the ex-King to inflict damage on his successor, prudence indicated a diplomatic approach after the abdication. But the royal family, abetted it must be said by the government, showed its usual incompetence in personal matters by heaping humiliation on the Windsors. They denied a royal title to the Duchess, pointedly ignored their wedding, and generally did their best to ostracise them.

For its part the government attempted to contain the Windsors during the years after the abdication. Special Branch monitored their movements, their visitors and their engagements. Several officers were detailed to 'protect' them, though the Home Secretary, Simon, was so embarrassed about this that he arranged for the costs to be met by the King.[99] They examined the Windsors' mail and reported on the number of abusive and threatening letters received, mostly by the Duchess.[100] This intelligence may have been reassuring to the authorities, but it also carried a warning to avoid antagonising the exiles, especially the angry Duchess who felt tempted to retaliate. In a midnight conversation overheard by one of the security officers shortly after the abdication she threatened: ' I will return to England and fight it out to the bitter end. The Coronation will be a flop compared to the story that I shall tell the British press.'[101]

For the government the Duke continued to be a headache because he remained an object of enduring interest to the Germans who still believed that he commanded influence in Britain. The Duke's irritation at being frozen out by the British establishment only made him more susceptible to German overtures. Once he and the Duchess had married, they lost no time in attempting to rehabilitate themselves by assuming a role as representatives of Britain around the world. In September 1937, when the Duke decided to visit the United States, he explained that he intended to make a study of labour conditions there, the excuse he employed for subsequent trips to Germany. Accordingly, he wrote to the ambassador in Washington, expecting to be accommodated at the embassy and expressing a hope to meet him: 'our visit will be of a purely private nature although we naturally hope to call on the President and Mrs Roosevelt,' he wrote.[102] Although the government regarded such a visit as undesirable, it saw no point in objecting; but it made sure that the BBC would not accept the opportunity to broadcast a talk by the Duke in America and that he and the Duchess would not be officially received in Canada or the United States.[103]

Ministers took even more alarm at the Windsors' proposed trip to Germany in October 1937, for the Duke made no secret of his continued ambition to secure peace by bringing Britain and Germany into an alliance. Nevile Henderson, the British ambassador, left Berlin to avoid meeting them and embassy staff were instructed not to entertain the Windsors.[104] Warned by Sir Eric Phipps that the Germans were skilful propagandists, the Duke merely promised to be careful and to refrain from making speeches.[105] Despite this, the Nazis, realising he could not resist a meeting with Hitler, manipulated the visit to their advantage. 'Poor dear,' commented Noël Coward, 'What a monumental ass he has always been!'[106]

The Windsors' reception in Germany made the authorities all the more anxious to exclude them from Britain, not only because of the perceived threat to the royal family, but because they might become a focus of opposition to the National Government. Six months after the abdication Mosley had not abandoned his aim of forming a King's Party, according to intelligence reports; the BUF remained loyal to the Crown 'but that did not necessarily mean loyalty to the present monarch'.[107] To this end fascist propaganda was designed to remind working men of the interest Edward VIII had taken in them and that he 'was forced to abdicate because of his determination to do something for them'. This complemented Mosley's attempt to exploit the economic discontent of manual workers in the late-1930s.

To make matters worse, from December 1937 onwards the Duke himself began to pressurise the government. 'When I decided to give up the throne last December,' he wrote, 'I realised that the only dignified and sensible course for me to follow was to leave the country for a period. But I never intended, nor would I ever have agreed, to renounce my native land or any right to return to it for all time.'[108] Employing a mixture of conciliation and threat, he complained about the petty injustices heaped upon him and his wife by the royal family, and suggested that if his grievances became known there would be a revival in his favour. Protesting that he would do nothing to embarrass his brother, he insisted. 'I would never remain long in any country where I felt my presence was unwelcome.'[109] The Duke may have been deluding himself about his popularity in Britain, for he had faded quickly from attention in view of the enormous publicity devoted to King George and Queen Elizabeth. In the year following the abdication they featured in no fewer than 89 of the 101 newsreels made by Movietone News, more than twice as many as in the previous year.[110] However, as late as January 1939 the Gallup Polls found that 61 per cent of people wanted the Windsors to live in Britain, with only 16 per cent opposed.

The real obstacle to the Duke's return lay among cabinet ministers who were annoyed not least because they felt he had deceived them over the financial arrangements made at the time of the abdication when he had claimed to be badly off. In 1937 the Home Secretary told him frankly that he could not regard himself as bound by the original settlement.[111] The government therefore used the new financial arrangements as a threat to make him behave. As the pressure for a return to Britain mounted, they wheeled out a new weapon in the shape of taxation, warning the Duke that if he resided for any length of time in Britain he would become liable for tax on the whole of his income for a full year.[112] In view of the Duke's anxiety about money this appeared a powerful deterrent, but he refused to abandon his cause for long. In August 1938 he reminded the prime minister that, as he had given his brother a clear field by staying abroad for twenty months, he now proposed to visit Britain in November.[113] Apparently Chamberlain accepted that as the new King's position was 'firmly established' the visit would not cause embarrassment.[114] However, George VI told his prime minister: 'I think you know that neither the Queen nor Queen Mary have any desire to meet the Duchess of Windsor and therefore any visit made for the purpose of introducing her to members of the Royal Family becomes impossible7[115]

Eventually Chamberlain managed to postpone the visit by pointing out that both he and Mrs Chamberlain had received many hostile letters aroused by speculation in the press. Subsequently the Duke agreed to make a short visit in the spring of 1939 to 'break the ice'; he emphasised that he and the Duchess had received two thousand Christmas cards, which proved that people wanted to see them, and that further postponement would only provoke controversy.[116] Yet in February Chamberlain once again put him off, saying that he was anxious that the trip should be a success and 'not provoke a heated controversy among the public. I have been forced to the conclusion that this would inevitably arise if you came here now.'[117] Angered by this rebuff, the Duke replied: 'I will never allow this attitude on [the

Royal Family's] part to be used as a reason for keeping me out of my country.'[118] The prime minister may well have been deceiving the Duke by using opposition from his family as the grounds for rejecting a visit which would have been damaging to the government. However, he managed to keep him away until the autumn of 1939 when the issue was overtaken by events in Europe.

This stubborn and protracted resistance to the Duke's return seems extraordinary in view of the apparently smooth transition accomplished by the new royal couple in the later 1930s. Initially George VI presented an unprepossessing spectacle; he suffered from nerves, a bad stutter and poor health; as he admitted himself: 'I'm quite unprepared for it. David has been trained for this all his life. I've never even seen a state paper.'[119] Fortunately for him the idea of a family on the throne once again proved extremely popular. And, as Baldwin had realised, the new King was content to follow his father in taking a strict and proper view of his duty. On the other hand the new incumbents did not lack political opinions. Ironically, in view of the accusations of Nazi sympathies levelled against Mrs Simpson, Queen Elizabeth proved to be unexpectedly strong-minded beneath her charm, and harboured most of the prejudices of the circles in which she had grown up. She disapproved of the French because of their unreliability, their Republicanism, their Socialism and their responsibility for dragging Britain into a war in which her brother had been killed.[120] Not that this mattered except that from time to time the Queen was inclined to get carried away by her convictions. In 1931 when Baldwin was waging his struggle with Beaverbrook over Empire Free Trade, the then Duchess of York despatched a busload of her servants to assist Baldwin's candidate, Duff Cooper, at a crucial by-election.[121]

After the coronation when Baldwin stepped down as prime minister, the King and Queen became totally loyal to his successor, Neville Chamberlain, and especially to his foreign policy. This caused embarrassment at the time of the Munich Settlement in September 1938 when George VI rather naively proposed to mark his admiration by going to greet the prime minister on his return from Germany. His advisers tried to persuade him that this would be a mistake and that Chamberlain had actually failed in his handling of the Czech issue; they feared that the Queen's partisanship was having an unhealthy effect on her husband at this time.[122] In the event the King settled for a welcome for the prime minister at Buckingham Palace where he and the Queen appeared on the balcony with him. Although even this infringed constitutional propriety, at the time the King's act attracted little comment amid the general rejoicing. Subsequently, however, the ignominious collapse of the Munich agreement made him look foolish and it left him too closely associated with the diehard advocates of appeasement. When Chamberlain fell from power in 1940, to the dismay of the royal couple, their preference for Lord Halifax as his successor was not concealed; they found Churchill an awkward and embarrassing choice. Despite some errors of judgement, however, they had largely avoided the kind of interference in politics to which Edward VIII had been so prone.

The approach of war during 1938 and 1939 stimulated fresh speculation in the press about the return of the Duke of Windsor to Britain. In fact, the only organisation openly campaigning for this was The Octavians whose membership comprised only a few hundred people, including many fascists. Their only prominent member was Sir Compton Mackenzie.[123] The Octavians circulated propaganda proclaiming 'He Should Be With Us', and complained about the exclusion of the ex-King from public affairs: 'The Duke is universally beloved. Resentment at the treatment accorded to him is too deep to be killed by a policy of silence ... The suggestion that the Duke is happy in exile is an insult to the man who has always identified himself with his native land.'[124] Such material naturally encouraged suspicions that the Nazis were propagating the idea that the royal family wanted to be reunited. Special Branch acquired an anonymous document circulating among trade union leaders which spelt out the danger posed by the Duke's return: 'For over a year the Nazi regime in Germany has been working this move, knowing that the admittance of the Windsors to this country would weaken the whole framework of England, as there would be factions for and against the ex-King; the Royal Family would be considerably belittled and even the Crown seriously imperilled. Thus a weakened England is a Nazi War aim.'[125]

Special Branch evidently took the signs of pro-Windsor activity seriously. Although the British Union of Fascists had shown itself publicly loyal to George VI since 1936, it made no secret of its support for his predecessor: 'As far as the Fascists themselves are concerned, the return of the Duke is being looked forward to with enthusiasm ... it is practically certain that some form of welcome and support will be forthcoming.'[126] The security services believed that the Communists were preparing to disrupt any welcome organised by the fascists and intended to condemn the Duke as a pro-Nazi. These turned out to be well-founded fears. When war broke out it proved difficult to decide whether the Duke would do more damage by returning to Britain than by remaining at loose on the Continent; either way he was a potential figurehead for the movement promoting a compromise peace with Hitler.

FOURTEEN

'Mind Britain's Business': Appeasement and the Peace Campaign

'We wanted peace and we could have had it, and with honour, and Mosley was the man who could have given it to us.'

John Charnley, *Blackshirts and Roses* (1990), p 84

The picture of the British Union of Fascists abandoning its 'respectable' phase in 1934 and thereafter marooning itself hopelessly on the lunatic fringe of British politics is a compelling but misleading one. During the later 1930s Britain certainly saw a rapid proliferation of small, fanatical, pro-Nazi groups, but although Mosley felt apprehensive about being outflanked by them, his movement remained distinct from them. Eventually he was to be damaged by association with them, but he never lost sight of the need to keep in touch with mainstream opinion if he were to have any chance of power. To this end, as we have seen, the British Union of Fascists attempted to develop a more conventional party machine from 1935 onwards, though still refusing to abandon its militarist element. This trend was accentuated by Mosley's campaigns to keep Britain out of another Continental war, a policy which exercised a strong appeal to respectable opinion which would otherwise have shunned street politics and anti-Semitism; it was this that helped to take the BUF back towards the political mainstream during the later 1930s, thereby strengthening its links with the political establishment that Mosley saw as a means to achieving power. As a result, by 1939 his movement had effected a significant recovery which was only checked by the outbreak of war.

The potential for this development had always been present in Mosley's principled reaction to the mass slaughter of the Great War. His own military record put him in a strong position to oppose any return to a strategy involving the use of mass British armies on the Continent, and in the early 1920s he had been a staunch advocate of the League of Nations, approving the imposition of sanctions against Italy, for example, over her occupation of Corfu in 1923.[1] On the surface, British post-war policy seemed to reflect precisely these sentiments. Britain embarked on a disarmament programme which reduced her army to barely 200,000 men by the early 1930s, and cut defence spending from £2,198 million in 1918–19 to £115 million by 1924–5, where it remained until 1936–7. Officially Britain embraced the League of Nations as a means of resolving disputes without recourse to war.

In practice, however, British governments merely paid lip-service to the League; they preferred their old habits of secret diplomacy and feared that if the League ever gained real authority it would eventually use it to the detriment of the British Empire. Meanwhile, her disarmament policy had led Britain into a position of some confusion by the early 1930s. With reduced forces the country faced additional responsibilities in the Middle East, the threat of Japanese expansion in the Far East following the lapse of the Anglo-Japanese alliance, rivalry with Italy in the Mediterranean, and a recovery of Germany's armed forces in defiance of the Treaty of Versailles. A dangerous gap thus opened up between Britain's interests and her commitments under the Treaty of Versailles and the Locarno Agreements on the one hand, and her strategic planning and resources on the other.

Inter-war governments attempted to cope by what is generally known as the appeasement of Germany and Italy, a policy based on the assumption that once a limited list of justified grievances arising out of the post-war peace settlement had been resolved, Germany would settle down as a stable democratic state, and the causes of conflict would disappear. Although Mosley's policy involved more than merely appeasement, it amounted to much the same in practice; he argued consistently that Britain should appease from a position of strength and thus adopt a rearmament programme. To this extent his views have gained credibility from the re-evaluation of appeasement in recent years which tends to condemn the Churchillian policy of fighting Nazi Germany to a finish as damaging to British interests, and portrays appeasement as a realistic response to Britain's dilemma and as unavoidable in view of popular hostility to war.

However, this sympathetic view is deeply flawed by its tendency to ignore the incompetence with which appeasement was implemented by successive foreign secretaries under the Baldwin and Chamberlain governments, by its exaggeration of Britain's military weakness, and by its misrepresentation of public opinion as largely pacifist which, if true, would give the politicians an alibi for their failures to resist the dictators. In any case, British politicians pursued appeasement because they thought it was right not because they respected public opinion. The fashionable defence of the appeasers also sees their approach as that of rational men, overlooking the highly emotive and ideological elements in their policy. In fact, National Government opinion in general, and the circle around Neville Chamberlain in particular, was strongly influenced by a crude perception of inter-war Europe as a choice between Communism and Fascism, heavily laced with anti-Semitism: 'we should let gallant little Germany glut her fill of the reds in the East and keep decadent France quiet while she does so,' commented the MP, Henry 'Chips' Channon, a typical Chamberlainite appeaser, in 1936.[2]

During the 1920s and early 1930s all British governments followed an uncontroversial policy of appeasing Germany. But Hitler's arrival in power in 1933 posed awkward questions for disarmament and for appeasement. The very fact that the democratic regime in Germany had collapsed suggested that appeasement had failed. Logically it should have been abandoned at this point. But the alternative view held that appeasement had not succeeded because it had not yet tackled the fundamental German grievances and should therefore be accelerated. In effect this view was adopted by British governments with the enthusiastic backing of the fascists. In the event, Hitler himself initiated an acceleration of the process in 1933 by abandoning the Disarmament Convention at Geneva and withdrawing from the League of Nations. At this stage British policy began to unravel; for a time she was actually pursuing disarmament and rearmament simultaneously. The National Government's incompetence was illustrated by the Naval Agreement of 1935 which encouraged Germany to build up to 35 per cent of British strength in ships. Meanwhile in 1934 the Defence Requirements Committee had reported, urging the government to rationalise its commitments by accepting that Germany, not Japan, would be Britain's key opponent. To this end it recommended an expansion of the Royal Air Force, particularly its bombing capacity, and the re-creation of an Expeditionary Force of four or five divisions for use in Europe. Under the influence of the Chancellor, Neville Chamberlain, the expeditionary force was rejected in favour of concentration on the RAF, a policy which handicapped British diplomacy by convincing the other powers of Britain's deep reluctance to intervene even in support of her treaty obligations.

However inadequate, this step towards rearmament suggested that Britain was once again contemplating the necessity for a Continental war, something deeply repugnant to people in all parties and at all social levels. In this demoralising situation the Mosleyites felt confident that they had identified the path to lasting peace. They saw the causes of war in the traditional rivalry for trade and economic advantage currently championed by the United States and covertly promoted by international financiers and Jews. A reorientation of Britain's economic strategy would therefore obviate the problem. Like Germany and Italy, Britain could reduce friction by withdrawing from the struggle for world markets and become largely self-sufficient as she developed her domestic and imperial resources.[3] In the fascist scheme of things each great power must expand in its own proper sphere: Japan in northern China, Italy in north Africa, and Germany in central and eastern Europe. On the assumption that Germany's aims were limited in scope, and in any case posed no threat to Britain, she could be given a free hand.

Though appealingly neat, this approach was not as uncomplicated as it seemed, for it was not clear just how far Germany would be led in the search for the raw materials she undoubtedly needed. Nor did it take account of Germany's demand for the return of her colonies, which were largely bereft of material resources but would pose obvious strategic threats to Britain if surrendered. This prospect sat awkwardly with the reassuring analysis offered by Mosley. In practice most British fascists uncritically endorsed every territorial claim made by Germany and Italy, as well as the Nationalist takeover of Spain, regardless of the strategic dangers they posed to Britain. Ultimately, they insisted, like the National Government, that each advance by these powers helped to stabilise Europe and consolidate the barrier to Soviet aggrandisement.

One casualty of this approach was the rejection of any role for the League of Nations which, as the upholder of the territorial status quo, represented an obstacle to the revisionism promoted by the dictators; peace could be better secured by cooperation between Britain, Italy and Germany.[4] Consequently fascists poured contempt on the League, which Major-General Fuller denounced as a 'Judaic-Masonic ideal', and upon its chief British champion, Sir Anthony Eden, the minister responsible for League affairs, whom Mosley derided as 'that tailor's dummy stuffed with straw'.[5]

The issue came dramatically to a head during 1935 when it became clear that Mussolini was intent on seizing the kingdom of Abyssinia. Privately British ministers felt reluctant to intervene as no vital British interest appeared to be involved. But they pursued a duplicitous line which eventually destroyed the government's whole diplomatic and strategic policy as well as its domestic credibility. Since the Italian invasion was a blatant act of aggression against a member of the League, the Foreign Secretary, Sir Samuel Hoare, announced in September, to wide approval, that Britain would uphold the League's principles by resisting it. When Mussolini invaded in October Britain reluctantly adopted sanctions, but made no attempt to stop the oil on which Italy was so reliant or to close the Suez Canal. With an eye on the general election planned for November, the cabinet's policy was largely designed to satisfy public opinion, which strongly backed the League. However, once the election was safely out of the way, Hoare shocked British opinion by agreeing a notorious pact with Pierre Laval, his French opposite number, designed to let Mussolini get away with his aggression. Although the government ditched the Hoare–Laval Pact in the ensuing controversy, along with the Foreign Secretary himself, Britain was left pursuing an ineffective sanctions policy in which her government had no confidence.

Yet, however feeble, sanctions suddenly forced Britain to contemplate the possibility that an overreaction by the blustering Mussolini might force her into war with a major power. This was why, on returning from Italy in late August 1935 Mosley gave orders to launch a new campaign under the slogan 'Mind Britain's Business'. Fascist opinion felt genuinely outraged at official policy partly because it seemed so contrary to British interests, which dictated friendship with Italy, and also because, morally, the issue amounted to a struggle between civilisation and barbarism. Fascist propaganda claimed that it had been a mistake even to admit Abyssinia to the League; since the Emperor had little effective control over the provinces, Abyssinia was not a state in the western sense; in particular he had failed to tackle the widespread slavery that existed there.[6] According to Captain Gordon-Canning, government policy meant that 'British men must fight side by side with Negro barbarians against a white race whose friendship has long been at our disposal.'[7] Fascists also believed that in view of her population growth, Italy had a perfect right to expand in Africa, and to prevent her would only be to exacerbate tensions within Europe. 'We should mind our own business', wrote Fuller, 'and leave Italy to mind hers.'[8]

On 1 September Mosley launched his campaign with four major rallies in the London parks, and he subsequently spoke three to four times each week.[9] All across the country BUF members staged poster parades to warn of the imminent war and chalked peace slogans on pavements, walls and railway bridges. There is no doubt that their message was widely endorsed among right-wing politicians, not merely a pro-fascist minority, who feared the country risked being dragged into war by Anthony Eden to save the face of the League of Nations.[10] L. S. Amery summed up the view when he declared in his constituency that he would not send a single Birmingham lad to die for Abyssinia.[11] The Italians also received a good deal of sympathetic treatment in the Rothermere press and in journals such as the *Saturday Review*, emphasising how astonished they were by British hostility towards them.[12] In January 1936 Special Branch reported that Ian Dundas had gone to Rome to encourage Mussolini to offer London terms to resolve the conflict and that Mosley was en route with the same object in view.[13]

By 1936 this activity had had the effect of promoting a rapprochement between the BUF and respectable Conservative opinion, which largely shared the view that sanctions ought to be abandoned and that the demise of the League would be no bad thing. However, whether this first peace campaign represented a real breakthrough, as some of Mosley's followers claimed, is less clear. Reynall Bellamy noted that the newspapers had been forced to give the BUF much more attention and he pointed to the huge rallies Mosley addressed, such as the one at Norwich attended by 10,000 people.[14] But although this created the impression of an upsurge of support, what it really reflected was the heightened political awareness provoked by sudden fears about a war with Italy. Although 'Mind Britain's Business' was well calculated to exploit the uncertainty and incompetence of the sanctions policy, the BUF conspicuously failed to challenge the government at the November election. While Mosley correctly saw that many people shrank from another war, he had miscalculated over this particular issue and more generally over the depth of anti-war sentiment.

Apologists for the appeasers, then and subsequently, have claimed that the Baldwin and Chamberlain governments were deterred from rearming and standing up to the dictators by popular pacifism. Strictly speaking, however, the politicians pursued the appeasement of the dictators because they thought it in British interests and regarded public opinion as a nuisance. Although Gallup polls did not appear until the later 1930s and were, in any case, disregarded by politicians, we have some indication of the popular mood from the participation of eleven million people in the misleadingly entitled 'Peace Ballot' organised by the League of Nations Union in June 1935. By a two-to-one margin the respondents supported the view that aggression by one state upon another ought to be resisted by sanctions, including military ones.

Mussolini's attack on Abyssinia seemed a flagrant example of unprovoked aggression, and the extensive publicity in the press about Italian atrocities, including the use of gas against poorly armed natives, only turned opinion further against him. In this sense 1935–6 probably marked the start of a gradual decline in pacifist opinion in Britain as people reluctantly readjusted to the idea of a just war. If anything, the government lagged behind public opinion, not the other way round. Consequently, campaigning for peace over the Abyssinian war was not the best means of reviving fascist fortunes. It also raised uncomfortable questions for a self-professed virile, patriotic movement. 'The most despicable thing of all', Mosley argued, 'was to find former conscientious objectors, now passed military age, clamouring to send our young men to a war on behalf of Abyssinia.'[15] However, BUF speakers had to be primed to reply to the challenge: 'what would fascists do if war did break out?' The official answer to this was that they would fight for their country.[16] But during the next four years some of their younger members became detached from a campaign that encouraged others to cast aspersions on their patriotism.

In the event the prospect of war diminished during 1936 as the Italians overran Abyssinia. Increasingly the issue was whether sanctions should be dropped and recognition given to the Italian regime. The chief obstacle to this was Eden who had succeeded Hoare as Foreign Secretary. However, when Neville Chamberlain became prime minister in May 1937, he urgently promoted renewed friendship with Italy, a policy enthusiastically endorsed by British fascists. To this end Chamberlain adopted remarkably duplicitous tactics involving the systematic undermining of his own ministers and he pursued his aims through Sir Joseph Ball, a former MI5 officer who had helped the Conservatives over the Zinoviev Letter in 1924.

Ball had been recruited into the party's Central Office by J. C. C. Davidson in 1927 and became head of the research department, but actually ran an intelligence agency designed, among other things, to infiltrate the Labour Party.[17] Chamberlain used Ball's operation as his personal weapon against critics in his own party, including ministers, and to manipulate the press into supporting his policy. The journal, *Truth*, which had been purchased in 1936, became the regular vehicle for his propaganda. Over the next four years Ball used it to smear Winston Churchill and Leslie Hore-Belisha, the War Minister, and to circulate rumours that the *Daily Mirror*, an outspoken critic of appeasement, was under Jewish control. But Chamberlain's first victim was Eden. In 1937 he had the telephones of Eden and his supporters tapped, and he used Ball to court the Italians who were naturally delighted to find the British prime minister undermining his own foreign secretary.[18] The frustration of his policy towards Mussolini eventually drove Eden to resignation in 1938 to a chorus of approval from British fascists. But they had already hailed the decisive failure of the League of Nations as a vindication of Mosley's stand over Abyssinia and more generally of his peace policy.[19]

However, the government's miscalculations over Abyssinia had disastrous results. By creating divisions between Britain and both the French and the Italians, they encouraged Hitler to risk making a major challenge to the status quo by marching his troops into the Rhineland in March 1936. At a stroke this destroyed France's security against another attack across her eastern frontier and violated the Treaties of Versailles and Locarno. Welcoming the remilitarisation, Mosley urged Britain to press ahead with a complete and final settlement with Germany by restoring her colonies. According to Admiral Sir Barry Domvile: 'The timid stress the fact that Germany has broken many agreements and can never be trusted. That line of thought gets us nowhere. Provided we are armed adequately, we run no risk in co-operating with that country to which we are most closely related.'[20] For fascists the danger lay in repeating Britain's pre-1914 error by encircling Germany through collaboration with France and Russia.

However, Hitler's initiatives from 1936 accelerated a shift in the orientation of the British fascists away from Italy towards Germany as the dominant expression of fascism. They repeatedly endorsed his acts of aggression and accused the Jews of causing the deterioration in Anglo–German relations. Growing rank-and-file enthusiasm for all things Nazi was signified by the adoption of a new title, 'The British Union of Fascists and National Socialists', in June 1936 and by the growing influence of extreme anti-Semites including Joyce, Chesterton and Beckett as a result of the organisational changes. However, Mosley, who had previously regarded Nazism as a Teutonic form of fascism, unduly driven by anti-Semitism, and by implication not one that Britain should follow, was not unaware of the dangers. Over the next three years, as Hitler posed an increasing threat to British interests, it became clear that he had made a crucial error in becoming an apologist for German expansionism.

For a time during 1936–7 the threat of Nazi Germany was obscured by the debate over the civil war in Spain. Following the victory of the left-wing parties in the elections of February 1936, Spain descended towards chaos as landowners and the Catholic Church refused to accept their loss of power. During the summer plans for a coup were laid and in July the troops in Spanish Morocco under General Francisco Franco rebelled against the elected government. For the right in Britain the civil war assumed immediate significance as another opportunity to check the spread of Communism and without the complications entailed in support for Hitler. By refusing to accept that the elected Republican government of Spain was a democratic one many politicians found it easy to reject any obligation to recognise it. They denied that Spanish Nationalists were fascists at all, seeing them, as Sir Charles Petrie put it, merely as traditionalists and Christians who wanted to rebuild their country and restore law and order; there was therefore nothing to alarm Britain in their victory. 'What Spain needs,' argued Major-General Fuller, 'is a strong Government not a democratic one.'[21] On this the British fascists were in complete agreement with many Conservatives. 'I hope to God Franco wins and the sooner the better,' Sir Arnold Wilson, the MP for Hitchin, was reported as saying. 'It will be a disaster for Conservatism if [Franco] is defeated by the forces of communism and anarchy,' wrote 'Chips' Channon.[22]

A new pressure group, 'The Friends of National Spain' quickly won the support of many MPs including Patrick Donner, Henry Page Croft, Alan Lennox-Boyd, Patrick Hannon, Viscount Castlereagh, Henry Channon, Alfred Denville, Sir Arnold Wilson and Victor Cazalet, as well as Lord Londonderry, the Earl of Home, Francis Yeats-Brown and Douglas Jerrold.[23] They pressed the British government to stick to its policy of neutrality, which meant allowing Italy and Germany to supply arms to the Nationalists, and eventually to recognise Franco's regime as the legitimate government. Around a hundred MPs were mobilised to maintain the pressure, but much work was done privately, notably by Franco's envoy, the Duke of Alba. An extremely well-connected figure who also held the British dukedom of Berwick, Alba shot pheasants with Page Croft whom he used as a channel to the Foreign Secretary; he was especially keen to reassure the British that Franco would never cede Spanish territory to a foreign power.[24]

Despite this the Friends of National Spain felt they were losing the argument as a result of the pro-Republicanism in the liberal press, the various 'Aid Spain' campaigns and the recruitment of British volunteers for the Republican army. When Mosley addressed the subject at Limehouse in February 1937 a lady in the audience told him that her husband had been asked to go to Spain for the Republican cause. Amid laughter he advised her: 'You keep the Labour Party's hands off your old man.'[25] But the more Italy and Germany poured in supplies for the Nationalists, while France and Britain stood by, the more opinion sympathised with the Republican cause. Even the Conservative Party contained a voluble minority led by the Duchess of Atholl who argued that Britain should not allow another democracy to be overthrown in favour of a dictatorship, and that if Hitler and Mussolini engineered a victory for Franco they would have a stranglehold over Spain; this would threaten Britain's routes to the empire and leave France vulnerable to hostile fascist powers on three sides.[26] For this the 'Red Duchess' was denounced as a warmonger and became marginalised in her party in the process.

Taken together the Spanish Civil War, the remilitarisation of the Rhineland and German rearmament greatly stimulated British fears about the military threat posed by Hitler. Under pressure from Conservative opponents of appeasement, as well as the Liberal and Labour press, the apologists for Hitler were forced into a systematic effort to present the Nazi regime in a favourable light. In the summer of 1935 Sir Thomas Moore had suggested starting a German study group for MPs to promote peace: 'the very recent call from the Prince of Wales for a closer understanding of Germany makes it a suitable opportunity,' he told the Marquis of Clydesdale.[27] From this emerged the Anglo-German Fellowship (AGF), founded in the autumn under the chairmanship of Lord Mount Temple, formerly Wilfred Ashley MP, and with a merchant banker, E. W. D. Tennant, and later Professor T. P. Conwell-Evans as secretaries. It was an article of faith for Nazi sympathisers that deteriorating relations between the two countries were largely the result of misunderstandings created by the left-wing press; the AGF aimed to correct this by fostering contacts in politics, business, sport and the professions with a view to maintaining European peace. Membership did 'not necessarily imply approval of National Socialism', and Mount Temple emphasised the AGF's disapproval of German anti-Semitism.[28]

By 1936 the Anglo-German Fellowship boasted forty-one corporate members including Thomas Cook & Sons, the Dunlop Rubber Company, Price Waterhouse, Unilever, the Midland Bank, Lazard Brothers, Firth-Vickers Stainless Steels and British Empire Steel Products; Unilever donated £600 and ICI £550.[29] Among the many MPs were the Marquis of Clydesdale, Sir Thomas Moore, A. T. Bower, Loel Guinness, Sir Ernest Bennett, Sir Assheton Pownall, Sir Robert Bird, Charles Taylor, J. R. J. Macnamara, Sir Robert Gower, Duncan Sandys, Sir Frank Sanderson, Rear Admiral Sir Murray Sueter, Wing Commander A. W. H. James, Ronald Tree, Sir Alfred Knox, Norman Hulbert and Peter Agnew. The Fellowship also recruited ministers such as Lord Londonderry, known derisively as 'The Londonderry Herr', and other peers including Lord Brocket, Lords David and Malcolm Douglas-Hamilton, Lord Redesdale, Lord Galloway, the Duke of Wellington, Lady Downe, Lord Nuffield, the Earl of Glasgow and Lord Rennell of Rodd, along with Professor Raymond Beazley, Captain Luttman-Johnson and Douglas Jerrold.[30]

However, the AGF's titled and well-connected membership did nothing to reduce the suspicions in the Foreign Office about its contacts with Goebbels and other leading Nazis, and, as a result, the organisation was infiltrated by the intelligence services as well as by the Soviet government. Guy Burgess, who had attached himself to Jack Macnamara, the young Tory member for Chelmsford, became an early member. Later in 1935 Kim Philby publicly broke with his left-wing friends so as to ease his entry into the AGF. Both men supplied reports on the organisation's activities and leading personalities to their masters. Burgess even managed to mix business with pleasure when he and Macnamara departed on 'fact-finding' missions to Germany, which became 'homosexual escapades with sympathetic members of the Hitler Youth'.[31]

But was the Anglo-German Fellowship important enough to justify this attention? A self-consciously elitist organisation aimed at people of standing, it had recruited some 600 members by 1937. 'We want "Names" otherwise how can we have any influence with the Government or the Foreign Office?' as one official put it.[32] Its forte was the monthly 'At Homes' and the lavish dinners graced by Joachim von Ribbentrop, the Duke of Saxe-Coburg-Gotha, Rudolf Hess (Hitler's deputy), Field Marshal von Blomberg (German War Minister) and the Duke and Duchess of Brunswick. Exchanges were organised with the Hitler Youth, the British Legion, German ex-servicemen, and a sister organisation, the Deutsch-Englische Gesellschaft which arranged social functions in Berlin.[33] Members also organised country-house parties where they potted game birds with delighted visiting Nazis, discreetly raised the swastika among the rhododendrons, dressed up in jackboots, and drank toasts to the Führer.

Such activities appealed to a clutch of society hostesses including Lady Emerald Cunard, Lady Sybil Colefax, Lady Londonderry and Nancy Astor who happily entertained von Ribbentrop and helped to make Nazism fashionable in smart circles. Most of these hostesses, along with the Redesdales, Lady Ravensdale, Mrs Ronnie Greville, Lady Diana Cooper and Sir Frank and Lady Newnes, eagerly accepted invitations to Nuremberg rallies and to Nazi dinners in Berlin; it was there that Tennant spotted 'the young and beautiful Miss Unity Mitford who really believes that Hitler is divine in the Biblical sense'.[34] Returning full of enthusiasm from their visits, Lady Londonderry and others filled the *Anglo-German Review* with gushing pieces about Hitler's yearning for peace and his admiration for England. 'The harm these silly hostesses do is immense,' complained Harold Nicolson who felt they gave foreigners the impression that British policy was settled in their drawing rooms.[35] The admiration was mutual. Nazi visitors were easily flattered at being accepted by aristocratic society, and Goering hailed Diana Mitford as the most perfect specimen of Aryan womanhood he had ever seen.[36]

The AGF's defence of the Nazi regime drew heavily on historical analysis. Mount Temple argued that although Bismarck had given the Germans a political federation, he had stopped short of developing a mass movement to sustain it; the creation of a truly popular national entity was therefore the current aim – and a liberal one, he suggested. But this object necessarily involved resolving the position of those Germans who had been marooned in Austria and Czechoslovakia. However, although the apologists for Germany believed that her territorial expansion posed no threat to the peace of Europe, they recognised that it made her appear a threat.[37] Lord Brocket insisted it was wrong to judge Hitler on the basis of *Mein Kampf* simply because it had been written so long ago.[38] 'No one in Germany, including Hitler himself, regards the "extreme" foreign policy in *Mein Kampf* as a guide to German foreign policy today,' wrote Professor A. P. Laurie.[39]

Unhappily for Brocket and Laurie, by 1938 such a claim was looking increasingly implausible. When Arthur Bryant proposed to reissue *Mein Kampf* as a volume for the Conservative Party's National Book Association, he drew fire from the Duchess of Atholl who pointed out that his version carefully omitted several sections about the expansion of Germany which had already been implemented.[40] But, as Lord Redesdale pointed out, the ultimate justification for Nazi expansionism lay in Hitler's success in lifting Germans from the depths of despair after the war and restoring their self-respect. 'Has any one of his critics stopped to consider . . . what Europe would be like today if Germany had gone Red?' he demanded, 'By holding Bolshevism on the flanks of Western Civilisation, a tragedy was averted.'[41]

Despite its efforts to present Germany in a sympathetic light, the Anglo-German Fellowship never managed to resolve the main obstacle to improved relations: Nazi persecution of the Jews. As early as 1935 Tennant had explained how embarrassing this was, and he even indicated that on visits to Germany he did not intend to listen to attacks on the Jews.[42] Yet the Nazis simply took this as proof that 'the power of the Jews in England is even greater than they had suspected'. They complained that the British failed to understand their problem because, lacking Germany's land frontier, they could not appreciate a society's vulnerability to outsiders who threatened its culture and its industry; in any case, they felt the British continued to be too relaxed about Communism.[43] On this question mutual understanding proved largely elusive right up to 1939.

The AGF's main achievement during 1937 was to push the sensitive issue of Germany's lost colonies to the fore once again. A government committee under Lord Plymouth had considered the idea in 1936, but Baldwin, aware how controversial this would be among Conservatives, dropped it.[44] Even for fascists the return of the German colonies caused embarrassment, but the BUF argued that as Britain was not allowed to develop the mandated territories she had received under the peace settlement, they were hardly worth retaining: 'Germany, on the other hand, must expand or starve; she must have access to raw materials. If she is not permitted to do so peacefully she will do so by war.'[45]

The *Anglo-German Review* returned to the argument with several articles by General von Ritter on 'Why We Need Colonies and Raw Materials'; he pointed out that Britain had damaged Germany's commerce by adopting a preferential trade system in the Ottawa agreements in 1932 and thus exacerbated her sense of grievance.[46] This was a timely initiative because the new premier, Neville Chamberlain, seemed much keener to resolve differences with Germany than his predecessor. However, colonial appeasement still offended many imperialists who at the party conference in October 1937, responded to the call by Sir Henry Page Croft to reject any sacrifice of colonies. In fact, the territories involved were of so little material value that Hitler never pressed for their return, preferring to use them as a live grievance helpful for putting the British on the defensive over Versailles.

Despite its efforts to promote peace, the BUF continued to languish in the provinces throughout 1937, though it was livelier in London.[47] By the end of the year the movement had around 6,000 members and 200 active branches. However, the circulation of its journals was much higher – 14,000 for *Action* and 12,000 for *The Blackshirt*.[48] Mosley refused to be deflected from his course. His confidence made sense in the context of Neville Chamberlain's assumption of the premiership in May 1937, a development which went some way to lancing the boil of disaffection among rebellious right-wing Tories who appreciated the new sense of urgency he brought to the appeasement of Germany. Mosley also welcomed the change because he recognised Chamberlain's determination to recover Italian friendship, even if that meant losing his Foreign Secretary. As Chamberlain and his circle fully shared the anti-Semitism of the far right and showed no moral repugnance for the dictators, fascists naturally felt reassured.

This rapprochement, of course, made it more difficult for the fascists to attack the government; but Mosley was determined to keep his movement respectable and patriotic, and by 1938 it began to look as though the peace campaign would bring significant rewards. Special Branch noted that Mosley had taken confidence from the fact that National Government policy now reflected BUF views quite closely. He believed he could capitalise on this because potential recruits would be impressed by the realisation that BUF influence was an efficacious means of achieving peace.[49] This implied some change in the composition of the movement. By September 1939 Special Branch reported that the BUF had been enrolling new recruits, though it was also losing some members in the East End where its patriotic working-class supporters remained hostile towards Germany.[50] As the peace campaign reached its climax in 1939 the movement was looking more middle-class and respectable than it had since 1934.

The rapprochement between Mosley and the Chamberlain government during the last two years of peace was accentuated by the growing polarisation within the Conservative Party as a result of Winston Churchill's protracted onslaught on disarmament and appeasement. As a 'warmonger' he offered the fascists a convenient, high-profile target: 'Churchill has become the mouthpiece of the Money Power,' as *Action* put it in January 1938.[51] Fascists began to turn up in Churchill's Epping constituency to shout 'Mind Britain's Business', to which he responded: 'We are minding our own business. We don't want organisations which seem chiefly to be minding Germany's business.'[52] This was far from being an unequal contest. To later generations brought up on the myths about Churchill as a patriot who sacrificed his chance of office by his principled stand against fascism and appeasement throughout the 1930s it comes as a surprise to realise what a handicap he was to the anti-appeasement cause.

The fundamental reason for this was ideological. In the inter-war divide Churchill found himself on the same side as Mosley in the sense that he regarded fascism as a necessary bulwark against Communism. Consequently his opposition to fascism was always of a strictly limited and qualified character, and it lacked a moral or ideological dimension. Essentially, Churchill regarded the Nazis as a threat to Britain and her empire; but beyond that fascism was not really objectionable. He shared the widespread admiration for Mussolini for checking the advance of Communism and he could barely suppress his appreciation for authoritarian government. He refused to see the moral dimension to the invasion of Abyssinia, regarding it as a marginal issue which ought not to be allowed to jeopardise Britain's friendship with Italy. He dismissed the civil war in Spain as a typical case of Bolshevik manipulation of weak, left-wing constitutional governments: 'This procedure is well known and well proved. It is part of the Communist drill book.'[53] Like many fascists Churchill insisted that an elected regime such as that in Spain was not entitled to support if it became subordinate to Communism, and if it failed to protect life and order it lost all legitimacy; if Franco could revive Spain as Mussolini had done for Italy, that would be in Britain's interests. Churchill even remained blind to the danger that a fascist regime in Spain could pose a severe strategic threat to Britain and France in the Mediterranean. His partisanship may have been reinforced by his close relationship with Franco's envoy, the Duke of Alba, a frequent visitor to Chartwell. In this context Churchill's role as an opponent of the appeasement of Hitler appears more an exceptional than a natural aspect of his politics, and it is for this reason that he could never have been a credible leader for a popular campaign against Chamberlainite policy.

This failing was all the more significant because any Popular Front strategy designed to check appeasement had to be a cross-party one. Yet Churchill never managed to rally a notable body of rebels even among fellow Conservatives. His position as a Conservative was complicated by his role as Chancellor in 1924–9 when he had been responsible for drastic cuts in expenditure on armaments which he now wished to reverse. Fellow Tories understandably had misgivings about Churchill's habit of using his causes as a means of personal promotion. To them his relentless attack on Baldwin's Indian policy smacked of opportunism and ingratitude, especially after he had been so generously restored to high office after returning to the party in 1923. In fact, Churchill showed himself an inept opportunist, always liable to spoil his chances by snatching at a prospect of power, the abdication crisis of 1936 being a classic example. Inevitably his campaign over rearmament and appeasement were seen in this perspective. As a result, Churchill signally failed to mobilise anti-appeasers in his own party, let alone to link up with Liberal and Labour members who shared the same view; the notion of a body of 'Eminent Churchillians' is a myth created by later historians. He had a few acolytes such as Brendan Bracken and several Liberal friends including Lady Violet Bonham-Carter and Sir Archibald Sinclair who were anti-appeasers. But anti-appeasement Tories such as Eden took some care to avoid association with him for fear of damaging their case by turning it into a personal crusade.

It is also difficult for later generations, brought up on Churchill's reputation as a wartime leader and grandiose patriotic orator, to appreciate how
unconvincing he often was to contemporaries. An entirely manufactured
speaker, Churchill could only speak to a prepared script, and consequently
he often misjudged his audience or bored them by excessive repetition. This
was true in parliament where he could be effective when well-briefed on
details, but frequently sank beneath his overblown rhetoric. In a characteristic passage in a debate in November 1936 he denounced government policy,
saying: 'they go on in strange paradox, decided only to be undecided,
resolved to be irresolute, adamant for drift, solid for fluidity.'[54] This was
magnificent, but it was not debating as understood in the Commons. 'He
can only think in phrases,' scoffed L. S. Amery, 'and close argument is really
lost on him.'[55]

Above all, Churchill's role as a rebel was increasingly hampered by his
desperate desire to get back into office. He felt obliged to pull his punches
for fear of antagonising his constituency party in Epping where his critics
kept in touch with Conservative Central Office; by 1938 he even contemplated being forced to resign and fight a by-election.[56] In any case, once the
government had embarked on a serious rearmament programme, Churchill's
real objection to their policy diminished. Although he criticised the Munich
Settlement in 1938, he privately told Henry Page Croft: 'I was at a loss to
understand how anyone could urge a course different to that which
Chamberlain took.'[57] Thereafter he lived in expectations of a call to join the
cabinet. In March 1939 he told Margot Asquith that the government had
adopted his policy, 'and consequently I am in very good relations with them'.
In April he virtually asked the Chief Whip for a post.[58] But Churchill was
deluding himself. Chamberlain kept him in hopes of office but continued to
do what he could to undermine his reputation.

Churchill's shortcomings as an anti-appeaser were highlighted by the more
dogged and courageous rebellion of the Duchess of Atholl, the member for
Kinross and West Perth. She had already earned herself the epithet 'The Red
Duchess' by defending the Republican cause in Spain on the grounds that it
was a democratic coalition of parties not a Communist or anarchist government.[59] The Duchess participated in the All-Party Committee for Spanish
Relief which eventually brought 4,000 children to Britain, and her Penguin
Special, *Searchlight on Spain*, published in June 1938, sold 100,000 copies in
the first week. However, during 1937 relations with her local party broke down
because of her refusal to accept their resolution supporting the National
Government's foreign policy.[60] By May 1938 her constituency had decided
to adopt another candidate; under this pressure she resigned the Party Whip
for a second time and fought an unsuccessful by-election in December.

Churchill himself doubtless felt that the sharp deterioration in the international and domestic situation during 1938 strengthened his position vis-à-vis Chamberlain. Eden's resignation as Foreign Secretary in February damaged the prime minister because it seemed to reflect his failure to support the League and underlined his susceptibility for the dictators. This was especially so as Chamberlain took the opportunity to bring more fascist sympathisers into government, including Alan Lennox-Boyd, Henry 'Chips' Channon and Earl Winterton. In March domestic politics was immediately overtaken by Hitler's occupation of Austria. Mosley adopted the widely held view that no one could reasonably object to this: 'what on earth does it matter to us if Germans unite with others of that race?'[61] Yet although most Conservatives accepted the *Anschluss* as inevitable, they felt unhappy because it further undermined confidence in Chamberlain's policy, which had been based on the assumption that by cultivating Italy, Britain could keep Austria out of Hitler's clutches.[62]

Now that Hitler was accelerating the process of appeasement the appeasers were quick to identify Czechoslovakia as his next target. Only five days after the *Anschluss* a junior minister, Lennox-Boyd, made an extraordinary declaration that it had ceased to be practical for Britain to guarantee Czech territory against Germany ; this was tantamount to exciting Hitler to make the next move.[63] Since Lennox-Boyd had no departmental responsibility for foreign affairs, he was doubtless expressing Chamberlain's view, and consequently he got away with this serious indiscretion.

Hitler's subsequent demand for the Sudetenland and its German population received unqualified approval from fascists and from many Tories who believed it would remove the obstacles to Anglo-German friendship. The Anglo-German Fellowship emphasised how oppressed the Sudetenland Germans had been; above all, it argued, Britain must avoid allowing France to entangle her in this dispute simply because she was already committed to Russia.[64] In his pamphlet, 'Should Britain Fight?', Lord Lymington argued that from the founding of their state the Czechs had never respected the rights of minorities to be free from discrimination.[65] Mosley once again insisted that Britain could not intervene to prevent one group of Germans practising self-determination by joining with another.[66] On this basis he launched a major new campaign, 'Britain First', in July 1938.

Interestingly, the Blackshirts became so convinced of the effectiveness of this cause that they largely ignored the Munich Settlement in September and continued to portray both Labour and Tory opponents as warmongers. Urging the need for a complete revision of the Treaty of Versailles, they argued that Britain should accept Hitler's promises on disarmament as genuine and avoid the encirclement of Germany by France and Russia.[67]

Women played an especially prominent role in this campaign, partly because some male Blackshirts had defected to more extreme organisations or were diverted by conscription. Capitalising on their motherhood, the women took the initiative in organising poster parades with the slogan: 'Our Children Were Young In 1914 – Have We Brought Them Up For War?' They also infiltrated other organisations not open to male influence, including Women's Institutes, Women's Citizens' Associations, Co-operative Societies and parent groups, in order to foster resistance to war.[68]

However, this peace campaign was increasingly undermined by the inexorable approach of war. From late 1937 onwards many urban BUF branches were weakened when young Blackshirts joined the Territorial Army; and their subsequent activity fluctuated according to whether the TA was holding training camps.[69] In Huddersfield Leslie Grundy disciplined a Blackshirt, who was a peacetime member of the Royal Artillery, for declaring his refusal to fight Germans, fearing that this would make the BUF vulnerable to accusations of treachery.[70] The popular mood shifted uneasily after April 1938 when the local authorities started acquiring supplies of gas masks, organising air raid precautions, training ARP wardens and demonstrating how to make homes proof against gas. By the summer they had instructed all civilians to attend to be fitted with gas masks.[71] At the risk of being unpatriotic the BUF derided gas masks as a waste of time and condemned evacuation schemes as impractical. Peace campaigners may have taken comfort from the knowledge that their views enjoyed the sympathy of the prime minister himself who notoriously declaimed: 'How horrible, fantastic, incredible it is that we should be digging trenches and trying on gas masks here because of a quarrel in a far-away country between people of whom we know nothing.'[72] Meanwhile, the BUF's campaign was undermined by the rapidly expanding rearmament programme, which helped reduce unemployment, and by the introduction of conscription in April 1939 which carried off more young activists; the only compensation lay in the new middle-class recruits it was now attracting.[73]

On the other hand, the announcement of the Munich Settlement in September 1938 had made an extraordinary impact on British society because of the immense relief it brought to a country teetering on the brink of war. The Anglo-German Fellowship hailed Munich for putting an end to the entire post-war hostility between Britain and Germany and establishing a new era of cooperation. In *The Times* Mount Temple, Londonderry, Domvile, Redesdale and Captain Ramsay described the agreement as 'nothing more than a rectification of the most flagrant injustice of the Peace Treaties. It took nothing from the Czechs to which that country could rightfully lay claim and gave nothing to Germany which could have been rightfully withheld.'[74] While Chamberlain was fêted by the King and Queen on the balcony of Buckingham Palace, clergymen across the country held services of thanksgiving at which they preached to the text: 'Blessed are the peace-makers for they shall be called the Children of God.' As one put it: 'The hand of God was upon us; one aged man was God-inspired to stand between Europe and her destruction.'[75]

Yet such language rapidly appeared embarrassing. A little reflection suggested that the situation had not been saved at all. As Lord Lloyd told the Foreign Secretary, Britain had apparently accepted Hitler's right to incor-porate every German minority: 'Where is this yielding to end? Poland, Hungary, Roumania all have their German minorities not to mention Italy and Switzerland . . . You will have opened a path for Germany to the Black Sea.'[76] Munich also revived the alarming suggestion that if Britain was ready to hand over other people's territory to appease Hitler, she could hardly refuse to surrender some of her own; hence a resurgence of fears that Chamberlain would offer to return Tanganyika.[77] However, in the agitated state of his party this would have been too damaging to the premier, and once again the scare subsided leaving colonial appeasement unresolved.

Munich turned out to be a turning point for the apologists for Nazi Germany in more ways than one. Leading Nazis admitted to being disap-pointed by the role of the Anglo-German Fellowship in September 1938; at a time of crisis in relations between the two countries it seemed to command little real influence.[78] These misgivings had been coming to a head for some months as the Nazis grew increasingly irritated by criticism of them in the newspapers, especially over their treatment of the Jews.[79] In November when the AGF voiced its concern over *Kristallnacht*, its German delegates returned to Berlin shocked at the 'narrow-minded views of the British public'. An exasperated Chips Channon complained: 'I must say Hitler never helps, and always makes Chamberlain's task more difficult.'[80] Lord Mount Temple himself resigned as AGF president in protest at the persecution of German Jews, several hostesses withdrew from its functions, and within weeks the organisation lost half its members, leaving 'only a lot of useless fanatics' according to one informant.[81]

Moreover, while the leading ministerial appeasers stubbornly clung to their beliefs, in the country the case for peace was now beginning to collapse. This was underlined by several 'Popular Front' by-elections at Oxford in October, at Bridgwater in November and at West Perth and Kinross in December where anti-appeasers challenged Chamberlainite candidates. Alarmed by the government's dramatic defeat at Bridgwater, several fascists anxiously trav-elled to Scotland to thwart the re-election of the rebellious Duchess of Atholl.[82] Her narrow defeat in a badly timed contest shortly before Christmas was celebrated by fascists, but it underlined the dangerous split among

Conservative supporters. Although few Tory MPs had publicly criticised Munich, many privately entertained serious misgivings about appeasement. Chamberlain's support was increasingly held together by the fear of war, combined with sheer party discipline, rather than by confidence in his policy.

For those who sympathised with Nazi Germany these intimations of Chamberlain's political mortality made them conscious of their own increasingly exposed position. The more resolute advocates of peace like Lord Londonderry, who had left the government by this time, were reduced to blaming Britain for not trying hard enough to extend the hand of friendship to Germany. They increasingly focused on economic appeasement which seemed to offer an immediate means of improving relations.[83] They claimed that Britain was being manipulated by American imperialists to block Germany's search for raw materials and restrict her trade. Lord Lymington claimed that the West was encircling Germany and Italy, buying less from them, expanding trade with Russia, granting loans to Romania and despatching trade missions to the Balkans.[84]

During the ten months between Munich and the outbreak of war Mosley played a careful game by trying to consolidate his links with mainstream politics. He advanced this aim by reducing the number of BUF candidates from one hundred to sixty and by switching some of them from National Government constituencies to seats held by 'Socialist warmongers'. Mosley evidently hoped this would open the way to an unofficial understanding with the Conservatives. William Joyce believed that he 'wants to get back into the Conservative Party . . . he is under full sail for a "safe" and profitable haven.'[85] That some respectable Tories favoured this development is evident from the readiness of MPs such as Lieutenant Colonel J. T. C. Moore-Brabazon to speak up for Mosley in the Commons where he accused the newspapers of a conspiracy to ignore his speeches.[86] In March 1939 Moore-Brabazon got in touch with BUF officers, asking to meet Mosley, and he subsequently conferred with him and other Nazi sympathisers. As late as 26 July 1939 Moore-Brabazon, along with two other Tory MPs, Sir Jocelyn Lucas and Captain Maule Ramsay, dined with Sir Oswald, Lady Maud Mosley, Admiral Domvile, Major-General Fuller and Professor A. P. Laurie in order to co-ordinate pro-peace activities.[87]

This desire on Molsey's part to maintain his links with respectable figures has to be seen in the context of the remarkable proliferation of pro-Nazi, pro-peace and anti-Semitic pressure groups in Britain during late 1938 and 1939. In these months the Nordic League, the Anglo-German Fellowship, the Link, English Array, the Imperial Fascist League, the White Knights of Britain and the National Socialist League were joined by the British Council Against European Commitments, the *New Pioneer*, the British People's Party, the Right Club and the Nationalist Association, to mention only a few examples. Although the BUF maintained contact with these organisations, largely because it was anxious not to be left out, it is significant that many of them regarded Mosley with suspicion, refusing to see him as an acceptable leader; in effect he was being outflanked by more extreme organisations during the last months of peace.

Not that any of these groups made much public impact. Established in the aftermath of Munich, the British Council Against European Commitments was funded by Lord Lymington who recruited John Beckett, William Joyce, George Pitt-Rivers, Major-General Fuller and A. K. Chesterton – almost a roll-call of former BUF leaders.[88] In December the group began publishing the *New Pioneer*, a journal bankrolled by Lymington and carrying pro-peace and anti-Semitic propaganda written by a phalanx of pro-fascists including Admiral Domvile, Joyce, Fuller, Chesterton, Ben Greene, Patrick Donner MP, Francis Yeats-Brown, Anthony Ludovici and Rolf Gardiner. In a typical piece entitled 'The War of the Jewish Revenge', Chesterton vigorously fostered defeatism about the prospective European war and made allegations about a conspiracy that he believed had obstructed Chamberlain's search for peace since Munich.[89] This notion that something sinister now had the prime minister in its grip became the dominating idea in the months prior to the war. In April 1939 there appeared the ambitiously named British People's Party, led and funded by the eccentric Marquis of Tavistock. John Beckett joined, because he needed Tavistock's money, as did two other ex-Socialists, John Scanlon and Ben Greene. The British People's Party combined anti-Semitism and military defeatism with a left-wing social policy; it published the *People's Post* in 1939–40 and ran a pro-peace candidate in a by-election at Hythe in July.[90] Among a range of ineffectual organisations the BPP was notably inadequate.

One of the more bizarre manifestations of pre-war extremism surfaced in May 1939. The Right Club was the inspiration of a hitherto obscure Scot, Captain Archibald Henry Maule Ramsay, who emerged from the landed, aristocratic and military background that produced so many Scottish fascists. After serving inconspicuously as MP for Peebles and South Midlothian since 1931, Ramsay was awoken to international issues around 1937 largely by the Spanish Civil War, which offended his Christian principles.[91] This rapidly led him to discover the dangers of Communism and to embroil himself in foolish accusations about Jewish conspiracies; by 1938 Ramsay had emerged as a speaker for the Nordic League and The Link and a leading apologist for Hitler. 'Captain Ramsay is definitely unbalanced and suffers from persecution mania so far as the Jewish problem is concerned,' reported Special Branch, which kept an eye on his activities.[92]

Like most fascist sympathisers, Ramsay maintained his loyalty to the

National Government until the spring of 1939, but at that stage he concluded that Chamberlain had succumbed to Jewish pressure and broken his pledges by introducing conscription. Thereafter he dedicated himself to purging the Conservative Party of Jewish influence and attempting to coordinate the proliferating pro-Nazi and pro-peace organisations, initially through the Nordic League.[93] In May he decided to establish a secret society, the Right Club, to further these ends. The new organisation was the product of the same thinking as the January Club and the Anglo-German Fellowship in the sense that it intended to influence members of the establishment; and although it kept its membership list secret, apparently to protect supporters from the Jews, the Right Club was easily penetrated by informants from MI5 and the Board of Deputies of British Jews. Members' names – ladies were on a separate list – were locked in a ledger, called the 'Red Book'; they were appointed as Wardens and Stewards, and received badges depicting an eagle killing a snake and the 'P.J.' initials. The Right Club list initially comprised 135 male and 100 female members recruited from May to August mostly from people already prominent in extremist organisations, notably the Nordic League, The Link, the *New Pioneer* group, and the Anglo-German Fellowship.[94] Among them were the Duke of Wellington, William Joyce, Captain Luttman-Johnson, Lord Ronald Graham (a son of the Duke of Montrose), Jock Houston, A. K. Chesterton, Anthony Ludovici, Francis Yeats-Brown, Lord Redesdale, Lord Semphill, and a clutch of MPs: Peter Agnew, J. J. Stourton, Sir Ernest Bennett, Colonel Charles Kerr (later Lord Teviot), Lord Colum Crichton-Stuart, John MacKie, Colonel Harold Mitchell, Sir Thomas Hunter, Sir Samuel Chapman, Sir Albert Edmondson and Mrs Mavis Tate.

Although the association of the Right Club with spying during the war gives it a sinister reputation, it was not an especially significant movement at this stage. Its membership was far smaller than that of The Link or even the Anglo-German Fellowship, and, though frankly elitist in aspiration, its recruits were not highly connected; among the MPs, Charles Kerr and Sir Albert Edmondson were junior whips and Harold Mitchell was a Conservative Party vice-chairman. Many were simultaneously members of three or four different extremist groups or were simply deserters from the BUF and the Anglo-German Fellowship: a stage army of increasingly desperate fascists and pro-Nazis. The club was a symptom of the undoubted need to coordinate the rapidly fragmenting anti-war movement and to provide it with some focus and leadership.

In fact, while Captain Ramsay and his associates busied themselves ineffectually with propaganda and private dinners, a rather more professional operation was under way to preserve the peace of Europe by means of clandestine negotiations with Germany, conducted partly on a freelance basis but also by men acting with the connivance and encouragement of the government itself. Neville Chamberlain, his Foreign Secretary, Lord Halifax, and the Under-Secretary, R. A. Butler, pursued a double policy in this period: while ostensibly preparing for war and blocking Hitler's next advances, they engaged in a frenetic round of diplomacy designed to ensure that Britain would never be called upon to honour the commitments she had given to support Poland and Romania from the Nazi threat.[95] Their task became complicated because so many fascists now had the same idea. During 1939 talks were conducted by a succession of regular visitors to Germany including Lord Brocket, the Duke of Buccleuch, Lord Redesdale, the Duke of Westminster, Sir Arnold Wilson MP, Ernest Tennant (of the AGF), Arthur Bryant, Henry Drummond Wolff and Lord Aberconway.[96] 'The Prime Minister and Halifax want to settle by negotiation but it would be dangerous for such negotiations to be undertaken otherwise than by the normal channels,' explained Sir Joseph Ball, who admitted that the unofficial conversations conducted by Brocket, Buccleuch and others 'are potentially dangerous in that they may encourage that section of opinion in Germany which has always held that Britain will never fight'.[97]

This was a considerable understatement. British diplomacy was extremely amateurish and confused at this time. The ministers used Brocket, for example, to keep them in touch with German thinking; but when he told the Germans, without authorisation, that Britain would not fight for Poland, the British position was hopelessly undermined. As late as July 1939 Halifax sent the historian, Arthur Bryant, to Germany, ostensibly on a holiday but in fact to meet two Nazi officials, Dr Kurt Blohm, the former Hitler Youth Leader and Walter Hewel, a close friend of Hitler, in Salzburg. Bryant contradicted Brocket and others by emphasising that Britain would uphold her pledge to Poland.[98] Bryant's activities also suggest that the efforts of those fascists who enjoyed official connections were now directed towards self-preservation. Bryant himself, as well as Luttman-Johnson, Yeats-Brown and Hugh Sellon all tried to obtain employment in government posts at home or abroad at this time.[99] Formerly employed by the Conservative Central Office, Bryant was engaged by the Publicity Department of the Foreign Office shortly before the war. When asked by George Strauss MP why he had employed Bryant, 'a man whose Fascist sympathies are so well known', R. A. Butler gave a characteristically evasive reply, but was not, apparently, embarrassed. Yeats-Brown, on the other hand, complained that he had been rejected because 'the Foreign Office thinks me too Fascist for the post of Press Attaché in Rome'.[100]

Meanwhile Sir Joseph Ball, acting on behalf of the prime minister, sanctioned four extensive visits to Germany by the former MP and BUF supporter, Henry Drummond Wolff, during the first half of 1939. Drummond Wolff's connection with Ball had arisen after his resignation as an MP in 1935 when he involved himself with reforms at Conservative Central Office. He objected especially to the Anglo-American Trade Agreement of 1938, which he claimed was 'regarded as a declaration of war in Germany and Italy'.[101] When Drummond Wolff returned from a visit to Goering in January 1939 he reported that Hitler was particularly anxious to obtain trade preferences for Germany, commercial credits, the resolution of the refugee problem and the return of the colonies.[102] In March Drummond Wolff urged Ball to encourage the prime minister to stand firm for a settlement on the understanding that this meant ending the economic boycott and the encirclement of Germany by the United States and Britain; this, he claimed, was dictated by the Jews who 'at the moment control to a large extent the Roosevelt administration'. Ball appeared to endorse his diagnosis.[103] A further visit to Berlin was authorised in May when Drummond Wolff saw Helmuth Wohltat (Goering's principal adviser) and Walter Hewel (political assistant to Hitler), and had three and a half hours with Goering himself. The chief point to emerge from all this was the priority given to a peaceful solution to the problem of Danzig and the Polish Corridor by the Germans. 'You ought to depart for Germany without delay,' Ball told him at the start of June.[104]

Drummond Wolff was an acceptable envoy, especially as he acted with authorisation from Chamberlain, but his obvious partiality for the Nazis made him little more than a vehicle for their demands. The Germans also used the businessman, Ernest Tennant, of the Anglo-German Fellowship, who met von Ribbentrop at his castle near Salzburg in July, to convey the message that they regarded the Polish guarantee as highly provocative.[105] As late as August Chamberlain and Halifax despatched another secret mission of seven businessmen led by Lord Aberconway to meet Goering on the island of Sylt off the German coast. Their brief was to offer another Munich-type settlement, granting Hitler what he wanted in Poland provided he refrained from invading the country.[106] This was particularly inept. It convinced Hitler that the British would not honour their commitment to Poland. In any case, since he regarded Munich as a humiliation and was intent on a war in the east, Hitler was merely irritated by Chamberlain's diplomatic efforts to offer him a way out.

The tactical shift towards economic appeasement represented a logical response to the final discrediting of territorial appeasement as a result of Hitler's action in March 1939 when German troops marched into Prague and dismantled what remained of the Czech state. After the celebration of Chamberlain's triumph at Munich this was so shocking and humiliating for

Britain that several apologists for Hitler, including the Marquis of Clydesdale, Yeats-Brown, Lord Esher and G. Ward Price of the *Daily Mail*, repudiated appeasement even if they could not entirely reconcile themselves to preparations for war. 'I have reluctantly become convinced that Nazism is out for nothing short of world domination,' wrote Clydesdale, 'and in its endeavours to achieve this end will go to any extreme.'[107] Yet many fascists remained obdurate in the face of a marked shift in popular attitudes. At a lunch with Lady Plymouth and the Duchess of Grafton, Admiral Domvile felt irritated by their enthusiastic chatter about the coming war: 'The thing is settled, you might think – all the absurdity and amateurism of land girls, nurses etc was trotted out – I was bored but it is interesting to see how permeated these people are with the war germ. Israel has done its work well.'[108] Domvile became even more irritated when questions were asked in parliament by Geoffrey Mander as to whether The Link received German funding and was an instrument of Nazi propaganda. When the Home Secretary, Samuel Hoare, endorsed the charges, Domvile threatened legal action and insisted: 'That The Link is pro-British to the core goes without saying.'[109] This was the nub: aspersions were now openly cast upon the patriotism on which most fascists prided themselves. As yet, however, most of them failed to recognise how precarious their position had become. The only prominent fascist who decided to throw in his lot with Hitler was William Joyce whose MI5 contacts warned him in August 1939 that if emergency regulations empowering the authorities to intern opponents of war came into effect he would probably be detained. Short of money and increasingly despondent, he left for Berlin just in time.

By contrast, a mood of almost irrational optimism settled upon some of the more naive fascists during the months leading up to war. As late as June The Link continued to organise trips to Nuremberg and Salzburg for its members. On 20 April Captain Luttman-Johnson celebrated the Führer's fiftieth birthday: 'I think we shall avoid war in spite of the Liberal-Communist warmongers,' he wrote.[110] Lord Brocket, Major-General Fuller and the Duke of Buccleuch accepted invitations to attend the birthday festivities, against Foreign Office advice; despite being Lord Steward of the Royal Household, Buccleuch went without consulting Buckingham Palace, but was ordered not to attend the celebrations on his arrival. However, Brocket and Fuller admired the parade of Germany's motorised army divisions: 'I hope you were pleased with your children,' Hitler reportedly told Fuller.[111] In a new book published in 1939, *The Case for Germany*, A. P. Laurie painted a romantic picture of Hitler as comparable to a poor Scot who had worked his way up from humble origins. Laurie claimed that as Nazi Germany was based on the idea of racial purity, Hitler had no desire to introduce other races and thus no interest in making conquests.[112] Laurie and other fascists simply professed themselves unconcerned by Hitler's latest act of aggression. Luttman-Johnson had welcomed the reports of German troops entering Prague. 'It is splendid news. Another great blow to Communism and Freemasonry,' he wrote in his diary. The *Anglo-German Review* insisted: 'The passing of Czechoslovakia calls for no regrets. A misbegotten state founded on broken promises violating by its very existence the sacred right of self-determination of peoples . . . who shall sorrow for that?'[113]

Mosley himself blandly refused to accept that Germany was guilty of unprovoked aggression; Czechoslovakia had collapsed through internal disruption, he claimed. As for the government's guarantees to Poland in March and Romania in April, he derided them as 'nothing short of a suicide pact'.[114] Poland, Mosley argued, was a country in pawn to international finance whose foreign policy was controlled by the owners of her major investments and state loans – American, British and French financial interests; this was why they were lining up against Germany. Why, he demanded, should Britain shed blood 'for the sake of this rotting confederacy of cash and corruption?'[115] In April he embarked on a tour of northern England to spread the message that Britain had nothing to fear from Germany. It was indicative of Mosley's links with respectable England that he had no difficulty gaining invitations to speak from middle-class organisations where he was warmly applauded. Addressing the Hexham Rotary Club in Northumberland he offered a persuasive recipe for preserving Britain's interests and keeping the peace: 'Why have we to be allied to every little country in the East of Europe? We are trying to build a wall around Germany and Italy . . . this strangulation policy will throw Europe into war.'[116] He offered what was undoubtedly still appealing, the chance of returning Germany's colonies and concentrating on the British Empire in return for a new disarmament pact with Germany. Tackled about Britain's moral responsibility to come to the aid of small nations he unhesitatingly resorted to his personal credentials: 'I can conceive of no greater moral question than whether we who fought in the last war are going to sentence the youth of Britain to die in another.'[117]

The enthusiastic response to such speeches convinced many Blackshirts that their movement was once again surging ahead despite being boycotted by the national press.[118] Nor were they entirely deluding themselves. As opinion polarised over the prospect of war, some of Mosley's natural supporters concluded that Hitler posed an imminent threat to Britain, but thousands of uncommitted people attended his meetings anxious for reassurance that peace remained a possibility. Special Branch confirmed that BUF membership was growing all over the country during the summer of 1939, though its estimates were approximate and the turnover of members was high.[119] On the eve of war the movement had something between 22,500 and 36,000 members. On the other hand, the enthusiasm manifested at Mosley's rallies failed to translate into tangible votes for peace. In July the newly formed British People's Party decided to run Harry St John Philby (father of Kim) at a by-election at Hythe. Admiral Domvile, Lady Pearson and many BUF members flocked to the Kent town to assist him. In his campaign Philby criticised Chamberlain on the grounds that after Munich he 'just sat back to see what would happen', while Lord Tavistock attacked the government over the ARP and National Service.[120] However, the BPP campaign was an amateurish effort; its agent, John Beckett, even wrote false returns on the canvassing cards, saying: 'That's done, Let's go to the pub!'[121] The 576 votes cast for Philby suggested that the BPP's collection of eccentrics had made little impact.

Yet the by-election did nothing to dampen the euphoria among the fascists who journeyed to London for the climax of Mosley's peace campaign, a rally at Earl's Court on 16 July, which was hailed as the biggest indoor meeting ever held.[122] When the doors opened at 6.30 some 9,000–10,000 people paid between one and ten shillings for seats, the rest being admitted free to make a total audience of around 20,000. Observers described them as noticeably respectable and middle-class, rather like the audience at a Conservative or Liberal meeting.[123] 'The hall was laid out à la Nuremberg,' noted a delighted Domvile. After an hour of patriotic songs, Mosley was announced by a fanfare of trumpets; he was played in by a drum and fife band and saluted by rows of stewards: 'as he passed you noted the deep-set eyes, the twinkling smile, short white teeth, thick neck, well-pomaded black hair.'[124] In his two-hour oration Mosley potted all the familiar targets – Jews, pacifists and Communists. He insisted that Hitler was not mad – if he had wanted to attack Britain he would have done so last September when she was helpless. Mosley had clearly decided he had to tread a careful line between patriotism and rebellion: 'We fight for Britain, yes, but a million Britons shall never die in your Jews' quarrel.'

Despite this, Mosley could not quite bring himself to offer the government his backing if war broke out. It was a tacit admission that he expected the crisis created by war to give the BUF its best opportunity to obtain power. For this reason he intended to maintain his campaign for peace; the remarkable thing was that he got away with it for nine months of the war.

FIFTEEN

The Open Conspiracy:
Fascism and the Phoney War

'Why don't the Government give them a fair trial and shoot them
if they are guilty of treason?'

Lady Redesdale, 13 December 1940

On 1 September 1939 German troops crossed the Polish frontier, thereby
making Britain's guarantee operative. That morning Neville Chamberlain
told Winston Churchill that he was forming a small war cabinet in which
he would be included. But two days passed without further developments.
'I have not heard anything from you since our talk on Friday,' Churchill
wrote plaintively, 'when I understood I was to serve as your colleague.'[1] In
effect the prime minister was muzzling his leading critic while he fought to
avoid war. Polish requests for help were ignored while the government tried
to persuade Mussolini to call a conference, promising to rewrite the entire
Treaty of Versailles if the Germans withdrew their troops. However, parliament grew restive at the inexcusable delay, and on 3 September Chamberlain
was finally obliged to announce Britain's entry into war in a lacklustre radio
broadcast. 'War declared at 11.00,' wrote Admiral Domvile in his diary.
'Shocking. The usual excuses – all Hitler. I despair of common sense.'[2]

Within hours of the prime minister's reluctant declaration the air-raid
sirens sounded, alerting the civilian population to the devastating wave of
bombing they had been taught to expect. But it proved a false alarm in more
senses than one. Although war had been declared, it was hardly being waged.
It would be six months before British armies advanced into battle. Despite
its guarantee to Poland, the government had no plans to assist the Poles,
and for some months the RAF dropped nothing but propaganda leaflets on
Germany. Chamberlain even tried to restrain the French from attacking
Germany because he hoped to negotiate a compromise peace rather than
escalate the conflict in the east into a major war. 'Although we cannot in
the circumstances avoid declaring war,' Sir Samuel Hoare told a German
journalist, 'we can always fulfil the letter of a declaration without immediately going all out.'[3] In ministerial circles it was an article of faith that Hitler

was not committed to all-out war with Britain, a notion that gained credibility from the olive branches held out by Hitler on 29 September and 6 October. It was tempting to believe that he was so delighted by his success in overrunning Poland that he would spare himself the trouble of marching his troops through the Low Countries by offering a deal to France and Britain. 'It soon became apparent', wrote Captain Ramsay, 'that no war was being conducted by Germany against this country.' Later Ramsay cited Hitler's decision to halt the advance of his Panzer Corps on 22 May 1940 to allow the British troops to make their escape from Dunkirk as further proof of his thesis.[4]

In this way Chamberlain managed for eight months to maintain what became derisively known as the 'Phoney War'. He retained control of government through his circle of devoted appeasers including Lord Halifax, R. A. Butler, Samuel Hoare and Horace Wilson, supported by lesser figures including Lord Dunglass and 'Chips' Channon. Churchill and Eden were brought back into office largely to reassure the public and the newspapers, but not to change the government's policy. In the pages of *Truth* Chamberlain's agent, Sir Joseph Ball, did his best to discredit the premier's opponents even though they had joined his government. 'Winston Drops A Brick' was typical of a series of such attacks.[5] When Leslie Hore-Belisha was sacked as War Minister in January 1940 – a victim of military conservatism, royal prejudice and anti-Semitism – *Truth* gleefully reported: 'Belisha Is No Loss.'[6] These cabinet reshuffles indicated that the appeasers were still in control, though desperately unhappy about being manoeuvred into war. They remained determined to engineer another Munich-type settlement, though since this was the last thing Hitler wanted it was an unrealistic aim. They convinced themselves that if Hitler were left to pursue his campaigns in the east, he would soon be willing to negotiate a deal with Britain, not least because Germany was not organised for a prolonged war, and shortages of crucial resources would seriously hamper her war effort. When that stage came Halifax hoped to use Mussolini as the mediator in peace talks, the sacrifice of Malta and Gibraltar being the price of his cooperation.

Naturally Chamberlain's ministers could not advocate their peace policy publicly: the British Union of Fascists did that for them. In his official message to his members Mosley condemned the war as contrary to British interests and brought about by 'the dope machine of Jewish finance'.[7] However, he tempered his defiance with compliance. 'I am not offering to fight in the quarrel of Jewish finance in a war from which Britain could withdraw at any moment she likes with her Empire intact and her people safe,' he wrote. But he urged: 'our members should do what the law requires of them, and, if they are members of the Forces or Services of the Crown, they should obey their orders but carry on working for peace if they are free to do so.' In fact Mosley was especially keen on having members within the armed forces, the police and the Home Guard where he believed they might play a key role. According to Special Branch, 'Mosley displays his usual optimism regarding his certainty that the BUF will be within reach of power in under two years.'[8] After 3 September a steady stream of new members joined, although many existing ones resigned and others simply ceased to be active.

Clearly, fascists responded to the outbreak of war in widely differing ways. At one end of the spectrum William Joyce decided: 'I am determined to throw my lot in with Germany and become a German.' On 26 August he and his wife, Margaret, benefiting from an MI5 tip-off, probably from Maxwell Knight, boarded a cross-Channel ferry en route to Germany. This was wise, for MI5 had had a Home Office warrant to tap Joyce's telephone and intercept his mail since September 1938, and consequently knew he had been in touch with German intelligence agents.[9] In Berlin he joined two other British fascists, John Amery and Norman Baillie-Stewart.

However, for many fascists the call of patriotism had overcome their sympathy for Nazi Germany. Francis Yeats-Brown felt invigorated by watching ARP exercises: 'we were no longer arrogant, bleating pacifists,' he enthused, 'but English again, and getting down to our own affairs, including the protection of our homes.' Arnold Leese condemned the Nazi-Soviet Pact, opposed any restoration of colonies to Germany, and was genuinely outraged when aspersions were cast on his patriotism.[10] Others were more ambivalent and confused, the most famous example being Unity Mitford who felt so devastated by war between the two countries she loved that she retreated into the English Garden in Munich and shot herself. The bullet lodged in her brain without killing her, and she returned to Britain for the remaining years of her life. The Marquis of Graham joined the RNVS and served on destroyers in the Mediterranean, but when on leave he and his brother, Lord Ronald Graham, who were Right Club members, continued to involve themselves in pro-peace activities.[11] Similarly the Marquis of Clydesdale, who succeeded as Duke of Hamilton in 1940, belatedly declared himself opposed to Hitler; while holding the rank of wing commander in the RAF he publicly promoted a negotiated peace with Germany, an initiative undertaken with the approval of the prime minister.[12]

Lord Lymington found great difficulty in adjusting to the new situation. In the *New Pioneer* he repeatedly urged peace, complained about the evacuation of civilians and the costs of the refugees, and expressed disgust at the enthusiasm for VAD work that he saw in the Hampshire villages which were in no danger of bombing. He also continued to stir hostility towards the Jews: 'some few will doubtless spy for the highest bidder.' However, by November Lymington had toned down his propaganda and stopped making positive references to Hitler; by December he had brought himself to refer to the 'justice' of the decision to enter the war, and in January *New Pioneer* ceased publication. Privately, however, Lymington continued to attend peace meetings with Domvile and Mosley.[13]

On the face of it the forces of the extreme right were withdrawing from the struggle, though this concealed a good deal of redeployment from one organisation to another. The National Socialist League was wound up in August, quickly followed by the Anglo-German Fellowship; on 4 September Domvile dissolved The Link, Leese closed the Imperial Fascist League offices, and the Nordic League had disbanded by 11 September. However, some members of the Nordic League moved over to the BUF and the Right Club, while many fascists took cover by joining the Peace Pledge Union. Others operated informally, attempting to discourage people from carrying gas masks, and mocking the evacuation and ARP arrangements as unnecessary on the grounds that Hitler had promised he would never be the first to use gas. And although Domvile patriotically declared, 'The King's enemies became our enemies', he continued to work for peace after The Link had been dissolved.[14] A BUF branch in Westminster was found to be stocking steel helmets and white ARP badges for distribution to East End members who were to pose as ARP wardens and take the opportunity to beat up Jews during air raids.[15]

By and large, however, fascist sympathisers campaigned openly for a negotiated peace. They were joined by several new propagandist organisations including Union and Reconstruction, led by Arthur Bryant and Henry Drummond Wolff, and the British Council for a Christian Settlement in Europe under Lord Tavistock, Robert Gordon-Canning and John Beckett.[16] The BUF and the British People's Party carried on much as before, as did the Right Club despite Captain Ramsay's claim that it had ceased to function. After an interview with Chamberlain, Ramsay busied himself gathering evidence of a plot to oust the prime minister; he also wrote doggerel on 'Land of Dope and Jewry', and circulated leaflets entitled 'Do You Know?' and 'Have You Noticed?' The BPP condemned the war in the *People's Post* and its leader, Lord Tavistock, made no pretence of supporting the war effort; he diverted quantities of scarce fodder to feed his deer at Woburn Abbey, refused to plough his land for food, and declined to sacrifice the railings in Bedford Square.[17]

For the BUF the Phoney War period offered ideal conditions for the dissemination of its propaganda. Mosley addressed large 'Stop the War' meetings right up to the spring of 1940 without hindrance, while his members continued to sell *Action* on street corners, although purchasers behaved more furtively than before and did not stop to ask questions.[18] 'Not a single German bomb has been dropped on British soil in the first fortnight of the war,' *Action* triumphantly informed its readers; and it joined with Captain Ramsay in urging the government to resist demands to bomb Germany, especially civilian targets.[19] However, the organisation suffered a check as three hundred organisers were claimed by the armed forces or other wartime duties. In Canterbury, where Reynall Bellamy worked in the Royal Army Service Corps, his colonel assured him that the local fascist leader would be spared by the invading German troops by a safe conduct signed by Hitler. 'Are you quite sure of your facts?' Bellamy asked. 'Absolutely reliable source,' the colonel replied, whereupon Bellamy explained that he was the local fascist leader.[20]

In effect the BUF kept a foot in both the war and the peace camps, encouraging members to do their duty and thus deprive the authorities of an excuse for banning it, while also spreading highly defeatist propaganda. It relentlessly emphasised the negative consequences of war including higher unemployment, punitive taxation, profiteering, inflation, swollen bureaucracy and rationing.[21] Nor did BUF speakers pull their punches; Anne Brock-Griggs told a Bethnal Green audience: 'you don't see any of the rotten Government leaders in khaki ... As for the swine Churchill, we well remember Gallipoli and the Dardanelles, the rotten murderer.'[22]

Why, then, did the authorities tolerate the peace campaign for so long? In addition to the pro-Nazi activity, there was a certain amount of left-wing pacifism, as represented by the Peace Pledge Union; the government could hardly have suppressed one but not the other without provoking widespread protest. By joining the PPU many fascists believed they had taken out a timely insurance. In any case, repression would have been an overreaction in the early stages of the war, for it seemed certain that as the German military threat loomed larger, the peacemongers would lose what limited support they enjoyed. On the other hand, according to the Mass Observation surveys, a large section of the public found a negotiated peace attractive, and there was a risk that Mosley might capitalise on this as the war dragged on.[23]

Yet the BUF signally failed to mobilise this sentiment when it intervened in three by-elections during the Phoney War. At Silvertown in February 1940 T. P. 'Tommy' Moran polled a derisory 151 votes despite holding many outdoor meetings in the constituency.[24] In March Mosley addressed packed meetings at North East Leeds, but his candidate, Sidney Allen, who was dubbed 'an agent of Hitler', won 722 or 2.9 per cent of the vote.[25] At the Middleton and Prestwich by-election, which took place in May amidst mounting invasion scares, Mosley was attacked by a crowd, apparently intent on lynching him, and the BUF managed only 418 votes or 1.3 per cent.[26] As a result of the party truce either Conservative or Labour candidates stood down at these by-elections, thus leaving an opportunity for small parties and Independents to gather a protest vote, but the BUF had not managed to exploit the opportunity to any significant extent. The surprising thing is that Mosley persisted with these efforts, but he may have seen them as a useful way of demonstrating that his movement was not subversive.

However, there was also an element of self-interest in the government's surprisingly relaxed attitude towards Mosley's peace campaign. Captain Ramsay speculated that ministers saw Mosley as a safety valve for the expression of pro-Nazi opinion.[27] Certainly, his propaganda posed no real threat; indeed, it prepared the way for the settlement with Hitler that Chamberlain devoutly hoped to achieve. On the outbreak of war the police had seized some copies of Mosley's pamphlets, but although the Home Office regarded them as mischievous and defeatist, Sir John Anderson, the Home Secretary, told MPs it would be a mistake to suppress or to ban the BUF. Privately he noted: 'It is very difficult to put one's finger on any particular matter in it which is unusually objectionable, many of the arguments used to support the peace policy are very specious and even good, so far as they go.'[28]

Nor was there much pressure from the security services in the early stages of the war. MI5 drew up a list of just twenty-three people it considered suitable for detention and Special Branch identified eighteen individuals including William Joyce and Captain Luttman-Johnson. But by 14 September the authorities had detained only fourteen, mostly obscure figures suspected of espionage, only two of whom, William F. Craven and G. Eric Thomas, were BUF members.[29] Subsequently two members of the Nordic League and the Right Club, Victor Rowe and Oliver Gilbert, were detained, though on the basis of slight evidence.[30] This meagre haul puts into perspective the Churchill government's decision to arrest hundreds of Mosley's members in May 1940; in September 1939 they were apparently not seen as a threat to security. To some extent the shift of policy reflected departmental rivalries. The security services, who were embarrassed about finding so few spies and fifth columnists, felt the need to make a mark; but they were obstructed by the Home Office officials who regarded them as rather dim ex-army officers who were prone to exaggerate the likelihood of fascist subversion. It required an invasion scare and a change of government to give MI5 the extra clout it needed.

One can understand why the Home Office refused to be stampeded by the security services' reports on the pro-peace movement. In October 1939 the Metropolitan Police suggested that Mosley was quite content for the war to continue, on the grounds that domestic discontent, accentuated by military failure, would eventually generate a revolt which would destabilise the government and create an opportunity for the BUF.[31] At the same time the Right Club was reported to be contacting sympathisers in the armed forces to spread its propaganda: 'There is talk of a military coup d'état, but there seems to be a lack of agreement among members on the question of leadership. Sir Oswald Mosley they regard with suspicion. Captain Ramsay is definitely unbalanced and suffers from persecution mania so far as the Jewish problem is concerned.'[32]

But was the talk about revolts and coups merely a pious hope rather than indicative of an organised plan? In February 1940 several Special Branch informants claimed that Mosley intended to form cells in every factory and on every street so as to enable him to take advantage of the confusion if government broke down; they detected a 'strong hint of a march to power by armed force'. In what one informant described as a 'strong revolutionary speech' Mosley mocked Chamberlain and Churchill as politicians floating on the current – 'being full of wind they keep on the surface'. He also made veiled references to marching to power with 'our brother parties', which won loud applause.[33] Ramsay also claimed to have cells working in all important government departments by the spring of 1940.[34] Yet such evidence must be interpreted with caution. Mosley was a skilled actor doing his best to boost the morale of his beleaguered followers at a time when they faced an uncertain future. Excitable reports of speeches should be set against the impression obtained by Special Branch officers when they paid a visit to Mosley's headquarters at the end of January and found nothing much going on; the switchboard was quiet and the postman delivered only five letters.[35] It is of course possible that the BUF was increasingly conducting its work in secret, though in view of the flock of informants now monitoring its activities it seems unlikely that plans for a violent coup could have been missed.

Yet, by March 1940 they were again fuelling speculation about Mosley's intentions. Apparently he continued to expect that military setbacks would create a national collapse or crisis which would accelerate his path to power. 'My conclusion may sound fantastic,' admitted one informant, 'but I rather feel that he is relying on the calling up of BU members to provide eventually an armed force which will effect revolution.'[36] But the informant conceded: 'it was not what he said but what he meant that interested me.' In private conversations with senior colleagues at this time Mosley expatiated grandiloquently about how, at the right moment, he would engineer a Communist uprising in order to enable the fascists to intervene by force on the pretext of 'saving the country'.[37] He anticipated support from the RAF, which he described as almost unanimously sympathetic to the BUF, as well as from the army. Undoubtedly Mosley had supporters within the RAF; but these reports suggest that his tendency to fantasise was getting the better of him. Alternatively, he may simply have been pandering to his members who looked eagerly for a whiff of grapeshot to scatter the reviled politicians. It must be significant that after his detention the authorities made no attempt to accuse him of plotting a violent coup, which suggests that he was guilty of no more than loose talk.

In fact, the real strength of the peace campaign lay in its influence behind the scenes in parliament, the government and the royal family. During the Phoney War ministers became the target of a battalion of aristocratic peacemongers including Lords Brocket and Queenborough, the Earl of Mar, the Marquises of Tavistock and Londonderry, and the Dukes of Buccleuch, Westminster and Hamilton, to name but a few. R. A. Butler left Arthur Bryant in no doubt that he was anxious to maintain friendly relations with the peace party: 'I am hoping you will feel that you have immediate access to me and those I serve,' he told him. He even asked the pro-Nazi Bryant to draft a statement of war aims for him.[38] At the end of September 1939 Butler had a long conversation with Buccleuch who urged the need for a negotiated peace: 'I had a distinct impression that even Halifax was not unfavourable.'[39] Butler gave the Duke to understand that an acceptable settlement would not involve restoring Czechoslovakian territory or returning Danzig and the Corridor to Poland. 'Why therefore must we remain committed to war for these aims?' demanded Buccleuch.[40] He answered himself by ruefully admitting: 'I suppose Winston can successfully veto any move towards peace.' Churchill reportedly warned the Duke of Westminster, who had hosted several gatherings of titled peacemongers at his London house in September: 'very hard experiences lie before those who preach defeatism and set themselves against the will of the nation.'[41]

One of the earliest initiatives, which gains significance in the light of the Hess affair in 1941, centred around the Marquis of Clydesdale MP (who became Duke of Hamilton in May 1940). Despite serving in the forces, Clydesdale, along with his brothers, Lords Malcolm and David Douglas-Hamilton, strongly believed that Britain was fighting the wrong war. 'I cannot help feeling that if we could get rid of Hitler,' wrote Lord Malcolm, 'the step would be short to discussing with Germany the best means to combat the Russian menace.'[42] Lord Malcolm had a contact in Stockholm who offered to act as an intermediary and bring together 'German and English moderates' to devise a peace plan based on a German withdrawal from Poland and the replacement of Hitler.[43] According to Lord David Douglas-Hamilton, who had contacts in Germany, the opposition to Hitler was ready to offer peace but had to be convinced of a positive response from Britain.

With this in mind, Clydesdale composed a letter, originally intended to be signed by young officers, which was eventually printed in his name in *The Times* on 6 October.[44] He took care to offer a patriotic preamble: 'We believe we speak for the young men and women of the Empire in saying that Britain had no choice but to accept the challenge of Hitler's aggression against one country in Europe after another.' But he went on to say:

> the moment the menace of aggression and bad faith has been removed, war against Germany becomes wrong and meaningless ... we do not grudge Germany Lebensraum, provided that Lebensraum is not made the grave of other nations. We should be ready to search for and find a just colonial settlement.

Before publication Clydesdale put his draft letter to Halifax who advised on it, while Lord Dunglass, Chamberlain's Parliamentary Private Secretary, obtained the approval of Chamberlain himself.[45] Although nothing came of this, the letter underlined how closely the prime minister and Halifax were involved with the peace movement.

Such sympathy in high places naturally encouraged the peace party to persist in its efforts. In December Buccleuch, who was Lord Steward of the Royal Household, delivered a 'full and strong' letter to Buckingham Palace complaining that Britain had gone to war because Halifax had been persuaded that 'the Nazis were determined on world domination, the subjection of Britain, and must be fought at once ... How much better to have allowed Germany to come up against Soviet Russia instead of pushing them into that alliance.'[46] Admitting that he had earlier received a 'friendly warning on behalf of Your Majesty', Buccleuch offered his resignation. But if he was hoping to elicit some sympathy for his views he was disappointed, for the King made no response until May 1940. In January the Duke complained to Bryant: 'I have had no reply and am wondering how to follow it up ... I am afraid people there have told [the King] I am pro-Nazi which is all rot.'[47]

The King's caution about replying to Buccleuch may have been connected with the rumours now circulating about a possible coup to replace George VI with the Duke of Windsor, who was being as indiscreet as ever in disseminating his belief in peace and his conviction that Britain would be defeated in the war. Frustrated by the palace, Buccleuch persisted in trying to persuade Downing Street of the need to negotiate a settlement, as late as April 1940, because of the inevitability of military defeat: 'why not do so now, when comparatively little damage has been done and when there is still time to avert economic ruin?'[48] As these remarks suggest, there were wider considerations behind the distaste for war among the aristocrats. They anticipated a repetition of the social and political upheavals that had attended the First World War. Lord Brocket reminded Chamberlain that 'middle and upper class people here see no hope for the future owing to the appalling taxation which a long war makes necessary.'[49] In this he was correct, for the experience of war changed the political agenda and decisively discredited the National Government.

Even in the House of Commons there was some pressure for a negotiated peace in the autumn of 1939. L. S. Amery complained about 'a certain amount of pretty sorry defeatism', which had surfaced in the 1922 Committee.[50] A Labour MP, Richard Stokes, despatched a circular entitled 'What are we fighting for?', arguing that Britain should pull out and leave Russia and Germany to fight it out; if Germany were defeated, according to Stokes, this would leave Russia too strong: 'Are we really content to bring our civilisation to ruin in order that the Hammer and Sickle shall fly from the North Sea to the Pacific?' Privately Arthur Bryant issued a similar warning: 'there is little or no possibility of an industrialised nation like Germany meeting a second defeat without going Bolshevik.'[51] In November Stokes and George Lansbury led some twenty Labour members in sending Chamberlain a memoir calling for a conference with Germany and the other powers. He attracted the approval of Lord Beaverbrook, proprietor of the *Daily Express*, who offered to finance a campaign in January if Stokes put his proposals to the Labour Party conference. An unscrupulous opportunist, Beaverbrook professed to be a supporter of Chamberlain, but opposed entry into the war; he shared Mosley's view that a well-armed Britain had nothing to fear from Germany and should concentrate on the empire, leaving the other powers to fight for control on the Continent.[52] He had encouraged other left-wingers, Jimmy Maxton and John McGovern, to run as pro-peace candidates at by-elections. However, Beaverbrook put all this behind him in 1941 when Churchill gave him a ministerial post.

On the other hand, those who publicly associated themselves with peace soon became vulnerable to patriotic attacks. In March 1940 Bryant published *Unfinished Victory* in which he blamed Britain for causing the war by misunderstanding Hitler; but when the book was condemned as 'pure and open Nazi propaganda' the chastened author hastily bought up copies to keep himself out of the public eye.[53] 'It is disheartening . . . to be stigmatised as a pro-Nazi dupe, traitor, biased or merely ignorant of German wiles and cunning,' complained Buccleuch; from his lonely refuge in Drumlanrig

Castle in Dumfries, he asked Bryant: 'Do you think I should come out more in public?'[54] The Duke at least had no constituents to worry about. When the Tory member for Ayr, Sir Thomas Moore, was dubbed 'Hitler's Friend' by the *Sunday Pictorial*, his constituency executive called him to task. At Bristol West the Conservative Association reprimanded their member, Cyril Culverwell, for involving himself with Brocket, Westminster and Buccleuch and deselected him in 1944.[55] Before long the press began outing fascist suspects. The *Daily Mirror*, *News Chronicle* and *Daily Herald* attacked Mary Allen, demanding her dismissal from the Women's Voluntary Service because of her role as a speaker at BUF peace rallies.[56] Asked for her view of Hitler, Allen replied: 'I have no opinion to give. Once my country is at war its enemies are my enemies.'

Despite attracting public opprobrium, however, the more discreet opponents of war and fascist sympathisers continued to penetrate the British establishment. After appointing Beaverbrook as Minister for Aircraft Production in 1941, Churchill replaced him in 1942 with Mosley's long-standing ally, J. C. T. Moore-Brabazon, though he may have calculated that it was advantageous to keep potential troublemakers in the government. When a vacancy occurred at Brighton in April 1940 the local Conservatives selected as their candidate Lord Erskine who was linked to the BUF as a member of the January Club. Erskine's father, the Earl of Mar, who regularly attended meetings with Mosley, Ramsay and Domvile, openly donated money to the BUF 'as a token of my appreciation of your ceaseless and strenuous work to protect Britain'.[57] One month after Erskine's unopposed election as MP he and his father could well have been detained as subversives under Regulation 18B. It seems likely that the Brighton Tories got to know of their activities because in November 1941 Erskine suddenly resigned his seat with no explanation, and a fresh candidate was adopted with indecent haste.[58]

But the most remarkable Phoney War fascist was Major-General 'Boney' Fuller, who had been a BUF candidate and was now involved with the Nordic League and the *New Pioneer*. On 27 September, the day after he dined with the Mosleys, Fuller met General Sir Edmund Ironside, Chief of the Imperial General Staff, who wanted to make him his deputy but was overruled by the war cabinet.[59] Fuller's fascist record since 1934 and his current opposition to the policy of outright defeat of Germany made him a stronger candidate for internment than for appointment as deputy CIGS; but his near-appointment is less surprising in the light of the fact that Ironside himself had been involved with the Anglo-German Fellowship and evidently looked indulgently on his opinions. 'Ironside is with us,' Fuller assured Admiral Domvile when they met in November.[60]

Insofar as there was an organised peace party during the Phoney War it consisted in a series of private meetings among fascist sympathisers held between October 1939 and May 1940. Later, during his detention, Mosley claimed he had hardly met Captain Ramsay, but they had, in fact, been in regular contact at these fortnightly gatherings along with Admiral Domvile, Lord Lymington, Lord Tavistock, the Earl of Mar, Neil Francis-Hawkins, R. C. Gordon-Canning, Charles Grey, George Pitt-Rivers, Mary Allen, Major-General Fuller, Lady Pearson and Lord Ronald Graham. The names were recorded by Domvile in a diary which survived because he hid it under his henhouse just before the police arrived to arrest him in May 1940. MI5 gave the impression that these gatherings were very sinister; one 'very reliable informant' claimed that Mary Allen had attended meetings with Ramsay and Domvile where 'the object was to secure the greatest possible collaboration and make preparations for a fascist coup d'état'.[61] The very fact that the peacemongers met at private houses in Ladbroke Grove under the auspices of the Anti-Vivisection Society, a BUF front run by the ex-suffragette Norah Elam and her husband, looked suspect. However, the authorities failed to produce convincing evidence, despite the fact that the gatherings were so intensively monitored that the pro-Nazis were sometimes in danger of being outnumbered by representatives of the security forces. Mosley and Ramsay certainly recognised the need to coordinate their scattered forces, but the secret gatherings amounted to little more than discussion groups. Beyond agreeing to contest several by-elections, which was scarcely a sign of sinister intent, they possessed neither a strategy nor a leader. Ramsay only strengthened his reputation as a foolish fanatic by his repeated interventions in the House of Commons on the subject of Jews.

By contrast, Mosley gradually emerged as the leading figure through force of intellect and personality. Many of the participants had previously worked under him in the BUF, while aristocrats such as Mar, Tavistock, Brocket and Buccleuch were rather naive and unworldly men easily eclipsed by Mosley. He demonstrated his dominance by attracting representatives of all the 'patriotic' societies to a lunch for five hundred people at the Criterion on 1 March 1940, where Domvile, Fuller, Lord Ronald Graham, Viscountess Downe, Lady Pearson, Yeats-Brown, Ben Greene and George Pitt-Rivers were among the guests. Mosley delighted his audience by openly ridiculing Britain's decision to enter the war and insisting that Hitler had no hostile designs towards her.[62] Yet they still harboured doubts about him. 'Frankly Mosley is more like a Leader than anybody I have seen in this country,' wrote Charles Grey, the fascist editor of *The Aeroplane*, 'and yet I can't quite convince myself that he is the man to save the country.'[63] Grey suspected a foreign strain, probably Italian, in him, and admitted that many critics suspected his reluctance to 'advocate an all-out pogrom'.

The optimistic mood at the Criterion lunch in March was apparently shared in ministerial circles. 'Peace [is] in the Air,' pronounced *Truth*, claiming that the atmosphere had changed all over Europe: 'Let us get it clear that peace is not a "threat", an "intrigue", or an "offensive".'[64] Meeting privately with Domvile and Tavistock, Mosley referred to the possibility of Lloyd George returning to negotiate a settlement with Germany.[65] During recent weeks several fresh peace initiatives had been launched. *The Patriot* published a somewhat bizarre list of what purported to be Hitler's latest terms, including independence for India, withdrawal from Egypt, surrender of the Palestine mandate, plebiscites in Cyprus, the Falklands and the West Indies, complete freedom for Ireland and the restoration of Canada to France.[66] A more realistic proposal emerged via Lord Tavistock who circulated peace terms received from Henning Thomson, an employee of the German legation in Dublin. This involved the restoration of independence to Czechoslavakia and Poland, a plebiscite in Austria, Germany's readmittance to the League of Nations and disarmament talks, the return of her colonies and improved access to raw materials.[67] When he passed this to Halifax, the Permanent Secretary, Sir Alexander Cadogan, dismissed Tavistock as a 'half-wit'; but this did not deter the Foreign Secretary from authorising Tavistock to visit Dublin to see whether the offer was genuine. Although Tavistock's son may have been right in describing him as a harmless crank, the fact is that he was operating with a measure of approval from Halifax, which may well have conferred some protection on him when the peace party was rounded up two months later.[68]

The chief threat to these efforts was, of course, Churchill. Up to this point Chamberlain had managed him shrewdly by restoring him to his old post at the Admiralty where Churchill quickly demonstrated that he retained his penchant for imaginative but ill-considered naval-military offensives. Only four days after taking office he proposed to use the navy to force a passage into the Baltic – an idea that had been discarded in 1914 as quite impractical. His next big idea, the Norwegian campaign, proved to be a thoroughgoing fiasco which destroyed the government and brought the Phoney War to an abrupt end. During a two-day debate on the campaign on 8 and 9 May 1940, Chamberlain frankly admitted it had been a serious setback, presumably to underline Churchill's responsibility. However, after eight months of uninspired leadership these tactics backfired. Chamberlain's whips failed to appreciate how disenchanted many MPs had become, especially those who had joined the armed forces and thus realised how poorly prepared for war the country had been. At the end of the debate the government's majority was reduced from 213 to 81, with 41 Conservatives voting against the government and 60 abstaining.

Chamberlain still hoped to survive as premier by forming a new national government with Labour and the Liberals. However, this was scuppered when Clement Attlee telephoned from Bournemouth, where the Labour Party was holding its conference, refusing to serve under him. This forced Chamberlain into resignation. There were now two alternative leaders of whom Lord Halifax, who enjoyed the support of most Tory MPs, seemed the more likely. But from the public's point of view Halifax was too close to Chamberlain; in any case, marooned in the House of Lords, he would have been embarrassed by Churchill, striking a prime ministerial pose in the Commons. On the other hand, much of the political establishment loathed Churchill as a diehard warmonger. Queen Mary declared she 'would not stay with that dreadful Mr Churchill', while Butler considered it a 'national disaster' that someone as unreliable as him should become prime minister.[69] Despite this, when Halifax backed down, the way was clear for Churchill to take over.

Whether he would survive the war as premier, however, remained doubtful. The formation of the new Coalition left most of the leading appeasers and defeatists still entrenched in government and no less convinced of the desirability of peace. On Chamberlain's fall from office Dunglass and Channon drank a toast to 'The King Over the Water', while Butler insisted that 'diehards like Churchill [will] not be allowed to prevent Britain making a compromise settlement'.[70] A British prime minister usually enjoys security of tenure by virtue of being leader of the majority party in the House of Commons; but Churchill was not the leader of any party at this stage. If the military situation deteriorated further, Halifax stood waiting to take over. Charles Grey was not alone in doubting the Coalition's ability to meet the awesome military challenge Britain faced: 'It certainly is not going to lead the nation to victory,' he wrote.[71] Indeed, after the fall of France in June 1940 things appeared so hopeless that the new war cabinet felt obliged to consider surrendering British territory in the Mediterranean and Africa as the price for peace; even Churchill was tempted to accept these losses 'if we could get out of this jam'.[72]

If only for purposes of stiffening civilian morale, the new Coalition had to demonstrate its resolute approach to winning the war. Five days after becoming prime minister, Churchill told the war cabinet he wanted to see suspect persons 'behind barbed wire'. In fact, an Emergency Powers (Defence) Bill had been introduced in September 1939 to empower the Home Secretary to detain anyone he had reason to suspect of hostile associations or involvement in 'acts prejudicial to public safety or to the defence of the realm'. However, only minimal use had been made of these powers, and at cabinet meetings as late as 15 and 18 May 1940 Sir John Anderson refused to take action against the fascists because there was no evidence to link them with fifth-column activities. However, by this time the retreat of the British forces in France and Belgium had provoked a sudden panic over a possible German invasion and heightened fears about a 'Fifth Column' operating in Britain. It was widely believed that the Nazis had infiltrated their spies amongst the 70,000 aliens and refugees admitted before the war. Security officers collected reports about mysterious radio messages supposedly broadcast to Belgium and Holland, unexplained signs appearing on telegraph poles at night, and suspicious crop patterns which might be designed to guide enemy aeroplanes. John Charnley's family was rumoured to have painted a swastika on the roof of the local BUF headquarters so that the German bombers would be able to avoid it.[73]

Amid all this spurious evidence about spies and fifth-column activities, the security services at last produced the proof that had hitherto been lacking. On 20 May Maxwell Knight of MI5 raided a flat at 47 Gloucester Place, where Tyler Kent, a clerk at the American embassy, was in bed with his mistress, Mrs Irene Danischewsky. He arrested Kent and his accomplice, Anna Wolkoff, the daughter of a Russian admiral, Nicholas Wolkoff, who ran the Russian Tea Rooms in South Kensington. The British had been aware for some time that Kent had been stealing documents from his embassy which he sold to the Russians to sustain his extravagant lifestyle; they had not alerted the Americans earlier because Ambassador Joseph Kennedy was himself under MI5 surveillance on account of his defeatist, anti-British views. The Wolkoffs were also known to the authorities as members of the Right Club.

The raid on 20 May unearthed some 1,500 stolen documents at Tyler Kent's flat including copies of eight letters from Churchill to President Roosevelt whose contents had been passed to the German ambassador in Rome. Kent intended to use them to expose and discredit Roosevelt's increasingly pro-British policy. The link with the peace party was strengthened by the discovery that Captain Ramsay had, rather foolishly, deposited his list of Right Club members with Kent, which, in the eyes of MI5, made it look like a network of spies. It seems that Ramsay, who blamed Roosevelt for pushing Britain into the war, intended to reveal in parliament that, before becoming prime minister, Churchill and Roosevelt had corresponded about overthrowing Chamberlain's government and ending the Phoney War.[74] Though hardly enough to bring Churchill down, this would certainly have provoked his enemies in the Conservative ranks.

The revelations about the activities of Kent and Wolkoff proved decisive. Two days after the raid the cabinet agreed to amend Regulation 18B of the Emergency Powers Act to allow for the detention of members of organisations 'subject to foreign influence or control' or whose leaders 'have or have had association with persons concerned in the government of, or sympathetic with the system of government of, any power with which His Majesty is at war'. This cumbersome language seems to indicate that the authorities' real target was the British Union of Fascists rather than the Right Club. Although Mosley was, as far as is known, innocent of any action likely to assist the enemy, his connection with Ramsay during the previous eight months now made him vulnerable.

On 23 May Mosley noticed several policemen waiting outside his flat in Dolphin Square. They had a warrant for his arrest. He gathered some clothes before being taken to New Scotland Yard where police confiscated a Walther automatic pistol and a truncheon from him. 'Sir Oswald was most affable', according to Special Branch, and assured them he had been expecting arrest and had ensured that BUF records would not fall into the hands of the authorities.[75] He was then removed to Brixton Prison while the police searched Savehay Farm, the Mosleys' home at Denham in Buckinghamshire. There they seized no fewer than nine guns, including rifles, pistols and revolvers, as well as ammunition, truncheons and swordsticks. Also on 23 May Captain Ramsay was seized on the steps of his London home on his return from Scotland. Arnold Leese, however, escaped immediate arrest and went on the run, moving from house to house for several months. He was finally caught in November after a violent struggle when visiting his home in Guildford.[76] Jock Houston evaded the police for five months by going to live with his girlfriend in Windsor. But by the end of May most of the prominent figures in the BUF had been detained including Francis-Hawkins, Mick Clarke, Raven Thompson, Anne Brock-Griggs and Norah Elam. Altogether 747 members were arrested. After a three-day search of headquarters police carried off quantities of documents, though much material had already been removed; *Action* published its last edition on 6 June, and in July the organisation was banned.

Although the detention of pro-fascists made sense in the context of the invasion scare that gripped Britain in May 1940, it is difficult to explain the policy convincingly. Churchill's many biographers tend to ignore the subject altogether and he himself soon became embarrassed by the whole thing, partly because he realised that two of his cousins by marriage, Diana Mosley and George Pitt-Rivers, were among the detainees. He accepted that MI5 had failed to come up with evidence of fifth-column activities by most of those detained, and he admitted that imprisonment without charges being brought or trial by jury was 'in the highest degree odious ... the foundation of all totalitarian government whether Nazi or Communist'.[77] Several writers have rejected the suggestion that Churchill's policy was influenced by political considerations, but this seems naive; it would have been most surprising if he had not, in the circumstances, seen the political implications of the detention of the leading fascists.[78] The political rationale that had led the Chamberlain government to be indulgent towards the peace party had now been reversed. This is not to say that Churchill originally intended detention to serve as a weapon against his opponents in parliament and the government, but he was surely the beneficiary of it subsequently. The main crop of arrests during May and June left many prominent pro-Nazis still at liberty, though under surveillance, and counting themselves very lucky not to have been incarcerated in Brixton. Moreover, a number of those who escaped detention were subject to restrictions on their movements – a clear warning that the authorities would take further action if they failed to behave themselves.

At the time many fascists blamed their arrest on the Labour Party which was thought to have made it a condition for joining the Coalition.[79] In 1945 Aneurin Bevan claimed: 'if we hadn't forced Churchill to imprison Mosley – who knows what he might have achieved?' However, despite the bitterness about 'upper-class traitors' and the lingering resentment towards Mosley in the Labour movement, there is no evidence that Attlee even raised the issue when he agreed to serve under Churchill. 'I was resolved that I would not, by haggling, be responsible for any failure to act promptly,' he wrote. Although there was some discussion about appointments, he and Churchill do not appear to have discussed policy matters.[80]

The slender evidence of fifth-column activities inevitably provoked public challenges to the government's policy, not to mention outrage among the detainees themselves. 'I would welcome a trial,' wrote Captain Luttman-Johnson. 'I should say that 93 per cent of the arrested 18bs are guilty of nothing more than indiscretions for which at the most they would have got two months from a magistrate.'[81] Yeats-Brown wrote to *The Times* protesting: 'Their lot is hard if they are innocent, and not hard enough if they are guilty of treason. Why, for instance was Sir Barry Domvile arrested? It is true he encouraged Anglo-German friendship before the war, but does that make this distinguished Admiral a traitor?'[82] In parliament Commander Robert Bower and other MPs criticised Regulation 18B for giving the Home Secretary powers to detain without trial, though they risked drawing accusations of pro-Nazism on to their own heads.[83] Other influential figures chose to express their disquiet privately. In the autumn of 1940 Viscountess Downe was lunching with the Chaplain from Sandringham who told her: 'A very high personage would like you to know that no traitorous tendency of any kind has been found in connection with your friend Sir Oswald Mosley, but it is expedient to detain him, if only for his own safety at the present time.'[84]

Henry Page Croft, who had received a peerage and been appointed Under-Secretary at the War Office by Churchill, was required to answer for the Home Office in the House of Lords. In July 1940 he refused to do this on the grounds that he could not defend the government's policy towards people 'arrested without any evidence that they are ill-affected to the State or that they have given or are likely to give help to our enemies'.[85] Pointing out that the sole grounds for detention appeared to be membership of a fascist organisation, Page Croft argued: 'the British Government never regarded the movement as illegal . . . when war broke out they were permitted without hindrance to sell their newspaper, *Action*, at street corners and to hold public meetings'; and he concluded, 'if any Fascist – past or present – has been helping the King's enemies, impeding the war effort or actively promoting disaffection . . . he or she should be punished without mercy . . . the guilty [should] be punished and the innocent set at once at liberty.' Though his case was compelling, Page Croft overlooked the fact that the basis for detention was not what people had done in the past but what they might do in the future. In any case, the government could not risk bringing the detainees to trial, not only because of lack of evidence, but also because of the risk of revealing how far the political establishment, the armed forces and the royal family had been implicated in the anti-war movement or had fascist connections; apart from many backbench MPs, several ministers including Moore-Brabazon, Beaverbrook, Butler and Halifax would all have been vulnerable.

Unfortunately for Mosley and the other detainees, by May 1940 the dire military situation had created a demand for traitors. American diplomats in France and Britain now took it for granted that Britain would suffer a defeat followed by the installation of a vassal regime by Hitler. Joseph Kennedy was quoted as saying: 'It is possible some other government, that of Sir Oswald Mosley for example, might turn over anything Hitler wanted to save England from destruction.'[86] Churchill himself referred to Mosley becoming 'Hitler's puppet' in the event of a German invasion. This was a careless remark, but Churchill found it useful to frighten Roosevelt with the thought that a British government under Mosley would surrender the navy, 'leaving Germany and Japan the masters of the New World'. In fact, it was highly improbable that the Germans would have chosen Mosley to lead a client regime. They had no high opinion of him, and would have found Halifax, Hoare or even Lloyd George much more suitable figureheads.

Although Mosley undoubtedly hoped to capitalise on the crisis created by the war to lever himself into power, there is no evidence that he conspired to secure a British defeat. His contacts with the Nazis, even in the 1930s, were very limited, although Diana had acted as a line of communication with Hitler. Mosley's refusal to accept that there was any rational justification for fighting Germany was shared by many people who were not fascists. Moreover, his campaign for peace had been conducted quite openly, and his private meetings with Ramsay and Domvile were kept under close surveillance by the security services who discovered no evidence of treasonable activity. Of course, as much of the relevant material was destroyed, or is still withheld, it is possible that there is something incriminating yet to be revealed, but it is significant that the record kept by one of the participants, Admiral Domvile, in his diaries tends to confirm the impression that the peacemongers did little more than talk among themselves.

According to the Home Secretary the detention policy was designed to apprehend BUF activists and organisers, not rank-and-file members, though in practice it was a rather hit-and-miss affair.[87] As MI5 operated with a card index and out-of-date membership lists, this is hardly surprising. One Special Branch officer based at Leeds recalled that the arrests had not been indiscriminate but carefully targeted so as to claim three members in the West Leeds branch, five at York, two in Huddersfield and four at Barnsley.[88] However, since four out of five branch organisers were thought to be serving in the forces by the time the arrests were made, only the older men and those under eighteen were affected. To Leonard Wise, who saw non-activists arrested while activists remained at large, the policy appeared quite arbitrary.[89] Maxwell Knight relied on BUF members who were willing to turn informants, and he also liked to place female agents in subversive organisations. Joan Miller, Marjorie Amos and Helene Louise Munch were infiltrated into the Right Club where they gained the confidence of Anna Wolkoff.[90] Yet despite this, only twenty of the Right Club's 350 members were interned.

Individual experience certainly makes the whole policy appear erratic. In Kingston the police called for Blanche Greaves, an obvious target as the BUF's Woman District Leader, in normal working hours; she was, in fact, away on her honeymoon and they never returned for her. Eric Piercey was arrested after returning from his sixth cross-Channel trip to rescue soldiers from Dunkirk. Louise Irving's husband was detained in June 1940, only to be released in December 1941 and almost immediately called up for military service.[91] Special Branch looked with great suspicion on Mary Allen who was a close associate of Mosley and Domvile and a frequent speaker at BUF peace meetings. Yet the Home Office saw no grounds to detain Allen whom they described unflatteringly as 'a terribly conceited woman, a crank with a tremendous grievance ... trailing round in a ridiculous uniform'.[92] But since Allen was well-known to the newspapers, due to her connection with the women's police, MPs demanded to know why she had not been arrested. Her home at St Just on the Cornish coast seemed suspicious in itself. Eventually, in July Allen was restricted to a five-mile radius of her home, subject to permission from the chief constable, and was banned from using motor cars, bicycles, telephone or wireless until 1942.[93]

Some suspects were left at large in the hope that they would lead to further discoveries, especially the female fascists whom the misogynists of MI5 regarded as particularly dangerous. This was why Diana Mosley escaped arrest until the end of July despite security reports describing her as 'this extremely dangerous and sinister young woman' and 'far cleverer and more dangerous than her husband and will stick at nothing to achieve her ambitions'.[94] Irritated by the delay, Diana's ex-father-in-law, Lord Moyne, seized the opportunity to take revenge for the insult she had inflicted on his family by informing on her: 'It has been on my conscience for some time that the Authorities concerned are aware of the extremely dangerous character of my former daughter-in-law, now Lady Mosley.'[95] He sent summaries of Diana's conversations with the governess and details of her visits to Germany extracted from her diary; Diana appeared to be well-informed about German plans for a breakthrough in France, expressed delight that the British army would be caught in a pincer movement, and foresaw that Britain would be starved into submission by the destruction of the docks in Liverpool and London. Yet despite this encouragement, the authorities preferred to leave Diana at Savehay Farm where they tapped her telephone; this showed she was making some attempt to keep the BUF organisation going but nothing very incriminating.[96] The eventual decision to intern her was embarrassing because she was a nursing mother and had an eighteen-month-old child; but she decided to leave both baby and child with her nanny rather than take the baby into Holloway.[97]

Yet the most remarkable aspect of the detentions under Regulation 18B was not who was arrested but who was not. Virtually all the leading aristocratic fascists including Tavistock, Buccleuch, Lymington, Westminster, Brocket, Mar, Queenborough and Downe remained at large, though they were kept under surveillance. Influence undoubtedly counted in some cases. Lady Pearson, who was a BUF parliamentary candidate, spent only a few days in prison. Her brother, the irascible Henry Page Croft, who was now a minister, angrily confronted the Home Secretary over his 'stupidity and indecency' in arresting her; he secured her release, though her movements were restricted.[98] Two suspects probably benefited from their royal connections. Police searched the home of Viscountess Downe, who appeared to fit the requirements for detention as a BUF candidate; but she had been a lady-in-waiting to Queen Mary. In the case of the Duke of Buccleuch, George VI suddenly wrote on 12 May, after a four-month silence, accepting his resignation as Lord Steward of the Royal Household; presumably the King judged it politic to distance himself from someone who was regarded as pro-Nazi.[99]

The escape of Lord Tavistock, who succeeded as Duke of Bedford in August 1940, also seems inexplicable in the light of the imprisonment of other members of the People's Party and the British Council for a Christian Settlement in Europe, notably John Beckett and Ben Greene. Greene applied for habeas corpus and was released in January 1941 because he had been accused on false evidence; Beckett remained in detention until 1943; but Tavistock went free. 'I can only suppose my father was spared . . . out of reluctance to lock up someone with such an old and respected title or because those in authority recognised his basic futility,' wrote his son. Tavistock's links with Halifax may have been more relevant. The Foreign Secretary sent pro-Nazi and anti-war correspondence he received from ordinary people straight to Special Branch, but presumably did not see Tavistock's activities in the same light.[100] Viscount Lymington, who also escaped detention, had distanced himself from the peace party by abandoning the *New Pioneer* in January and joining his local Home Guard as a platoon commander. However, in October he was abruptly required to resign by the Commander for Hampshire. The reason is not clear, but Lymington believed he had been accused of fifth-column tendencies, which was not improbable in view of the company he had been keeping previously.[101]

Among the non-aristocratic non-detainees four cases stand out. Mosley was doubtless correct in thinking that Bill Allen was not arrested 'because he had done so much for [MI5]'.[102] Air Commodore Sir J. A. Chamier was the highest ranking BUF member in the RAF and a January Club member. His escape is unexplained. Ten serving officers in the army and the RAF were arrested, although most BUF servicemen were ignored.[103] In the case of Sir Arthur Bryant, who had given plentiful evidence of pro-Nazi sympathies, the authorities sought advice on whether to intern him from his fellow historian, Hugh Trevor-Roper, who assured them it was unnecessary as Bryant would 'change with the times'.[104] It would have been awkward to have arrested a man who had worked so closely with R. A. Butler. Finally, Major-General Fuller's record in the BUF, as one of its candidates, as a contributor to fascist journals, and as a member of the Domvile–Ramsay circle during the war made him an obvious candidate for detainment under Regulation 18B. As late as 23 May Fuller attended one of the private pro-peace meetings; but on hearing of Ramsay's arrest he promptly went home and subsequently told the *Evening Standard* that he had gone to hear a lecture about egg-farming.[105]

Initially most of the male prisoners were accommodated in Brixton and the women in Holloway, though a few went to Wandsworth, Walton and Stafford; in 1941 many rank-and-file fascists were sent to camps on the Isle of Man, but the leaders were kept in London. 'Every waking hour is a punishment,' complained Luttman-Johnson. 'Everything jars. You are treated like an insane child by underbred and brainless warders.' Arnold Leese, furious at his arrest, refused to do any work in Wandsworth where he went on a hunger strike and was forcibly fed.[106] However, Mosley took his incarceration more philosophically. Conditions were soon relaxed because the authorities regarded the prisoners as being detained rather than imprisoned under Regulation 18B. Inmates were allowed to associate with one another at meals and in recreation periods, they wore their own clothes, wrote two letters a week, had at least one weekly visit, received food parcels and bought in meals if they could afford it. After his release in 1943 Luttman-Johnson sent pheasants for Domvile and grouse for Ramsay. Nellie Driver, restricted to prison food, claimed she was fed horse meat and fish pie that was rejected even by the cats.[107] The authorities also permitted Mosley to have a wireless set for evening recreation, though the Governor instructed him not to tune into foreign stations. When he discovered that other detainees were attending Mosley's cell to learn Italian and German this was stopped.[108] Once a month Mosley visited Diana and eventually he was allowed to join her in a disused wing at Holloway. The press quickly dubbed this 'Lady Mosley's Suite' and stoked up popular feeling by circulating imaginary accounts about the luxurious lifestyle enjoyed by the detainees; at a time of strict rationing stories of the food arriving from expensive restaurants for the Mosleys inevitably aroused anger. They successfully sued the *Daily Mirror* and the *Sunday Pictorial* over these reports.

Although the detainees were not brought to trial, they were given the opportunity to appear before an Advisory Committee set up by the Home Office to review their cases. Officially it was necessary under Regulation 18B for the Home Secretary to demonstrate that they satisfied several criteria: membership of an organisation which was subject to foreign influence or control, that their leaders had associated with an enemy power or had sympathised with its system of government, that there was a danger that the organisation could be used for purposes prejudicial to the defence of the realm or to the prosecution of the war.[109] In effect this was a political exercise designed to keep the detainees out of circulation for the good of public morale. Before the hearings Norman Birkett QC, who chaired the Advisory Committee, realised how thin MI5's case against Mosley was. He therefore concentrated on gathering background material on the BUF and evidence to show that its activities had been prejudicial to war aims and the war effort. Meanwhile Mosley collected material designed to show that he had advocated rearmament, urged his members to do their duty, and maintained the BUF as a purely British movement.[110]

In his five-day appearance before Birkett in July Mosley vigorously rehearsed his patriotic record, but was less at ease when denying foreign influence in the movement. He claimed that he had nothing to do with finance: 'my general directions were that no money should be accepted except from British subjects and that no conditions should be attached.' It was not until July that Special Branch produced evidence of the Italian funds channelled through Allen, Dundas and Tabor.[111] At the end Mosley enquired: 'is it suggested that we are traitors who would take up arms and fight with the Germans if they landed?' Birkett replied: 'speaking for myself, you can entirely dismiss that suggestion.' Although the hearings had established nothing very incriminating, the Advisory Committee required only a general impression of Mosley's politics to justify recommending his continued detention.[112]

Diana appealed against her detention in July though the case did not come before the Committee until October. She was at best evasive and at worst untruthful. She claimed she had never been an active member of the BUF. Questioned closely about her foreign contacts Diana even denied meeting fascists in Italy. When asked: 'Is Hitler still a friend of yours?' she replied, 'I have not seen him for some time', though she was known to have obtained a concession from him to set up a wireless station quite recently.[113] The contempt Diana displayed towards the Advisory Committee made it all the easier for them to conclude that she would be a great danger if released: she had acted as a channel of communication between Mosley and the Nazis, after his arrest she had helped to keep the BUF going, and she had expressed fascist and pro-German sentiments.[114]

Little is known about the hearings of Captain Ramsay, who also appeared early in July, as the records remain closed. To judge from his own account, which he released to the Speaker and the House of Commons, Ramsay remained trapped in his fantasy world. Ignoring the charges against him, he simply rehearsed his political creed. He insisted that after warning Chamberlain about the plots to subvert his peace policy in July 1939, he had the prime minister's authority to collect evidence; he regarded Chamberlain's fall from power as proof of the Jewish conspiracy to ensure an all-out war against Germany.[115]

The experience of being incarcerated in prison with no prospect of a trial forced the fascist detainees to recognise that Britain had, for a time, turned itself into the kind of totalitarian state they had so admired. Yet they lost no time in appealing to the despised parliamentarians to secure their release or at least the amelioration of their conditions. However, most members of parliament ignored them. Nellie Driver, who spent two years in Holloway and the Isle of Man, was visited by her MP, Sidney Silverman; and during Lady Pearson's brief detention her sister approached Mavis Tate (who was herself listed as a member of the Right Club), Dr Edith Summerskill and Lady Davidson, though only the last visited her.[116] Luttman-Johnson appealed to his former MP, the Duchess of Atholl, to intercede on his behalf, while Mosley contacted Earl Winterton who was not his MP but had shown sympathy for the fascists.[117]

In the Commons Robert Bower, Sir Thomas Moore, Irving Albery, Richard Stokes, Rear Admiral Tufton Beamish, Earl Winterton, Captain William Shaw, Captain Piers Loftus and Commander Sir Archibald Southby criticised Regulation 18B and pressed the Home Secretary to ameliorate the detainees' conditions. Bower accused him of an abuse of his powers of arrest and detention; he also urged the case of Ben Greene who, he claimed, had been imprisoned on the basis of false evidence, and he challenged the detention of Squadron Leader Rutland in January 1942.[118] After several talks with Domvile in 1942, Tufton Beamish told Herbert Morrison he had been treated unjustly and should be given the opportunity to prove his innocence, but the Home Secretary simply replied that he had already appeared before the Advisory Committee.[119]

MPs correctly sensed that after nineteen months there was some feeling that the detainees had been punished enough and that the government was secure enough to adopt a more lenient attitude. In fact the number of BUF members still in prison had been reduced to 200 by December 1941, and to 130 by April 1942. The Mosleys expected to be released once the hysteria about a German invasion had subsided and the enquiries had failed to turn up anything incriminating. However, they overlooked the fact that detention had developed a political momentum which could not easily be reversed. Although Churchill felt embarrassed at their incarceration, he was unwilling to upset his Labour colleagues or antagonise their followers. Nonetheless, Churchill was the Mosleys' best weapon. Tom Mitford, Diana's brother, had dinner with him at Downing Street in December 1941 to press for their release; Lady Redesdale worked on Clementine Churchill; and Walter Monckton and Lady Ravensdale, Mosley's sister-in-law, also used their influence. This seems to have had some effect, for Churchill intervened with the Home Secretary to allow interned couples to be reunited in Holloway.[120] After a visit from Lady Redesdale in October 1943 Diana observed: 'We shall have to get Brenden [*sic*] moving', an apparent reference to Churchill's acolyte, Brendan Bracken.[121] At this stage the deterioration in Mosley's health had opened up a new prospect of release.

Churchill's relaxed attitude towards the detainees probably reflected his belief that the influence of the peace party had dwindled. The most dramatic bid for a negotiated settlement with Germany was made in 1941. On the night of 10 May the Luftwaffe took advantage of a full moon to bomb the Houses of Parliament. But on the same night Hitler's deputy, Rudolf Hess, flew in a Messerschmitt 110 from Augsburg across the North Sea and over the Cheviot Hills into Scotland. Just after 11.00 p.m. he bailed out over Bonnytown Moor, coming down near the village of Eaglesham south of Glasgow. However, Hess had miscalculated and was eight miles from his target – Dungavel House, the seat of the Duke of Hamilton. Apprehended by a local farmworker, Donald Maclean, and the Home Guard, he asked to be taken to the Duke. After meeting Hess the following day, Hamilton flew south to brief Churchill, who was at Ditchley Park in Oxfordshire having dinner before settling down to watch a Marx Brothers film. In view of the fact that the implication of the peace bid was the removal of Churchill from office, the prime minister's apparent reluctance to treat the episode seriously looks odd. 'Hess or no Hess,' he reportedly told Hamilton, 'I am going to see the Marx Brothers.'[122]

On 13 May Sir Ivone Kirkpatrick, a German expert from the Foreign Office who knew Hess, interviewed him with Hamilton present. According to the Duke Hess had already tried three times to fly to England since December 1940 with a view to persuading him to 'get together leading members of my party to talk things over with a view to making peace proposals'.[123] The offer provided that Germany be given a free hand in Europe and England in the Empire, subject to the return of German colonies; Russia was to satisfy Germany's demands, Britain was to evacuate Iraq, British and German nationals whose property had been expropriated were to be indemnified, and the negotiations were to be conducted with any British government other than one led by Churchill 'who had planned war since 1938, and [whose] colleagues who had lent themselves to his war policy were not persons with whom the Führer could negotiate'.[124]

Kirkpatrick's view of Hess as 'stupid and eccentric' and a man who was no longer close to Hitler has been accepted by subsequent writers.[125] However, at the time the Duke, who was understandably embarrassed at being the target of such a high-level peace mission, took the bid seriously and he insisted: 'I had no recollection of ever having seen [Hess] before.' He protested to Churchill: 'If in a public place . . . a harlot flings her arms around your neck and whispers something in your ear, it is only natural that some of your friends and acquaintances may wonder whether you have ever met this individual before and what she whispered in your ear.' At this the prime minister 'was somewhat amused'.[126] However, Hamilton was being rather disingenuous as, despite denials, he had apparently met Hess at the

Berlin Olympic Games.[127] As a former member of the Anglo-German Fellowship (although he denied this too) the Duke had been energetic in promoting closer relations with the Nazis; he was a friend of Albrecht and Karl Haushofer who had visited Dungavel and collaborated with Hess over the mission; he maintained an airstrip at Dungavel; he had publicly advocated peace during the war; and, apart from his political connections, he was the premier Scottish peer and Buccleuch's successor as Lord Steward of the Royal Household. While none of this meant the Duke was involved in planning the Hess flight, it amply explains why, from a German perspective, he seemed a credible British figurehead for a negotiated peace.

Despite the many suspicious aspects, there are strong grounds for regarding the mission as a wholly unrealistic venture. Hess himself admitted that he had come without Hitler's knowledge. A negotiated peace would only have become feasible following a coup against Hitler as well as the overthrow of Churchill. In fact, the affair generated far more controversy in Germany than in Britain. A furious Hitler declared Hess mentally deranged; the episode made him appear foolish and caused defections within the Nazi Party.[128] It also threatened to offend Mussolini by suggesting Germany's readiness to bypass him by making a separate peace. Having already abandoned the idea of invading Britain, Hitler was planning to invade Russia in June, calculating that his success there would eventually force the British to sue for peace.

However, the crucial question in assessing the Hess mission is whether an effective peace party now existed in Britain capable of taking up the initiative. By 1941 this appeared improbable. With many leading peace advocates in prison and others subject to restrictions and under surveillance it is difficult to see how a peace party could have functioned. Suspects were still being arrested as late as 1942. Peacemongers like Arthur Bryant and Drummond Wolff who had started new pressure groups had abandoned them by this time. Nor were the political links of the peace party intact. Chamberlain had died, Hoare was exiled to Madrid, and Churchill had despatched Halifax to Washington, leaving Butler alone in the government. The public's hostility towards any public figures who were compromised by sympathy towards Germany had become obvious in the expanding sales of the anti-appeasement newspaper, the *Daily Mirror*, and in the success of *Guilty Men* (1940), a much-reprinted attack on the leading appeasers. In June 1941 Gallup polls showed that no fewer than 87 per cent of the population backed the Coalition, while Anthony Eden and Sir Stafford Cripps were the most favoured alternatives to Churchill.

After Chamberlain's death Churchill had strengthened his position by becoming Conservative leader, and his colleagues recognised that his popularity offered the best chance of defending the party over their pre-war record on appeasement and rearmament. Consequently, by 1941 the replacement of Churchill with a government ready to negotiate peace was wholly unrealistic. It would have required his dismissal by the King in favour of a pro-peace premier, an action inconceivable for the cautious George VI. It is true that Churchill's failure to exploit the propaganda value of the Hess mission seems rather odd. He made a brief reference to it in parliament on 27 January 1942, possibly as a warning to his political opponents. But apart from this it was not until September 1943 that Eden made a full statement on the Hess affair in parliament. The likeliest explanation for this is that the government deliberately used it to fortify Soviet resistance to Hitler. The Russians were very reluctant to believe that Hitler planned to attack them, but were fearful of Germany and Britain quietly settling their differences to their disadvantage; by keeping quiet about Hess the British encouraged the Russians to recognise that Hitler was securing his rear prior to launching an attack in the east.

If Churchill's hold on the premiership looked more secure by 1941 this was essentially a reflection of the limited improvement in the military situation since 1940. Having seen the country through the Battle of Britain in September 1940 his Coalition had earned itself a breathing space, if not an indefinite lease of life. During 1941 the British armies, having been chased out of Europe, took the field again in North Africa; though this was a marginal theatre in the war, at least it demonstrated that the German and Italian forces could be defeated. On 22 June Hitler's long hoped-for offensive against the Russians began, though at first the military experts were too influenced by their view of Soviet politics to appreciate its significance; it says little for the perspicacity of the Joint Intelligence Committee that it expected Moscow to fall to the Germans within three to six weeks at most. On top of the unexpected resistance of the Russians came the entry of the United States into the war following the Japanese attack on Pearl Harbor in December. Provided the three allies resisted the temptation to make a separate peace, their combined resources made their eventual victory fairly certain from 1942 onwards. Consequently, although the civilian population grew restive over the privations imposed by wartime, their support for Churchill as prime minister remained consistently high, reaching a low point of 78 per cent after the fall of Tobruk in June 1942.

Despite this, Churchill's room for manoeuvre with regard to the 18B detainees was limited. By this time hundreds of obscure fascists had already been released without provoking much attention, but the prominent figures posed a problem. The general public had become angered by the regular broadcasts from Germany by William Joyce, now known as Lord Haw Haw, who had announced his real name in April 1941. Some 80 per cent of households had a radio and by January 1940 six million people listened regularly, and eighteen million occasionally, to Joyce's 'Views on the News'. Many people simply equated Joyce and Mosley as traitors, however unfairly. Consequently, the authorities had to tread carefully. The first leading fascist to be released was Luttman-Johnson in the spring of 1943, followed by Domvile in July and Beckett in October: 'I hated leaving those poor chaps behind me,' wrote Domvile, 'I felt so mean.'[129] Mosley himself remained in Holloway until 20 November, and Leese until December, while Ramsay was detained until September 1944 whereupon he resumed his seat in the Commons.

By 1943 Mosley and the peace cause had become so discredited that Churchill saw no danger in releasing him. In November he told Herbert Morrison: 'I am convinced 18B should be completely abolished as the national emergency no longer justifies abrogation of individual rights of habeas corpus and trial by jury on definite charges'; but the Regulation was not finally revoked until May 1945. The recurrence of phlebitis in Mosley's leg gave Churchill the opportunity to release him on health grounds; he had lost three stone in weight and Churchill believed he might die in the coming winter.[130] However, Mass Observation reported that a majority of people opposed his release. Hostile demonstrations took place and protesters sent the Home Secretary bottles labelled 'Rat Poison' and 'Cure for Phlebitis'. An angry deputation of Labour MPs met Herbert Morrison, but as usual, the party leaders dealt firmly with the rebels.[131] Even so, 62 voted against the government in a division on 1 December.

Mosley's release was conditional on his refraining from all forms of political activity up to May 1945, avoidance of contact with his followers, restriction to a seven-mile radius of his home, and monthly reports to the police. He spent the next three years farming his 11,000-acre estate at Crowood in Wiltshire. Still only forty-seven when released, Mosley remained anxious to return to politics, and many of his followers, now martyrs for fascism after their detention, felt the same. By 1944 they had begun to meet as 'The Friends of Sir Oswald Mosley', and on 15 December 1945 some 1,150 of them gathered for a social and dance. However, the times were not propitious for the revival of the movement. William Joyce was executed at Wandsworth Prison on 3 January 1946, the last man to be hanged for high treason in Britain. In a country that had recently elected a Labour government that was concentrating on full employment, the National Health Service and the nationalisation of failing industries, fascism suddenly seemed very marginal indeed.

After considering whether to ban fascist organisations the Attlee government decided it would be impractical and was probably unnecessary anyway. Meanwhile, Mosley spoke at private meetings and circulated a modest monthly newsletter to supporters. But in 1946 he seized the opportunity presented by Churchill's famous 'Iron Curtain' speech at Fulton, Missouri, to justify the stance he had taken on the war, arguing that the dramatic extension of Soviet power validated the fascists' warnings about the damage to British interests once Germany had been removed as a major factor in European affairs. Finally, in October 1947 he relaunched his movement by publishing *The Alternative* and returning to the Farringdon Street Memorial Hall for a rally in November. In February 1948 he became the leader of what was now known as the Union Movement, campaigning for a united Europe and for imperial control of Africa.

Yet although Mosley found himself once again drawn back to the East End where he became embroiled in fights with Jews and Communists, his movement was not regarded as genuinely racist. Post-war anti-Semites looked to other organisations including the White Defence League and later the British National Party. In the 1950s A. K. Chesterton's League of Empire Loyalists recruited much of Mosley's former support. The onset of immigration from the West Indies during the later 1950s and 1960s offered the Union Movement fresh opportunities for attacking the political parties by advocating repatriation. However, when Mosley took his policy to the electorate at North Kensington in the 1959 election he received a humiliating 8 per cent of the vote and lost his deposit. The programme of the Union Movement never achieved the range, force and relevance of the British Union of Fascists in its heyday. In an era of full employment Mosley's economic strategy had been eclipsed, and he found himself caught halfway between the conventional parties and the racist fringe, boycotted by the media and irretrievably confined to the margins of British political life.

*

Whatever the reason for the failure of fascism to grow into a major movement in inter-war Britain, the explanation does not lie primarily in British political culture. The underlying obstacle was the limited nature of the economic depression and the improving material conditions enjoyed by most people even during the 1930s. This forced fascism to focus on limited sections of society who felt they had not benefited from the National Government's attempts to engineer a recovery. But the failure can also be explained partly in terms of timing and contingencies. In 1926 a prolonged general strike could well have destroyed Baldwin's government and created the opportunity fascists were looking for. The crisis of 1931 that led to the creation of the National Government came at a point when no significant fascist alternative existed. When Mosley produced what was by far the most coherent and compelling challenge in the autumn of 1932, he was just too late to catch the parliamentary system at its most vulnerable. Thereafter, Mosley was always looking for an economic crisis that did not quite materialise before war restored the country to full employment. In 1936 the abdication crisis showed just how vulnerable Britain's constitutional arrangements were; but, again, contingency, in the shape of the King's sudden withdrawal, snatched his opportunity away.

Despite attempts by Mosley to resuscitate his career and the emergence of several extreme right-wing movements in post-war Britain, fascism has never succeeded in posing the kind of challenge it did between the wars. Are we justified, then, in regarding the Second World War as the chief explanation for the absence of a significant fascist revival? The war had two very obvious effects. First, from 1935 to 1940 British fascists committed a crucial tactical error in allowing themselves to become apologists for Nazi Germany, thereby undermining their patriotic credentials. The argument that a well-armed Britain had nothing to fear from Germany had been too subtle to carry complete conviction; and it was overtaken by the inexorable expansion of Hitler's Germany and its continuing demand for the return of her colonies. Fascists were never very credible as advocates of peace, and the frustrations of the Phoney War and scares about fifth-columnists inevitably cast Mosley and his followers as traitors in the eyes of many people. Second, the atrocities committed in Germany towards Jews before 1939, combined with subsequent revelations about the Holocaust which resonated through the post-1945 era, went a long way to discrediting the racist ideas of fascism. The fascists themselves would no doubt have argued that this was further proof of the effectiveness of the Jewish propaganda machine, but those who have attempted to play down or disregard Nazi responsibility for the Holocaust have made little impact.

However, the Second World War weakened the fascist case in other and less obvious ways. Throughout the inter-war period fascists had sedulously propagated the notion that the emasculated politicians and their degenerate parliamentary system would prove hopelessly inadequate in the face of a real national crisis. Yet somehow Britain managed, without abandoning her traditional system, to develop a strong and, in some respects, authoritarian wartime strategy tempered with a stiff dose of liberalism. For all its faults, the House of Commons managed to make the government answerable and to subject it to occasional votes of confidence. Although the Labour members were officially on the government side, once Churchill's coalition had been established in May 1940, a hybrid Opposition emerged, led by Emmanuel Shinwell (Labour) and Lord Winterton (Conservative), who were charmingly known as 'arsenic and old lace'. At by-elections, the gap left by the main parties as a result of the truce was filled by a multitude of Independents and by the Common Wealth which humiliated the government by capturing several Conservative seats. Mass Observation and the Gallup opinion polls regularly recorded the public's fluctuating morale, its views on major issues and political personalities, and hostile reactions to official propaganda. While many newspapers had been discredited by their mindless support for appeasement, the *Daily Mirror* and the *News Chronicle* retained their credibility as consistent critics of official policy.

Moreover, though the government often appeared omnipotent it knew it could not afford to take the civilian population for granted. After an initial 'patriotic' dip in strike activity in 1940, no doubt due to the departure of many working men for the forces, the number of stoppages and working days lost rose year by year to 1945, and there was a marked increase in trade union membership. It was an absolute necessity for the Coalition to win the cooperation, or at least acquiescence, of the civilian population by a series of concessions on the economic front. The fashionable school that regards the wartime social reforms and the Beveridge Report as unnecessary or as a costly error simply misses the point. By 1940 Britain's military position was so dire that she could not hope to win the war unless she managed to mobilise her full resources in terms of money, manpower and industrial and agricultural output. Ever since the Napoleonic wars Britain's capacity to tax herself reasonably efficiently had been one of the keys to military victory, although she was perversely unwilling to take pride in her achievement. She repeated this success in the Second World War. It is often forgotten that while the wealthy paid high rates of tax, income tax was also levied on the modest incomes of most manual workers; 1943 saw the introduction of 'Pay As You Earn', a brilliant innovation designed to produce an immediate yield for a cash-strapped government.

The mobilisation of Britain's scarce manpower resources was marked by a judicious mixture of concessions and controls. Wages were raised, food was rationed and subsidised, from 1941 workers were required to register, skilled men accepted dilution of labour by unskilled, and those in vital occupations were exempted from the call-up. Most strikingly, the government decided, admittedly reluctantly, to impose industrial conscription on women who were called up for work by age groups from 1941 onwards in order to remedy the huge manpower shortage faced by industry. Within a few months almost half the entire labour force was employed by the government. Neither politicians, nor trade unionists nor women themselves were especially enthusiastic about this, but they were sufficiently persuaded to cooperate in a policy that was a crucial part of Britain's success in the war.

Neither Nazi Germany, nor Fascist Italy nor Soviet Russia were able to mobilise their human resources and win the cooperation of the population as effectively as Britain did; their authoritarian politics and conventional thinking about gender roles became real obstacles to a mass war. By contrast, wartime Britain demonstrated the flexibility and interplay between popular discontent and the needs of the government that enable a complex modern state to wage war effectively; liberalism worked after all, and it was probably the only thing that did. By rising to the challenge parliamentary democracy decisively discredited the fashionable thesis that disparaged it as an outworn tradition.

Other factors also help to explain the demise of post-1945 fascism. In some respects the aftermath of the Second World War did lead to a recrudescence of the kind of developments that had animated fascists in the 1920s, notably the shocking election result in 1945, the growing influence of Socialism and the trade unions at home, the extension of Soviet influence in Europe, and the retreat of British imperial control beginning with Indian independence in 1947. Many apologists for the Nazi regime had warned that once German power was removed from central Europe, nothing would prevent the Soviet Union enjoying hegemony over much of the Continent.

However, the spirited anti-Soviet policy and the huge military expenditure adopted by the incoming Labour government and its Foreign Secretary, Ernest Bevin, deprived right-wing critics of their momentum. Perhaps more surprisingly in view of the controversies of the 1930s, not even Churchill attempted to take up the cause of empire. The loss of India failed to provoke much public response, perhaps because by the 1940s the moral case for self-government had been accepted and because after the war the scale of the effort required to suppress nationalism in India seemed wholly unacceptable. Towards the end of the century a revisionist school emerged highly critical of Churchill for his determination to fight Nazi Germany to the finish on the grounds that his stubbornness weakened Britain and thus led directly to the loss of empire. This extraordinary view assumed that Britain both could and should have maintained her rule over Asia and Africa indefinitely. But it overlooked the fact that the argument had been fought and decisively lost by 1935; after that decolonisation was really only a matter of timing.

Britain's relatively relaxed acceptance of the loss of empire also suggests that many of the influential people who had backed fascism before 1939 had either withdrawn from public activity or lost their political influence in postwar Britain. Dukes were at a discount even in the Conservative Party, and fascists did not enjoy the opportunities they had previously done. One does not have to accept without qualification the idea of a post-war age of consensus between Labour and the Conservatives to recognise that the 1945 election had shocked Conservatives and led them to move towards the centre.

Churchill himself now adopted a conciliatory policy, despite some chilling rhetoric designed to stir the party faithful. He did not promote extreme right-wingers, and when the party came to appoint his successors to the leadership in 1955 and 1957 they chose from among the liberal Tories. The formation of the League of Empire Loyalists, a lonely voice raised to save the empire, underlines how marginal the right had now become in Conservative politics. Aspiring ministers who felt endangered by their earlier involvement with fascism did their best to erase it from the record; and their bland obituaries in *The Times* suggest that they enjoyed a large measure of success. After 1945 Britain had a new national story which made the earlier fascist thesis about conspiracy, decline, decadence and rejuvenation appear irrelevant and defeatist.

NOTES

Introduction

1. Martin Francis, *Times Literary Supplement*, 17 August 2001.

1. *The Origins of British Fascism*

1. K. D. Ewing and C. A. Gearty, *The Struggle for Civil Liberties* (2000), 6–8.
2. Ibid., 40–1.
3. See Martin Pugh, *The March of the Women: A Revisionist Analysis of the Campaign for Women's Suffrage, 1866–1914* (2000), 206–10.
4. S. Gopal, *British Policy in India 1858–1905* (1965), 121 [Lord Mayo], 126 [Lord Lytton], 122 [Fitzjames Stephen].
5. E. D. Hart, 'The Decline of Feudalism', *Fascist Quarterly*, April 1935; A. L. Glasfurd, 'Fascism and the English Tradition', *Fascist Quarterly*, July 1935; A. K. Chesterton, 'Fascist Principles in the Middle Ages – Why England Flourished Under the Guilds', *Action*, 13 August 1936; 'English Array', memorandum, n.d., Lymington Papers F178.
6. Speech at Birmingham, 12 May 1904.
7. Pugh, *March of the Women*, 48–52.
8. See the discussion in Paul Hayes, 'The Contribution of British Intellectuals to Fascism', in K. Lunn and R. C. Thurlow (eds.), *British Fascism* (1980); Dan Stone, *Breeding Superman: Nietzsche, Race and Eugenics in Edwardian and Inter-war Britain* (2002).
9. Houston Stewart Chamberlain, *The Foundations of the Nineteenth Century* (1899), 261.
10. Stone, *Breeding Superman*, 125–6.
11. Ian Kershaw, *Hitler 1889–1936* (1999), 135, 151.
12. Quoted in Stone, *Breeding Superman*, 45.

13. Quoted in Michael Ffinch, *G. K. Chesterton* (1986), 335.
14. Leo Maxse in *National Review*, 61, July 1913, 808.
15. Ffinch, *Chesterton*, 155; Stone, *Breeding Superman*, 125–6.
16. Bentley Gilbert, *The Evolution of National Insurance* (1966), 77.
17. Quoted in G. R. Searle, 'Critics of Edwardian Society: the Case of the Radical Right', in Alan O'Day (ed.), *The Edwardian Age* (1979), 89.
18. John Charmley, *Lord Lloyd and the Decline of the British Empire* (1987), 31, 37.
19. G. R. Searle, *Corruption in British Politics 1895–1930* (1987), 222–31.
20. Stone, *Breeding Superman*, 44–5.
21. Pugh, *March of the Women*, 56–7.
22. Quoted in Robert Blake, *The Unknown Prime Minister* (1955), 130.

2. *Decadence, Democracy and Revolution*

1. Winston Churchill, *The World Crisis 1911–1918*, vol. I (1931 edn), 130.
2. *Daily Mail*, 25 August 1914.
3. *Daily Mail*, 21 May 1915.
4. Colin Clifford, *The Asquiths* (2002), 343.
5. Christopher St John, *Ethel Smythe* (1959), 221.
6. Martin Pugh, *Electoral Reform in War and Peace 1906–1918* (1978), 57–66.
7. K. D. Ewing and C. A. Gearty, *The Struggle for Civil Liberties* (2000), 51–62.
8. Queen's Hall speech, 19 September 1914.
9. Pugh, *Electoral Reform*, 113–14, 125–6.
10. *The Workers' Dreadnought*, 15 September 1923.
11. *The Times*, 8 May 1920.
12. *The Times*, 10 May 1920.
13. *National Review*, 73, August 1919, 819.
14. Gisela Lebzelter, *Political Anti-Semitism in England 1918–1939* (1978), 21–6.
15. Ibid., 50–6.
16. Arnold Leese, *Out of Step: Events in the Two Lives of an Anti-Jewish Camel Doctor* (1951), 48–50; Francis Beckett, *The Rebel Who Lost His Cause* (1999), 53–4.
17. *The Patriot*, 23 March 1922; *National Review*, 79, May 1922; *National Review*, 81, May 1923; PRO CAB 24/6425.
18. Nesta Webster, *World Revolution: The Plots Against Civilisation* (1921), 278–9; *The Patriot*, 18 May 1922; *English Review*, 39, December 1924, 697–705.

19. Quoted in Philip Williamson, *Stanley Baldwin* (1999), 148.
20. *Daily Mail*, 2 May 1927.
21. David Baker, *Ideology of Obsession: A. K. Chesterton and British Fascism* (1996), 71.
22. E. P. Hewitt, 'The Failure of Democracy', *English Review*, 37, December 1923, 739; *English Review*, editorial, 39, July 1924; Duke of Northumberland, *National Review*, 91, June 1928.
23. *Saturday Review*, 27 April 1918, 357; *English Review*, 29, December 1919, 463–4.
24. *Daily Mail*, editorial, 7 April 1927.
25. *Daily Mail*, 7 April 1927; *English Review*, 46, June 1928, 394–5.
26. A. Ludovici, 'The Folly of Feminine Franchise', *English Review*, 37, October 1923.
27. *Saturday Review*, 27 April 1918.
28. Douglas Jerrold, 'The Feminist Movement', *English Review*, 25, March 1918, 317; John Charmley, *Lord Lloyd and the Decline of the British Empire* (1987), 67; Duchess of Atholl, House of Commons Debates, vol. 170, 29 February 1924, c. 872.
29. Austin Harrison, 'Woman Understood', *English Review*, 37, September 1923, 339–40.
30. Ludovici, 'Feminine Franchise', 577–8.
31. *Daily Express*, 12 November 1924.
32. Barbara Cartland, *The Isthmus Years* (1942), 106.
33. House of Commons Debates, vol. 145, 4 August 1921, c. 1800, 1803–4.
34. Cartland, *Isthmus Years*, 15–16.
35. *Good Housekeeping*, November 1934.
36. *National Review*, 90, December 1927, 514–15.
37. *English Review*, 46, June 1928, 394–5.
38. *Daily Mail*, 7, 11, 20, 23, 28 April 1927.

3. *The Advent of Mussolini*

1. Dennis Mack Smith, *Mussolini* (1980), 25–8.
2. Mack Smith, *Mussolini*, 60–1.
3. 'An Interview with Mussolini', *English Review*, XLVIII, April 1929; Haig quoted in *Fascist Bulletin*, 27 March 1926; Colin Clifford, *The Asquiths* (2002), 470; Dr C. Pellizzi, 'Aims and Origins of the Fascists', *English Review*, 35, December 1922.
4. Austin Harrison, 'Parliament Regained', *English Review*, 35, December 1922, 567–8.
5. *Daily Mail*, 2 May 1927; editorial and E. Corradini, 'How Italy Has

Put Down Bolshevism', *English Review*, 35, December 1922.

6. Duke of Northumberland, 'Whitewash', *National Review*, 79, February 1923.

7. *English Review*, 37, 1923, 492.

8. Nigel Copsey, *Anti-Fascism in Britain* (2000), 6.

9. *National Review*, 77, June 1921, 448.

10. *Daily Mail*, 17 September 1923.

11. *National Review*, 83, August 1924, 819.

12. E. Corradini, 'The Political Revolution in Italy', *National Review*, 81, March 1923.

13. Lord Sydenham, 'The Fascist State', *English Review*, 48, February 1929.

14. John Brown, 'Freedom in Italy', *English Review*, 105, December 1935.

15. Editorial, *National Review*, 83, May 1924; *The Times*, 21 January 1927.

16. Sir Frank Fox, 'Mussolini's Work in Italy', *National Review*, 90, November 1927, 472.

17. Noel Skelton, 'The Safeguarding of British Democracy', *English Review*, 43, July 1926, 26.

18. Although nineteenth-century Italian politicians were noted for their keen Anglophilia, the only obvious British feature of their 1848 constitution was the idea of 'the King in Parliament'. As ministers were not responsible to the elected parliament, this scarcely seems consistent with British thinking. In fact, Cavour had been more influenced by the French and Belgian systems and was more favourably impressed by the conduct of the French parliament than that at Westminster. I am grateful to Dr Eugenio Biagini for advice on this point which is fully discussed in his revised edition of Derek Beales, *The Risorgimento and the Unification of Italy* (2002).

19. Skelton, 'Safeguarding of British Democracy', 25.

20. Editorial, *National Review*, 81, July 1923, 644.

21. *Daily Mail*, 2 May 1927.

22. Editorial, *National Review*, 89, June 1927, 486–7; editorial and Henry Page Croft, 'The Plight of Agriculture', *National Review*, 89, August 1927; *English Review*, 47, April 1929, 421–3.

23. Quoted in Mack Smith, *Mussolini*, 94.

24. *Daily Mail*, 17 September 1923.

25. *National Review*, 87, April 1926, 166–7.

26. Christabel Pankhurst, *The World's Unrest: Visions of the Dawn* (1926), 21.

27. Ibid., 21–6.

28. *Daily Mail*, 2 May 1928.

29. L. Villari, 'The Campaign Against Italy', *National Review*, 89, April 1927.
30. *The Times*, 21 January 1927.
31. Ibid.
32. Ibid.
33. *Daily Mail*, 17 September 1923.
34. Ibid.
35. *Daily Mail*, 2 May 1928.
36. Pellizzi, 'Aims and Origins of the Fascists'.
37. H. A. McClure Smith, 'The Spirit and Form of Fascism', *English Review*, 43, 1928, 53–7.
38. Lord Sydenham, 'The Fascist State', *English Review*, 48, February 1929, 163–5.
39. Sir Charles Petrie, *Monarchy* (1933), 18.
40. Ibid., 158–9.

4. *Boy Scout Fascism*

1. Robert Blakeney, 'Fascism', *Nineteenth Century*, 97, January 1925, 132.
2. Peter Martland, *Lord Haw Haw: The English Voice of Nazi Germany* (2003), 8–10; Francis Selwyn, *Hitler's Englishman* (1987), 17–29.
3. See Martin Petter, '"Temporary Gentlemen" in the Aftermath of the Great War: Rank, Status and the Ex-officer Problem, *Historical Journal*, 37, 1994, 127–52.
4. Quoted in Julie Wheelwright, 'Colonel Barker: A Case Study in the Contradictions of Fascism', in Tony Kushner and Kenneth Lunn (eds.), *The Politics of Marginality* (1990), 42.
5. Ibid., 43.
6. See Nigel Copley, *Anti-Fascism in Britain* (2000), 6–11.
7. See *Sunday Dispatch*, 10 March 1929; *Empire News and Sunday Chronicle*, 19 February 1956.
8. *Empire News and Sunday Chronicle*, 19 February 1956.
9. *Sunday Dispatch*, 10 March 1929.
10. *Empire News and Sunday Chronicle*, 25 March 1956.
11. *Sunday Dispatch*, 17 March 1929.
12. Ibid.
13. *Sunday Dispatch*, 10 March 1929.
14. Wheelwright, 'Barker', 47.
15. Diana Mosley, *A Life of Contrasts* (2002), 65.
16. Arnold Leese, *Out of Step: Events in the Two Lives of an Anti-Jewish Camel Doctor* (1951), 49.

17. Ian Kershaw, *Hitler 1889–1936* (1999), 150, 245, 317.
18. *Fascist Bulletin*, 12 June 1926.
19. *British Lion*, August 1927.
20. *Fascist Bulletin*, 20 June 1925.
21. Robert Smith to the Lord Chancellor, 17 June 1926, PRO HO 144/19069.
22. See PRO HO 144/19069.
23. *Nineteenth Century*, 97, January 1925, 138.
24. Ibid., 139.
25. *Brighton and Hove Herald*, 20 March 1926.
26. Robert Benewick, *The Fascist Movement in Britain* (1972), 38.
27. Sir Charles Burn (1859–1930) was MP for Torquay 1910–23; in 1925 he adopted his wife's family name, becoming Sir Charles Forbes-Leith of Fyvie; Philip Murphy, *Alan Lennox-Boyd: A Biography* (1999), 14–15.
28. National Archives of Scotland, Sir John Gilmour Papers GD 383, memorandum, 12 November 1924.
29. Ibid.
30. PRO HO 144/22282, Note for Secretary of State, 31 October 1939.
31. PRO HO 144/22282, LSB to Bovenden, 30 August 1930.
32. PRO HO 144/20158/310.
33. House of Commons Debates, vol. 188, 16 November 1925, c.25–6; 30 November 1925, c.1823–4; 3 December 1925, c.2487–8.
34. Sir Patrick Hannon (1874–1963) was member for Birmingham Moseley 1918–45; *The Times*, 11 January 1963; Simon Haxey, *Tory MP* (1939), refers to his business connections, 43–6, 55, 62, 86, 219.
35. See J. A. Turner, 'The British Commonwealth Union and the General Election of 1918', *English Historical Review*, CCCLXVIII, 1978; on the Women's Party see Martin Pugh, *The Pankhursts* (2001), 351–4.
36. See Appointments Diary, 29 February 1924, 5 February 1925, 7, 13 and 20 May 1925, House of Lords Record Office, Hannon Papers 123; *Fascist Bulletin*, 13 June 1926.
37. *Birmingham Post*, 8 May 1925.
38. *Birmingham Mail*, 8 May 1925.
39. Special Branch Report by Maxwell Knight, 15 June 1944, PRO KV 2/245/331b.
40. *Fascist Bulletin*, July 1926.
41. *British Lion*, 23 October 1926.
42. *British Lion*, 9 October 1926.
43. See Julie Gottlieb, *Feminine Fascism: Women in Britain's Fascist Movement 1923–1945* (2000), 296.

44. House of Commons Debates, vol. 188, 18 November 1925, c.406.

45. Leese, *Out of Step*, 50.

46. Diary of Miss K. B. M. Alexander, 29 February 1916, Peter Liddle Collection, University of Leeds.

47. *Fascist Bulletin*, 21 November 1925.

48. PRO HO 144/19069; *British Lion*, 25 September 1926, 3 October 1926.

49. *British Lion*, December 1927.

50. PRO HO 144/19069, Robert Smith to the Lord Chancellor, 17 June 1926.

51. PRO HO 144/19069, memorandum, 22 January 1929; Robert Smith letter, 11 January 1929.

52. *Nineteenth Century*, 97, January 1925, 139.

53. Quoted in Gottlieb, *Feminine Fascism*, 20.

54. *Evening News*, 7 May 1927.

55. *Harrogate Advertiser*, 5 November 1926.

56. Gottlieb, *Feminine Fascism*, 93–135.

57. *Fascist Bulletin*, 13 June 1925.

58. *Fascist Bulletin*, 11 July 1925.

59. *Fascist Bulletin*, 3 October 1925.

60. *Fascist Bulletin*, 17 October 1925.

61. *The Patriot*, 29 April 1927; *Evening News*, 24 April 1926.

62. *Fascist Bulletin*, 31 October 1925.

63. PRO HO 144/19069, Rippon-Seymour letter, 12 May 1926.

64. PRO HO 144/19069, 'To All Commanders: Work Done by Fascists in the General Strike', 26 May 1926; H. Boyd to Lord Stamfordham, 23 June 1926.

65. *Birmingham Post*, 8 May 1925; *Daily Herald*, 29 January 1926; *Fascist Bulletin*, 1 May 1926.

66. PRO HO 45/25386, 37–40.

67. *Fascist Bulletin*, 22 May 1926; *The Patriot*, 3 June 1926.

68. *British Lion*, 18 December 1926.

69. *British Lion*, August 1927.

70. PRO HO 144/19069, Lintorn-Orman to Joynson-Hicks, 4 February 1927.

71. PRO HO 144/19069, press reports, 18 January 1927; also *Evening News*, 1 March 1926, 20 April 1926; *Daily Mail*, 1 March 1926; *Daily Sketch*, 19 May 1927; *Daily Herald*, 31 July 1925, 11 and 29 October 1925, 19 November 1925, 6 March 1929.

72. *Morning Post*, 5 May 1927; *Sunday Worker*, 3 May 1927.

73. PRO HO 144/19069 includes reports from *Daily Herald*, 10 March 1927.

74. *Sunday Dispatch*, 17 March 1929.
75. Leese, *Out of Step*, 49–50.
76. Ibid., 48–50.
77. PRO HO 45/24967, 'The Imperial Fascist League', 16 March 1942.
78. PRO HO 45/24967, Special Branch Report, 9 March 1936.
79. Ibid.
80. *The Fascist*, editorial, March 1929.
81. *The Fascist*, April and May 1929.
82. *The Fascist*, April 1929.
83. *The Fascist*, June 1929.
84. *The Fascist*, July 1929.
85. PRO HO 45/24967, Special Branch Report, 9 March 1936.
86. Leese, *Out of Step*, 51.
87. 'To the Electors of North East Hants Parliamentary Division', 14 February 1934, Lymington Papers F416.
88. 'English Array', undated memorandum, Lymington Papers F178, F179.
89. Mosley to Lymington, 7 October 1937, Lymington Papers F391; Neil Francis-Hawkins to Lymington, 12 February 1938, Lymington Papers F181; D. P. Ratcliffe to Lymington, 23 February 138, Lymington Papers F188; Dan Stone, 'The English Mistery, the BUF and the Dilemmas of British Fascism', *Journal of Modern History*, 75, 2003, 336–58.
90. 'English Array', Lymington Papers F178.
91. Kershaw, *Hitler 1889–1936*, 317.
92. *The Fascist*, October 1929.
93. For example, *The Patriot*, 2 and 16 September 1926.
94. PRO HO 144/19069, *Daily Herald*, 29 January 1926.

5. Boiled Shirt Fascism

1. W. D. Rubinstein, 'Henry Page Croft and the National Party 1917–1922', *Journal of Contemporary History*, 9, 1974, 129–48.
2. *Saturday Review*, 5 April 1919, 321.
3. Austin Harrison, 'The Crushing of the Middle Classes', *English Review*, 29, 1919, 463–4.
4. Martin Petter, '"Temporary Gentlemen" in the Aftermath of the Great War: Rank, Status and the Ex-officer Problem', *Historical Journal*, 37, 1994, 127–52.
5. Harrison, 'Crushing of the Middle Classes', 463.
6. Richard Lomas, *A Power in the Land: The Percys* (1999); R. C. Bosanquet in *Archaeologia Aeliana*, 8, 1931, 1–5.

7. *The Patriot*, 9 February 1922.

8. *The Patriot*, from editorial, 23 February 1922, 1–2.

9. See *The Patriot*, 23 February 1922; 30 March 1922; *National Review*, 79, May 1922; 87, April 1924; 97, July 1931.

10. *The Patriot*, 20 April 1922.

11. *The Patriot*, 16 March 1922, 18 January 1923, 5 July 1923, 20 December 1923.

12. Arthur Kitson, 'Bolshevism and Its Allies', *National Review*, 89, July 1927.

13. Ibid.

14. Ibid.

15. *The Patriot*, 29 June 1922, 6 July 1922.

16. *The Patriot*, 12 October 1922.

17. *The Patriot*, 8 June 1922.

18. *Daily Notes*, 1924, quoted in David Jarvis, 'Stanley Baldwin and the Ideology of the Conservative Response to Socialism, 1918–1931', unpublished Lancaster University PhD thesis, 1991, 132.

19. See *English Review*, editorial, 36, June 1923, 498; 39, 1924, 705; *National Review*, 82, January 1924, 703–4.

20. *National Review*, 77, July 1921, 617–27; *The Patriot*, 11 January 1923, 365–6.

21. *English Review*, editorial, 37, 1923, 138.

22. *The Patriot*, 16 November 1922, 241.

23. *English Review*, 39, July 1924; *The Patriot*, 23 February 1922.

24. *National Review*, editorial, 89, July 1927; *National Review*, 89, August 1927, 903.

25. Rothermere to Beaverbrook, 26 April 1922, Beaverbrook Papers C 283.

26. *National Review*, editorial, 83, April 1928, 198.

27. *Manchester Guardian*, 18 March 1922.

28. *Newcastle Journal*, 3 October 1924, quoted in John Ramsden, *The Age of Balfour and Baldwin 1902–40* (1978), 209.

29. *The Patriot*, editorial, 23 March 1922, 1–2.

30. Francis Yeats-Brown to Arthur Bryant, 28 May 1937, Bryant Papers E 39.

31. Arthur Bryant to Yeats-Brown, 10 June 1937, Bryant Papers E 39.

32. *English Review*, XLI, September 1925, 399.

33. *English Review*, 30, May 1920, 542; 40, June 1925.

34. *English Review*, 30, January 1920, 86.

35. Rothermere to Beaverbrook, 19 December 1923, Beaverbrook Papers C 282.

36. *The Times*, 12 December 1923.

37. Ibid.
38. *The Patriot*, 8 January 1924, 341; 17 January 1924, 369, 373–4.
39. *The New Vote*, 4 February 1924, quoted in Jarvis, thesis, 139.
40. *Morning Post*, 11 October 1924.
41. *National Review*, 83, June 1924, 483.
42. Quoted in Keith Feiling, *Neville Chamberlain* (1946), 111.
43. Philip Snowden, *An Autobiography* (1934), 710.
44. David Marquand, *Ramsay MacDonald* (1977), 381–8; Ramsden, *Balfour and Baldwin*, 202–6.
45. *Daily Mail*, editorial, 25 October 1924.
46. Ibid.
47. *Daily Mail*, 27 October 1924.
48. *National Review*, 84, December 1924, 489.
49. Rothermere to Beaverbrook, 1 November 1924 and December 1924, n.d., Beaverbrook Papers C 282.
50. For a discussion of Joynson-Hicks see David Cesarani, 'Joynson-Hicks and the Radical Right in England after the First World War', in Tony Kushner and Kenneth Lunn (eds.), *Traditions of Intolerance* (1989), 118–39.
51. Ibid., 129–31.
52. *National Review*, 78, January 1922, 614–20; *English Review*, 46, January 1928, 135.
53. *The Patriot*, 'The Indian Danger', 9 February 1922; *English Review*, 'The Wrecking of India', 37, 1923; 'The Passing of India', 41, July 1925.
54. *National Review*, editorial, 83, April 1924, 177–8.
55. John Charmley, *Lord Lloyd and the Decline of the British Empire* (1987), 158–65.
56. Roger W. Louis, *In the Name of God Go!* (1992), 77–8.
57. *The Patriot*, 8 February 1923, 8; *National Review*, editorial, 81, March 1923, 322–3.
58. *National Review*, 89, April 1927, 215.

6. *The General Strike: The Fascist Crisis Denied*

1. Viscountess Lee, diary, 4 April 1921, quoted in David Jarvis, 'Stanley Baldwin and the Ideology of the Conservative Response to Socialism, 1918–1931', unpublished Lancaster University PhD thesis, 1991, 135.
2. Memorandum, 12 November 1924, Gilmour Papers, GD 383.
3. Wilfred Ashley, 'The Menace of Communism', *English Review*, 40, 1925, 633.

4. Duke of Northumberland, 'The Coming Storm', *National Review*, 86, September 1925, 54–6.

5. 'General Strike: Russian Gold', n.d., Baldwin Papers 12.

6. Memorandum, n.d. 1928, Baldwin Papers 12.

7. Henry Pelling, *A History of British Trade Unionism* (1963), 159.

8. *English Review*, 40, 1925, 631–3.

9. Quoted in Harold Nicolson, *King George V* (1952), 415.

10. *The Patriot*, 24 September 1925, 446; *Fascist Bulletin*, 20 June 1925; 11 July 1925.

11. *English Review*, 41, November 1925, 627.

12. *National Review*, 86, September 1925, 49.

13. PRO HO 45/12336, 3 December 1925.

14. PRO HO 45/12336, Notes of a conference of Home Office with OMS, 5 and 7 December 1925.

15. *The Times*, 1 October 1925.

16. See *Daily Mail*, 25 and 26 September 1925; *The Times*, 26 September 1925; *Daily Herald*, 26 September 1925.

17. *The Times*, 5 and 8 October 1925.

18. *The Times*, 15 February 1926; *Daily Mail*, 25 September 1925.

19. *The Times*, 25 September 1925.

20. *Fascist Bulletin*, 17 October 1925; PRO HO 45/12336, 7 December 1925.

21. *Morning Post*, 7 October 1925.

22. PRO HO 45/12336, 7 December 1925.

23. Ibid., 3 December 1925.

24. *Manchester Guardian*, 4 May 1926.

25. *Daily Herald*, 16 February 1926.

26. PRO MEPO 2/1838, 26 May 1926.

27. *Fascist Bulletin*, 17 October 1925; *Morning Post*, 7 October 1925.

28. *Fascist Bulletin*, 25 May 1926.

29. *Fascist Bulletin*, 31 October 1925.

30. PRO HO 144/19069, Rippon-Seymour to Joynson-Hicks, 12 May 1926; H. R. Boyd to Lord Stamfordham, 12 June 1926.

31. PRO HO 144/19069, Rippon-Seymour to Stanley Baldwin, 12 May 1926.

32. Nicolson, *George V*, 420.

33. Quoted in J. Barnes and K. Middlemas, *Baldwin* (1969), 411.

34. *Picture Post*, 7 April 1951.

35. Jessica Mitford, *Hons and Rebels* (1960), 56.

36. PRO CAB 23/53, 28 April 1926.

37. Barnes and Middlemas, *Baldwin*, 411.

38. *Manchester Guardian*, 6 May 1926.
39. PRO HO 144/6902, Situation Reports, file 2, 7 May 1926.
40. *Manchester Guardian*, 7 May 1926.
41. *Manchester Guardian*, 8 May 1926.
42. PRO HO 144/6902, 7 May 1926.
43. PRO HO 144/6902, 9 May 1926
44. PRO HO 144/6902, 10 and 11 May 1926.
45. 'Report of the Proceedings at Downing Street', 12 May 1926, PRO LAB 27/9.
46. *British Lion*, June 1926.
47. PRO HO 144/6902, 7 May 1926.
48. PRO HO 144/21933, memoranda, 20 July 1927, 10 and 16 August 1927.
49. *New York Times*, 24 May 1926.
50. Mitford, *Hons and Rebels*, 20.
51. Ibid.
52. Philip Murphy, *Alan Lennox-Boyd: A Biography* (1999), 16; *National Review*, 87, June 1926, 492.
53. PRO WO 32/3455.
54. Nicolson, *George V*, 418.
55. PRO WO 32/3455, 8 May 1926.
56. Ibid.
57. PRO HO 144/6902, 10 May 1926.
58. PRO HO 144/6902, 11 May 1926.
59. PRO WO 32/3455.
60. PRO WO 32/3455, Section IV: Comments.
61. PRO HO 144/6902, 7 May 1926.
62. I am grateful to Professor David French for clarifying this point.
63. PRO WO 32/3455, Section IV: Comments.
64. Ibid.
65. *English Review*, 42, June 1926, 734; *The Patriot*, 20 May 1926, 417–18.
66. PRO HO 144/6902/493562, file 2.
67. 'General Strike: Russian Gold', Baldwin Papers 12.
68. *National Review*, 87, July 1926, 639.
69. *National Review*, 87, October 1926, 276.
70. Winston Churchill to his Woodford constituents, quoted in Jarvis, thesis, 218.
71. *The Times*, 21 January 1927.
72. PRO HO 45/12336, report, 1 June 1926; Joynson-Hicks to Lord Hardinge, 30 June 1926.
73. *Fascist Bulletin*, 20 November 1926.

74. PRO HO 144/13864, memorandum on Workers' Defence Group; memorandum, 27 February 1927; memorandum, 17 November 1927.
75. *Morning Post*, 14 February 1927.
76. PRO LAB 27/9, C. W. K. MacMullan, memorandum, 38–40; David Harrison, 'The General Strike and the Law', *English Review*, 42, June 1926, 747–8.
77. *English Review*, 42, June 1926, 741–2.

7. *'Boneless Wonders': The Crisis of 1929–31*

1. The Earl of Listowel, interview with the author, 2 May 1996.
2. See Martin Pugh, 'Class Traitors: Conservative Recruits to Labour 1900–1930', *English Historical Review*, CXIII, February 1998.
3. Oliver Baldwin, *The Questing Beast* (1932), 214.
4. Robert Skidelsky, *Oswald Mosley* (1975), 23.
5. Ibid., 69–75.
6. Martin Pugh, *Women and the Women's Movement in Britain, 1914–1959* (1992), 142–4.
7. Skidelsky, *Mosley*, 83.
8. Quoted in Diana Mosley, *A Life of Contrasts* (2002), 92.
9. Oswald Mosley, *My Life* (1969), 24.
10. Nicholas Mosley, *The Rules of the Game* (1983), 32–3.
11. Ibid., 247–8.
12. Ibid., 96.
13. 17 April 1921, quoted in Skidelsky, *Mosley*, 110–11.
14. House of Commons Debates, vol. 169, 17 January 1924, c.370.
15. Edon Wertheimer, *Portrait of the Labour Party* (1929), viii–x.
16. *Birmingham Mail*, 22 October 1924.
17. *Smethwick Telephone*, 27 November 1926.
18. *National Review*, 90, February 1928, 828.
19. *English Review*, 45, July 1927, 7–8; *National Review*, 89, June 1927, 671–2; 89, July 1927, 903–5; 92, March 1929, 37.
20. *National Review*, 89, April 1927, 215.
21. H. H. Little to Sir L. Maclachland, 3 June 1927, Baldwin Papers 51; *English Review*, 48, July 1928, 20–1.
22. W. J. Brown, 'Democracy in Danger', *Saturday Review*, 31 January 1931, 145.
23. *Saturday Review*, 7 February 1931, 180.
24. *National Review*, 94, April 1930, 1126.
25. Quoted in Skidelsky, *Mosley*, 206.

26. Draft speech, 15 December 1930, Nicholas Mosley Deposit, Box 8.
27. Austen Chamberlain to Ida Chamberlain, 25 May 1930, in Robert C. Self (ed.), *The Austen Chamberlain Diary Letters* (1995), 345.
28. Quoted in Skidelsky, *Mosley*, 224.
29. Stuart Ball, *Baldwin and the Conservative Party* (1988), 222–3.
30. Patrick Hannon to Lord Beaverbrook (copy), 7 October 1930, Hannon Papers 17/1.
31. Lady Houston to Lord Lloyd, 11 November 1930, Lloyd Papers 19/2.
32. *English Review*, 51, November 1930, 568–9.
33. *Saturday Review*, 7 and 14 February 1931.
34. Mary S. Lovell, *The Mitford Girls* (2001), 134.
35. Harold Nicolson, *Diaries and Letters*, vol. I: *1930–39* (1966), 75, 28 May 1931.
36. Ibid., 76, 30 May 1931.
37. Quoted in Skidelsky, *Mosley*, 251.
38. Lord Beaverbrook to Neville Chamberlain, 7 May 1931, Hannon Papers 17/1.
39. Skidelsky, *Mosley*, 252.
40. Nicolson, *Diaries*, 80, 17 July 1931.
41. Harold Nicolson, *King George V* (1952), 460–2.
42. House of Commons Debates, vol. 256, 8 September 1931, c.72–82.
43. Nicolson, *Diaries*, 91, 21 September 1931.
44. Oswald Mosley, 'Old Parties or New?', *Political Quarterly*, vol. 3, January–March 1932, 30.
45. Nicolson, *Diaries*, 97, 24 September 1931.
46. Ibid., 115, 19 April 1932.
47. Ibid., 106, 6 January 1932.
48. J. S. Barnes, 'Fascism', *National Review*, 92, February 1929, 845.
49. *Saturday Review*, 29 August 1931.

8. *'Hurrah for the Blackshirts!': The British Union of Fascists 1932–4*

1. Nicholas Mosley, *Rules of the Game* (1983), 211.
2. Ibid., 210; Robert Skidelsky, *Oswald Mosley* (1975), 284–5.
3. Earl of Portsmouth, *A Knot of Roots* (1965), 159.
4. Diana Mosley, *A Life of Contrasts* (1977), 92; Mary S. Lovell, *The Mitford Girls* (2001), 132.
5. Mosley, *Rules*, 240.
6. Ibid., 242.
7. Lovell, *Mitford Girls*, 153–4.
8. Mosley, *Rules*, 230.

9. Oswald Mosley, *The Greater Britain* (1932), 17.

10. Speech at Edinburgh, *The Times*, 2 June 1934.

11. R. R. Bellamy, *Mosley's Blackshirts* (1986), 60.

12. *The Blackshirt*, 1 February 1933; *The Times*, 25 January 1933.

13. Mosley, *Greater Britain*, 20.

14. *The Blackshirt*, 1 February 1933; *The Times*, 23 April 1934; Mosley, *Greater Britain*, 43.

15. Report, 22 January 1934, PRO HO 45/25386.

16. Arnold Leese, *Out of Step* (1951), 52.

17. Mosley, *Greater Britain*, 21.

18. *The Observer*, 21 January 1934.

19. Martin Pugh, *Women and the Women's Movement in Britain 1914–1959* (1992), 143–4.

20. A. Leese to his wife, 16 June 1942, Myra Story Papers 01/28/1; Cimmie's maternal grandfather was Levi Zebidee Leiter who belonged to a Dutch Protestant sect called Mennonites: Nicholas Mosley, *Beyond the Pale* (1983), 13.

21. *Daily Mail*, 7 July 1934.

22. Mosley, *Beyond the Pale*, 71.

23. Mosley, *Life of Contrasts*, 131.

24. Leslie Grundy, 'Don't Let Your Conscience Be Your Guide', 43, British Union Collection 5/3.

25. John Charnley, *Blackshirts and Roses* (1990), 48–9; Grundy, 'Conscience', 31.

26. Charnley, *Blackshirts and Roses*, 48–9.

27. Mosley, *Rules*, 57–8.

28. Ibid., 185.

29. *Manchester Guardian*, 26 October 1931.

30. Francis Selwyn, *Hitler's Englishman* (1987), 17–21, 26, 35; David Baker, *The Ideology of Obsession: A. K. Chesterton and British Fascism* (1996), 122–8.

31. *Saturday Review*, 10 February 1934.

32. Louise Irving, *Mosley's Men* (1986), 47; Oswald Mosley, *Sunday Dispatch*, 21 January 1934.

33. Mosley, *Rules*, 232.

34. Kent Constabulary to Home Office, 8 March 1934, PRO HO 144/19070.

35. Chief Constable to Under-Secretary of State, 14 November 1933, PRO HO 144/19070.

36. *The Times*, 3 November 1933.

37. See letters by Major-General Fuller, 16 November 1933 and Sir John Gilmour, 23 November 1933, PRO HO 144/19070.

38. *The Times*, 25 January 1933.

39. *News Chronicle*, 4 February 1936.

40. *News Chronicle*, 5 February 1936.

41. *News Chronicle*, 6 February 1936.

42. *News Chronicle*, 5 February 1936.

43. *News Chronicle*, 4 February 1936.

44. *News Chronicle*, 8 February 1936.

45. Minute by Lieutenant General Sir Walter Kirke, May 1936; Oswald Mosley to the Secretary of State for War, 22 May 1936, PRO WO 32/4608.

46. G. D. Roseway to Oswald Mosley, 16 July 1936; CO Hampshire Regiment to HQ 128 Infantry Brigade, 26 May 1936; War Office Circular Letter, 21 August 1936, PRO WO 32/4608.

47. See Saunders Papers (Dorset BUF), British Union Collection, Sheffield University; Stuart Rawnsley Interviews, Bradford University Library Special Collections.

48. Nellie Driver, 10, Stuart Rawnsley Interview.

49. B. Rowe, 5, Stuart Rawnsley Interview, 24 August 1978.

50. Nellie Driver, 'From the Shadows of Exile', unpublished autobiography, 21, 23; B. Rowe, 3, Stuart Rawnsley Interview; Julie Gottlieb, *Feminine Fascism: Women in Britain's Fascist Movement 1923–1945* (2000), 55.

51. Arthur Fawcett, 15, Stuart Rawnsley Interview.

52. B. Rowe, 5, Stuart Rawnsley Interview.

53. Nellie Driver, 'Shadows of Exile', 21; B. Rowe, 6, Stuart Rawnsley Interview; G. P. Southerst, 13, Stuart Rawnsley Interview, 16 February 1977.

54. R. R. Bellamy, in J. Christian (ed.), *Mosley's Blackshirts: The Inside Story of the British Union of Fascists 1932–1940* (1986), 62; 'The British Union of Fascists in Yorkshire 1934–40', Trevelyan Schools Project (1960), 2–4.

55. 'British Union of Fascists in Yorkshire', 2–4.

56. B. Rowe, 3, Stuart Rawnsley Interview; Leonard Wise, in J. Christian (ed.), *Mosley's Blackshirts*, 2–3.

57. Arthur Fawcett, 22, Stuart Rawnsley Interview, 24 August 1978; Thomas Pickles, 4, Stuart Rawnsley Interview, 10 September 1977.

58. Robert Richard, 'Geordie Recollections 1932–1939', 6–11, British Union Collection.

59. *The Times*, 22 January 1934.

60. *Daily Mail*, 25 April 1934.

61. Naomi Mitchison, 'Fascists at Olympia', 1934, Labour Party Archives, 329.8.

62. *Sunday Dispatch*, 29 April 1934.
63. Leonard Wise, in J. Christian (ed.), *Mosley's Blackshirts*, 3.
64. Nellie Driver, 'Shadows of Exile', 29; Charnley, *Blackshirts and Roses*, 43–4.
65. *The Blackshirt*, 30 September 1933.
66. J. Christian (ed.), *Mosley's Blackshirts*, 10, 21, 60.
67. *Saturday Review*, 18 March 1933, 27 May 1933, 21 July 1933.
68. *Saturday Review*, 10 February 1934.
69. *The Blackshirt*, 21 October 1933.
70. *The Blackshirt*, 4, 18 May 1934.
71. *The Times*, 7 April 1934, 13 June 1934, 2 July 1934; *Daily Mail*, 2 July 1934.
72. R. R. Bellamy, 'We Marched with Mosley', 89, British Union Collection 5/5.
73. *The Blackshirt*, 19 August 1933.
74. *The Blackshirt*, 23 February 1934; Bellamy, 'We Marched', 90; George Hoggarth, in J. Christian (ed.), *Mosley's Blackshirts*, 43–4.
75. Mosley, *Greater Britain*, 41.
76. Gottlieb, *Feminine Fascism*, 56.
77. Ibid., 53–4.
78. Robert Saunders Papers, file E/1; Gottlieb, *Feminine Fascism*, 46–7.
79. Nellie Driver, 'Shadows of Exile', 12.
80. Oswald Mosley, *My Life* (1968), 344.
81. Nellie Driver, 'Shadows of Exile', 32.
82. Ann Page, in J. Christian (ed.), *Mosley's Blackshirts*, 16; Gottlieb, *Feminine Fascism*, 44.
83. Nellie Driver, 'Shadows of Exile', 32.
84. Minutes, Grand Council of the Primrose League, 7 June 1934; *Morning Post*, 21 May 1934.
85. *The Blackshirt*, 29 June 1934.
86. Cecile Hamilton, *Life Errant* (1935), 68; Emmeline Pethick-Lawrence, *My Part in a Changing World* (1938), preface.
87. Martin Pugh, *The Pankhursts* (2001), 356, 381; Norah Elam, *Fascist Quarterly*, July 1935, 290–4.
88. *The Blackshirt*, 22 February 1935; Ann Page, in J. Christian (ed.), *Mosley's Blackshirts*, 15–16.
89. *The Blackshirt*, 7 September 1934; Anne Brock-Griggs, *Fascist Quarterly*, October 1935, 435–44.
90. *The Blackshirt*, 19 August 1933, 19 October 1934.
91. Gottlieb, *Feminine Fascism*, 114–15.
92. Jessica Mitford, *Hons and Rebels* (1960), 60.

93. Ibid., 61.

94. Mosley, *Life of Contrasts*, 103.

95. Lovell, *Mitford Girls*, 185.

96. Mitford, *Hons and Rebels*, 62–3.

97. Robert Campbell to the Duchess of Atholl, 10 May 1938, Atholl Papers 95/2.

98. Leigh Vaughan-Henry to Oswald Mosley, 25 July 1934, Nicholas Mosley Papers box 8.

99. Ibid.

100. *The Times*, 22 March 1934.

101. R. Forgan to H. Luttman-Johnson, 23 December 1923, Oswald Mosley to H. Luttman-Johnson, 5 April 1934, William Joyce to H. Luttman-Johnson, 8 February 1935, Luttman-Johnson Papers 1.

102. H. Luttman-Johnson to Mrs Luttman-Johnson, 3 July 1940, Luttman-Johnson Papers 2, fol. 1.

103. See Luttman-Johnson Papers 8; Philip Murphy, *Alan Lennox-Boyd: A Biography* (1999), 43; *The Times*, 15 July 1936.

104. T. E. Lawrence to H. Luttman-Johnson, 17 May 1934, Luttman-Johnson Papers 1.

105. House of Commons Debates, 290, 14 June 1934, c.1940.

106. R. R. Bellamy, 'We Marched with Mosley', 105, British Union Collection 5/5.

107. Charles Chenevix Trench to H. Luttman-Johnson, 7 March 1934, Luttman-Johnson Papers 1.

108. Norman Thwaites to H. Luttman-Johnson, 3 February 1935, Harold Goad to H. Luttman-Johnson, 11 January 1934, Sir Charles Petrie to H. Luttman-Johnson, 28 June 1938, Luttman-Johnson Papers 1.

109. R. Forgan to H. Luttman-Johnson, 27 December 1933, Luttman-Johnson Papers 1.

110. Robert Skidelsky, *Oswald Mosley* (1975), 330.

111. Norman Thwaites to H. Luttman-Johnson, 3 February 1935, J. B. Morton to H. Luttman-Johnson, 3 May 1934, Luttman-Johnson Papers 1.

112. John Hone to H. Luttman-Johnson, 23 October 1935, Luttman-Johnson Papers 1.

113. *Daily Mail*, 25 April 1934; Commissioner of the Metropolitan Police report to Home Secretary, 1 May 1934, PRO HO 144/20140; *Saturday Review*, 16 June 1934; *National Review*, 103, July 1934; *English Review*, 59, July 1934.

114. Admiral Sir Roger Keyes was adopted at Portsmouth in January 1934:

Winston Churchill to Henry Page Croft, 19 January 1934, Page Croft Papers 1/8; *National Review*, 101, July 1933, 615.

115. Lymington believed he had been pushed out: Lymington to Drummond Wolff, 24 August 1935, Drummond Wolff Papers II/629.

116. E. A. Loveridge to Henry Drummond Wolff, 7 August 1935, Drummond Wolff Papers I/50.

117. Murphy, *Lennox-Boyd*, 42–3.

118. *National Review*, 99, August 1932 (Page Croft), December 1932 (Robert Boothby).

119. Cuthbert Headlam Diary, 13 February 1934, Headlam Papers D/He/30.

120. *Saturday Review*, 8 April 1933; see also F. J. C. Hearnshaw on the failure of democracy, *National Review*, 101, July 1933, 53–9.

121. *English Review*, 57, October 1933, 342–4.

122. *Saturday Review*, 15 October 1932.

123. *Saturday Review*, 30 September 1933.

124. *Saturday Review*, 10 February 1934, 28 April 1934, 5 May 1934.

125. Mosley, *Rules*, 205.

126. Dino Grandi to Benito Mussolini (copy), 30 January 1934, Nicholas Mosley Papers, Box 8.

127. Ibid.

128. *Daily Mail*, 15 January 1934.

129. *Sunday Dispatch*, 22 April 1934.

130. *Sunday Dispatch*, 29 April 1934.

131. R. R. Bellamy, 'We Marched with Mosley', 120, British Union Collection 5/5; Mosley, *Beyond the Pale*, 45.

132. *Saturday Review*, 5 May 1934.

133. *Daily Mail*, 25 April 1934.

134. *Morning Post*, 6 October 1934; further letters from disaffected Tories: *Morning Post*, 22 October 1934.

135. *Daily Telegraph*, 18 June 1934.

136. Arthur Beavan, in J. Christian (ed.), *Mosley's Blackshirts*, 58.

137. Mosley, *Beyond the Pale*, 32.

138. Oswald Mosley, *The Greater Britain* (1934), preface.

139. *Sunday Dispatch*, 21 January 1934; G. C. Webber, 'Patterns of Membership and Support for the British Union of Fascists', *Journal of Contemporary History*, 19, 1984.

140. A. S. Hutchinson to Sir Geoffrey Fry, 11 February 1935, Baldwin Papers 9/5.2.10.

141. Oswald Mosley to the editor of *The Spectator*, 22 June 1946, Diana

Mosley Papers box 2; Dino Grandi to Benito Mussolini (copies), 30 January 1935 and 1 March 1935, Nicholas Mosley Papers, Box 8.

142. PRO HO 283/10.

143. G. P. Southerst, 13, Stuart Rawnsley Interview, 16 February 1977.

144. Selwyn, *Hitler's Englishman*, 49.

145. Mosley, *Beyond the Pale*, 45; Richard Thurlow, *Fascism in Britain: A History 1918–1985* (1987), 139.

146. Note of Home Office conference, 23 November 1933, PRO HO 45/25386.

147. PRO HO 45/25386/15.

148. Francis Beckett, *The Rebel Who Lost His Cause* (1999), 121, 135, 139–40.

149. Draft memorandum for the cabinet by Hugh Trenchard, 12 January 1934; extract from cabinet discussion, 30 May 1934; undated draft: PRO HO 45/25386/20.

150. Commissioner of the Metropolitan Police to Under-Secretary, Home Office, 26 February 1934, Gilmour Papers GD 383/48 and PRO HO 144/20158/107.

151. Memorandum, 2 March 1934, PRO HO 144/20158/102/3.

152. Note of Home Office conference, 23 November 1933, PRO HO 45/25386.

153. Sir Hugh Trenchard, undated draft, PRO HO 45/25386/20.

9. *'Where Are the Bodies?': The Politics of Violence 1934–7*

1. *News Chronicle*, 9 June 1934.

2. 'Fascists at Olympia' (1934), 12, Labour Party Archives, 329.8.

3. Ibid., 11; House of Commons Debates, 290, 14 June 1934, c.1936.

4. *The Times*, 8 June 1934; *Daily Telegraph*, 9 June 1934.

5. Reports 28 May, 4 and 7 June 1934, PRO MEPO 2/4319; *Daily Worker*, 24 April 1934, 15 and 17 May 1934.

6. House of Commons Debates, 290, 14 June 1934, c.1928.

7. See Nigel Copsey, *Anti-Fascism in Britain* (2000), 15–17; Francis Beckett, *The Rebel Who Lost His Cause* (1999), 129–30; Andrew Thorpe, 'The Membership of the Communist Party of Great Britain 1920–1945', *Historical Journal*, 43, 2000, 781.

8. Robert Saunders to E. Burch, 22 February 1937, Saunders Papers A6/147.

9. House of Commons Debates, 198, 18 December 1908, c.2206–8, 19 December 1908, c.2330–4.

10. *Daily Telegraph*, 15 June 1934.

11. Robert Skidelsky, *Oswald Mosley* (1975), 370.

12. *Daily Express*, 8 June 1934.
13. House of Commons Debates, 290, 14 June 1934, c.1943–4, 1984, 2035–6.
14. *News Chronicle*, 8 and 9 June 1934.
15. Sir Charles Petrie, *Chapters of Life* (1950), 167; *Morning Post*, 3 May 1934.
16. *Morning Post*, 12 June 1934; *National Review*, 103, July 1934.
17. *English Review*, 59, July 1934, 9–10; *Saturday Review*, 16 June 1934; *National Review*, 103, July 1934.
18. Report 1 August 1934, PRO HO 144/20142/108; *The Blackshirt*, 22 June 1934.
19. House of Commons Debates, vol. 290, 11 June 1934, c.341–3.
20. Ibid., 14 June 1934, c.1916–18.
21. Ibid., c.1943, 2010, 2034, 2038.
22. Ibid., c.1940, 2018, 2032.
23. Ibid., c.2011, 2033, 2036–7.
24. Ibid., c.1969.
25. Headlam Diary, 14 June 1934; House of Commons debates, vol. 290, 14 June 1934, c.1980.
26. 13 June 1934, PRO HO 45/2538.
27. PRO CAB 23/79, 24 (34).
28. Notes on cabinet meeting, 31 July 1934, PRO HO 45/25387.
29. PRO HO 144/20141.
30. *News Chronicle*, 18 August 1934.
31. See Stafford Cripps Papers, 519.
32. Chief of the Metropolitan Police to the Home Secretary, 18 July 1934, PRO HO 45/25387.
33. Ibid.
34. Report 1 August 1934, PRO HO 144/20142/108.
35. John Strachey, memorandum, 20 September 1934, Cripps Papers 553/A.
36. Headlam Diary, 14 June 1934.
37. *The Blackshirt*, 15, 22 and 29 June 1934, 7 September 1934.
38. See A. J. Trythall, *'Boney' Fuller: The Intellectual General 1878–1966* (1977), 181–4, 200.
39. See the discussion in G. C. Webber, 'Patterns of Membership and Support for the British Union of Fascists', *Journal of Contemporary History*, 19, 1984, 575–606.
40. Robert Saunders Papers A1/301–2.
41. Report, 25 October 1935, PRO HO 144/20145.
42. Special Branch, 29 October 1935, PRO HO 144/20145.
43. John Charnley, *Blackshirts and Roses* (1990), 61.

44. 'Apathy', undated typed memorandum, 1934, Nicholas Mosley Papers, Box 8.

45. J. F. C. Fuller to Oswald Mosley, summer 1935, Nicholas Mosley Papers, Box 8.

46. *Sunday Dispatch*, 17 June 1934.

47. S. J. Taylor. *The Great Outsiders: Northcliffe, Harmsworth and the Daily Mail* (1996), 298.

48. Rothermere to Mosley, 14 July 1934, in the *Daily Mail*, 19 July 1934; *Sunday Dispatch*, 6 May 1934.

49. Richard Bellamy, 'We Marched with Mosley', 121–3, British Union Collection 5/5.

50. This was confirmed by Mosley's Italian backers: Count Grandi, typed memorandum, 30 January 1934, Nicholas Mosley Papers, 'The Italian Papers', Box 8.

51. Rothermere to Mosley, 14 July 1934 in the *Daily Mail*, 19 July 1934.

52. Report no. III, PRO HO 144/20142/215.

53. PRO HO 144/20142/215, 222 and 225.

54. *Daily Mail*, 2 and 6 July 1934.

55. *The Blackshirt*, 2 November 1934.

56. *Sussex Herald*, 22 June 1934; *Hemel Hempstead Gazette*, 10 October 1935; *Kentish Observer*, 10 October 1935; PRO HO 144/20142/82.

57. *Dorset County Echo*, 29 January 1935; *Southern Times*, 2 February 1935.

58. Special Branch, 20 October 1935, PRO HO 144/20145.

59. 'Fascist Meeting at West Ham Town Hall', 24 July 1935, PRO HO 144/20145.

60. *The Times*, 27 May 1935.

61. Trenchard to the Home Secretary, 29 June 1934, PRO HO 45/25387.

62. Robert Saunders Papers A2/343–50.

63. Leslie Grundy, 'Don't Let Your Conscience Be Your Guide', 32, British Union Collection 5/3.

64. William Joyce, 24 October 1934, PRO HO 144/20145.

65. Memorandum, 16 September 1934, PRO HO 144/20145.

66. *Daily Telegraph*, 22 June 1934; *Sunday Dispatch*, 24 June 1934.

67. Inspector J. Holmes, PRO HO 144/21060/92242.

68. Cripps to Strachey (copy), 16 October 1934, Cripps Papers 553/A.

69. 11 July 1936, PRO CAB 24/250 Cabinet Papers 189.

70. Report, 27 October 1936, PRO HO 144/21062/259.

71. Sir Philip Game, 9 June 1936, PRO HO 144/21379.

72. Special Branch report, 7 May 1937, PRO HO 144/21380.

73. Sir Philip Game to Sir John Simon 12 October 1936, PRO HO 144/20159.

74. *News Chronicle*, 23 February 1934; *Manchester Guardian*, 8 October 1936.

75. File on 'The Public Order Act 1936', Diana Mosley Papers, Box 4.

76. K. D. Ewing and C. A. Gearty, *The Struggle for Civil Liberties* (2000), 314–15.

77. Ibid., 323.

78. *Mosley's Blackshirts: The Inside Story of the British Union of Fascists 1932–1946* (1986), 47.

79. Bellamy, 'We Marched', 191.

80. 'Report on the Organisation of the BUF', undated 1934, Nicholas Mosley Papers, Box 8.

81. Special Instructions, 30 September 1936, Saunders Papers A2/295.

82. Special Branch, 11 January 1937, PRO HO 144/21063.

83. *Action*, 9 January 1937.

84. *Action*, 30 January 1937.

85. *Action*, 20 March 1937; Special Branch, 27 April 1937, PRO HO 144/21060.

86. Charnley, *Blackshirts and Roses*, 80–1.

87. Ewing and Gearty, *Civil Liberties*, 322.

88. For an example of photographs see T. Linehan, *East London for Mosley* (1996), 108–9.

89. Robert Richard, 'Geordie Recollections 1932–39', typescript, 37, British Union Collection 5/4.

90. Memorandum 28 September 1937, PRO HO 45/24999.

91. See files dated 24 April 1937, 16 September 1937, 16 December 1937, PRO HO 45/24999.

10. *'Drinking Tea With Treason': Fascism and the Defence of Empire*

1. Templewood Papers RF3, 12–13.

2. Lord Sydenham, *English Review*, 41, July 1925, 54.

3. Lord Sydenham, 'The Passing of India', *English Review*, 37, January 1923, 48.

4. 'The Irish Travesty', *National Review*, 78, January 1922, 614–15; *English Review*, 46, January 1928, 135.

5. *National Review*, 78, January 1922, 620.

6. John Charmley, *Lord Lloyd and the Decline of the British Empire* (1987), 84.

7. Ibid., 158–9.

8. Ibid., 163–5.

9. See William Roger Louis, *In the Name of God Go!: Leo Amery and the British Empire in the Age of Churchill* (1992), 19–20.

10. Ibid., 27.
11. See Mosley's speeches at Stoke: *Daily Mail*, 9 April 1934; and *Preston Guardian*, 15 December 1934.
12. *The Blackshirt*, April 1933.
13. *See* William Joyce, *Fascism and India* (BUF, 1937).
14. Joyce, *India*; Oswald Mosley, *The Greater Britain* (1932), 144.
15. *Preston Guardian*, 15 December 1934; Mosley, *Greater Britain*, 142–3; *Daily Mail*, 9 April 1934.
16. Undated memorandum, 'Notes on the Indian position in relation to the Princes', Lymington Papers F421.
17. Ibid.
18. *Daily Telegraph*, 3 March 1930.
19. *Daily Telegraph*, 5, 8, 10, 15 March 1930.
20. Lord Lloyd to the Duke of Atholl, 15 June 1933, Atholl Papers 9/1; Duchess of Atholl, notes, 14 February 1935, Atholl Papers 9/4.
21. *Daily Mail*, 21 January 1931.
22. Lord Lloyd to Baldwin (copy), 5 March 1931, Lloyd Papers 19/2.
23. Churchill, 12 December 1930, in Martin Gilbert, *Winston S. Churchill*, vol. V: *1922–1939* (1976), 377.
24. Lord Middleton to Lord Lloyd, 19 December 1931, Lloyd Papers 19/2.
25. Duke of Atholl to Colonel Butter, 18 April 1933, Atholl Papers 9/1.
26. *Daily Mail*, 21 January 1931; *English Review*, LVII, August 1933, 123.
27. J. Wentworth Day, *Lady Houston DBE: The Woman Who Won the War* (1958), 86, 165.
28. *Saturday Review*, 11 November 1933, 490.
29. Day, *Houston*, 81.
30. Ibid., 21.
31. Ibid., 157; it lampooned her for her patriotism and poor grammar; Mosley refused to apologise.
32. Lady Houston to Lloyd, 21 November 1932, Lloyd Papers 19/2; Day, *Houston*, 175.
33. Day, *Houston*, 178.
34. Lloyd to Lady Houston, 10 October 1933 (copy), Lloyd Papers 19/2.
35. Lloyd to Lady Houston, 19 June 1934 (copy), Lloyd Papers 19/2; Day, *Houston*, 185.
36. Day, *Houston*, 115, 122, 132–44.
37. *Daily Express*, 27 June 1983.
38. Memorandum, 14 October 1932, Hamilton Papers 5397; Day, *Houston*, 203–23.
39. 'The Houston-Everest Flight', 1 June 1933, Hamilton Papers 5397.
40. Clydesdale to Londonderry (copy), 12 November 1932, and

Londonderry to Clydesdale, n.d., Hamilton Papers 5397.

41. Day, *Houston*, 58–70; Lady Houston to Lord Burnham, 18 July 1933, Hamilton Papers 5403.

42. Lady Houston to Clydesdale, 16 May 1933, Hamilton Papers 5433.

43. *Saturday Review*, 13 May 1933, 453.

44. *Saturday Review*, 8 April 1933, 331.

45. Speech, 5 October 1932, Hamilton Papers 5397.

46. Letter to Commander Fellowes (copy), 27 May 1935, Hamilton Papers 5399.

47. Clydesdale to R. C. Greig (copy), 11 August 1933, Hamilton Papers 5433.

48. Colonel C. Butter to the Duke of Atholl, 19 April 1933, Atholl Papers 9/1; *National Review*, 101, July 1933.

49. John Ramsden (ed.), *Real Old Tory Politics: The Political Diaries of Robert Sanders, Lord Bayford 1910–1935* (1984), 249.

50. Louis, *Amery*, 109.

51. Duke of Atholl to Lloyd (copy), 14 June 1933, Atholl Papers 9/1; there is a file on the danger of default on pensions in the Atholl Papers 9/5.

52. Cuthbert Headlam's Diary, 26 May 1932, Headlam Papers D/He/28.

53. Duchess of Atholl to Colonel C. Butter, 14 August 1935, Atholl Papers 22/3.

54. Martin Gilbert, *Winston S. Churchill*, vol. V: *1922–1939* (1976), 607–8.

55. Memorandum, n.d., Lymington Papers F421.

56. Ibid.

57. *Action*, 6 March 1936.

11. *Corporatism, Capitalism and the Economic Depression*

1. Oswald Mosley, *The Greater Britain* (1932), 59–62.

2. R. I. McKibbin, *The Ideologies of Class* (1990), 266–7.

3. Ibid., 269.

4. See Philip Coupland, 'The Blackshirted Utopians', *Journal of Contemporary History*, 33, 1998; 'Left-Wing Fascism in Theory and Practice: The Case of the British Union of Fascists', *Twentieth Century British History*, 13, 2002.

5. Francis Beckett, *The Rebel Who Lost His Cause: The Tragedy of John Beckett* (1999), 115–25.

6. Quoted in Coupland, 'Left-Wing Fascism', 41; Beckett, *The Rebel*, 128; A. Raven Thompson, *Fascist Quarterly*, July 1935, 276–89.

7. Earl of Portsmouth, *A Knot of Roots* (1965), 125.

8. A. K. Chesterton in *Action*, 13 August 1936; E. D. Hart, 'The Decline

of Feudalism', *Fascist Quarterly*, April 1939, 195–201; A. L. Glasfurd, 'Fascism and the English Tradition', *Fascist Quarterly*, July 1935, 360–4.

9. Mosley, *Greater Britain*, 131–3.

10. *The Blackshirt*, 8 July 1933.

11. A. Raven Thompson, 'The Economics of British Fascism' (BUF, 1934), British Union Collection 3/THO; A. Raven Thompson, 'Corporate Economics', *Fascist Quarterly*, January 1935, 26–8.

12. *The Blackshirt*, 22 and 29 July 1933.

13. *The Blackshirt*, 26 August 1933.

14. *The Blackshirt*, 5 July 1935; see file in Nicholas Mosley Papers, Box 12.

15. *The Blackshirt*, 30 August 1935.

16. *The Blackshirt*, 24 May 1935.

17. Special Branch Report, 22 January 1934, PRO HO 45/25386.

18. John Beckett, 'Fascism and Trade Unionism' (BUF, 1935), British Union Collection 3/BEC; John Beckett, 'Fascism and the Trade Unions', *Fascist Quarterly*, July 1935, 327–36.

19. Stuart Rawnsley, 'The Membership of the British Union of Fascists', in K. Lunn and R. Thurlow (eds.), *British Fascism* (1980), 160–1; Thomas P. Linehan, *East London for Mosley: The British Union of Fascists in East London and South West Essex 1933–1940* (1966), 201, 211–12.

20. Linehan, *East London*, 262.

21. Nellie Driver, 'From the Shadows of Exile', n.d., 30.

22. J. Christian (ed.), *Mosley's Blackshirts: The Inside Story of the British Union of Fascists 1932–46* (1986), 46.

23. Ibid., 27, 30, 56; Arthur Fawcett, 2, Stuart Rawnsley Interview; Linehan, *East London*, 44.

24. Leslie Grundy, 'Don't Let Your Conscience Be Your Guide', typescript, British Union Collection 5/3, 18, 25–8.

25. J. Christian (ed.), *Mosley's Blackshirts*, 42.

26. Austin Harrison in *English Review*, 36, June 1923, 340.

27. Editorial, *National Review*, 83, March 1929, 37.

28. Portsmouth, *Knot of Roots*, 122.

29. Sir Charles Petrie, *Chapters of Life* (1950), 150–1.

30. Ibid., 129.

31. Ernest Remnant, *English Review*, 45, July 1927, 7–8.

32. *English Review*, 54, April 1937, 420–32.

33. Viscount Lymington, *Famine in England* (1938), 42.

34. Ibid., 123.

35. *The Blackshirt*, 5 July 1935.

36. Mosley, *Greater Britain*, 72, 79.

37. Douglas Jerrold, *English Review*, 57, October 1933, 342.

38. *Action*, 4 June 1936.
39. Jonathan Brown, 'Agricultural Policy and the National Farmers Union, 1908–1939', J. R. Wordie (ed.), *Agriculture and Politics in England, 1815–1939* (2000), 179–80.
40. Ibid., 186–7.
41. *National Review*, 94, March 1930, 990.
42. Mosley, *Greater Britain*, 127.
43. *National Review*, 98, October 1932, 493.
44. Brown, 'Agricultural Policy', 192–3.
45. *Action*, 4 February 1939.
46. Portsmouth, *Knot of Roots*, 131.
47. *Action*, 4 February 1939.
48. Lord Lymington to Ramsay MacDonald, copy, 18 February 1933, and 'Notes on the Milk Marketing Board', Lymington Papers F416.
49. *The Blackshirt*, 31 August 1934.
50. *The Blackshirt*, 1 March 1935.
51. *The Blackshirt*, 19 July 1935.
52. *Action*, 21 February 1936.
53. 'To Poultry Breeders' (BUF, 1937), British Union Collection 3/L.
54. *The Blackshirt*, 15 June 1934, 27 July 1934.
55. Special Branch Report, 26 June 1935, PRO HO 144/20145; *The Blackshirt*, 25 October 1935.
56. John Beckett and A. Raven Thompson, 'The Private Trader and Co-operation: The Distributive Trades' (BUF, 1936), British Union Collection 3/BEC.
57. *Action*, 12 February 1938.
58. *Action*, 4 June 1936.
59. *The Blackshirt*, 29 June 1934, 6 March 1936; Beckett and Raven Thompson, 'Private Trader and Co-operation'.
60. *Action*, 5 March 1938.
61. Ralph Jebb to District Leader, 29 July 1937, Robert Saunders Papers A3/152.
62. Linehan, *East London*, 33–7, 65–6, 73–6.
63. *Action*, 2 April 1938.
64. *Action*, 20 January 1938.
65. *Action*, 1 May 1937.
66. 2 and 3 December 1936, Robert Saunders Papers A2/298–9; *Action*, 5 December 1936; 'Why Did Wholesale Combines Ban *Action*?', British Union Collection 3/L.
67. *Action*, 8 May 1937.
68. *Action*, 19 June 1937, 6 January 1938.

69. *Action*, 6 January 1938.
70. *Action*, 4 and 18 June 1938, 2 July 1938.
71. *Action*, 21 and 28 August 1937.
72. Linehan, *East London*, 211–12.
73. Minutes, 17 June 1937, PRO HO 144/21063.

12. *Anti-Semitism and the Reorganisation of Fascism 1936–8*

1. *Evening Standard*, 2 and 5 November 1936.
2. *Evening Standard*, 2 November 1936.
3. Michael Ffinch, *G. K. Chesterton* (1986), 334–5.
4. John Buchan, *The Thirty-Nine Steps* (1915), 7.
5. Harry Defries, *Conservative Party Attitudes to Jews, 1900–1950* (2001), 121.
6. Geoffrey Alderman, *Modern British Jewry* (1992), 273.
7. *Action*, 17 September 1936.
8. Geoffrey Searle, *Corruption in British Politics 1895–1930* (1987), 209–11, 244–6, 332–3; Bernard Wasserstein, *Herbert Samuel* (1992), 143–6, 170–1.
9. Quoted in Peter Stansky, *Sassoon: The World of Philip and Sybil* (2003), 122; House of Commons Debates, vol. 334, 4 April 1938, c.6–7; *Daily Herald*, 2 December 1954; Mrs Diana Spens to Robert Bower, n.d., Bower Papers 1/5.
10. Francis Selwyn, *Hitler's Englishman* (1987), 32; *'Chips': The Diaries of Sir Henry Channon* (1993), ed. Robert Rhodes James, 23–4 (27 January 1935), 120–1 (27 April 1937).
11. Stansky, *Sassoon*, 214.
12. Ibid., 106–7.
13. See *Baffy: The Diaries of Blanche Dugdale 1936–1947* (1973), ed. N. A. Rose.
14. Defries, *Conservative Party Attitudes*, 41–66.
15. V. D. Lipman, *A History of the Jews in Britain* (1990), 129.
16. See W. D. Rubinstein, 'Jews Among Top British Wealth Holders 1857–1969', *Jewish Social Studies*, 34, 1972.
17. G. P. Southerst, 15, Stuart Rawnsley Interview, 16 February 1977.
18. *Daily Express*, 24 March 1933.
19. Lipman, *History of the Jews*, 192–4.
20. William Joyce, 'Fascism and Jewry' (?1936), British Union Collection 3/JOY.
21. *Manchester Guardian*, 24 October 1932.
22. Robert Skidelsky, *Oswald Mosley* (1975), 291.

23. Nicholas Mosley, *Beyond the Pale* (1983), 28.

24. Typed Memorandum, 'Apathy' (?1934), Nicholas Mosley Papers, Box 8.

25. *Fascist Quarterly*, January 1935; A. J. Trythall, *'Boney' Fuller: The Intellectual General 1878–1966* (1977), 184; Thomas Linehan, *British Fascism 1918–1939* (2000), 193.

26. *Fascist Quarterly*, April–June 1937, 5.

27. Quoted in Selwyn, *Hitler's Englishman*, 61–2.

28. *The Blackshirt*, 1 April 1933, 16 May 1933.

29. Joyce, 'Fascism and Jewry'.

30. *The Blackshirt*, 2 November 1934.

31. *Daily Mail*, 12 July 1934.

32. 'Fascism – 100 Questions Asked and Answered', Diana Mosley Papers, Box 2.

33. 'Apathy', typed memorandum, by G. S. Guerault, Nicholas Mosley Papers, Box 8.

34. Ibid.

35. 'Report on the British Union of Fascists', n.d., 11, Nicholas Mosley Papers, Box 8.

36. Special Branch Report, 16 June 1935, PRO HO 144/20145.

37. Special Branch Report, 18 December 1935, PRO HO 144/20146.

38. Special Branch Reports, 24 October 1935, PRO HO 144/20145, and 29 June 1937, PRO HO 144/21063.

39. 'Apathy', Nicholas Mosley Papers, Box 8; Leigh Vaughan-Henry to Oswald Mosley, 25 July 1934, Nicholas Mosley Papers, Box 8.

40. Richard Thurlow, *Fascism in Britain: A History 1918–1985* (1987), 141–3.

41. 'Apathy', Nicholas Mosley Papers, Box 8.

42. 'Report on the Organisation of the British Union of Fascists', n.d., Nicholas Mosley Papers, Box 8.

43. Ibid.

44. Special Branch Report, 26 June 1935, PRO HO 144/20145.

45. Quoted in *Daily Mail*, 7 June 1946.

46. Report on 'The Fascist Movement in the UK February–July 1936', PRO HO 144/21060; Special Branch Report, 12 May 1937, PRO HO 144/21063; PRO HO 283/7.

47. Special Branch Report, 20 January 1936 and 3 March 1936, PRO HO 144/20146; Francis Beckett, *The Rebel Who Lost His Cause* (1999), 134.

48. Saunders Papers A3/158.

49. 'Report on the Organisation of the British Union of Fascists', n.d., Nicholas Mosley Papers, Box 8.

50. Special Branch Report, 17 January 1936, PRO HO 144/20146.

51. Special Branch Report, 20 January 1936, PRO HO 144/20146.

52. Ibid.
53. Saunders Papers A1/267, 268; A2/303; A3/152.
54. Special Branch Report, 17 January 1936, PRO HO 144/20146; *Fascist Quarterly*, January–April 1937, 4–5.
55. J. F. C. Fuller to Captain Luttman-Johnson, 30 June 1937, Luttman-Johnson Papers 1.
56. John Charnley, *Blackshirts and Roses* (1990), 42; Julie Gottlieb, 'Motherly Hate: Gendering Anti-Semitism in the British Union of Fascists', *Gender and History*, 14, 2002, 297.
57. Special Branch Report, 24 October 1935, PRO HO 144/20145.
58. 'The British Union of Fascists in Yorkshire 1934–40', Trevelyan Scholarship Project, 1960, 4–7.
59. Nigel Copsey, *Anti-Fascism in Britain* (2000), 46–7.
60. Sir John Simon, 'Aide Memoir – Jew Baiting', 16 July 1936, PRO HO 144/2178.
61. Donald Somervell, 22 July 1936, Nathan Laski, 26 July 1936, PRO HO 144/2178.
62. Report, 18 July 1937, PRO HO 144/2178.
63. Minutes, 4 September 1936, PRO HO 144/21379.
64. B. Rowe, Stuart Rawnsley Interview, 24 August 1978.
65. Minutes, 12 June 1936, PRO HO 144/21060.
66. *Daily Herald*, 28 September 1936; Special Branch Report, 12 September 1936, PRO HO 144/21379.
67. Memorandum, 11 September 1936, PRO HO 144/21379.
68. Memorandum, 24 October 1934, PRO HO 45/24967.
69. Sir John Simon, 'Aide Memoir – Jew Baiting', 16 July 1936, PRO HO 144/2178.
70. PRO HO 45/24967; Thurlow, *Fascism in Britain*, 75–6.
71. Linehan, *British Fascism*, 136–7.
72. Philip Game, 9 June 1936, PRO HO 144/21379.
73. Special Branch Report, 16 September 1936, PRO HO 144/21379.
74. Copsey, *Anti-Fascism*, 54–5.
75. Thomas Linehan, 'Fascist Perceptions of Cable Street', Tony Kushner and Nadia Valman, *Remembering Cable Street* (2000), 23–9; Special Branch Report, 5 November 1936 PRO HO 144/21379.
76. PRO HO 144/21061/692.
77. Special Branch Report, 12 March 1937, PRO HO 144/21380.
78. 'Draft Election Manifesto for Municipal Elections 1936–37', Nicholas Mosley Papers, Box 8.
79. Ibid.
80. Memorandum, 24 April 1937, PRO HO 144/21063.

81. Special Branch Report, 12 March 1937, PRO HO 144/21063; Special Branch Report 11 March 1937, PRO KV 2/245/28a.
82. Ibid.
83. Special Branch Report, 7 May 1937, PRO HO 144/21380.
84. Memorandum, 5 May 1937, PRO HO 144/21063.
85. Chief Commissioner Metropolitan Police, 29 June 1937, PRO HO 144/2178.
86. *News Chronicle*, 6 August 1937.
87. Special Branch Report, June 1938, PRO HO 144/21381.
88. E. W. Tennant to von Ribbentrop (copy), 7 September 1935, Mount Temple Papers BR81/9; Lord Mount Temple, speech, April 1933, Mount Temple Papers 81/15; *The Times*, 19 November 1938.
89. Special Branch Report, 2 September 1938, PRO HO 144/21281.
90. Lineham, *British Fascism*, 179–80.
91. Selwyn, *Hitler's Englishman*, 68–73; Linehan, *British Fascism*, 138–9.
92. Nordic League file, 23 May 1939, PRO HO 144/22454; Thurlow, *Fascism in Britain*, 78–83.
93. Ibid.
94. Nordic League file, 5 June 1939, PRO HO 144/22454.
95. Ibid.
96. Sir Barry Domvile, *From Admiral to Cabin Boy* (1947), 23, 43.
97. See *Anglo-German Review*, August 1937.
98. *Anglo-German Review*, March and April 1938, January and June 1939.
99. Sir Barry Domvile's Diary, 27 February 1939, Domvile Papers 56.
100. R. Cockett, 'Ball, Chamberlain and *Truth*', *Historical Journal*, 33, 1990, 131–42.
101. A. P. Laurie, *The Case for Germany* (1939), 31–2; Jessica Mitford, *Hons and Rebels* (1960), 80; Arthur Bryant, *Unfinished Victory* (1940), 144–5.
102. *Action*, 25 March 1939.
103. *New Pioneer*, May 1939.
104. *New Pioneer*, January 1939.
105. *Action*, 7, 14 and 21 January 1939.

13. 'Who is King here? Baldwin or I?'

1. Harold Nicolson, *King George V* (1952), 384.
2. Templewood Papers RF3, 13.
3. Nicolson, *George V*, 300–1.
4. J. H. Thomas, *My Story* (1937), 154.
5. J. R. Clynes, *Memories 1869–1924* (1937), 326.
6. Nicolson, *George V*, 384.

7. Clynes, 343–4.
8. Nicolson, *George V*, 418–19.
9. Sir Charles Petrie, *Monarchy* (1933), 58, 74.
10. *The Star*, 10 January 1923.
11. Ibid.
12. Quoted in Philip Ziegler, *King Edward VIII* (1990), 54.
13. Ibid., 94–103.
14. Ibid., 185–6.
15. Ibid., 184.
16. John Aird's Diary, 31 May 1934, in Ziegler, *Edward VIII*, 208–9.
17. *Guardian*, 30 January 2003.
18. *The Blackshirt*, 8 July 1933; A. L. Glasfurd, 'Fascism and the English Tradition', *Fascist Quarterly*, July 1939, 361.
19. *The Fascist*, July 1930.
20. *National Review*, 83, June 1929, 541–2.
21. Petrie, *Monarchy*, 25, 28.
22. 'An Essay in English Royalism', Lymington Papers F179.
23. 'The English Mistery', 1 December 1934, Lymington Papers F417; 'Notes on the correspondence with the Government between 28 November 1934 and 26 May 1935', Lymington Papers F417.
24. J. H. Blaksley, 'The Tory Ideal', *National Review*, 83, June 1929, 542.
25. Petrie, *Monarchy*, 77, 81.
26. Ibid., 291–3.
27. *The Blackshirt*, 10 May 1935.
28. *English Review*, 60, May 1935, 578.
29. *Saturday Review*, 2 May 1936.
30. *Saturday Review*, 6 June 1936.
31. Ibid.
32. *Saturday Review*, 13 June 1936.
33. *Saturday Review*, 8 August 1936 and 19 September 1936.
34. Bruce Lockhart Diaries, vol. 1, 263, in Ziegler, *Edward VIII*, 206.
35. Charles Douglas-Home, *Dignified and Efficient: The British Monarchy in the Twentieth Century* (2000), 112.
36. *The Blackshirt*, 21 June 1935.
37. Templewood Papers RF3, 16.
38. See the discussion in Gerwin Strobl, *The Germanic Isle: Nazi Perceptions of Britain* (2000).
39. Ziegler, *Edward VIII*, 209.
40. Ibid., 220.
41. J. Barnes and K. Middlemas, *Baldwin* (1969), 976.

42. Ibid., 984.
43. PRO CAB 127/157, 'King Edward VIII. Notes by Sir Horace Wilson'.
44. Susan Williams, *The People's King: The True Story of the Abdication* (2003), 47, 50, 60.
45. Abdication Diary, Duff Cooper Papers 2/16, 4.
46. Ziegler, *Edward VIII*, 275.
47. *Documents on German Foreign Policy*, Series C, vol. IV (HMSO, 1962), 1016–17.
48. Quoted in Barnes and Middlemas, *Baldwin*, 979.
49. *Anglo-German Review*, December 1936.
50. PRO MEPO 10/35, Mrs N. M. Strickland, 2 September 1936.
51. Ibid.
52. Abdication Diary, Duff Cooper Papers 2/26, 16 November 1936.
53. See H. Samuel to Lord Salisbury, 19 September 1943, and Lord Salisbury to H. Samuel, 16 November 1936, Samuel Papers A/101.
54. Kenneth Harris, *Attlee* (1982), 132–3.
55. Abdication Diary, Duff Cooper Papers 2/16, 11.
56. Abdication Diary, Duff Cooper Papers 2/16, 12.
57. PRO CAB 127/157, 'King Edward VIII. Notes by Sir Horace Wilson'.
58. Lord Lymington to King Edward VIII (draft), 7 December 1936, Lymington Papers F250; Williams, *People's King*, 185–7.
59. Philip Murphy, *Alan Lennox-Boyd: A Biography* (1999), 48.
60. *The Times*, 5 December 1936; Barnes and Middlemas, *Baldwin*, 1011.
61. PRO PREM 1/457, minutes, 4 December 1936.
62. J. Wentworth Day, *Lady Houston DBE: The Woman Who Won the War* (1958), 246–7.
63. Abdication Diary, Duff Cooper Papers 2/16, 20.
64. John Charnley, *Blackshirts and* Roses (1990), 68; *Saturday Review*, 14 November and 5 and 12 December 1936.
65. Francis Beckett, *The Rebel Who Lost His Cause* (1999), 140–1.
66. Abdication Diary, 13, Duff Cooper Papers 2/16.
67. *Daily Express* and *Daily Mail*, 4 December 1936.
68. *Daily Mail*, 5 December 1936.
69. *Daily Express* and *Daily Mail*, 7 December 1936.
70. *Daily Mail*, 8 December 1936.
71. R. R. Bellamy, in J. Christian (ed.), 'We Marched with Mosley', 170, British Union Collection 5/5.
72. J. Christian (ed.), *Mosley's Blackshirts: The Inside Story of the British Union of Fascists 1932–46* (1986), 25; Williams, *The People's King*, 64–5.

73. Robert Richard, 'Geordie Recollections', 33, British Union Collection 5/4.

74. Leslie Grundy, 'Don't let your conscience be your guide', 46, British Union Collection 5/4.

75. R. R. Bellamy, 'We Marched with Mosley', 172, British Union Collection 5/5; Leslie Grundy, 'Don't Let Your Conscience Be Your Guide' 18, British Union Collection 5/4.

76. Domvile Diary, 9 and 19 December 1936, Domvile Papers 54.

77. 'Crisis', British Union Collection 3; *Daily Express*, 5 December 1936.

78. William Joyce, 'Crisis'.

79. *Daily Mail*, 4 and 5 December 1936; *News Chronicle*, 3 December 1936; *Daily Express*, 4 December 1936.

80. *Daily Express*, 5 December 1936; *Daily Mail*, 3, 4 and 7 December 1936.

81. *News Chronicle*, 3 and 5 December 1936.

82. *Daily Express*, 4 and 5 December 1936.

83. *News Chronicle*, 3 and 7 December 1936.

84. *Daily Mail*, 5 December 1936.

85. *News Chronicle*, 7 December 1936.

86. *Daily Express*, 5 December 1936.

87. PRO CAB 127/157; PRO PREM 11/451, memorandum by Sir Horace Wilson, 4 December 1936.

88. PRO PREM 1/451, minutes, 4 December 1936.

89. *Daily Express* and *Daily Mail*, 4 December 1936.

90. PRO PREM 1/457.

91. PRO PREM 1/448.

92. PRO PREM 1/457, minutes, 5 December 1936.

93. Martin Gilbert, *Winston Churchill*, vol. V: *1922–39* (1976), 822–3.

94. *Daily Express*, 8 December 1936; *Daily Mail*, 9 December 1936.

95. PRO PREM 1/451, 'Most Secret' by Sir Horace Wilson, 10 December 1936.

96. John Charnley, *Blackshirts and Roses* (1990), 69.

97. *Saturday Review*, 12 and 19 December 1936, and 2 January 1937.

98. *Daily Mail*, 5 December 1936; Williams, *The People's King*, 250–1.

99. PRO MEPO 11/35, Sir John Simon to the King (copy), 10 December 1936.

100. PRO MEPO 10/35, D. Storrier to Sir Philip Game, 26 January 1938.

101. PRO MEPO 10/35, Canning to Sir Philip Game, 19 December 1936.

102. PRO PREM 1/464, Duke of Windsor, 29 September 1937.

103. PRO PREM 1/464, dated 9 September 1937.

104. PRO PREM 1/464, Foreign Office telegram, 6 October 1937.

105. PRO PREM 1/464, telegram, 5 October 1937.

106. Quoted in Michael De-la-Noy, *The Queen Behind the Throne* (1994), 98.

107. Minutes, 17 June 1937, PRO HO 144/21063.

108. PRO PREM 1/465, Duke of Windsor to Neville Chamberlain, 22 December 1937.

109. Ibid.

110. J. M. Golby and A. W. Purdue, *The Monarchy and the British People* (1988), 110.

111. PRO PREM 1/463, Sir John Simon to the Duke of Windsor, 10 March 1937.

112. PRO PREM 1/465, G. Curry to Horace Wilson, 11 January 1938.

113. PRO PREM 1/467, Duke of Windsor to Neville Chamberlain, 29 August 1938.

114. PRO PREM 1/467, memorandum by Duke of Windsor, 9 January 1939.

115. PRO PREM 11/467, King George VI to Neville Chamberlain, 14 December 1938.

116. PRO PREM 1/467, memorandum by Duke of Windsor, 9 January 1939.

117. PRO PREM 1/467, Neville Chamberlain to the Duke of Windsor, 22 February 1939.

118. PRO PREM 1/467, Duke of Windsor to Neville Chamberlain, 24 February 1939.

119. Golby and Purdue, *Monarchy*, 111.

120. Douglas-Home, *Dignified*, 138.

121. De-la-Noy, *The Queen*, 62.

122. Douglas-Home, *Dignified*, 137–8.

123. PRO MEPO 10/35, Special Branch report, 5 January 1939.

124. PRO MEPO 10/35, undated leaflet by The Octavians.

125. PRO MEPO 10/35, undated memorandum.

126. PRO MEPO 10/35, Special Branch report, 5 January 1939.

14. *'Mind Britain's Business': Appeasement and the Peace Campaign*

1. Nicholas Mosley, *Rules of the Game* (1982), 11, 27, 47.

2. Harold Nicolson, *Diaries and Letters*, vol. I: *1930–39* (1966), 273.

3. J. F. C. Fuller, 'Fascism and War', *Fascist Quarterly*, April 1935, 147–8; William Joyce, 'Collective Security', *Fascist Quarterly*, October 1935, 422–30.

4. Joyce, *Fascist Quarterly*, October 1935, 422–30.

5. *Action*, 15 May 1937; R. R. Bellamy, 'We Marched with Mosley', 135, British Union Collection 5/5.

6. *The Blackshirt*, 19 July 1935, 16 August 1935; Bellamy, 'We Marched', 137–9.

7. *The Blackshirt*, 9 August 1935.

8. *The Blackshirt*, 23 August 1935.

9. *The Blackshirt*, 30 August 1935.

10. *Saturday Review*, 6 July 1935, 10 August 1935; Douglas Jerrold to Captain Luttman-Johnson, 26 November 1935, Luttman-Johnson Papers 1.

11. *National Review*, 105, November 1935, 564.

12. *Saturday Review*, 19 October 1935, 25 March 1936.

13. Special Branch Report, 6 January 1936, PRO HO 144/20146.

14. Bellamy, 'We Marched', 155.

15. Speech at Porchester Hall, London, report, 29 October 1935, PRO HO 144/20145.

16. Saunders Papers A1/240.

17. R. B. Cockett, 'Ball, Chamberlain and *Truth*', *Historical Journal*, 33, 1990, 131–2.

18. William C. Mills, 'Sir Joseph Ball, Adrian Dingli and Neville Chamberlain's Secret Channel to Italy 1933–40', *International History Review*, 24, 2002, 302–3; *Truth*, 21 December 1938.

19. *Action*, 7 May 1936.

20. *Daily Telegraph*, 4 August 1936.

21. *National Review*, 107, September 1936, 273–4; 109, December 1937, 731–8; J. F. C. Fuller, *Fascist Quarterly*, April–June 1937, 35–40.

22. *Manchester Guardian*, 11 June 1938; Channon's diary 21 April 1937, in R. R. James (ed.), *'Chips': The Diaries of Sir Henry Chips Channon* (1993), 120.

23. See Simon Haxey, *Tory MP* (1939), 214–18.

24. Duke of Alba to Henry Page Croft, 23 November 1937, Page Croft Papers AL/8; *Note Verbale*, 30 August 1938, Page Croft Papers AL/9; Memorandum, 21 January 1944, Page Croft Papers AL/17.

25. *Action*, 27 February 1937.

26. Duchess of Atholl to W. Halley (copy), 22 June 1936, Atholl Papers 95/2; Duchess of Atholl to Erik Georgeson (copy), 1 July 1938, Atholl Papers 95/2.

27. Sir T. Moore to Marquis of Clydesdale, 27 June 1935, Hamilton Papers 5000/4.

28. 'The Anglo-German Fellowship', Mount Temple Papers BR 81/1; Lord Mount Temple, *Anglo-German Review*, November 1936.

29. Annual Report 1935–36, Anglo–German Fellowship, PRO KV 5/3; Haxey, *Tory MP*, 230–2; *News Chronicle*, 20 July 1936.

30. Hamilton Papers 5000/5/5–6; Annual Report 1935–36, Anglo–German Fellowship; *Anglo–German Review*, January 1938; Haxey, *Tory MP*, 207–9.

31. Christopher Andrew and Oleg Gordievsky, *KGB: Inside Story* (1990), 175–6, 168–70; Andrew Boyle, *Climate of Treason* (1979), 139.

32. Elwin Wright quoted in Haxey, *Tory MP*, 199. This is why it looked askance at Domvile and The Link: Conwell-Evans to Mount Temple, 18 January 1938, Mount Temple Papers BR 81/9; Domvile regarded the AGF Council as 'a useless body': Domvile Diary, 26 May 1936, Domvile Papers 54.

33. For an example see Mount Temple Papers BR 76/14.

34. E. W. D. Tennant, 'Notes on Hitler and His Policies', 8, Mount Temple Papers BR 81/10.

35. *Anglo–German Review*, February 1937; Norman Rose, *The Cliveden Set* (2000), 181.

36. *Yorkshire Evening News*, 3 December 1938.

37. *The Times*, 26 February 1938.

38. Anglo–German Fellowship meeting, 24 October 1938, PRO KV 5/3.

39. A. P. Laurie, *The Case for Germany* (1939), 44.

40. Duchess of Atholl to Arthur Bryant, 6 April 1939, 12 May 1939, Sir Arthur Bryant Papers C 46 and C 63.

41. *Anglo–German Review*, November 1936.

42. E. W. D. Tennant to von Ribbentrop (copy), 7 September 1935, Mount Temple Papers BR 81/9; Tennant, 'Notes on Hitler and His Policies', Mount Temple Papers BR 81/9.

43. Tennant, 'Notes', BR 81/9.

44. Saunders to H. Bartlett, 24 November 1936, Saunders Papers A6/63.

45. N. J. Crowson, *Facing Fascism: The Conservative Party and the Dictators 1935–40* (1997), 75.

46. *Anglo–German Review*, January 1937, September 1937.

47. Special Branch Report, 12 March 1937 and 17 June 1937, PRO HO 144/21063.

48. Special Branch Report, 3 February 1938, PRO HO 144/21281.

49. Special Branch Report, 7 April 1938, PRO HO 144/21281.

50. Special Branch Report, 14 October 1938, PRO HO 144/21281.

51. *Action*, 29 January 1938.

52. David A. Thomas, *Churchill: The Member for Woodford* (1995), 95.

53. *Evening Standard*, 10 August 1936.

54. House of Commons Debates, 12 November 1936, c.1107.

55. William Roger Louis, *In the Name of God, Go!* (1992), 104.

56. Thomas, *Churchill: Member for Woodford*, 92–5, 98–110.

57. W. Churchill to Henry Page Croft, 31 October 1938, Page Croft Papers 1/8.

58. Roy Jenkins, *Churchill* (2001), 539, 541.

59. 'My Answer', August 1937, Atholl Papers 22/2.

60. Duchess of Atholl, Letter to Members of the Kinross and West Perth Unionist Association, 6 May 1938, Atholl Papers 22/2.

61. *Action*, 12 March 1938.

62. Crowson, *Facing Fascism*, 88.

63. Philip Murphy, *Alan Lennox-Boyd: A Biography* (1999), 53.

64. *Anglo-German Review*, May 1938.

65. Lord Lymington, 'Should Britain Fight?', British Union Collection 3/LYM.

66. *Action*, 17 and 24 September 1938.

67. Robert Richard, 'Geordie Recollections', 47–8; 'ARP: Belisha Bluff and National Neglect' (BUF, 1938), British Union Collection.

68. Julie Gottlieb, *Feminine Fascism* (2000), 59–61, Anne Page, in J. Christian (ed.), 'Mosley's Blackshirts', 15–16.

69. Richard, 'Recollections', British Union Collection 5/4.

70. Leslie Grundy, 'Don't Let Your Conscience Be Your Guide', 37, British Union Collection 5/3.

71. *Hexham Courant*, 9 April 1938, 28 May 1938, 30 July 1938.

72. 'ARP: Belisha Bluff and National Neglect' (BUF, 1938), British Union Collection.

73. Thomas E. Linehan, *East London for Mosley* (1996), 160–1.

74. *Anglo-German Review*, October 1938; *The Times*, 26 February 1938.

75. *Hexham Courant*, 8 October 1938.

76. Lord Lloyd to Lord Halifax (copy), 12 September 1938, Lloyd Papers 19/5.

77. Lord William Scott to Sir Archibald Sinclair, 3 October 1938, Sinclair Papers THRS II 40/1.

78. 'The AGF and The Link', memorandum, 17 February 1939, PRO KV 5/3; Lord Nigel Douglas-Hamilton, memorandum re AGF, 14 August 1939, Hamilton Papers 5000/1/1.

79. E. W. D. Tennant, Notes, 10 April 1938, Mount Temple Papers BR 81/10.

80. Memorandum on AGF meeting, 23 November 1938, PRO KV 5/3; Channon's diary, 15 November 1938, in James (ed.), *Chips*, 177.

81. Ibid.; *The Times*, 19 November 1938.

82. Luttman-Johnson Diary, 22 December 1938, Luttman-Johnson Papers 5.

83. Crowson, *Facing Fascism*, 95, 153; *Anglo-German Review*, February 1939.

84. Articles by Lymington and Chesterton, *New Pioneer*, January 1939.

85. Special Branch Report, 14 October 1938, PRO HO 144/21281; W. Joyce to Dr Christian Bauer, 30 July 1939, PRO KV 2/245/167a.

86. House of Commons Debates, 343, 15 February 1939, c.1832; *Action*, 25 February 1939.

87. Special Branch Report, 23 March 1939, PRO HO 144/21281; Admiral Domvile's Diary, 26 July 1939, Domvile Papers 56; Richard Griffiths, *Patriotism Perverted: Captain Ramsay, the Right Club and British Anti-Semitism 1939–40* (1998), 113–14.

88. Special Branch Report, 14 October 1938, PRO HO 144/21281; Griffiths, *Patriotism Perverted*, 53–4.

89. *New Pioneer*, May 1939.

90. Duke of Bedford, *A Silver-Plated Spoon* (1959), 155–6; Griffiths, *Patriotism Perverted*, 55–8.

91. For his background see Griffiths, *Patriotism Perverted*, 77–89.

92. 'The Right Club', Nordic League file, 2 October 1939, PRO HO 144/22454.

93. Admiral Domvile's Diary, 10 July 1939, Domvile Papers 56.

94. For details see Griffiths, *Patriotism Perverted*, 121–66.

95. Paul Stafford, 'Political Autobiography and the Art of the Possible: R. A. Butler at the Foreign Office 1938–1939', *Historical Journal*, 28, 1985, 901–22; for an immediate disavowal of the Polish guarantee by Chamberlain's mouthpiece see *Truth*, 7 April 1939.

96. Sir Joseph Ball to Henry Drummond Wolff, 30 June 1939, Drummond Wolff Papers I/82.

97. Henry Drummond Wolff to Sir Joseph Ball (copy), 24 May 1939, Drummond Wolff Papers II/647; Memorandum, 24 July 1939, Drummond Wolff Papers V/883; Arthur Bryant to R. A. Butler, 14 October 1939, Bryant Papers C 69.

98. Arthur Bryant, confidential memorandum for the prime minister, 23 June 1939; memorandum, 3 July 1939; memorandum for the prime minister, 13 July 1939, Bryant Papers C 68.

99. Lord Halifax to Arthur Bryant, 5 April 1939; letter dated 25 April 1939; Lord Halifax to Arthur Bryant, 14 June 1939, Bryant Papers C 66; F. Yeats-Brown to Arthur Bryant, 23 June 1939, Bryant Papers E 39.

100. House of Commons Debates, 348, 19 June 1939, c. 1793–4; F. Yeats-Brown to Arthur Bryant, 29 July 1939, Bryant Papers E 39.

101. Personal and Confidential Statement by Drummond Wolff, 3, Drummond Wolff Papers IV/870.

102. Ibid.

103. H. Drummond Wolff to Sir Joseph Ball (copy), 17 and 20 March 1939, Drummond Wolff Papers II/639–40; Sir Joseph Ball to H. Drummond Wolff, 19 April 1939, Drummond Wolff Papers I/80.

104. H. Drummond Wolff to Sir Joseph Ball, 19 and 24 May 1939, Drummond Wolff Papers II/645, 647; Sir Joseph Ball to H. Drummond Wolff (copy), 2 June 1939, Drummond Wolff Papers I/81.

105. Lord Nigel Douglas-Hamilton, memorandum, 14 August 1939, re AGF, Hamilton Papers 5000/1/1; Lord James Douglas-Hamilton, 'Ribbentrop and War', *Journal of Contemporary History*, 5, 1970, 45–63.

106. Lord Aberconway, obituary, *Guardian*, 6 February 2003; Scott Newton, *Profits of Peace: The Political Economy of Anglo-German Appeasement* (1996), 123.

107. Marquis of Clydesdale to D. Simpson (copy), 1 June 1939, Hamilton Papers 5001/4; Admiral Domvile's Diary, 26 July 1939, Domvile Papers 56.

108. Admiral Domvile's Diary, 6 June 1939, Domvile Papers 56.

109. House of Commons Debates, 350, 3 August 1939, c.2649; Admiral Domvile's Diary, 30 March 1939 and 3 August 1939, Domvile Papers 56; Sir Barry Domvile, *From Admiral to Cabin Boy* (1947), 73–5; 'A Backbencher Looks Back', 24, undated typescript, Geoffrey Mander Papers, Bristol University.

110. Luttman-Johnson Diary, 20 April 1939, Luttman-Johnson Papers 5.

111. Stafford, 'R. A. Butler at the Foreign Office', 908; *News Chronicle*, 25 April 1939.

112. A. P. Laurie, *The Case for Germany* (1939), 19–20.

113. Luttman-Johnson Diary, 19 March 1939, Luttman-Johnson Papers 5; *Anglo-German Review*, March 1939.

114. *Action*, 25 March 1939, 8 April 1939.

115. *Action*, 8 August 1939.

116. *Hexham Courant*, 29 April 1939.

117. Ibid.

118. George Hoggard, in J. Christian (ed.), *Mosley's Blackshirts*, 45.

119. Special Branch Report, 12 June 1939, PRO HO 144/21281; G. C. Webber, 'Patterns of Membership and Support for the British Union of Fascists', *Journal of Contemporary History*, 19, 1984, 576–9.

120. Admiral Domvile's Diary, 14 July 1939, Domvile Papers 56; *Hythe Reporter*, 8 July 1939.

121. Francis Beckett, *The Rebel Who Lost His Cause* (1999), 159.

122. John Charnley, *Blackshirts and Roses* (1990), 84–7; Grundy, 'Don't Let Your Conscience', 52.

123. Special Branch Report, 16 July 1939, PRO HO 144/21281.

124. *Picture Post*, 29 July 1939; Admiral Domvile's Diary, 16 July 1939, Domvile Papers 56.

15. *The Open Conspiracy: Fascism and the Phoney War*

1. Winston Churchill, *The Second World War* (1959), 161.

2. Domvile's Diary, 3 September 1939, Domvile Papers 56.

3. Quoted in Scott Newton, *Profits of Peace: The Political Economy of Anglo-German Appeasement* (1996), 133–4.

4. A. H. M. Ramsay, *The Nameless War* (1954), 62, 67; House of Commons Debates, vol. 363, 15 February 1940, c.954.

5. *Truth*, 29 September 1939, 17 November 1939, 26 January 1940.

6. *Truth*, 13 December 1939, 12 January 1940.

7. 'Mosley's message to all British Union members', Nicholas Mosley Papers, Box 8.

8. PRO HO 144/21429.

9. Peter Martland, *Lord Haw Haw: The English Voice of Nazi Germany* (2003), 26–9.

10. Francis Yeats-Brown to Arthur Bryant, 8 October 1939, Bryant Papers E 39; see PRO HO 45/24967/105.

11. *The Times*, 13 February 1992; Richard Griffiths, *Patriotism Perverted: Captain Ramsay, the Right Club and British Anti-Semitism 1939–1940* (1998), 118, 224–5.

12. See his *Times* letter, 6 October 1939.

13. *New Pioneer*, October, November, December 1939; Domvile's Diary, 26 October 1939, Domvile Papers 56.

14. 'Nordic League' file, 2 October 1939, PRO HO 144/22454.

15. Julie Gottlieb, *Feminine Fascism: Women in Britain's Fascist Movement 1923–1945* (2000), 230.

16. H. Drummond Wolff to Arthur Bryant, 19 May 1940, Bryant Papers C 69.

17. *People's Post*, Nos. 5 and 6, 1940; Duke of Bedford, *A Silver-Plated Spoon* (1959), 162–3.

18. John Charnley. *Blackshirts and Roses* (1990), 89.

19. *Action*, 23 September 1939.

20. Leonard Wise, 3, and R. R. Bellamy, 66–7, in J. Christian (ed.), *Mosley's Blackshirts: The Inside Story of the British Union of Fascists* (1986).

21. *Action*, 19 October 1939.

22. Quoted in Gottlieb, *Feminine Fascism*, 236.
23. Mass Observation File Reports, No. 39 (Silvertown by-election), 12; No. 59 (North East Leeds by-election), 1.
24. *Action*, 22 and 29 February 1940.
25. *Action*, 14 and 21 March 1940.
26. *Action*, 16 and 22 May 1940.
27. 'The Right Club', 6 March 1940, PRO KV 22/884.
28. PRO HO 144/21429/44.
29. Brian Simpson, *In the Highest Degree Odious: Detention without Trial in Wartime Britain* (1992), 53–7.
30. Ibid., 71–3.
31. Metropolitan Police Report, 18 October 1939, PRO HO 144/21429.
32. Nordic League file, 2 October 1939, PRO HO 144/22454.
33. Special Branch Report, 1 February 1940, PRO HO 45/24895.
34. 'Right Club', 6 March 1940, PRO KV 2/884.
35. Special Branch Report, 31 January 1940, PRO HO 45/24895.
36. M/R, 'British Union', 15 March 1940, PRO KV 2/884.
37. Special Branch Report, 27 March 1940, PRO KV 2/884.
38. R. A. Butler to Arthur Bryant, 16 October 1939; Arthur Bryant to R. A. Butler (copy), 23 September 1939, Bryant Papers C 69.
39. Duke of Buccleuch to Arthur Bryant, 10 November 1939, Bryant Papers C 111/4.
40. Duke of Buccleuch to Arthur Bryant, 10 November 1939, Bryant Papers C 111/4.
41. L. Field, *Bendor: The Golden Duke of Westminster* (1983), 260–4; Andrew Roberts, *The Holy Fox* (1991), 179.
42. Lord Malcolm Douglas-Hamilton to Marquis of Clydesdale, 9 November 1939, Hamilton Papers 5001/7.
43. 'Mac' to Lord Malcolm Douglas-Hamilton, 30 October 1939 and Lord David Douglas-Hamilton to Marquis of Clydesdale, 16 and 22 September 1939, Hamilton Papers 5001/7.
44. Lord David Douglas-Hamilton to Marquis of Clydesdale, 16 and 22 September 1939, Hamilton Papers 5001/7.
45. Draft letter to Lord Halifax, 30 September 1939, Hamilton Papers 5001/5.
46. Duke of Buccleuch to King George VI, 12 December 1939; King George VI to Buccleuch, 12 May 1940, Royal Archives, PS/GVI/C/134/1 and 2.
47. Duke of Buccleuch to Arthur Bryant, 19 January 1940, Bryant Papers C 111/4.
48. Quoted in Crowson, *Facing Fascism: The Conservative Party and the*

European Dictators, 1935–40 (1997), 175.

49. Lord Brocket to Neville Chamberlain, 27 January 1940, PRO PREM 1/418.

50. L. S. Amery to R. T. Bower, 7 October 1939, Bower Papers I/4.

51. R. R. Stokes circular letter, 14 October 1939, Henry Graham White Papers GW/6/5/30; Arthur Bryant to R. A. Butler (copy), 18 October 1939, Bryant Papers C 69.

52. A. J. P. Taylor, *Beaverbrook* (1972), 403–6.

53. Duke of Buccleuch to Arthur Bryant, 12 March 1940, Bryant Papers C 111/4.

54. Duke of Buccleuch to Arthur Bryant, 10 November 1939, Bryant Papers C 111/4.

55. Crowson, *Facing Fascism*, 175–6, 182.

56. *Daily Mirror*, 26 April 1940; *News Chronicle*, 27 April 1940; *Daily Herald*, 26 April 1940.

57. *Action*, 26 October 1939.

58. *Brighton and Hove Herald*, 27 April 1940, 1 November 1941.

59. A. J. Trythall, *'Boney' Fuller: The Intellectual General* (1977), 215.

60. *Anglo-German Review*, January 1938; Griffiths, *Patriotism Perverted*, 221.

61. Special Branch Report, 25 June 1940, PRO HO 144/21933.

62. Report, 5 March 1940, PRO HO 45/24895.

63. Charles Grey to Captain Luttman-Johnson, 15 July 1940, Luttman-Johnson Papers 1.

64. *Truth*, 22 March 1940.

65. Admiral Domvile's Diary, 13 March 1940, Domvile Papers 56.

66. *The Patriot*, 22 February 1940.

67. *People's Post*, No. 6, 1940.

68. Bedford, *A Silver-Plated Spoon*, 158.

69. Quoted in Richard Lamb, *Churchill as War Leader: Right or Wrong?* (1991), 45.

70. *The Times*, 9 September 1965.

71. Charles Grey to Captain Luttman-Johnson, 15 May 1940, Luttman-Johnson Papers 1.

72. Neville Chamberlain's Diary, 26 May 1940, Chamberlain Papers NC2/24A.

73. R. V. Jones, *Most Secret War: British Security Intelligence 1939–45* (1978), 114–19; John Charnley, *Blackshirts and Roses* (1990), 89.

74. Ramsay, *Nameless War*, 73, 85; Anthony Masters, *The Man Who Was M* (1984), 84–5.

75. Special Branch Report, 25 May 1940, PRO KV 2/884.

76. A. Leese, *Out of Step* (1951), 62–3.

77. David Stafford, *Churchill and the Secret Service* (1997), 180–2.

78. Simpson, *In the Highest Degree Odious*, 151–2; Griffiths, *Patriotism Perverted*, 267.

79. Nicholas Mosley, *Beyond the Pale* (1983), 169–70; John Christian in J. Christian (ed.), *Mosley's Blackshirts*, 41.

80. See Kenneth Harris, *Attlee* (1982), 176; Ben Pimlott (ed.), *The Second World War Diary of Hugh Dalton 1940–45* (1986), 19; Ben Pimlott, *Hugh Dalton* (1985), 274–6.

81. Captain Luttman-Johnson to his wife, n.d., Luttman-Johnson Papers 2/14.

82. *The Times*, 14 November 1940; *The Patriot* made similar remarks regarding Ramsay, 30 May 1940.

83. R. T. Bower to Victor Gollancz (copy), 11 July 1947, Bower Papers 1/5.

84. Note dated 13 October 1967, Nicholas Mosley Papers, Box 17.

85. Henry Page Croft to Lord Caldecote, 26 July 1940, Page Croft Papers 1/6.

86. *Reynolds News*, 15 June 1958; see press cuttings in Diana Mosley Papers, Box 2.

87. House of Commons Debates, 365, 18 July 1940, c.386–7; 25 July 1940, c.966.

88. 'The British Union of Fascists in Yorkshire 1934–40', Trevelyan Scholarship Project, 1960, 19.

89. Anne Page, in J. Christian (ed.), *Mosley's Blackshirts*, 19; Leonard Wise, *Mosley's Blackshirts*, 6.

90. Gottlieb, *Feminine Fascism*, 230–1.

91. Ibid., 240; Mary Kenney, *Germany Calling* (2003), 102–3; Louise Irving, in J. Christian (ed.), *Mosley's Blackshirts*, 47.

92. Special Branch Report, 26 June 1940 and G. H. Stuart Bunning, 30 November 1940, PRO HO 144/21933.

93. PRO HO 144/21933/512110/26.

94. Allen Harker to Sir Alexander Maxwell, 27 June 1940, PRO HO 144/21995; DDMI Report, 5 June 1940, PRO KV 2/884.

95. Lord Moyne to Philip Swinton, 25 June 1940, PRO HO 144/21995.

96. Memorandum, 22 June 1940, PRO KV 2/884.

97. Mosley, *Beyond the Pale*, 166.

98. Gottlieb, *Feminine Fascism*, 248.

99. George VI to the Duke of Buccleuch, 12 May 1940, Royal Archives PS/GVI/C/134/2; Buccleuch to George VI, 19 May 1940, Royal Archives GVI/PRIV/C/03/B/23.

100. Bedford, *A Silver-Plated Spoon*, 157; Simpson, *In the Highest Degree*

Odious, 211–12; Roberts, *Holy Fox*, 152.

101. G. P. St Clair to Lymington, 25 October 1940, and Lymington to St Clair (copy), 28 October 1940, Lymington Papers F256.

102. Mosley, *Beyond the Pale*, 174.

103. Simpson, *In the Highest Degree Odious*, 213.

104. Andrew Roberts, *Eminent Churchillians* (1994), 315.

105. Griffiths, *Patriotism Perverted*, 268–9.

106. Captain Luttman-Johnson to his wife, n.d., Luttman-Johnson Papers 2; Leese, *Out of Step*, 64, 66.

107. A. H. M. Ramsay to Luttman-Johnson, April 1943, Luttman-Johnson Papers 1; Nellie Driver, 'From the Shadows of Exile', 58.

108. Governor's reports, 7 September 1940, 8 and 11 November 1940, PRO PCOM 9/878.

109. Norman Birkett, memorandum 5 June 1940, PRO HO 283/1 and 12.

110. Oswald Mosley to Diana Mosley, 19 June 1940, PRO KV 2/884.

111. Mosley, *Beyond the Pale*, 171–2; Special Branch Report, 16 July 1940, PRO HO 283/10.

112. Memorandum, 19 June 1940, PRO HO 283/18; Mosley, *Beyond the Pale*, 172.

113. 'Transcript of Diana Mosley's Appeal Against Internment', 2 October 1940, PRO HO 144/21995.

114. Memorandum 4 October 1940, PRO HO 144/21995.

115. Ramsay, *The Nameless War*, 99–102.

116. Driver, 'Shadows of Exile', 58; Gottlieb, *Feminine Fascism*, 243–4; Griffiths, *Patriotism Perverted*, 159–60.

117. Luttman-Johnson to the Duchess of Atholl (copy), n.d., Luttman-Johnson Papers 2/8, 9.

118. House of Commons Debates, 371, 24 April 1941, c.242; 15 May 1941, c.1239–40; 374, 11 November 1941, c. 2040–1; 377, 22 January 1942, c. 439, 441; 29 January 1942, c. 905–6.

119. House of Commons Debates, 377, 19 February 1942, c. 1885–6.

120. Mosley, *Beyond the Pale*, 204.

121. Report, 27 October 1943, PRO HO 144/21995.

122. Stafford, *Churchill and the Secret Service*, 219. Churchill's biographers neglect the whole topic; even Martin Gilbert offers no serious comment in his monumental biography: *The Finest Hour: Winston Churchill 1939–41* (1983), 1087–8.

123. 'Personal Report by Wing Commander the Duke of Hamilton', 11 May 1941, Royal Archives PS/GVI/C/199/17.

124. 'Record of the Interview with Herr Hess', 13 May 1941, Hamilton Papers 5004/2; House of Commons Debates, 392, 22 September 1943,

c.178–82.

125. Ivone Kirkpatrick in Hamilton Papers 5004/6; Hugh Trevor-Roper, *Sunday Times*, 24 May 1970.

126. Duke of Hamilton to Provost Michie, 23 May 1941 (copy), Hamilton Papers 5005/3.

127. R. R. James (ed.), *Chips: The Diaries of Sir Henry Channon* (1993), 13 May 1941, 304; Lynn Picknett, Clive Prince and Stephen Prior, *Double Standards: The Rudolph Hess Cover-Up* (2001), 141–3.

128. Ian Kershaw, *Hitler 1936–1945* (2000), 371–6.

129. Admiral Domvile to Luttman-Johnson, 7 August 1943, Luttman-Johnson Papers 1.

130. W. S. Churchill to H. Morrison, 25 November 1943, in Churchill, *The Second World War*, vol. V (1952), 635–6; Simpson, *In the Highest Degree Odious*, 389.

131. Ben Pimlott (ed.), *The Second World War Diary of Hugh Dalton 1940–45* (1986), 674–5.

SOURCES

Manuscript Sources

Wilfred Ashley [Lord Mount Temple] Papers – Hartley Library, Southampton University

Duchess of Atholl Papers – Blair Castle

Stanley Baldwin Papers – Cambridge University Library

T. P. H. Beamish Papers – Churchill College, Cambridge

Lord Beaverbrook Papers – House of Lords Record Office

R. R. Bellamy MSS – Sheffield University Special Collections

Robert Bower Papers – Churchill College, Cambridge

British Union Collection – Sheffield University Special Collections

Sir Arthur Bryant Papers – Liddell Hart Centre for Military Archives, King's College, London

Neville Chamberlain Papers – Birmingham University Library

Duff Cooper Papers – Churchill College, Cambridge

Sir Stafford Cripps Papers – Nuffield College, Oxford

Henry Page Croft Papers – Churchill College, Cambridge

Sir Barry Domvile Papers – National Maritime Museum, Greenwich

Nellie Driver MSS – J. B. Priestley Library, Bradford University

Sir John Gilmour Papers – National Archives of Scotland

Leslie Grundy MSS – Sheffield University Special Collections

Duke of Hamilton Papers – National Archives of Scotland

Sir Patrick Hannon Papers – House of Lords Record Office

Cuthbert Headlam Papers – Durham County Record Office

Sir Samuel Hoare [Viscount Templewood] Papers – Cambridge University Library

Labour Party Archives – National Museum of Labour History, Manchester

Lord Lloyd of Dolobran Papers – Churchill College, Cambridge

H. W. Luttman-Johnson Papers – Imperial War Museum

Viscount Lymington [Earl of Portsmouth] Papers – Hampshire County Record Office

J. T. C. Moore-Brabazon [Lord Brabazon of Tara] Papers – RAF Museum, Hendon

Diana Mosley Papers – Birmingham University Library

Nicholas Mosley Papers – Birmingham University Library

Public Record Office (Kew): CAB 21, 23, 24, 65, 127; HO 45, 144, 283; KV 2, 5; LAB 27; MEPO 2, 10; PCOM 9; PREM 1; WO 32

Robert Richard MSS – Sheffield University Special Collections

The Royal Archives, Windsor Castle (Buccleuch and Hamilton correspondence)

Herbert Samuel Papers – House of Lords Record Office

Robert Saunders Papers – Sheffield University Special Collections

Myra Story Papers – Imperial War Museum

Henry Drummond Wolff Papers – Brotherton Library, Leeds University

Other Unpublished Sources

Stuart Rawnsley Interview Transcripts – J. B. Priestley Library, Bradford University

'The British Union of Fascists in Yorkshire 1934–1940', Trevelyan Scholarship Project (1960) – J. B. Priestley Library, Bradford University

Mass Observation file reports (microfilm)

Newspapers and Journals

Action
Anglo-German Review
Birmingham Mail
Birmingham Post
The Blackshirt
Brighton and Hove Herald
British Lion
British Union Quarterly
Daily Express
Daily Herald
Daily Mail
Daily Telegraph
Empire News and Sunday Chronicle
English Review
Evening Standard

The Fascist
Fascist Bulletin
Fascist Quarterly
Hexham Courant
Morning Post
National Review
New Pioneer
News Chronicle
The Patriot
People's Post
Picture Post
Saturday Review
The Star
Sunday Dispatch
The Times
Truth

Works by Contemporaries

Mary Allen, *Lady in Blue* (1936)
Sir Ernest Barker, *Reflections on Government* (1942)
R. R. Bellamy, *Mosley's Blackshirts: The Inside Story of the British Union of Fascists 1932–46* (1986)
Sir Arthur Bryant, *Unfinished Victory* (1940)
John Buchan, *The Thirty-Nine Steps* (1915)
John Buchan, *Huntingtower* (1922)
Barbara Cartland, *The Isthmus Years* (1942)
'Cato', *Guilty Men* (1940)
Houston Stewart Chamberlain, *The Foundations of the Nineteenth Century* (1899)
John Charnley, *Blackshirts and Roses* (1990)
Sir Barry Domvile, *From Admiral to Cabin Boy* (1947)
Rex Welldon Finn, *The English Heritage* (1937)
H. E. Goad and M. Currey, *The Working of a Corporate State* (1934)
Simon Haxey, *Tory MP* (1939)
Harold Laski, *Democracy in Crisis* (1933)
Arnold Leese, *Out of Step: Events in the Two Lives of an Anti-Jewish Camel Doctor* (1951)
Anthony Ludovici, *A Defence of Aristocracy* (1915)
Anthony Ludovici, *Woman: A Vindication* (1923)
Anthony Ludovici, *A Defence of Conservatism* (1927)

Anthony Ludovici, *English Liberalism* (1939)
Arnold Lunn, *Revolutionary Socialism* (1939)
Viscount Lymington, *Famine in England* (1938)
Nancy Mitford, *Wigs on the Green* (1935)
Nancy Mitford, *Pigeon Pie* (1940)
Diana Mosley, *A Life of Contrasts* (2002)
Oswald Mosley, *The Greater Britain* (1932)
Oswald Mosley, *Fascism: 100 Questions Asked and Answered* (1936)
Oswald Mosley, *The Alternative* (1947)
Oswald Mosley, *My Life* (1969)
Bernard Newman, *Danger Spots of Europe* (1939)
Christabel Pankhurst, *The World's Unrest: Visions of the Dawn* (1926)
Sir Charles Petrie, *Monarchy* (1933)
Sir Charles Petrie, *Lords of the Inland Sea* (1937)
Sir Charles Petrie, *Chapters of Life* (1950)
Earl of Portsmouth, *A Knot of Roots* (1965)
G. Ward Price, *I Know These Dictators* (1937)
A. H. M. Ramsay, *The Nameless War* (1952)
Sir Ernest Simon (ed.), *Constructive Democracy* (1938)
Nesta Webster, *World Revolution: The Plots Against Civilisation* (1921)
Esme Wingfield-Stratford, *The Foundations of British Patriotism* (1940)

Autobiographies, Biographies and Diaries

David Baker, *Ideology of Obsession: A. K. Chesterton and British Fascism* (1996)
J. Barnes and K. Middlemas, *Baldwin* (1969)
Francis Beckett, *The Rebel Who Lost His Cause: The Tragedy of John Beckett MP* (1999)
Duke of Bedford, *A Silver-Plated Spoon* (1959)
Michael Bloch, *The Reign and Abdication of Edward VIII* (1990)
J. Christian (ed.), *Mosley's Blackshirts* (1986)
J. Wentworth Day, *Lady Houston DBE: The Woman Who Won the War* (1958)
Frances Donaldson, *Edward VIII* (1974)
David Dutton, *Simon: A Political Biography of Sir John Simon* (1992)
Michael Ffinch, *G. K. Chesterton* (1986)
L. Field, *Bendor: The Golden Duke of Westminster* (1983)
Martin Gilbert, *Winston S. Churchill*, vol. V: *1922–39 (1976)*; vol. VI. *1939–41* (1983)
Lavinia Greacen, *Chink: A Biography* (1989)
S. J. Hetherington, *Katharine Atholl 1874–1960* (1989)

Robert Rhodes James (ed.), *'Chips': The Diaries of Sir Henry Channon* (1993)

Mary Kenney, *Germany Calling: A Personal Biography of William Joyce, Lord Haw Haw* (2003)

Ian Kershaw, *Hitler 1889–1936: Hubris* (1998), *Hitler 1936–1945. Nemesis* (2000)

Roger William Louis, *In the Name of God Go!: Leo Amery and the British Empire in the Age of Churchill* (1992)

Mary S. Lovell, *The Mitford Girls* (2001)

David Marquand, *Ramsay MacDonald* (1977)

Peter Martland, *Lord Haw Haw: The English Voice of Nazi Germany* (2003)

Anthony Masters, *The Man Who Was M* (1984)

Jessica Mitford, *Hons and Rebels* (1960)

Nicholas Mosley, *Rules of the Game* (1982)

Nicholas Mosley, *Beyond the Pale* (1983)

Philip Murphy, *Alan Lennox-Boyd: A Biography* (1999)

Harold Nicolson, *King George V* (1952)

Harold Nicolson, *Diaries and Letters,* vol. I: *1930–39* (1966)

David Pryce-Jones, *Unity Mitford: A Quest* (1976)

John Ramsden (ed.), *Real Old Tory Politics: The Political Diaries of Robert Sanders, Lord Bayford, 1910–35* (1984)

Andrew Roberts, *The Holy Fox* (1991)

Andrew Roberts, *Eminent Churchillians* (1994)

Robert C. Self (ed.), *The Austen Chamberlain Diary Letters* (1995)

Francis Selwyn, *Hitler's Englishman: The Crime of Lord Haw-Haw* (1987)

Robert Skidelsky, *Oswald Mosley* (1975)

Denis Mack Smith, *Mussolini* (1981)

Peter Stansky, *Sassoon: The Worlds of Philip and Sybil* (2003)

A. J. P. Taylor, *Beaverbrook* (1972)

David A. Thomas, *Churchill: The Member for Woodford* (1995)

A. J. Trythall, *'Boney' Fuller: The Intellectual General 1878–1966* (1977)

Philip Williamson, *Baldwin* (1999)

Evelyn Wrench, *Francis Yeats-Brown 1886–1944* (1948)

Philip Ziegler, *King Edward VIII* (1990)

Selected Secondary Works

Paul Addison, *The Road to 1945* (1975)

Geoffrey Alderman, *Modern British Jewry* (1992)

Martin Allen, *Hidden Agenda: How the Duke of Windsor Betrayed the Allies* (2000)

Christopher Andrew and Oleg Gordievsky, *KGB: The Inside Story* (1990)

Stuart Ball, *Baldwin and the Conservative Party* (1988)

D. Beales and E. Biagini, *The Risorgimento and the Unification of Italy* (2002)

R. Benewick, *The Fascist Movement in Britain* (1969)

R. Bosworth, 'The British Press, the Conservatives and Mussolini 1920–34', *Journal of Contemporary History*, 5, 1970

Andrew Boyle, *Climate of Treason* (1979)

John Brewer, *Mosley's Men: The British Union of Fascists in the West Midlands* (1984)

Jonathan Brown, 'Agricultural Policy and the National Farmers' Union 1908–39', in J. R. Wordie (ed.), *Agriculture and Politics in England 1815–1939* (2000)

David Cannadine, *The Rise and Fall of the British Aristocracy* (1990)

David Carlton, 'Churchill and the Two Evil Empires', *Transactions of the Royal Historical Society*, XI, 2001.

Martin Ceadel, *Semi-Detached Idealists: The British Peace Movement and International Relations 1854–1945* (2000)

Richard Cockett, *Twilight of Truth: Chamberlain, Appeasement and the Manipulation of the Press* (1989)

Richard Cockett, 'Ball, Chamberlain and Truth', *Historical Journal*,, 33, 1990

Nigel Copsey, *Anti-Fascism in Britain* (2000)

Philip M. Coupland, 'The Blackshirted Utopians', *Journal of Contemporary History*, 33, 1998

Philip M. Coupland, 'Left-Wing Fascism in Theory and Practice: The Case of the British Union of Fascists', *Twentieth Century British History*, 13, 2002

M. Cronin (ed.), *The Failure of British Fascism* (1996)

Colin Cross, *The Fascists in Britain* (1961)

N. J. Crowson, *Facing Fascism: The Conservative Party and the European Dictators 1935–40* (1997)

Stephen Cullen, 'Political Violence: The Case of the British Union of Fascists', *Journal of Contemporary History*, 28, 1993

Harry Defries, *Conservative Party Attitudes to Jews 1900–1950* (2001)

Michael De-La-Noy, *The Queen Behind the Throne* (1994)

James Douglas-Hamilton, 'Ribbentrop and War', *Journal of Contemporary History*, 5, 1970

Charles Douglas-Home, *Dignified and Efficient: The British Monarchy in the Twentieth Century* (2000)

P. G. Edwards, 'The Foreign Office and Fascism, 1924–1929', *Journal of Contemporary History*, 5, 1970.

K. D. Ewing and C. A. Gearty, *The Struggle for Civil Liberties* (2000)

Julie Gottlieb, *Feminine Fascism: Women in Britain's Fascist Movement 1923–1945* (2000)

Julie Gottlieb, 'Motherly Hate: Gendering Anti-Semitism in the British Union of Fascists', *Gender and History*, 14, 2002

Julie Gottlieb and Thomas Linehan (eds.), *The Culture of Fascism* (2004)

E. H. H. Green, *The Crisis of Conservatism* (1995)

E. H. H. Green, *Ideologies of Conservatism* (2002)

Richard Griffiths, *Fellow Travellers of the Right* (1980)

Richard Griffiths, *Patriotism Perverted: Captain Ramsay, the Right Club and British Anti-Semitism 1939–1940* (1998)

Colin Holmes, *Anti-Semitism in British Society, 1876–1939* (1979)

Colin Holmes, *John Bull's Island: Immigration and British Society 1871–1971* (1988)

R. V. Jones, *Most Secret War: British Security Intelligence 1939–1945* (1978)

Tony Kushner and Kenneth Lunn (eds.), *Traditions of Intolerance* (1989)

Tony Kushner and Kenneth Lunn (eds.), *The Politics of Marginality* (1990)

Tony Kushner and Richard Thurlow (eds.), *British Fascism* (1980)

Tony Kushner and Nadia Valman, *Remembering Cable Street* (2000)

Walter Laqueur (ed.), *Fascism: A Reader's Guide* (1976)

Jon Lawrence, 'Fascist Violence and the Politics of Public Order in Inter-war Britain: the Olympia Debate Revisited', *Historical Research*, 76, 2003

Gisela Lebzelter, *Political Anti-Semitism in England 1918–1939* (1978)

D. S. Lewis, *Illusions of Grandeur: Mosley, Fascism and British Society 1931–81* (1987)

Thomas P. Linehan, *East London for Mosley* (1996)

Thomas P. Linehan, *British Fascism 1918–1939* (2000)

V. D. Lipman, *A History of the Jews in Britain* (1990)

Richard Lomas, *A Law in the Land: The Percys* (1999)

W. F. Mandle, 'Sir Oswald Mosley's Resignation from the Labour Government', *Historical Studies*, 10, 1963

W. F. Mandle, 'The Leadership of the British Union of Fascists', *Australian Journal of Politics and History*, 12, 1966

William C. Mills, 'Sir Joseph Ball, Adrian Dingli and Neville Chamberlain's "Secret Channel" to Italy 1937–40', *International History Review*, 24, 2002

Richard Moore-Colyer, 'Towards Mother Earth: Jorian Jenks, Organicism, the Right and the British Union of Fascists', *Journal of Contemporary History*, 39, 2004.

R. A. C. Parker, *Churchill and Appeasement* (2000)

Martin Petter, '"Temporary Gentlemen" in the Aftermath of the Great War: Rank, Status and the Ex-officer Problem', *Historical Journal*, 37, 1994

Lynne Picknet, Clive Prince and Stephen Prior, *Double Standards: The Rudolph Hess Cover-Up* (2001)

Martin Pugh, '"Class Traitors": Conservative Recruits to Labour 1900–1930', *English Historical Review*, CXIII, 1998

Martin Pugh, 'The British Union of Fascists and the Olympia Debate', *Historical Journal*, 41, 1998

Martin Pugh, *The Pankhursts* (2001)

Roland Quinault, 'Churchill and Democracy', *Transactions of the Royal Historical Society*, 11, 2001

John Ramsden, *The Age of Balfour and Baldwin 1902–40* (1978)

Norman Rose, *The Cliveden Set* (2000).

W. D. Rubinstein, 'Henry Page Croft and the National Party 1917–22', *Journal of Contemporary History*, 9, 1974

W. D. Rubinstein, *A History of the Jews in the English-Speaking World: Great Britain* (1998)

Markku Ruotsila, 'The Anti-Semitism of the Eighth Duke of Northumberland's *The Patriot* 1922–30', *Journal of Contemporary* History, 39, 2004

G. R. Searle, 'Critics of Edwardian Society: The Case of the Radical Right', in A. O'Day (ed.), *The Edwardian Age* (1979)

G. R. Searle, *Corruption in British Politics 1895–1930* (1987)

B. Semmel, *Imperialism and Social Reform* (1960)

Brian Simpson, *In the Highest Degree Odious: Detention without Trial in Wartime Britain* (1992)

Robert Skidelsky, *Politicians and the Slump* (1967)

Nick Smart, *The National Government 1931–1940* (1999)

Paul Stafford, 'Political Autobiography and the Art of the Possible: R. A. Butler at the Foreign Office, 1938–1939', *Historical Journal*, 28, 1985.

David Stafford, *Churchill and the Secret Service* (1997)

Dan Stone, *Breeding Superman: Nietzsche, Race and Eugenics in Edwardian and Inter-war Britain* (2002)

Dan Stone, 'The English Mistery, the British Union of Fascists and the Dilemmas of British Fascism', *Journal of Modern History*, 75, 2003.

Gerwin Strobl. *The Germanic Isle: Nazi Perspectives of Britain* (2000)

S. J. Taylor, *The Great Outsiders: Northcliffe, Rothermere and the Daily Mail* (1996)

Andrew Thorpe (ed.), *The Failure of Political Extremism in Inter-war Britain* (1989)

Andrew Thorpe, *The British General Election of 1931* (1991)

Andrew Thorpe, 'The Membership of the British Communist Party 1920–1945', *Historical Journal*, 43, 2000

Richard Thurlow, *Fascism in Britain: A History 1918–1985* (1987)

Richard Thurlow, 'The Evolution of the Mythical British Fifth Column,

1939–1946', *Twentieth Century British History*, 4, 1999

Nigel Todd, *In Excited Times: The People Against the Blackshirts* (1995)

Bernard Wasserstein, *Herbert Samuel* (1992)

G. C. Webber, 'Patterns of Membership and Support for the British Union of Fascists', *Journal of Contemporary History*, 19, 1984

G. C. Webber, *The Ideology of the British Right 1918–1939* (1986)

Susan Williams, *The People's King* (2003)

S. J. Woolf (ed.), *Fascism in Europe* (1981)

INDEX